Remembering: Cleveland's Jewish Voices

VOICES OF DIVERSITY
JOHN J. GRABOWSKI, EDITOR

You Can't Be Mexican: You Talk Just Like Me
FRANK S. MENDEZ

My Father Spoke Finglish at Work: Finnish Americans in Northeast Ohio
EDITED BY NOREEN SIPPOLA FAIRBURN

Remembering: Cleveland's Jewish Voices
EDITED BY SALLY H. WERTHEIM AND ALAN D. BENNETT FROM
DOCUMENTS SELECTED BY JUDAH RUBINSTEIN

Remembering:
Cleveland's Jewish Voices

Edited by

Sally H. Wertheim

and Alan D. Bennett

from documents selected by

Judah Rubinstein

*Published in cooperation with The Jewish Federation of
Cleveland and The Western Reserve Historical Society*

The Kent State University Press

KENT, OHIO

Library of Congress Catalog Card Number 2011000677
ISBN 978-1-60635-074-4
Manufactured in the United States of America

All photographs in this volume are drawn from *Merging Traditions: Jewish Life in Cleveland, Revised Edition* (Judah Rubinstein with Jane Avner, The Kent State University Press, 2004).

LIBRARY OF CONGRESS CATALOGING-IN-PUBLICATION DATA
Library of Congress Cataloging-in-Publication Data

Remembering Cleveland's Jewish voices / edited by Judah Rubinstein ; with the assistance of Sally Wertheim, Alan Bennett, and John Grabowski.
   p. cm. — (Voices of diversity)
   Includes index.
"Published in cooperation with The Jewish Community Federation of Cleveland and The Western Reserve Historical Society."
   ISBN 978-1-60635-074-4 (pbk. : alk. paper) ∞
   1. American literature—Jewish authors. 2. Jews—Ohio—Cleveland—Literary collections. 3. Jews—Ohio—Cleveland—Social life and customs. 4. Jews—Literary collections. 5. Cleveland (Ohio)—Literary collections. I. Rubinstein, Judah.
   PS508.J4R46 2011
   977.1'32004924—dc22
   2011000677

British Library Cataloging-in-Publication data are available.

15 14 13 12 11   5 4 3 2 1

To the memory of our friend and colleague

Judah Rubinstein,

whose passion to preserve Cleveland's written historical record

set us on this journey to complete his dream

The twenty-fifth anniversary of the Cleveland Jewish Archives, the principal repository for the history of the Jewish community of Northeastern Ohio. Left to right: Albert Ratner, Audrey Ratner, Judah Rubinstein, Sally Gries, Peggy Gries Wager, and Michael Wager (2001, Richard Palmer, Western Reserve Historical Society).

Contents

Series Editor's Foreword *John J. Grabowski*   xi

Foreword *Jewish Federation of Cleveland*   xiii

Acknowledgments   xv

Introduction   1
   The Jews of Cleveland: A Documentary Review

Historical Overview   5

SECTION ONE: ARTS AND CULTURE

  Jo Sinclair (1913–1995)   15
    Excerpt from *The Seasons: Death and Transfiguration*

  William Zorach (1887–1966)   28
    Excerpt from *Art Is My Life*

  Clara Lederer (1907–1987)   47
    Excerpt from *Their Paths Are Peace*

  David Guralnik (1920–2000)   53
    "The Yiddish Theater"

  Judah Rubinstein (1921–2003)   60
    "The Jewish Press in Cleveland"

SECTION TWO: CIVIC LIFE

  Sidney Z. Vincent (1912–1982)   67
    Excerpt from *A Tale of Ten Cities*

  Rose Pastor Stokes (1879–1933)   78
    Excerpt from *"I Belong to the Working Class"*

The Jewish Community Federation of Cleveland   100
   "Memorandum on Housing Situation, Lee-Harvard Area"
Alfred A. Benesch (1879–1973)   111
   "Oral History Interview"

SECTION THREE: WORK AND BUSINESS
Kaufman Hays (1835–1916)   127
   Excerpt from "Autobiography of Kaufman Hays"
Joseph Hays (1838–1916)   135
   Excerpt from Oral "Autobiography of Mr. Joseph Hays"
Julius C. Newman (ca. 1876–1958)   161
   Excerpt from *Smoke Dreams*
Howard W. Brody (1916–)   171
   "The Life and Times of a Jewish Farm Boy"

SECTION FOUR: JEWISH CONTINUITY
Lazarus Kohn (?–ca. 1846)   195
   Alsbacher Document: Ethical Testament, 1839
Laura Porath (1958–)   202
   Handwritten Account, May 2, 1975
Samuel M. Silver (1912–2008)   205
   Excerpt from *Portrait of a Rabbi*
Abba Hillel Silver (1893–1963)   223
   "What I Would Say . . . "
Leon Wiesenfeld (1885–1971)   232
   Excerpt from *Jewish Life in Cleveland in the 1920s and 1930s*
Libbie L. Braverman (1900–1999)   248
   Excerpt from *Libbie*
Louis Rosenblum (1923–)   263
   Excerpt from *Involvement in the Soviet Jewry Movement*

SECTION FIVE: PHILANTHROPY AND SERVICE
Michael Sharlitt (1884–1966)   283
   Excerpt from *As I Remember*
A. R. Warner, Jas. F. Jackson, and Martin Marks   292
   Petition to the Trustees, Western Reserve University
Lillian Strauss (?–1959)   296
   "I Remember Hiram House"

Henry L. Zucker (1910–1998)   303
   "The Federation Idea: Cleveland Model"
Montefiore Home   317
   Documents from the Montefiore Archives
Menorah Park   321
   Menorah Park, "Rules for Synagogue," ca. 1920
Mt. Sinai Hospital   323
   Chronology of the Beginnings of the Mt. Sinai
   Hospital, 1915

Appendix: Chronological List of Documents   329
Index   331

Series Editor's Foreword

JOHN J. GRABOWSKI

Remembering: Cleveland's Jewish Voices is the third volume to be published in the series "Voices of Diversity." It is the first to take the form of an anthology of previously published material as well as unpublished manuscripts. As such, it represents a variety of voices, some of which have found audiences in libraries and bookstores for many decades and a number that have remained somewhat sequestered in the archives.

It was the long-held dream of the late Judah Rubinstein to allow these voices to speak again and to do so in unison at a single forum. As *the* historian of the Greater Cleveland Jewish community, Judah became expert on the substantial literature that had been produced by the community. When asked some decades ago to prepare a history of the Jewish community of Cleveland, he demurred. One new work had recently been published. Moreover, he knew that perhaps the best way to record that history was not to impose yet another outside narrative but to allow the community to speak for itself.

The long gestation of that idea rests upon many factors, primary among them the breadth of material available. It proved hard to find an end point, a terminus for research, and equally difficult to select from the hundreds of textual memories those that best reflected the Jewish experience in northeastern Ohio. Judah was working on that process at the time of his death in 2003. Thereafter, his friends and colleagues, most notably Sally H. Wertheim, Alan D. Bennett, and Jane Avner, took up the work of bringing these voices to life once again. What follows in this volume is a testament to the power of the written word in giving voice to memory, as well as to the incredibly rich and diverse history of that portion of the Jewish Diaspora that came to settle in the Greater Cleveland area beginning in the 1830s.

Cleveland is a cosmopolitan city, and this anthology places the Jewish community within that context. Most important, it captures the internal diversity of life, opinion, and activity within the Jewish community of Cleveland itself. Certainly, the voices that speak herein are all Jewish, and they reflect strongly what it means to be Jewish in the United States. But they also address topics that range far and wide in the broader American experience. Those who remember in this volume include a farmer, businessmen, social workers, authors, religious leaders, political activists, and educators. They speak of neighborhoods, politics, schools, suburbanization, the struggle for civil and equal rights, the vicissitudes of business, and the importance of family and community. Some, such as Rabbi Abba Hillel Silver, are internationally renowned. Others, such as Lillian Strauss, achieved fame and recognition in smaller venues—in her case, the venue was a settlement house. However, despite their diversity—in terms of fame, wealth, and the years in which they lived—they have one other aspect in common outside of their faith. Each remembered and each gave voice to his or her memories through the written word. And thus, as participants in a broader history, they provide us with a vital chronicle of that history.

I and my colleagues are honored to bring Judah Rubinstein's work to publication. By doing so, we remember him as a friend, mentor, and scholar and we hear his voice again, speaking to us about his love of history, books, and the many memories he had of his community.

Foreword

JEWISH FEDERATION OF CLEVELAND

In 1977 the members of the rock group Fleetwood Mac spoke only of the future in their song "Don't Stop." The lyrics "Don't you look back" argued that tomorrow rather than yesterday was the primary focus of life.

This song could be counted as one of the major anthems of the younger generations. A *Billboard* chart topper, it has been popular since its release nearly three decades ago, was used as the campaign theme for a winning U.S. presidential candidate, and has become embedded in pop culture. Yet it is not a very Jewish message. We are a people who look forward to perfecting the world, but we do so with a firm grounding in tradition, one that requires us to study and respect the text handed down over the generations.

Moving beyond religious teachings, all too often there is a desire to forget about or not bother with the past. The here and now is what matters. We have new challenges, a fast-paced world, ever changing, not like the slower days of yesteryear. What could those times teach us about what we face?

Well, the pages that follow do speak to us over the decades since they were written. The institutions discussed, the personalities recalled, and the historical events described all serve to remind us that we are a unique Jewish community, shaped by our predecessors. In our time, we will also shape the community we pass on to the next generation, albeit in somewhat different mediums and timeframes—our papers, DVDs, tweets, e-mails, Facebook postings, and You-Tube videos will be for someone else to edit and compile. If we have done our jobs well, the members of the next generation will also realize how the actions and outcomes of yesterday continue to affect their tomorrows.

The Jewish Federation of Cleveland is grateful to Dr. Sally H. Wertheim, one of our past board chairs and a historian of education herself, and Dr. Alan D. Bennett, retired executive vice president of the Bureau of Jewish Education, for the editing of this volume. We dedicate the volume to the memory of Judah Rubinstein, the Federation's long-serving historian and archivist, who enabled us to preserve our past to inform our future.

STEPHEN H. HOFFMAN
President, Jewish Federation of Cleveland

Acknowledgments

We acknowledge, with respect and appreciation, the Cleveland Jewish voices—builders and shapers whose own words attest to their work and their experiences and whose words you will now be privileged to read.

We are grateful also to the many researchers, historians, and archivists who secured and protected the documents used in preparing this chronicle. We thank, too, the Jewish Federation of Cleveland for its support of the Cleveland Jewish Archives since its inception. As guardian of Cleveland's Jewish past and as protector of the future, the federation and its president, Stephen H. Hoffman, have been instrumental in helping this volume move from dream to reality.

There would be no *Remembering: Cleveland's Jewish Voices* save for John J. Grabowski, Krieger Mueller Associate Professor of Applied History at Case Western Reserve University and historian and vice president for collections, Western Reserve Historical Society. It was his determination to see the completion of Judah Rubinstein's documentation of Jewish Cleveland that informed the process leading to this publication, another in The Kent State University Press series that John edits. His attention to detail, ability to manipulate the parts to reach the whole, dedication to historical scholarship, and knowledge about The Kent State University Press have been critical to this publication.

The Western Reserve Historical Society and its Jewish Archives have been essential and instrumental partners in this volume's development and production. Its vast collection of Jewish documents, including personal papers and community records, makes the Jewish Archives the primary source for scholarship about Cleveland's Jewish community.

We are especially grateful to Jane Avner, former director of the Jewish Archives, for continuing what would have been the next phase of Judah Rubinstein's work. Although, sadly, Judah's death interrupted the effort, it is fortunate that Jane had worked with him prior to his death. Her diligence and professionalism made it possible for us to carry on Judah's undertaking after she left the archives.

We express our gratitude to Sean Martin, current associate curator for Jewish history at the Historical Society, who was of great help in this as in other projects, and who contributed to the historical preface. His understanding of and familiarity with the Jewish Archives and with Cleveland's Jewish history, plus his own contributions to the manuscript, added immeasurably to the result.

We recognize and thank the unsung heroines and heroes of the Western Reserve Historical Society staff whose behind-the-scenes, sometimes mundane work contributed significantly to this volume.

The editors express their gratitude, appreciation, and esteem to all—from the voices of the past to those more directly involved—for their part in bringing this volume to publication.

SALLY H. WERTHEIM AND ALAN D. BENNETT

In the interim between the completion of the mauscript and its publication, my coeditor and friend, ALAN D. BENNETT, *became seriously ill and died. Alan's death is a great loss to his family, many friends, colleagues, and students. I appreciate the opportunities I have had to collaborate with him over the years. I had hoped and expected that he would be able to see the results of all the work he contributed to the publication of this book. That, sadly, was not to be the case.*
—*Sally H. Wertheim*

Introduction

The Jews of Cleveland: A Documentary Review

Three publications, each of which provides a unique perspective on the origin, development, and achievements of one of the foremost Jewish communities in North America, recount the remarkable story of Cleveland's Jewish population. In text and in photographs, the authors—Allan Peskin,[1] Sidney Z. Vincent and Judah Rubinstein,[2] and Lloyd P. Gartner[3]—have chronicled a journey that moves from small beginnings to giant accomplishments, from refugee immigrant community to proud partner helping to nurture the greater Cleveland community while strengthening itself. (In addition, the chapter by Sidney Z. Vincent entitled "Cleveland—City without Jews" in Eugene J. Lipman and Albert Vorspan's 1962 volume provides an important analysis of a transitional phase in the history of Cleveland and of Cleveland Jewry.)[4]

An updated and expanded edition of the Vincent and Rubinstein volume, published after Rubinstein's death, continues and expands upon his unique approach to understanding a community at its core through contemporaneous photographs.[5] The volume is a worthy tribute to Rubinstein's tireless effort to tell the stories of real people pursuing their everyday activities and, in that way, illuminating the community's soul.

At the same time, Rubinstein understood and respected the significance of the written record and valued the inestimable contribution that all historical artifacts make to the academic discipline. That appreciation led him to a new undertaking nearly a decade ago: identifying documents that elucidate aspects of the story. He diligently searched the archives of the Western Reserve Historical Society and drew on his own vast knowledge of the Cleveland

Jewish community to select the most instructive documents to include in a planned publication. He died before he could complete the work.

Rubinstein prepared several preliminary lists of documents that he culled from the files. The artifacts he chose represent aspects of early Jewish communal life in Cleveland ranging from social welfare to labor, from religious life to cultural activities, from the role of women to family life, from politics to social interactions—and more. From his lists, together with a few additional selections, we present here twenty-seven documents that we believe comprise major indexes of Jewish life over more than a century and a half since the first venturesome band of fifteen Jewish souls, seeking liberty in a new land, set foot on the territory that General Moses Cleaveland had mapped out for the Connecticut Land Company some four decades earlier.[6] As the Alsbacher document shows, it was a journey fraught with potential danger for the continuation of the Jewish heritage in the New World. Other documents in this volume attest to the fact that the immigrants successfully met their challenges and laid the groundwork for today's vibrant Cleveland Jewish community.

We have arranged the documents thematically. Each group of documents provides a limited but compelling view of a salient feature of a century and a half of Jewish communal existence. We have tried to be consistent in assigning documents to categories of Jewish endeavor, although many do not neatly fit into a single category. The appendix lists the documents chronologically for additional reference.

Judah Rubinstein was our friend. We are grateful for the opportunity to carry his work forward.

SALLY H. WERTHEIM
ALAN D. BENNETT
Cleveland, Ohio

NOTES

1. Allan Peskin, *This Tempting Freedom* (Cleveland, OH: Fairmount Temple Anshe Chesed, 1973).
2. Sidney Z. Vincent and Judah Rubinstein, *Merging Traditions: Jewish Life in Cleveland* (Cleveland, OH: Western Reserve Historical Society and Jewish Community Federation of Cleveland, 1978).
3. Lloyd P. Gartner, *History of the Jews of Cleveland* (Cleveland, OH: Western Reserve Historical Society and Jewish Theological Seminary of America, 1978).
4. Eugene J. Lipman and Albert Vorspan, eds., *A Tale of Ten Cities* (New York: Union of American Hebrew Congregations, 1962), pp. 45–77.
5. Judah Rubinstein, with Jane Avner, *Merging Traditions: Jewish Life in Cleveland* (Kent, OH: Kent State University Press, 2003).
6. Nineteen Jews left Unsleben, Bavaria, arriving in New York in 1839. Fifteen of them then traveled to Cleveland, joining three of their townsmen who were already in the city.

Historical Overview

[handwritten margin notes: 1839 – Come to cleve; 1841 – First Temple]

Early Jewish immigration to Cleveland, mainly from Germany, began with the arrival of the Alsbacher party from Unsleben, Bavaria, in July 1839. At the encouragement of Simson Thorman, a fur trader from Unsleben with a business in Cleveland, fifteen members of the party, soon to be seduced by the religious and political freedoms of the United States, made their home in the growing city on Lake Erie. In a document addressed to Moses and Yetta Alsbacher, Lazarus Kohn, the group's religious teacher in Unsleben, exhorted the emigrants, "Resist and withstand this tempting freedom and do not turn away from the religion of our fathers." In 1841, recalling their teacher's counsel, the group established the city's first Jewish congregation, the Israelitic Society of Cleveland, known today as Anshe Chesed. A second congregation, Tifereth Israel, was founded by members of Anshe Chesed in 1850, and thus, Jewish religious practice set the stage for the development of a rich and vibrant Jewish communal life that would play an important role in the development of northeastern Ohio. The readings in this volume reflect various aspects of that communal life and challenge us to consider how we might build upon the achievements of our predecessors.

A vital part of the economic, cultural, educational, and social life of the city, Cleveland's Jews have demonstrated significant individual and communal achievements. The documents here represent the communal life of Cleveland's Jews, encompassing their role in arts and cultural organizations, their participation in civic life, their economic development, and their commitment to philanthropy and social service. Arranged thematically, the readings attest to the fact that the immigrants successfully met the challenges of their new

5

world and laid the groundwork for the dynamic Jewish community of today's Cleveland. Each group of documents provides a limited but compelling view of a salient feature of more than a century and a half of Jewish communal existence. The readings may not fit neatly into the categories assigned, but brief introductions to each document, along with the appendix listing the documents chronologically, will guide the reader throughout the book. These documents comprise major indexes of Jewish life in northeastern Ohio since the late 1830s.

As the Alsbacher document shows, it was a journey fraught with potential danger for the continuation of the Jewish heritage in the New World. Taking care to found and foster the institutions necessary for Jewish continuity, Cleveland's Jews have proven themselves worthy stewards of the counsel of Lazarus Kohn.

The first Jewish immigrants demonstrated the entrepreneurial skills necessary to succeed in a new country. They worked as peddlers and shopkeepers and later moved into manufacturing businesses, especially the garment trade. Many were also bankers, clerks, bookkeepers, and dry goods merchants. Kaufman Hays and his brother Joseph Hays, whose autobiographies are excerpted in this volume, exemplify the successful entrepreneurs of the period. After joining Simson Thorman in business in 1860, the Hays brothers established a clothing store; Kaufman Hays later sold the store and became involved in finance, manufacturing, and local politics. Although few were as successful as the Hays family, members of the Jewish community gradually achieved a degree of professional success and economic stability and began moving farther out from the Central Market district to the Woodland neighborhood.

A second wave of Jewish immigration from Eastern Europe, fueled by the search for better economic opportunities and the desire to be free from political, social, and religious discrimination, occurred from the 1880s to 1924, a period that brought immigrants of all ethnic backgrounds and religious denominations from many countries to the United States. William Zorach, who would become a well-known artist, offers in this volume his description of growing up as an immigrant child from Eastern Europe in Cleveland, and Lillian Strauss recalls her time at Hiram House, a settlement house that served both Jews and non-Jews. The East European Jews arriving in Cleveland joined a German Jewish community that was already well established. More overtly traditional than their new German Jewish neighbors and often speaking a different language, Yiddish, the East European Jews challenged the community with their need for a range of separate Jewish organizations and social services. As elsewhere in American Jewish communities, this challenge led to distinct differences between the Germans and the East Europeans.

The earliest congregations established by the Germans, Anshe Chesed and Tifereth Israel, gradually focused on classical Reform Judaism in the nineteenth century, in an effort to appear similar to their Protestant neighbors. By contrast, East European Jews, once settled in Cleveland, established their own congregations, with significantly different practices than in the Reform congregations. Some of these congregations, most notably Anshe Emeth (today's Park Synagogue, founded by Polish Jews in 1857) and B'nai Jeshurun (founded by Hungarian Jews in 1866), eventually adopted some of the innovative practices of Reform Judaism and came to occupy a space between Orthodox tradition and Reform practice. Many others, though, adhered strictly to religious traditions as practiced by their ancestors in Eastern Europe. By the 1920s, over twenty congregations in the city could be identified as Orthodox, and Orthodox rabbinical leadership had begun to participate actively in the larger community. Rabbi Israel Porath, the area's most significant Orthodox leader, is remembered fondly in this volume by his granddaughter, Laura Porath. In the New World, congregations remained the most valued centers of Jewish life. In its internal religious diversity, the Jewish community demonstrated the importance of a foundation of American democracy—the freedom to worship.

East European Jews would ultimately change more than simply the religious landscape of the Jewish community. As early as the 1850s, members of the Jewish community founded social and charitable organizations, asserted their presence in the city, and then came to play leadership roles alongside others representing Cleveland's diverse ethnic populations. A local chapter of B'nai B'rith, a national Jewish service organization, was founded in 1853. A Jewish men's club, the Excelsior (a forerunner of the Oakwood Club), was founded in 1872. But the more recently arrived immigrants would see a need to establish their own groups, such as the Hungarian Benevolent and Social Union, founded in 1881. Such organizations met specific social, cultural, educational, and economic needs beyond the purview of the synagogue and assured the continuity of various forms of Jewish culture.

The influx of immigrants, the increased need for social services, and the growth of these kinds of associations together with business and labor groups provided the necessary social context for the organization and development of philanthropy in the early twentieth century. As Jews moved into industry, they faced exploitation as workers, as described here by Rose Pastor Stokes, but they also reaped the benefits of economic success, as described by cigar factory owner Julius C. Newman. Cleveland's burgeoning population required community leaders to develop institutions to meet the needs of all. Competition and rivalry began to appear among social service organizations originally founded to meet similar, specific needs. In 1903, Jewish community leaders formed an umbrella organization to pool resources and provide a system of social services to the area's Jewish community. Nine men, prominent in Cleveland's business, legal, and political activities and the leaders of Jewish charitable associations, met as a group to begin the process of legal incorporation for a federation. These leaders intended to help Jews connect to Jewish life and to improve the general social conditions of the world in which they lived. They aimed to spare contributors to Jewish charities the bother of rival solicitations by persuading those charities to participate in a single campaign that raised funds on behalf of its member agencies. One gift would touch many lives. The first campaign in 1904 raised $41,350 from 1,219 subscribers. The federated Jewish organization these men formed, the Federation of Jewish Charities (today, the Jewish Federation of Cleveland), provided support to eight agencies: the Jewish Orphan Asylum (later known as the Bellefaire Jewish Children's Bureau), the Montefiore Home for the Aged, the Denver Hospital for Consumptives, the Council Educational Alliance (later part of the Jewish Community Center), the Infant Orphan Mothers Society, the Council of Jewish Women, the Mt. Sinai Hospital, and the Hebrew Relief Association (later the Jewish Family Service Association). Indicative of their involvement in the larger community, one of the men involved in the establishment of the Federation of Jewish Charities, Martin Marks, was also instrumental in founding an institution intended to train social workers in the practical skills necessary to improve urban life, Western Reserve University's School of Social Science and Research (later renamed the Mandel School of Applied Social Sciences, after another well-known Jewish community philanthropist).

The establishment of the Federation of Jewish Charities was a sign of the community's maturity. By the early twentieth century, many of the immigrants had already become accustomed to life in the United States, and their children had begun to take on increasingly significant leadership roles. Alfred Benesch, the son of Czech Jewish immigrants, served on Cleveland's City Council in 1912 and went on to hold other key positions, most notably on Cleveland's Board of Education. As Jewish immigrants and their children began to find themselves in improved economic circumstances, they grew anxious to move away from the crowded conditions and dilapidated housing of the Woodland neighborhood. From 1918 to 1926, the Jewish population of Woodland declined precipitously, whereas that of the Glenville, Mt. Pleasant, and Kinsman neighborhoods increased dramatically. This move is reflected in the histories of some of the city's most prominent Jewish institutions. In Glenville, Mt. Sinai opened on 105th Street in 1916, and the Hebrew Orthodox Old Age Home moved to Lakeview Avenue in 1921. The Council Educational Alliance relocated to East 135th Street and Kinsman in 1928. The congregations followed, too. Glenville, Mt. Pleasant, and Kinsman were home to many smaller congregations of the Orthodox in the 1920s. Anshe Emeth built the Cleveland Jewish Center on East 105th Street in 1922, and Tifereth Israel dedicated its building on Ansel Road and 105th in 1924. The Cleveland Jewish Center combined religious, social, and cultural functions and became a symbol of an active, thriving community. The center also figures in the reminiscences of Leon Wiesenfeld, a local newspaper editor and community activist who offers a frank assessment of the split between Orthodox Jews and the growing Conservative movement. By 1926, the Federation of Jewish Charities had expanded to provide budgetary oversight to their member agencies and changed its name to the Jewish Welfare Federation. That same year, the Federation offered its first aid to Orthodox Jewish institutions, and the Hebrew Cultural Garden, the first of the ethnic gardens in Cleveland's Rockefeller Park, was dedicated during the visit to Cleveland of the Hebrew and Zionist poet Chaim Nachman Bialik, suggesting the roots of the Jewish community in the United States and the community's commitment to its Jewish identity. Both the consolidation of the work of the Federation and the move of Jewish institutions to the eastern side of the Cleveland area, coinciding with the many individual moves of Jewish families, illustrate the remarkable unity within the Cleveland Jewish community.

Cleveland's Jews paid close attention to events overseas throughout the 1930s and 1940s. Major Reform rabbis, including Barnett Brickner of Anshe Chesed and Abba Hillel Silver of The Temple–Tifereth Israel, campaigned indefatigably on behalf of Zionism and for the establishment of a Jewish state. Silver's attention to the international situation can be seen in an address reprinted here, focusing on the rabbi's response to the 1937 visit of German exchange students to Cleveland. The difficulties of coming of age in the 1930s are vividly evoked by Howard Brody, who grew up outside Cleveland on a farm in Ashtabula County, and Jo Sinclair, the pen name of Cleveland's Ruth Seid, who describes her exposure to other cultures while working on a Works Progress Administration (WPA) project at the Cleveland Public Library.

Although American Jews often expressed different views about Zionism and the best way to achieve the goal of protecting the global Jewish community, they agreed on the need to assist their own country during a time of war. More than 8,500 Jews from Cleveland served in the U.S. military during World War II. Immediately following the war, Cleveland's Jews contributed to the rescue and resettlement of European Jewry, and they were also very involved in the 1948 founding of the state of Israel.

After World War II, the eastward migration of the Jewish community continued. Jews had already begun to move to the inner-ring suburb of Cleveland Heights in the 1910s, but they faced restrictive covenants in Shaker Heights, Beachwood, and Pepper Pike. In the postwar period, barriers gradually broke down, and Jews moved beyond Cleveland Heights into Shaker Heights and farther east to Beachwood. Initially opposed to Jews moving in, the village of Beachwood filed a suit against Anshe Chesed when it tried to build a synagogue on Fairmount Boulevard. The village lost, and Anshe Chesed became popularly known as Fairmount Temple, one of the most prominent Jewish institutions in a town whose population was nearly 90 percent Jewish in the 1990s.

The move to the suburbs was nearly complete by the late 1950s. Though Sidney Z. Vincent, a Federation official and community activist whose work is included in this volume, had described Cleveland as a "city without Jews" in 1960, the Jewish community was alive and well in the eastern suburbs. Though the community had already become an integral part of American life, the distinctive features of language and religious tradition continued to define it in the postwar period. David Guralnik describes here the Yiddish theater of Mark Feder, a director who brought the best of Yiddish theater to Cleveland throughout the 1960s under the auspices of the Jewish Community Center. Orthodox congregations and schools, such as the Hebrew Academy, located along Taylor Road in Cleveland Heights and formed the heart of a bustling community. Other congregations, such as B'nai Jeshurun in its relocation to Pepper Pike from Cleveland Heights, moved farther out. Two new Reform congregations located in the suburbs—Temple Emanu El in University Heights in 1954 and Suburban Temple (a congregation born of differences in approaches toward religious education and Zionism) in Beachwood in 1955.

Communal institutions made the move as well, transforming themselves into organizations that could meet community needs using the most contemporary methods. Some of them moved east early, anticipating the future migration pattern. The Jewish Orphan Asylum relocated to the intersection of Belvoir and Fairmount in University Heights and became known as Belle-faire in 1929, a process described here by Michael Sharlitt, who directed the institution from 1922 to 1941. The Jewish Community Center, formed in 1948, was located in Glenville, but by 1960, it had moved to Cleveland Heights and today can be found on South Woodland Road in Beachwood. In the 1960s, The Temple–Tifereth Israel built a "branch" in Beachwood, now the primary site of the congregation's activities. The Jewish Orthodox Home for the Aged (previously the Hebrew Orthodox Old Age Home) became the Menorah Park Jewish Home for the Aged when it located on Cedar Road in Beachwood in 1968. The Montefiore Home, an older nursing facility for the Jewish elderly, was originally located in Woodland and then moved to Cleveland Heights. In 1991, the Montefiore Home opened in a campus next to Menorah Park. Also previously in Glenville and Cleveland Heights, the Cleveland College of Jewish Studies (today the Siegal College of Judaic Studies) located near other Jewish institutions on Shaker Boulevard in Beachwood in 1976. Cleveland's Orthodox Jewish community maintains two centers of activity, one on Taylor Road in Cleveland Heights and another developed in the 1990s near the intersection of Cedar and Green, straddling University Heights and Beachwood.

This eastward migration was not without its challenges. As Jews and other groups left inner-city neighborhoods for the suburbs, Cleveland be-came increasingly segregated. Jews often led the fight to establish integrated neighborhoods in the 1950s, as the memorandum published here from the Jewish Community Federation shows. The movement east, along with the ongoing challenge of maintaining Jewish community in stable and integrated neighborhoods, continues, as Jewish families have begun to move to Geauga, Lake, and Summit counties. The concentration of Jewish institutions in the eastern suburbs, especially Beachwood, continues to facilitate the coherence of a religiously and culturally diverse community.

Working with the disparate groups in Cleveland and with Jewish communi-ties throughout the world, especially in Israel, the Jewish Federation ensures Jewish continuity by, among other tasks, supporting social service efforts and Jewish education. The address included here by Henry L. Zucker outlines the reasons for the success of the Federation model in realizing philanthropic goals. Jewish social service professionals continued to provide for the needs of immigrants in the mid-twentieth century, aiding Holocaust survivors in the late 1940s and 1950s and offering support to the more than five thousand Soviet Jews arriving in Cleveland from the 1960s to 1990s. Federation officials provided assistance to the pioneering movement to aid Soviet Jews, led by

Louis Rosenblum and other members of Cleveland's west side Jewish community. The Jewish Education Center of Cleveland, an agency perceived as the education planning and budgeting arm of the Federation, offers financial and curricular support to Jewish day schools, professional development programs for educators, and support for research and planning; it builds on the legacy of educators such as Libbie Braverman, a champion of Reform Jewish education who served many years as education director at Anshe Chesed. Thus, the Jewish Community Federation of Cleveland, formed under that name in 1951 as the result of a merger between the Jewish Community Council and the Jewish Welfare Federation (organizations that grew out of the original Federation of Jewish Charities), eventually bridged the gap between Jews native to Cleveland and those who arrived with very different cultural backgrounds.

There is much to be learned here about how Cleveland's Jewish leaders developed a community that has been responsive to its members' needs and able to take a leading role in the larger society. Helping us to better understand the leadership challenges of both the past and the future, these documents also raise many questions, not the least of which concerns the Jewish community's ability to work in common for shared goals. Most important, they offer a model of community development that emphasizes the continuity of tradition in an increasingly diverse society.

SEAN MARTIN

Section One

Arts and Culture

Playbill, circa 1930, for Yiddish performances at the Manhattan Theater at East 106th Street and Superior in Cleveland's Glenville neighborhood (Western Reserve Historical Society).

Excerpt from *The Seasons: Death and Transfiguration*

Novelist Ruth Seid (pen name Jo Sinclair) showed early promise as a writer and was valedictorian at her Cleveland high school graduation in 1930. Her novels reflect her concern for Jews and for other minority groups and explore themes such as oppression, poverty, Jewish self-hatred, homophobia, and marginalization.

Wasteland, her first novel (1946), dealt with Jewish gender issues and self-hatred. It encouraged other writers to address Jewish themes and brought her a $10,000 Harper Prize; she shared the $10-a-week installments of this award with her parents, who continued to live in Cleveland. *The Changelings* (1955), which drew on Jewish experience to tell the story of a community in transition from white to African American, earned Sinclair a nomination for the Pulitzer Prize and received the 1956 Jewish Book Council of America Annual Award. *Sing at My Wake* (1951) continued her concern for minority groups, and *Anna Teller* (1960) told the story of a Jewish matriarch.

The new popularity of women's and ethnic literature in the 1980s and 1990s revived interest in Sinclair's work, bringing her writing to a new generation of readers.

In the following excerpt, Sinclair reveals her early consuming passion for learning and writing. However, an unresponsive educational system and a stultifying society frustrated her at every turn. She shunned formal college and created her own—free—school of higher education by devouring the holdings of the Cleveland Public Library, which liberated her from the repressions of the ghetto "of street, mind, and soul." With her first published short story, Ruth

Seid, iconoclast and rebel, became Jo Sinclair "as one more 'being different' for that Ruth trapped in a ghetto."

Source: "Some Biographical Notes on the Author (by the Author)," an excerpt from Jo Sinclair, *The Seasons: Death and Transfiguration* (New York: The Feminist Press of the City University of New York, 1993). Reprinted with permission for this edition only, The Feminist Press, New York.

SOME BIOGRAPHICAL NOTES ON THE AUTHOR (BY THE AUTHOR)

"Jo Sinclair" was born Ruth Seid in a Brooklyn, New York ghetto, in 1913. She was the youngest of the five children of Nathan and Ida Seid, Russian Jews who emigrated to America in the early 1900s.

She was three when her family moved to Cleveland, Ohio, where jobs were more plentiful for her carpenter father. Much of her life was spent there, and in the nearby countryside.

Following family and working-class traditions, she attended John Hay High School, a commercial school that trained students for office jobs. Wrong school for the girl who had been writing poems for herself since fourteen or so—rough, free-verse outbursts of frustration, anger, intense longing for "life." She was bored by her classes in shorthand, filing, bookkeeping, loved English and composition, was drawn at once to writing for the school newspaper.

Completely wrong school; not that there was ever a single question in her mind about attending college. In her rigidly traditional world, a decent child in a poor Jewish family always got a job immediately after graduating, to help with food and rent and clothes. Period. Except that this child would dream once in a while (but a quiet yearning, with none of the rage and bitterness of her poems) of going off to one of those fabulous universities she'd read about—in a flowers-and-trees city far from the barren neighborhoods in which she had always lived. Very quiet talking to herself: Sure, college probably might help, but she could do it even without those special teachers. Become the famous, rich author she had promised herself she would be someday—with money enough to help parents and to write at the same time.

Ruth Seid created her own college, via the Cleveland Public Library; always the branch within walking distance of home, so that she did not even have to pay for a streetcar ride, and could carry five or six books at a time back to the house after gleaning one more library shelf. It was all free—a must for the child who had always known that there was rarely enough money for extras in life.

Her "courses" of study in library books began early, and went on all her life. As she grew older, they included real and even great poetry (Keats was nothing like her own blurts in the heart). She read voraciously, with constant excitement and curiosity, every kind of book on the shelves—soon including plays and essays and biographies of authors, but always going back to the short-story collections and novels with which she had started this education of the fiercely insistent writer.

The college-library courses were enthralling lessons about the universe outside any ghetto of street, mind, and soul; lessons about the "other people"—who lived in what she called, in some of her poems, the "garden of world." And, after a while, she knew that the precious courses would never end for her, even if she *were* permitted into that garden someday, to live and work there rightfully. She would never want to graduate, and leave her special college for the writer and good human being she wanted so fervently to be for all her life.

But there was high school to leave right now; she was eager for that kind of graduation, which naturally would be followed by grown-up life action—to go into a new kind of writing. In 1930, valedictorian of her class, the naive girl of seventeen graduated into the Depression. So very naive: she looked at once for the obligatory job, the salary with which a decent child helps her family; and learned a great deal about that new word, *Depression.* (She had never seen it in a book.) Learned rather quickly: jobs were few, lasted briefly, and paid very little even if you managed to find one.

Much, much later, she could smile wryly at the roster of jobs the honor student searched out in the first years of what became known as the Great Depression. That period was crammed with fearfully difficult courses of rock-bottom poverty, lost homes, thousands of families "on relief"—including her own. But no smiling as that girl grew up and learned all about desperation, but kept reading her library books and writing.

Ruth Seid became Jo Sinclair with her first published short story, in early 1936. No money paid, and it was a magazine put out for the country's ghettos of poverty, bitterness, racial wars, and hatred. It was called *New Masses,* and, in all honesty, she did not want to be part of anonymous, shabby, huddling masses of people; she wanted to walk free and independent in the airy, flower-filled garden of world. But the story *was* a writing credit in a national magazine, so it felt like a little hope, even a kind of small guarantee of further publications. Yes, she would hang on to that pseudonym she had made up as one more "being

" for that Ruth trapped in a ghetto. She would keep using that shining
ne, but add the right credits to this first grubby one—and smash open
p!

it was now Jo Sinclair who was writing evenings and weekends. Days,
it was Ruth Seid who found and lost the weird mélange of brief jobs: making boxes in a factory; proofreading telephone directories; doing a sort of
bookkeeping in a neighborhood store that was supposed to sell spaghetti
and olive oil at the front, while the proprietor handed big sacks of sugar out
the back door to bootleggers. Once she was a salesgirl in a department store
during the Christmas rush. Once she counted votes half the night as a clerk
in an election booth.

That job was an excellent course—her first in politics—and it taught her
that she wanted to be a lifelong voter. Her first-ever vote was for Roosevelt,
of course, savior of poor people. And now, in the latest branch library, she
began reading the city newspapers, learning as much as possible about FDR's
rescue program for the unemployed.

It was Ruth who took her family off relief by using one of those programs
called the WPA. The magazine credit helped; she explained the pen name,
which in a sense proved she was a writer. So did her report on all the high-
school newspaper writing she had done. She ended up on a WPA project
called "The Foreign Language Newspaper Digest." Her job was editing the
awkward translations of articles into English from all the newspapers written
in the languages of Cleveland's ethnic groups. She'd had no idea there were
that many in her city. "Melting pot" in library books turned into real people,
who became friends as she learned their ways.

And there was a wondrous bonus for the perennial student. Her project
was housed in the main branch of the library, in downtown Cleveland—an
enormous and very beautiful building she had seen once but never entered.
(Too far from home for walking.) She had never even imagined so many
books in one place—floor after floor, wide marble staircases between—for
more beauty, so she never used the elevator. Intensely excited, she planned
to stay late and investigate all the riches, use her old branch card to borrow
as many books as were permitted.

The project itself was fascinating: new and complex courses in American
sociology, and world history and geography. She was working with men and
women who had come to this city as immigrants, like her parents, and lived
in their own ghettos. But they were different; they still loved their homelands,
and talked about them incessantly. Her parents never mentioned Russia. These

people read their own languages in special papers, as well as the Cleveland dailies, from which they could learn English. They seemed to touch two countries at once—America and the one they had left—and obviously loved both.

The student of a Ruth listed those newspapers she had never heard of before: Italian, Hungarian, Czech, Polish, Ukrainian, Spanish. (A Yiddish paper was there too—the same one her father read at home, but he never included one of the Cleveland newspapers, as her translator-friends did. He did not read much English, had never even wanted to learn the language. Interesting variety of ghettos!) The writer of a Jo filed away her new information about foreign Americans and homelands for future short stories. And maybe a novel some day?

She liked her colleagues a lot: their warmth and overt emotions, their quickness to trust and to become friends, their easy laughter, their honest and unabashed weeping at European troubles. They did not act like any of the unhappy, always worried ghetto Jews she knew. And, one day, she decided that there must be varied gardens of world for varied kinds of people. As she listened to the accented talk, she realized that she was learning about entirely different chunks of the world outside her cramped one. These people were probably some of the "others" she had read about, but this job brought them close and real, very alive; and she knew with happiness that the horizons of the writer were widening.

Jo wrote about Ruth's new friends—contented Americans who still had plenty of room in their souls for the lands they had left. She went on studying actual people, instead of just men and women in books, and imagined a new type of garden that bloomed in two countries, and seemed even lovelier for the sturdy bridge of love between them. Wonderful how chapters of books could turn into true life. Could any ordinary university have taught her that?

One day, listening to her colleagues as she edited their work, she heard about a faraway war that had started—too near their homelands, and getting nearer all the time. Many of them cried as they discussed their families, how they were bound to be killed or made refugees by tyrants like Mussolini and Franco; and she saw the name Hitler for the first time, in several of the articles they had translated.

At home, Ruth's heart ached for her friends, and Jo began writing new kinds of stories about those weeping men and women, the war swooping toward the parents and brothers they had left behind when they emigrated. It was the closest the student had come to a war. And this one felt so different than the ones she had read about. In books you could not hear crying, or see fear for endangered beloveds. Jo wanted to write that sorrow and fear so well that her readers would be able to hear and see people in torment.

She sold one of those stories (little kids being bombed in the Spanish Civil War) to *Esquire,* a rather new and "good" magazine—nothing at all like *New Masses,* her only other credit. And they paid writers! As she looked at that check for seventy-five dollars, marvelously shocked at the amount, she suddenly remembered that this magazine had been the real reason for her pen name. Picking up the first issue in a branch library, she had read that they would use only men writers. Ah, a challenge, Mr. Editor! With much care, over a few weeks, she had created *Jo*—chuckling at the thought that it could be used by men *or* women. And *Sinclair* sounded much better with Jo than Seid. (Besides which, she admired writers like Sinclair Lewis and Upton Sinclair.) So—would the editor question her phony name?

No. But it had taken her more than two years of submitting old type stories, and getting rejection slips for all of them, before *Esquire* accepted this new type she had learned how to write by watching and listening to suffering people. She was twenty-five when she sold her first paid story, and earned that kind of credit: a top magazine which published many of the famous authors she had studied in her libraries and used as teachers. And now Jo Sinclair was among those fabulous names! She even had the first proof that her writing was worth money, not only proper credits, if she worked the right way. New and joyous hope: could she leave the ghetto soon?

That life course turned still more hopeful as she began using this magnificent library for Jo, as well as for WPA-Ruth. During her wanderings in free time around the many departments on all the floors, she had discovered the general reference and reading room—enormous, with lots of tables and chairs and lamps for students like her. It was stocked with the finest magazines, and with newspapers from every big city—where she found book reviews, and interviews with successful authors recently published. On her lunch hour, she would gulp the sandwich from home and rush down the marble stairs to that magical room on the ground floor, study the work of writers good enough to be accepted by such magazines and reviewed in such newspapers.

Not enough time: she started going to the room after work, to spend hours enough with her new teachers of the best in today's writing. Her branch libraries had never held such treasures. The first time she read the *New York Times*—that Sunday *Book Review!*—was a revelation of glory. She felt as if she had been given a precious gift.

And the room continued to be crammed with similar gifts, as if from a god of writers. Each day, she felt inches closer to her dream garden. Wonderful sensation: as if her spiritual self were growing stronger, more courageous—the self she called "soul" in the poems she was still writing in bursts, between the different kinds of short stories.

That year (1938), she sold several more of those stories to two new magazines she found, that were being put out by the *Esquire* publishers: *Coronet* and *Ken*. Was paid for them, too (split the money with her happy, thrilled mother, as usual); but the really important factor was that accumulation of top credits.

Then a remarkable thing happened. The room began to hold extremely interesting levels beyond magazines and newspapers. By then, she had masked her shyness and her insecurity at being only a WPA worker, instead of a regular city patron, and had begun talking with the reference librarians. One day, she learned about grants for evening courses at Cleveland College, the downtown branch of Western Reserve University—which drew a lot of students who had to work days. Grants? That meant free courses!

The building was only a few blocks from the library. She examined it two or three times, coming early to the project; finally worked up enough courage to apply for a course in play writing. That was a new facet of writing, and she had longed to know the professional's way of tackling it ever since she'd read those dozens of library plays. Her tries on her own had been tough going. Maybe a real college would make it possible?

She was honest about her WPA job to the teacher they sent her to (a sensitive, very nice guy). He nodded with a gentle smile about her magazine credits and her pseudonym, but was much more interested in reading the copies of her one-act plays she had brought along—especially the very short one, raw with ghetto protest and frustration, that had been put on in 1935 by the Cleveland People's Theater as a curtain-raiser to *Waiting for Lefty*. (She knew the producer-founder, an unemployed actor who spent a lot of time in her branch library.)

The teacher said: "Shows talent, but a lot of the wrong technique. A play is not a short story. You'll have to learn that first off. Call me George, and I'll call you Jo. Can you make my class on Monday and Wednesday evenings, at seven?"

George became another friend, encouraged her tremendously in her work on a long one-acter she started while on the grant, taught her a great deal about writing for theater instead of for magazines. She worked earnestly on a first draft; and George was impressed enough with it to get her a second grant, on which to finish the play.

Miracle stuff happened. Near the end of the next semester, the dazed author saw *Listen to My Heart* by Jo Sinclair produced, under George's direction, in a packed college auditorium. (That really sensitive guy had used her pen name in the program.) A wonderful, deeply moving experience: her characters came as alive as real people when they spoke words she had written. A feeling of "thanks, oh Lord!" by the self who wanted so much to try every kind of writing the world of literature contained.

In the meantime, it was rather wonderful, too, that a "temporary" in a few evening classes had the student's status to make it possible to submit stories and poems to the school's literary magazine. Those local credits (always "by Jo Sinclair") in the *Cleveland College Skyline* made her feel more and more a true author: one who liked to sell for soul, as well as for money—and in hometown, as well as country wide.

Then, in the midst of those credits for play and stories and poems, a wry grin: hey!—here she was, getting a smattering of "higher learning" after all, for a split moment of that high-school dream about the bookkeeper going off to a great university for a writer's education. It seemed like an amusing but thrilling interval outside the thick walls of her bone-poor life.

But suddenly, that kind of life changed. The faraway war of her translator-friends came to her own homeland. The Depression dwindled, and the WPA program began to peter out, as the marching of men began and the country needed workers (especially women). Ruth left the project for a "real" job, found exactly the right one on her third try—with the help of Jo's credits—in the publicity department of the Greater Cleveland Chapter of the American Red Cross.

Such work seemed to put her on a smoother, shorter road toward the world of the "others," and she felt close enough sometimes to see open doors. She had read in many books that life is always a-changing, sooner or later; had never actually believed that until now. Now!—astounded by the indisputable proof that it *was* true, she even thought occasionally that she may have escaped from a few of her ghettos—especially the spiritual one, with its feeling of being in a lifetime prison.

This job was pretty perfect for somebody like her. It was crammed with the heart-need to help fight an extremely important war—fight not only for her America, but for the world's Jews and many others of those so-called

imperfect people being tortured and murdered by a Hitler. And she was battling the writer's way, with words for weapons: carefully done publicity for
the city newspapers, and optimistic stories and articles for the two national
Red Cross magazines.

The war years proved to be fine lessons in life for the patriot and decent
child. Though she was now living with very dear friends, outside any walled
neighborhood, she was still splitting a salary with parents and seeing her
family often; praying for her two brothers, off to the actual front lines, and
writing them letters regularly.

This different life was as stimulating as higher college courses for both her
selves. During the day, Ruth fought her country's war in the bustling Red Cross
building, and, on many evenings and weekends, Jo fought her own wonderful
inner war with the real writing of stories and poems. She was also studying the
making of novels (a daringly new facet befitting an author in a vastly changed
life), bringing home books for that course from the branch library near the
Cleveland Heights house she was sharing with these closest friends she had
ever had in the world. It was a time of continuing happiness—a first for her.
Among other marvels, she had fallen in love with gardening, in the backyard
of her home—discovered it was a perfect way of rest and replenishment after
hours of writing.

One Sunday morning, in her private bedroom-workroom on the third
floor (far from the activities of the family downstairs), it finally happened.
Overjoyed by how well the war was going on the early radio news, Jo started
a novel. Astonished (she had not planned to, quite yet), she went right on.
Like many of the novelists she had studied in her library books, she began
with an extremely detailed outline, a technique strange to her outside of
the brief outlines for short stories—completely different in concentration
and sustained work. Despite all the books she had read so carefully, she felt
tremulous and unsure about this difficult way of preparing for a piece of
writing. Intensely difficult, and even frightening; but she went on with the
outline. She had always been a stubborn writer, especially when some kind
of hope had triggered the work. This time, the devout hope came from a war
being won—for a whole world of tortured people and grabbed homelands.

Slowly, doggedly, over the next few weeks, she got to the writing of actual
chapters. As the war continued to go extremely well, she saw the shaping of a
first draft, the true beginning of a deeply felt book. Sometimes she discussed
the novel with her friends (book lovers, intellectuals), but never showed them

any of the manuscript. As usual, the writing was hers alone, completely private until the work was finished. But the discussions were good, even took away some of her unsureness.

Sometimes Ruth took breathers in the garden. Or Jo wrote much easier short stories, for a different way of resting. But gradually (as if the characters and plot pulled her in), the book took over all her free time. Not even a poem for explosive curse or prayer; there was just the harsh, slogging work on that first novel. Still quite scary in her heart, but in her mind she knew that this was the most challenging exciting course she had ever taken in her special college for the author.

It seemed to go on without any end in sight: her own war, in the midst of her country's. But an end did come for both. It took her almost three years to finish a last draft she could accept. And—double miracle—the American war was won, too—as if one victory had triggered the other. Ruth had her brothers home unharmed, and saw with gratitude that the universe was clean and full of beautiful values again, no longer tyrannized by evil leaders. Jo sent her manuscript out for a possible sale.

That first novel, *Wasteland,* won the ten-thousand-dollar Harper Prize Novel Award in 1946.

The war over, she could leave the Red Cross with a free conscience, and try out the girl's dream of being a free-lance writer. There was enough money to start. She was thirty-three when that major "life-changing-again" happened to her.

In the garden of world at last, all conceivable ghettos left behind, Jo Sinclair has written constantly. Over the next two decades, three more novels have been published: *Sing at My Wake, The Changelings,* and *Anna Teller.* A three-act play has been produced in a "real" theater. Between the big pieces of writing, new short stories and poems have been accepted (she still likes that selling for soul and money, that combination of national and local credits). By the sixties, a dozen anthologies have reprinted old stories. That meant books (much longer life than magazines), to add to her novels on library shelves—for oncoming students in their homemade colleges. She likes the thought of that, too: a kind of small "passing it on" to kids without money who would be as eager as she had been for those free courses.

And there are very meaningful payments to the spirit during those years of hard work. The writer has earned more awards (as if her right to live in the garden has been acknowledged often enough by the world to keep her safe in there): Best Novel of the Year—Jewish Book Council of America; Certificate of Recognition—National Conference of Christians and Jews; three-time winner, Best Novel of the Year—Ohioana Library; second prize in drama, TV Competition for Civil Rights—the Fund for the Republic; Literature Award—Cleveland Arts Prize; first Wolpaw Playwriting Grant—Cleveland Jewish Community Centers.

Jo feels humbly thankful that her work-songs continue, and that she can go on feeling that she will belong in the garden forever because the writing comes back at the right times, very like the orderly seasons of earth always come for gardeners like Ruth.

But of course there is no forever. Had she forgotten that life is change, sooner or later? Better pick up some of those library books she had studied long ago!—and read again that many once-famous authors had been subjected to these same publication silences that have sucked her in, and keep her imprisoned despite her persistent attempts to break free with new writing.

Naturally, she goes on working. By now, she knows with utter certainty that survival—for both her selves—is writing, no matter the changes in life, good or bad. This one is very bad, and especially so because she cannot figure out the mystery of why the silences began, and why they continue through months and months of disciplined work and the offering of well-done stories. Everything she sends in is rejected. Even the last draft of her fifth novel has been turned down—a particularly painful wound.

If only she could search out answers to the why. Could it be "a time to mourn"? There had been monumental deaths in her life recently. Her mother, and then, three years later, that dearest friend as beloved as a second mother. If so, how long does a gospel season go on? (The Book never gave the exact time it took for seasons to end.)

Ruth cannot find a realistic answer for that one about mourning. She dislikes mysteries, especially psychological ones; they make clear thinking too difficult. But she asks herself other questions that might explain some of this terrifying life change. Is the writer in a creative block? No. Jo has been working steadily all along. It's more as if the publishing world is blocked—at least where she is concerned.

Grim joke! But she tries one more question. Is fame so temporary that an award-established name like Jo Sinclair has been forgotten by old editors, and never heard of by new ones? No answer—not even with slightly comforting black humor this time. It all stays the sickening mystery.

Yet she goes on with the daily writing, clutching at spiritual weapons she has used before in her inner wars (gardening, Bach, Keats, and Faulkner for sleepless nights). She even grabs at a particular weapon that had been a favorite in very rough youthful battles; starts by thinking often of certain words in that book Ruth discovered on a shelf in one of her earliest libraries. The child's first bible, her introduction to Ecclesiastes.

One day, the woman tries to renew the strength and courage that the little girl took from those words. Between stints of work, she reads them in her own bible (one of the first of the books she began buying with *Wasteland* money): "To every thing there is a season, and a time to every purpose under the heavens. There is a time to keep silence, and a time to speak." And she can still smile wanly as she remembers that Jo translated "speak" into "sing."

The readings are reassuring, good for her. Except that one of those seasons does not change; and sometimes it feels as if "a time to mourn" will go on endlessly, that there will never, never be "a time to dance."

Nevertheless, that weapon helps get her through the years of near despair about the continuing publication silences. She even starts a new book, new in all ways of content and technique (as if she still half believes in those seasons of man). And then, one year—she is in her seventies—the singing begins again, but in a very different way. Life changes once more, now turns into a kind of renascence: two of her old novels are republished, are wanted in the world again as worthy books for a new generation to read.

It is a powerful, undeniable reminder that "there is a time to speak" is indeed gospel. *The Changelings* reappears in 1985 (the first publication was 1955); *Wasteland* in 1987 (that prize publication had come in 1946), by a second publisher.

Both selves of the weary survivor feel overwhelmed, unreal. But slowly, an old joy begins again in Jo's soul, in Ruth's heart, as that renascence continues like a fantastic rebirth: in 1989, *Anna Teller* (first out in 1960) earns a contract from one of those publishers. Now a favorite weapon of inner war glows like a beautiful sculpture in the spring sunlight of a new season: "There is a time of peace."

And (tasting wonderfully of the youthful writer's miracles) "there is a time to speak" goes on: in 1989 and early 1990, there are two more anthologies—out of the blue—with Jo Sinclair stories considered important enough to be taken out of old magazines and put into new books.

Is that actual singing she hears in the garden? Maybe a few more gospel words can answer that question for the writer: "There is a time to get, and a time to lose. There is a time to weep, and a time to laugh."

It is still 1990; and, yes, that *is* laughter as the singing comes true and clear with a finished book accepted: that new-in-all-ways memoir she had started in the midst of the silences. It is her first contract since 1960 for a new book. She is seventy-seven when that contract is signed, and she can give quiet thanks to all the gods in the universe for the lovely gift of this merging of old and new writing.

The whole human being has learned some important things: that forever is not necessary for survivors, that changing life can be explained calmly in the mind (there is a time to every purpose under the heavens). And she can know with that same calmness that "a time to mourn" is over.

She can even add her own new season for an honest believer in life's decreed changes: There is a time to stay, and a time to move on.

The author now lives near Philadelphia, with a very good friend. The moving-on was to a town close to New York for Jo; and yet countryside quiet, with a lot of backyard space, for the ardent gardener Ruth became years ago. Life changes, but the patterns of heart and soul remain constant. She is well into a new novel, and planning next year's garden. And, of course, there is an excellent library nearby.

WILLIAM ZORACH (1887–1966)

Excerpt from *Art Is My Life*

Born in Lithuania, the seventh of nine children, William Zorach was about four when his family moved to America. Ultimately settling in Cleveland, they adopted a new surname, Finkelstein, and Zorach's grade school teacher changed his first name to William. He left school at age fourteen to help support his family as a journeyman lithographer. In that trade, he met professional artists who understood that art would be his life.

He attended evening classes at the Cleveland School of Art from 1903 to 1906 while continuing as a lithographer. Realizing that his development could not progress without exposure to variant styles, Zorach left Cleveland in 1908 to study in New York. He returned to work in the Cleveland lithograph shop in 1910 to earn money for study in Paris. There, he experimented with the newer and freer modes of artistic expression that were to characterize his successful career.

Zorach turned to sculpture in 1922. His *Spirit of the Dance* at New York's Radio City Music Hall and his massive figure of Benjamin Franklin on the Washington, D.C., Post Office Department building are particularly celebrated. His most famous piece, *Mother and Child,* received a permanent home in New York's Metropolitan Museum of Art.

Here, Zorach remembers many of the buildings, people, joys, and tragedies of his Lithuanian hometown. He relives the memory of the inferior status of Jews and his own escape across the Russian-German border "because Jewish families had no rights and they dreaded having their sons drafted into the army."

He observes that his family was clueless about American ways, a failure that precipitated a clash between his Jewishness and his urge to become an

American. Art was his dream and his salvation despite the precarious art apprenticeships he endured in the early Cleveland years.

Source: An excerpt from William Zorach, *Art Is My Life: An Autobiography* (New York and Cleveland: World Publishing, 1967).

CHAPTER ONE

I remember the little village of Euberick in Lithuania where I was born. I remember our house, a low house with a slanting roof built into a bank in a river valley. It was made of logs and bricks and had a long dark hall where big black bears lay in wait for a little boy. There was an earthen floor and a huge brick oven with bunks over it where my mother tucked us in on cold nights.

Behind the house the land ran up the hillside, and my mother planted garden patches of beets and potatoes. At the top was a big barn in which flax was processed into rope. My father was a flaxmaker as was his father before him. My mother's people were farmers. She loved animals and growing things. When she was nineteen, her parents thought she had better be married or she would be a hopeless old maid. My father was brought around and they were married. She had never seen him before. My father owned a large barge, which he sailed and dragged with a tow rope up and down the Nieman River from Kovno to Konigsberg.

In the summers, we lived on the barge in a sort of poop deck on the stern. My mother's first child died when he was very small. I remember her saying he was a sweet child but fragile and could not stand living on the water. My oldest sister fell off the barge, but my father, who couldn't swim, caught hold of her long golden hair and saved her. I was the seventh child and the last one born in Russia; two more were born in America. All of us lived to a good age.

Recently my oldest brother who lives in Cleveland sent me a photograph of himself, his children, his grandchildren and various in-laws. My wife, Marguerite, looked at it and said, "That's not a family. That's a town."

I left Russia when I was four years old, but there are things I remember—the excitement of a fair and a little colt running beside a wagon galloping through the streets, of water being drawn from the village well by a long pole weighted with rocks, and trips to the village baker with my mother taking bread to be baked. One night there was a tapping on our windows, and my mother and father rushed out into the night. In the morning I saw hogs running about with scorched backs. Part of the village had burned in the night.

One incident stands out clearly in my memory; there was a beautiful castle outside the town surrounded by forests and a great, green meadow with grazing sheep. My brothers climbed the fence and began chasing the sheep. Suddenly soldiers with rifles strapped to their backs appeared and started chasing the boys. I was caught, impaled by my clothes on the spikes on top of the fence. I wept bitterly until a kind man came along and lifted me down.

I remember soldiers being billeted in our house—the Czar's troops. They spread their blankets on the floor of our big room and slept overnight. The soldiers all seemed to be very gay and everything was friendly. My mother asked them for a piece of pork fat. It was taboo in a Jewish house, so she hid it in the rafters and later tried it out for lard and rubbed it on us when we had sore throats.

Of the Russian language I remember only one word—the word for ice cream. And as for the trip to America I remember only the clanking of the chains at the German-Russian border as we slipped through in the night. We left because Jewish families had no rights and they dreaded having their sons drafted into the army. Too often, they never returned. I don't know that we suffered from persecution, but there was always terror of it in our minds. My father decided to go to America because his barge was confiscated, which meant the loss of his livelihood. He had been accused of smuggling a Bible into Russia—at least, that is the story. My father's brother had already gone to America, and my father and my oldest brother left to join him, leaving the rest of us behind.

Adjustment to American life was very difficult for my father. He had worked outdoors all his life and could not stand the confinement of a factory. My uncle, who had a store, fitted him up with a sixty-pound pack of notions, and he tramped from farm to farm, sleeping in barns and eating God knows how. Profits were terribly small, but he saved every cent so that he could send for his family in Europe. He had been in America three years, and he was walking down a country road thinking of my mother and the children in Russia and wondering if he could ever save enough to send for us when, behold—he saw five brand-new ten-dollar bills lying on the road before him—sent from heaven.

My mother landed in New York without one cent, only our tickets to Cleveland. On the train a man passed out boxes of candy and we children fell to. What a wonderful country! But when the man came around to collect payment there wasn't a cent. After much excitement, my mother sold a couple of silver spoons to a passenger and all was well.

We settled in Port Clinton, not far from Cleveland, in a house by the railroad tracks with fields and meadows on the other side. My family were totally Old World people. When they came here they had nothing, and they felt utterly lost in a completely strange country. In Russia they had inherited their house, all their copper utensils, their feather beds, their linens, silver, and pewter. Things like these were customarily handed down from generation to generation, and it was normal to be well supplied. They had their own land and their own garden. As average human beings in a low economic strata they were well off.

In America they started with nothing. My father and mother were very simple people, intelligent but without schooling. They could speak five languages but they could neither read nor write. Their education was traditionally Hebrew; they had learned the Bible by rote. They observed the Jewish holidays and traditions and said their prayers daily. My father was very much interested in the events of the world, but he was completely indifferent to commercial success. It was my mother who valued success—or perhaps it was security she wanted. Caring for a brood of children was an all-day and an all-night job. I remember getting up in the middle of the night and finding my mother scrubbing floors and washing clothes. My father drove around the country all day with a horse and wagon peddling notions. I can still see him sitting by lamplight in the kitchen, spreading out all the small change and counting the day's earnings.

My mother would argue with him and tell him he had started out with more money than he had come back with and ask, "Where is it?" And he would shout, "And how do I know?"

My mother was a handsome, outgoing woman, who made friends easily. I remember her trips to the docks to see fishermen. They would give her fish, and in return she would make gefilte fish and sweet and sour carp for them—things they had never heard of, and they found them delicious.

I started to go to school. When my teacher asked me my name I told her "Zorach."

"That's just too difficult to pronounce," she said. "We'll call you Willie." And William it has remained.

I did not adjust easily to life in America. The people I lived among were a mystery to me. School was a greater mystery. I was surrounded by unknown and often hostile forces and events, through which, with luck, I threaded my way but which I never quite understood. This was also true of my parents, and much of this must have been reflected in my childhood. At the same time I was exposed to the typical American boy's life. I remember sticking a pin in a bicycle tire to see what would happen and getting caught. And I remember getting into a row boat at the docks on Lake Erie and falling overboard. I was scared to death and soaking wet, but I never told anyone what I had done.

We sent for my cousins in Europe. When they arrived they were dressed in the clothes that children wore in Russia—long pants, boots, and gay over-shirts with belts. My aunt was scandalized and ashamed of such greenhorns. She immediately stripped them of their clothing and dressed them in all new clothes from the store—Americanized them right away. My family had probably been Americanized in the same way.

We lived in Port Clinton three years. My older brothers were growing up and spending too much time around the docks. My parents decided to move to Cleveland, where the children could work and keep out of trouble. They felt they couldn't afford to send them to school when they could be wage earners. My father took the horse and wagon and went ahead. My mother with all the children followed a week later. After we were settled, my father found people he could talk to and trade with in the outlying districts—Poles, Litvaks, and Russians who worked in the blast furnaces. But they had no money to buy his wares. Maybe there was too much competition or the people didn't save the money to pay for things. He began exchanging merchandise for scrap iron and junk, which he seemed to be able to sell. I went with him to hold the horse and help. My father would start for the outlying districts and farms. He liked wandering from farm to farm; he liked farmers and they liked him. He seemed to be more interested in traveling places than in the money he could make when he got there. As I got older, this job that had been so exciting bored me and humiliated me.

My father had come to this country at forty-five. He never mastered the language. He remained a Russian, kept his beard, wore felt boots, and in winter he was enveloped in a huge black overcoat tied around the waist with a rope. He was a little man but tremendously strong, with powerful hands. I remember when two men tried to rob him and he held them by the lapels of their coats, yelling, "Police!" until they were arrested.

One time he found a huge piece of machinery for sale. The man wanted sixteen dollars for it. It was too big a deal for my father. He went back to Cleveland, got himself a partner, and they bought the thing. They were afraid to drive through the city, afraid of the cops who were always poking in their wagon, and afraid the machinery might have been stolen. So they had me, a little kid, drive the wagon home. They worked on this treasure with a sledge hammer for three days to separate the brass from the iron and finally made three dollars apiece on the deal.

One time I said to my father, "Those people down the street have a big pile of junk in their yard—why do they just pile it up? Why don't they sell it?"

My father said, "They keep it, and when the price goes up they sell it. That's how they get rich."

"Why don't you do that? Why do you sell it every night?"

He said, "Oh, for that you have to have a lot of money."

He had to sell his junk every night and make a few cents to make it possible for us to eat.

My childhood was spent in the slums of Cleveland. Images appear, vanish, and reappear like the detailed patterns in tapestry or colors spotted on a canvas in a correlated design. The eye and mind wander over the surface picking out details from the overall pattern—a wide street with clanking streetcars, trolley wires overhead; towards evening, crowds coming home from work, hanging like bees on the running boards of the trolleys. At dusk, wagons drawn by six galloping horses; smells, kids yelling "Ho, ho, honey dumpers." Woodland Avenue, once a beautiful, wide, tree-lined street with handsome houses—then a dilapidated slum, a market street where farmers lined their produce up along the sidewalks and cried their wares. Across the street, houses seemed a long way off, set in back of dried up lawns full of tall dried grass and weeds. A small boy seldom walked around the street.

Those were the days of a saloon on every corner, and livery stables; kids would jump from upper windows into soft manure piles. Of our neighbors, some were colored, some were cooks, laborers, Italian vegetable men, and commission merchants.

I remember the agony of Hebrew lessons after school. On Sundays I would sit in torture reciting Hebrew while the Rabbi and his family ate a beautiful dinner.

The winters were crowded with snow storms, cold, sleet, slush; I suffered constantly from catarrh. I remember the dispensary and funerals, our neighbor dying of lockjaw. A little girl in my class who lived across the street died—just died—vanished out of life and was no more.

A little, wizened man, always well dressed and wearing a bowler hat, carrying a cane, and with a stogey in his mouth, was pursued by a gang of kids throwing stones and yelling, "Stogey, hey, Stogey." He always stopped and shook his fist at the kids.

Some people moved into a house across the street. Around five o'clock that evening we saw a disreputable woman sitting on the doorstep; a red light appeared in the window at night. Someone complained to the authorities. The house was raided and closed and the woman disappeared.

The Educational Alliance was further down the street. There was a Gymnasium, a playground, and a library where we could read books.

The little boy next door played the harmonica beautifully. I bought one and tried to learn, but I could only produce sounds—not music. A mother brought a little girl over to our house who sung popular songs such as, "Bill Bailey, won't you please come home." I was terribly impressed. A boy at a party would do fancy jigs to a tune. I wished I could jig. I tried but I was clumsy, my feet wouldn't move. I remember my frustration and thinking it was wonderful to sing and dance and play a mouth organ or a Jew's harp, but I couldn't seem to learn.

My mother was very enterprising. She was determined to own a house, a home of her own. She found a brick house in a run-down section of Cleveland, on Woodland Avenue. The street had been widened, the big trees cut down; the flower beds and lawns were black patches and ran to weeds. It was a good, residential house owned by a man named Peter Steers, an early-American type. He'd been a captain of a steamboat going down the Ohio to New Orleans. Now he was retired. He didn't have much money left, and he was alone in the world. My mother made a deal with the old man. She borrowed 300 dollars to give him on the condition that he could stay with us in his house as long as he lived. Old Mr. Steers looked after us children like a nurse. He'd wash our heads and bathe us. This was the beginning of my emancipation from being Jewish—there was a non-Jew in the family and we had only known Jews before. When we'd talk Yiddish he'd say, "What are you chattering about? Talk United States."

He was an old Southern gentleman who slept with a loaded gun under his pillow and "God bless our home" over his door. He played the banjo and sang old Southern melodies and entertained us with tales of steamboating on the Mississippi, the Civil War, and philosophy. He was a Democrat and easily made a Democrat out of me. He took me to political rallies, where I heard Teddy Roosevelt hold forth and saw Bob LaFollette stride up and down the platform like a caged lion. He took me to Rigoletto and Sappho and to a vaudeville show, where I had such a hilarious time that he was embarrassed and said that he would never take me again.

My mother used to take in boarders and roomers to help out, and she rented the upstairs to an Italian family. The neighborhood was a mixed one—

Italians, Irish, Russians, Jews, and all kinds of laborers and, later, colored people. There were street brawls, knifings, and gay times when the streets were turned into colorful Italian festivals. And there were always Jewish weddings. A Jewish wedding was a very festive occasion: it meant all kinds of marvelous food and gaiety. My father was very lively at these weddings. He danced the Kasotsky—a version of the classical Tartar dance, a whirling dance on bent knees. It is about the liveliest dance there is. My father would always end up with a somersault in the air, and everyone would applaud. Years later, when I began to dance in Greenwich Village, I found that, without any training, I, too, could dance this dance—but not like my father.

The street we lived on was used as a local produce market. Farmers lined the sidewalks with their vegetables and wares. There was no place for the horses. They were packed one alongside the other on the street with traffic jammed around them. My mother took them off the streets and tied them in our back yard. It took courage and skill. There were twenty or thirty horses in the yard at a time and sometimes the muck was up to our ankles, but my parents made a little money that way, ten or fifteen cents a horse.

There were beautiful spider webs in the sheds. I loved the spiders and loved watching them. I remember my father getting a broom to sweep them off. I was heartbroken and protested and he stopped, but the next morning the spiders were all gone.

I raised bantams in the back yard. I loved the gay-colored, cocky little fellows, but I never wanted anyone to eat the eggs. I imagine the family solved that problem as they had the one of the spider webs, without hurting me.

There were some fresh kids, living next door, who had a bulldog. One day he took a bite out of my sister's leg, and my mother insisted he be shot so that my sister wouldn't get hydrophobia. There was much ill feeling over this, and one day these kids set an old couch afire alongside our barn. The first thing we knew, the whole barn was in flames. My father got his horse out and ran into the street shouting, "Fire!" Everyone was coming home from work, the trolley cars were packed inside and out, and people thought it was a joke to see an old Jew running out waving his arms and shouting, "Fire!" But the fire engines came and put the fire out.

If our neighborhood had become very international, it also had become very tough. Once, when one of my brothers came home from work, he was attacked and beaten up by a bunch of rowdies. He said nothing, but when this began happening every night, he became more and more miserable and finally told my father. My father and a couple of my older brothers went out that night. They took crowbars and went after this gang. We heard the crowbars flying and clanking around the street. After that my brother had no more trouble.

My father used to be harassed and attacked and stoned. Boys yelled "Sheeny" at him on the streets. I remember some kids getting him into their yard to buy a sack of junk. It was supposed to be iron, but when he looked in, it was only rocks. When he wouldn't fall for it, they began pelting him with the rocks. He ran down the street yelling, with the kids after him. Everyone thought it was a joke. All this made me very self-conscious and embarrassed. I didn't know how to live with it, and I was miserable for my father and myself.

These were the days of Tom L. Johnson and the streetcar strikes. Johnson was a reform mayor. He promised the people a three-cent fare if he could take over the lines for the city. The strikes were terrific. Quantities of strike breakers were imported and it was war. Streets were littered with rubbish ten feet high, rails and streets were torn up; effigies labeled "scab" were strung on trolley wires. I remember a boy watering his horse yelled, "Scab!" at a motorman. The motorman stopped his car, chased the boy, and shot him dead. The company got the man released, and he ran cars in Cleveland for many years, but I would never set foot in his car: I remembered. During the strike a man gave me a bar of soap and told me to grease the tracks. I thought it would be fun, but my father saw me and yanked me off warning me I'd be killed if caught.

I was in the third grade when I started as a wage earner, selling papers and shining shoes. After school a bunch of us boys raced to the public square and fought for the late editions. We hopped street cars, yelled, "Extra!" and developed strong lungs and legs. Life as a newsboy meant having amazing contacts in the world of people—medicine men selling snake oil, corn doctors, socialist orators, and Negro evangelists predicting the end of the world. I remember a quack doctor riding through the streets in a carriage drawn by four beautiful horses and throwing handfuls of nickels to the crowd. I sold papers to Bob Fitzsimmons and Mark Hanna. I watched the sleigh races on Euclid Avenue on snowy winter Sundays. I ran errands and carried heavy bags for salesmen until I thought my arms would be pulled out of their sockets. But with it all, I was no businessman; I made very little money, and every cent I made I gave to my mother.

Some kids asked me one day, "How much do you rake off selling papers?" They told me they kept part of the money and never gave their mother all. I was horrified. I couldn't think of doing such a thing.

The day McKinley was shot, I was delivering my papers. Women rushed out into the streets, weeping. Boys were rushing about selling the latest editions, crying, "Extra! Extra!"

And I had to go right on with my paper route.

Sunday newspapers were two for a nickel, and you sold them for a nickel apiece. Once when I bought two from a kid and gave him a quarter, he lit out, hopped a car, and disappeared. I caught up with him on the public square and demanded my change. He denied I had given him a quarter. Finally I knocked him down on the sidewalk and began pommeling him. A man grabbed me, slammed my head against a lamppost till I saw stars, and handed me over to a policeman, who took me to jail.

I told the policeman, "This fellow cheated me; it is not my fault."

He said, "You were disturbing the peace."

They put me in jail in a cell with a little colored boy who had run away from school. He was weeping and I was weeping. Fortunately, an uncle of mine had been riding by on a streetcar and had seen the policeman taking me away.

As soon as my father heard what had happened, he rushed over to see Harry Bernstein, the wardheeler for the Republican party. "Czar Bernstein" organized the immigrants, got them citizen papers, got them out of trouble, and delivered the vote. Harry Bernstein called someone up, and I was let out.

I was very miserable. There was no justice in the world; a crime had been committed against me, and I was the one to suffer. My parents were very sympathetic. They knew I wouldn't do anything wrong. But when I went back to school and told my teacher why I had been absent, she made a scene and treated me as if I were a criminal. I had committed the unpardonable crime of getting arrested.

I had to go to court the next day. A man there told me to plead guilty. "Then they'll give you a lecture and let you off."

I did—and the judge gave me a long lecture on how I was starting a criminal career and dismissed me.

I used to get up at six in the morning to go on my paper route. One terribly stormy day my mother stopped me. "You can't go out on a day like this." I didn't go and somehow that seems to have been the end of my life as a newsboy.

School was a world I never understood and never seemed to fit into. In the lower grades some of my teachers were very nice girls, and gay. They had flirtations with the firemen in the next block and used to send me down with notes. We were happy with these teachers. After the fourth grade the teachers were older and more removed from the children. We did not understand them, nor did they know how to handle us. Discipline was lax both in school and out. The kids were uncontrolled. There were gang wars and lots of trouble. Kids would line up at either end of the block and throw rocks at each other, and any unprotected kid was jumped upon. I remember our principal walking some of the boys home because of the gangs waiting for them. Those of us who weren't in the gang had to run the gauntlet.

I used to love poetry and recitation. And I remember every poem, song, and recitation from those days—Sir Walter Scott, William Cullen Bryant, and Longfellow. The rest of school was a mystery to me, a morass through which I stumbled and fought my way. Arithmetic was a trap, grammar another. It was German grammar that absolutely defeated me—German was taught in the public schools in Cleveland at that time. I was never any good at examinations; my brain would cease to function the minute an examination paper was put in front of me.

My seventh grade teacher, Miss Alice Sterling, was nice and took a great interest in me because I drew. I used to make drawings for her and often went out to her house to help her with such things as taking down screens in the fall. She was no disciplinarian; the kids in her class were a pretty tough lot, and she simply couldn't control them. Despite Miss Sterling's interest in me, I was disturbed and unhappy. I'm not sure now whether I quit or whether the school gave me up as a hopeless case. Anyway I remember feeling that I was through with school, that my parents needed my help, and that I should go out and get a job.

I was shy and big for my age. I wandered around the streets of Cleveland from one end of town to the other. I hung around railroad tracks and shops. I'd see signs, "boy wanted," but was too shy to go in and ask for the job. Finally through other boys, I began to get jobs, the jobs nobody else wanted and jobs I was not fitted for. They never lasted more than a few days or a week, and I penetrated into almost all the lower branches of industry. I got a machine shop job; a boy told me, "Watch yourself. The last kid working that punch machine lost all his fingers on one hand." I stuck a bar into the machine and broke it. I was fired. I had a job in a hat factory and got bored to death dusting hats. There was a job in a brass factory working with buffing wheels in an atmosphere dense with metal dust, which filled the lungs and eyes and left one coated from head to foot with brass. My job was to dip the hot brass in benzine and roll it in sawdust. It was so painful to the hands that I was in agony. I quit.

After these experiences, school didn't look as black as it used to. I wrote a long letter to Miss Sterling and told her I wanted to come back. I don't know what I said but it touched her deeply. I went back to the seventh grade, which was very illuminating to me because most of the children were half my size. That year the class was made up of an entirely different breed of children; everything was peaceful and lovely. Miss Sterling kept me happy by letting me draw copies of Millet and other masters, and I covered the blackboards with drawings. She wasn't teaching drawing—just encouraging me.

At an early age my art took the form of woodcarving. I began working on back fences and barn walls. The kids in the neighborhood thought I was good, but at school there was a boy who was a whiz at drawing cowboys and Indians. I was much in awe of him but was also inspired. I decorated books, papers, blackboards, even the backs of my hands with Indians and such. No surface was safe from me. I even drew all over a geography book and was sent to the principal. She took one look and said, "You will have to pay for this book." I paid five cents, and they let me keep the book. It was the first book I ever owned, and I still have it.

When we bought our house there were pseudo-classical chromos on the walls. They were my introduction to art. A scene by Turner hung over my bed; I always looked at it. My family could not see keeping a potential wage earner in school. I must learn a trade. They knew nothing of art—this habit of mine of drawing was just something that got me into trouble. The eighth grade teacher agreed with them, but Miss Sterling thought otherwise. She persuaded the supervisor of art to write me a letter of introduction to the Morgan Lithograph shop.

I went down with my letter. The office boy said no boys were wanted, but by this time I recognized the brushoff.

I said, "I have an important letter for the superintendent."

He took me up to the foreman of the printing department, who looked at the letter and took me over to the Art Department and introduced me to George Groll, the head of the department—a little round fat man with a moon face and a bad limp. He chewed on a cigar and rolled it around in his mouth while he read the letter. He told me to come back and bring some of my drawings. I had nothing but kid stuff—drawings of battleships, Indians, and copies from Prang's textbooks. I rushed home and got my sister and brother to pose for me while I drew their profiles. I went into our stuffy, unused parlor and made two careful drawings of a couple of plaster Indian busts that sat on the mantel. I also made a copy of a picture of George Washington. I took this little folder of drawings down to Groll. He was impressed and told me to come back on Monday and go to work. He said he couldn't put me on as an apprentice because of the union but would give me a job as errand boy at three dollars a week.

There had been a fire in the shop, and I was set to clean out the debris. I worked very hard, swept floors, ran errands not only for Groll but for all the men in the shop. I was so happy to be around art and artists that I made myself invaluable. I was there before anyone, kept the place in order, mixed colors, collected bits of crayon and boiled them into a liquid to be used in lettering. I was never allowed to touch a stone, but I practiced on them in the early morning before anyone was around.

An apprentice worked six months for nothing, then six months for three dollars a week, and then he started getting six dollars a week. That was his salary until he was raised to nine dollars a week after he had been working three years.

When I was put on as an apprentice, the whole shop walked out on strike. According to union rules, I was one apprentice too many. The strike lasted a whole year and almost wrecked the firm. I never saw such a bunch of incompetents as were brought in as strikebreakers—old has-beens, drunks, and an anarchist from Italy who only wanted to talk. They just about ruined the company.

Lithography in those days was one of the legitimate ways of making a living for artists who couldn't make a go of it by painting alone. In his youth Arthur B. Davies had worked in this same shop. Many fine artists drifted in and out of lithograph shops. Some stayed on for the security. I worked with a fine, sensitive fellow named Lisle. I used to be heartbroken when he'd do a beautiful job and the foreman would come around and wreck it—dig in and prettify it, harden it and take all the art out of it.

I worked with old man Archibald Willard, who painted the famous "Spirit of '76," and with Bill Sommers, who was a fine artist all his life. From him I learned the differences between a real artist and a commercial artist.

Then there was Billy Crane, an old time commercial artist who was not so much of an artist himself but was determined to make me one. Billy Crane came from a family of actors and theatrical designers. He had been a very successful scenic artist. He had just left his wife, run away with a very beautiful redheaded girl, come to Cleveland, and gone to work in the lithograph shop. They were very proud to have him and gave him a private room. He took a great interest in me, and I spent a lot of time with him. I ran his errands, bought his cigars (he had expensive taste in cigars) and kept him supplied with Bromo Seltzer, to which I thought he was addicted as a substitute for drink. He was very difficult in lots of ways. It seemed to me as if he was always raping the cleaning women in the building, or at least chasing them around with rape in mind.

He would never pay his bills and would send me out to tell the people to whom he owed money that he would pay them next week. These things were very embarrassing to a kid and I'd revolt. I'd refuse to do it.

Then he'd kick me out of his room and run me down the stairs shouting, "You goddamned ungrateful Jew bastard, don't you come here again."

It was tough on a kid. I felt that he was my master, a man who was going to teach me how to be an artist. I felt like a lost soul.

One day he said to me, "While I am out to lunch, you paint a picture out of the window."

I used to see him take his brush, twirl it around in the color, and give the brush a swish. I thought this was the way it was done. I took the brush, put it in the paint, gave it a backward swipe, and put the paint on the paper.

When he came back he said, "What the hell's going on here?"

The whole place was spattered with paint. "Isn't that the way you do it?" I asked.

He laughed and said, "Well, you don't have to do what I do."

He sent me out in the country on weekends to paint and draw. He'd say, "You come back with a picture, or I'll break your neck."

One time he saw me sketching in the park and came over to help me and talk to me about painting.

One day Crane said to me, "I need some carmine—has Groll got any downstairs?"

"Yes," I said, "he's got some nice colors in his desk."

He said, "Run down and get me some."

I was very innocent—after all the company was supplying him with colors and materials. I never questioned his right to them. I got the carmine.

Later Groll asked me, "Did you take a tube of carmine out of my desk?"

"Yes," I said, "Billy Crane wanted it."

He hit the ceiling. Did he bawl me out. Did he lay it on.

"That's an expensive color; you had no business giving it to Crane. Don't you ever do that again. Who the hell are you working for—me or him?"

I told Billy Crane and he rushed down and jumped on Groll—told him to shut up and mind his own business, if he didn't like what he was doing, he'd get out and leave him and his damned shop. I made myself scarce.

Some Cleveland businessmen got the bright idea of having a group of artists paint a series of pictures of the life of Christ. They commissioned five of the most famous American artists to paint scenes from the life of Christ, and they planned to send the pictures around the country as an exhibition and charge admission. Billy Crane was to paint Christ in the Garden of Gethsemane. He sent me out to find him a studio where he could paint this huge picture—about eight by twelve feet. Imagine this man sending a kid out to find a studio for him and taking whatever he found. I went all over town and told people I knew an artist who wanted a studio. They just looked at me. I knocked at doors and asked if they knew of a studio. Finally in a market section in an old tenement I saw a sign "Floor to rent." I told Crane about it and he rented it—an apartment on the fourth floor.

Crane had his beautiful, red-haired girl pose for the head of Christ and had me pose for the figure.

He'd say, "You want to help me, Billy? Take this brush and paint a rock." This was a kind gesture to make me feel I had a real part in the picture. We worked every Saturday and Sunday. I swept the room, cleaned his palette, washed his brushes, and did endless little chores.

His Christ had no beard and he began to worry about it. So he sent me out to find a Jewish character with a beard. I went down the street in this Jewish neighborhood stopping every man with a beard, and I'd say, "A man I know is painting a head of Christ and needs a model. Will you pose for him?" I had a pretty hard time; people thought I was nuts. Finally I thought of my father. He had a fine head and a beard. My father went down and posed for the beard. Crane finished the picture, but the enterprise was a complete flop. The paintings finally ended up in the barn of a Mr. Wade, one of the sponsors, and then one day the barn burned down.

I was going to art school nights all this time and learning to use my natural ability for art. I was clever at drawing, and during the strike I was doing professional work in the shop—work that men were being well paid for. I had been working for a year when the strike was called and went right into doing the big jobs even though I was only paid as an apprentice. The union men came around to see me one time when I wasn't home.

Old man Steers said, "Billy, don't you pay any attention to those fellows. The minute the strike is over, they'll put you right out of the shop and you'll never get back in again—you'll just be drifting." Finally the men came back one by one and the strike was broken.

There came a time when I found it hard to concentrate on the work in the shop. My mind began to run in too many directions—art and daydreams. One of the workmen was quite a gay blade and always telling about his affairs with women. One day I asked him what he thought about when he worked on a stone. I expected an entertaining answer.

He jumped, "What the hell do you think I'm thinking about, you damn fool? I'm thinking about my work."

I thought that one over and tried it too.

I must have been eighteen the fall I went to New York to study art at the National Academy of Design. I had finished my apprenticeship and managed to save, after paying my mother room and board, one hundred sixty dollars. Abe Warshawsky, a neighbor who was already an artist, was going to Paris and suggested that I go to New York with him and he would find me a place to board with his cousins, the Benders.

Abe took me to his cousins on 116th Street, near the Academy. I gave Mrs. Bender my hundred sixty dollars. Later I found out she gave it to her brother, a saloon keeper, from whom she had borrowed money. Mr. Bender was a gambler and an unscrupulous character who left his family penniless most of the time. That winter I slept in a clothes closet. It seemed to be the only available space.

I would get up in the morning and little Jessie Bender, who was seven and an enchanting little black-eyed, black-haired sprite, would say, "Willie, there's nothing for breakfast."

I would say, "All right, just give me a piece of bread."

She'd say, "But there is no bread."

"Then give me a glass of water." And I would take a glass of water and go to art school on that.

To get away from the misery of this family and because of my absorption in art, I would take the morning classes, the afternoon classes, and the evening classes. Afterward, I'd come home to a meager supper and go to bed. On Friday evenings, Zadu, the old grandfather, would come up from the lower East Side and bring a big basket of food. That kept us from starving. I lived with this family for one whole winter. When I came home the following spring, my parents were shocked. I looked like a famine victim. I suppose I could have sent home for money and eaten at restaurants, but it never occurred to me. I just accepted the situation and did nothing about it. I was used to poverty. Besides my mother had told me never to eat in restaurants—the food was poison. I guess I accepted that, too.

I worked hard. I won a prize in drawing in the Men's Day Class and an honorable mention in painting. I was becoming a pretty good painter in my way. My instructor was E. M. Ward, a very old-time genre painter of black-smith shops and such. Then there was Francis C. Jones, a prissy little man who minced around the studio, said everyone was doing nicely and rushed out. He was a well-to-do artist who owned big apartment houses and studios on Fifty-seventh Street.

Ward always came in, sat down, looked from side to side, and said, "Where's your plumb line?"

If a student said, "I don't have one," he would roar, "If you ain't got one, borrow one."

I wonder now how I ever learned anything about art from these instruc-tors. Instruction in those days was a matter of anatomy and correction of drawing from the viewpoint of realism only. The halls of the Academy were lined with the most perfect and meticulous drawings from casts and from life made by prize students no one has ever heard from since.

I remember there were parties at the Academy. Sometimes I would stand and look in the door, but I would never go in. It wasn't just that I was im-mature and too serious minded. I just had no interest outside of art and drawing and going to museums.

After a winter at the Academy I went back to Cleveland and the lithograph shop. It worked out well. Summer is the season when the lithograph shops are busy making posters for the coming winter. I could work all summer, save my money, and go back to study art in the winter in New York.

I went back to the Academy the second year, and this time I rented a room and ate in restaurants. That year I met a man, a successful writer, who asked me if he could get a room in the same rooming house where I was. He said he wanted to get away from his friends, who were drinking too much, living too fast a life, and disturbing him so that he couldn't write. He rented this room and isolated himself. He was wonderful at cooking and I certainly enjoyed my meals with him. He liked my company because I was so unbeliev-ably naive and I made no demands upon him. And I was a perfect audience for his stories. I was enthralled just listening to him. Calvin Johnson was a typical western type, looked like Bill Cody and wrote railroad stories for *The Saturday Evening Post* and the Street and Smith pulp magazines.

My second year at the Academy I also went to classes morning, afternoon, and night, but I began to branch out. I went to the Metropolitan Museum and copied old masters. I copied Franz Hals. I copied the Dutch masters and Rembrandt and Velasquez. I copied Raeburn and still have the picture. A man came up to me one time and asked if I would make some copies of Mauve for him—sheep pictures. I made six copies of these sheep for him, and he paid me twenty-five dollars apiece for them, which was quite something for me at that time. I was very embarrassed by people standing in back of me and watching me paint. There was a young man who took care of the students' locker room in the basement. I told him how much people disturbed me by watching over my shoulder.

He said, "Remember this, if you think you don't know anything, they know still less about what art is."

I was convinced of this when a man standing back of me said, "Is that the first coat?"

After that people watching me never disturbed me. That year for the first time I began to wander around the galleries and become familiar with what was going on in the art world of the day.

I sound like a desperately serious young man without a thought in my head but work. Years after in New York I met a young woman who said, "Why, you're the young man my friend in the Cleveland Library was so in love with."

I was completely astonished. To me at that time librarians were all old women.

"But I was just a baby," I said.

"Nonsense," she said. "You were eighteen and she was twenty. To her you were the most charming, delightful, and serious young man she had ever met and she never forgot you." I couldn't even remember her. But evidently my picture of myself isn't totally objective.

When I returned to Cleveland and the lithograph shop that summer, I found things had changed. The foreman, Frank Seamons, had married a woman with illusions of grandeur, one who wanted things—an expensive apartment, a gay social life. Seamons and another man had left and started a shop of their own. They decided to make posters for the movies. It was a new idea and as it turned out, a very profitable one. Frank Seamons had no children of his own and had always taken a fatherly interest in me.

Our foreman, Groll, when I came back to the shop offered me a dollar raise. One day he came over to my stone and seemed much, much more friendly than usual. He had always been aloof and gruff.

I asked my friend, Elmer, "What's come over Groll?"

Elmer told me, "You know why he's nice to you, don't you? He's afraid you're going to go over to Seamons in that new shop and he'll lose you."

I was making ten dollars a week. Frank Seamons sent for me and said, "How much are they paying you, Willie?"

"I'm getting ten dollars a week," I said.

He said, "I'll give you fifteen if you'll come and work for me."

So I went to work for Seamons.

When Groll found out, he sent for me.

Groll kept going up and Seamons had offered to top any offer he made. In the end, I stayed with Seamons for thirty-two dollars a week. I guess I was worth it. I worked overtime and Saturdays and Sundays. I worked sixteen hours a day. Out of this I paid my mother fifteen a week for board and the rest I saved to go to Paris and study.

CLARA LEDERER (1907–1987)

Excerpt from *Their Paths Are Peace*

The Cleveland Cultural Gardens comprise a chain of national and ethnic plantings along what is today Martin Luther King Jr. Boulevard—formerly Rockefeller Parkway. The gardens, created in 1925 and officially recognized by Cleveland in 1927, convey the diversity of the city's population. Many of the gardens fell into disarray starting in the early 1960s. Refurbishment projects are restoring some of them. The Hebrew Garden, partially restored in the 1970s, does not yet match the beauty of the original that Clara Lederer described.

Lederer's depiction of the Hebrew Cultural Garden is a panorama of Jewish culture. The artistic integration of plantings, plaques, and statuary extols wisdom, Jewish thought and letters, the Hebrew language, Zionist aspiration, and Jewish poets and composers. A special grouping celebrates Jewish women. Lederer chronicles and credits the participation of Jewish individuals and organizations that worked to present Jewish values to the public in this aesthetic and symbolic setting.

Source: An excerpt from Clara Lederer, *Their Paths Are Peace: The Story of the Cleveland Cultural Gardens* (Cleveland, OH: Cleveland Cultural Gardens Federation, 1954). Reprinted with the permission of the Executive Board of the Cleveland Cultural Gardens Federation, Avon, OH.

HEBREW CULTURAL GARDEN

First to be established under the new conception of a chain of gardens was the Hebrew Cultural Garden, the site for which was dedicated in 1926.

Located across the roadway and just southwest of the Shakespeare Garden, it is an oriental garden in three sections in a circular forest-tree setting. The stone walks are laid out to form the chief motif—the six-pointed Star, or Shield, of David.

A hexagonal pool in the center reflects a pink Georgia marble fountain, its seven slender columns representing the seven Pillars of Wisdom, and inscribed with the quotation, in Hebrew characters, from Solomon's Book of Proverbs: "Wisdom hath built herself a house; she hath hewn her out seven pillars."

The garden was designed by Landscape Architect T. Ashburton Tripp.

At four points of the Star of David are bronze portrait reliefs of world renowned philosophers. Moses Maimonides, Biblical scholar and physician, was born in Cordova, Spain, in 1135 and died in Cairo, Egypt, in 1204. Baruch Spinoza (1632–1677), Spanish-born philosopher of Amsterdam, was a major dynamic force in the development of Western Civilization and moulder of the thoughts of such great figures as Lessing, Goethe, and Coleridge. Moses Mendelssohn (1729–1786), grandfather of the composer, represents a modern school of Jewish thought, and translated the Bible into German. Achad Ha'am (pseudonym of Asher Ginsburg, 1856–1927) was the leader of cultural Zionism and a great writer who was responsible for the revival of the Hebrew language. The olive tree, the tree most characteristic of Hebrew history, figures prominently in the planting of the Philosophers' Circle.

A smaller, adjoining garden on the left, the "music section," is planted in the shape of a Hebrew harp, or lyre. It was dedicated in July of 1937 with the unveiling of a monument bearing one plaque of three portrait heads of Jewish composers. These are Jacques Halevy (1799–1862), teacher of Gounod and Bizet, and composer of the opera, The Jewess; Giacomo Meyerbeer (1791–1864), who wrote L'Africana, Les Hugenots, and Le Prophete; and Karl Goldmark (1830–1915), author of Queen of Sheba, and uncle of the wife of former Chief Justice Louis Brandeis. Funds for this plaque were provided by the Gan Ivri Women's League.

To the right of the main section is the Poet's Corner, a ravine rock garden containing Palestinian plants and bronze tablets with appropriate inscriptions from Hebrew literature. This completes the general design of the Hebrew Garden. A dominating feature of this rock garden is a large boulder, set with a circular plaque, a bronze bas-relief, to the memory of Rebecca Gratz of Philadelphia. She was the founder of the first Jewish religious school in America, and is famous as the prototype of Rebecca, the heroine of Scott's Ivanhoe. She lived from 1781 to 1869. The Gratz plaque is flanked by plaques of Henrietta Szold and Emma Lazarus.

The dedication of the Hebrew Garden site occurred during an important event: the visit of Chaim Nachman Bialik to Cleveland. Acclaimed as the greatest Hebrew poet since the Prophet Isaiah, Bialik had come from Palestine on an American tour in the cause of Zionism. On May 5, 1926, in the presence of a large crowd despite steady rainfall, Bialik planted three Cedars of Lebanon in the future Poet's Corner of the Hebrew Garden, and delivered an eloquent address in Hebrew, translated by the late Rabbi Solomon Goldman. City Manager William R. Hopkins, in his speech of greeting, paid tribute to the contributions of Hebrew writers to world culture. Edmund Vance Cooke, Cleveland poet, Councilman A. R. Hatton, and A. H. Friedland, superintendent of Cleveland's Hebrew schools, also participated.

In his address, Bialik, Hebrew translator of Shakespeare's "Julius Caesar," emphasized the joint literary domination of Shakespeare and the Hebrew Bible in modern culture, noting at the same time that the Hebrew Garden site faced the Shakespeare Garden.

"Today Chaim Bialik plants the older poetry into a newer earth," said Mr. Cooke, referring to the Cedars of Lebanon, "immortal in a truer sense than material reality, immortal in song and story . . . the symbolism of their evergreen fragrance representing an ancient faith." Mr. Cooke concluded his address with the words, "And the significance of it all is that this ceremony occurs not in hoary Palestine, or in dreamy Stratford-on-Avon, but in this modern, throbbing, vital City of Cleveland, unsurpassed in its modernity by any city in the world."

In memory of Julius Schweid, Cleveland civic and Jewish communal leader, a plaque of Israel's renowned poet, Chaim Nachman Bialik was dedicated in the Hebrew Garden on July 25, 1954, more than 28 years after Bialik's visit to the site of the garden. The plaque, designed by Dr. Bernard Cooper, was the gift of a sponsoring committee of which Edward J. Schweid and Dr. Haskell H. Schweid, sons of Julius Schweid, were members.

The formal opening of the Philosophers' Circle of the Hebrew Garden, October 30, 1927, was a national event. Ceremonies were participated in by noted Jews from all parts of the world, by civic leaders, and by rabbis of Cleveland. Speakers included Dr. Judah L. Magnes, chancellor of the Hebrew University in Jerusalem, Henrietta Szold, founder of Hadassah, Rabbi Barnett R. Brickner, Rabbi Solomon Goldman, Rabbi Abba Hillel Silver, and Rabbi Abraham Nowak, of Cleveland. Miss Szold and Rabbi Magnes planted cedars at the Achad Ha'am plaque. Rabbi Brickner unveiled the Mendelssohn plaque, a gift of the Gan Ivri Women's League. Rabbi Silver unveiled the

Achad Ha'am plaque, given by the Cleveland Zionist District and Cleveland Hebrew schools; Rabbi Goldman unveiled the Maimonides plaque, memorial gift made to the garden by Mrs. Rae Roodman.

The Spinoza plaque, gift of the Cleveland Lodge of B'nai B'rith had previously been unveiled with impressive ceremony to mark the 250th anniversary of the philosopher's death. A. H. Friedland, noted Cleveland poet and educator, delivered the principal address.

Both the Gratz monument and the rock garden were dedicated in September, 1932, as part of the Sir Walter Scott centennial celebration. Park Commissioner John Brown accepted the memorial for the city. Max E. Meisel delivered the address on Rebecca Gratz. Mrs. Jennie K. Zwick made the presentation of the plaque, a gift of the Gan Ivri League. Dr. William Auld of Elyria gave the address on Sir Walter Scott.

Completing a grouping of memorials to famous Jewish women in this section are bronze plaques of Henrietta Szold and Emma Lazarus. The Henrietta Szold plaque was dedicated June 4, 1950, the 90th anniversary of her birth. She was founder of Hadassah and creator of the Youth Aliyah. The plaque was a gift of the Cleveland Chapter of Hadassah.

Mrs. Albert P. Schoolman of New York, member of the Hadassah National Board, spoke on Henrietta Szold. Greetings were by Albert A. Woldman, director of Ohio Industrial Relations Department. Mrs. Lewis W. Phillips was chairman of the Henrietta Szold Committee.

The Emma Lazarus plaque was dedicated June 16, 1949, to mark the 100th anniversary of her birth. The Federation of Jewish Women's Organizations presented the plaque, which is inscribed with a phrase from the sonnet of Emma Lazarus which is affixed in bronze to the pedestal of the Statue of Liberty:

> "Give me your tired, your poor,
> Your huddled masses yearning to breathe free,
> The wretched refuse of your teeming shore.
> Send these, the homeless, tempest-tost to me,
> I lift my lamp beside the golden door."

These words reflect the spirit of the Cultural Gardens, which symbolically, also "lifts its lamp beside the golden door."

To the right of the Philosophers' Circle and at the entrance to the rock garden is a bronze memorial plaque of Milton B. Schweid. The tablet is inscribed with a quotation from Ecclesiasticus, concluding with the following lines:

"Bountifulness is as a garden of abundance. And benevolence endureth forever."

Also in this section is a boulder to which is affixed a plaque inscribed with a passage from the writings of Emma Lazarus:

"The Soul at Peace Reflects the Peace Without, Forgetting Grief as Sunset Skies Forget the Morning's Transient Shower."

The boulder was presented to the Hebrew Garden by Cleveland B'nai B'rith Auxiliary, Cleveland Heights B'nai B'rith Auxiliary, and Balfour B'nai B'rith Auxiliary, honoring the Women's Grand Lodge District No. 2 B'nai B'rith.

Dr. Chaim Weizmann, who in 1949 became Israel's first president, in 1927 visited the Garden and planted several Cedars of Lebanon. This planting was sponsored by the Keren Hayesod Women's Club. The Gan Ivri Women's League took part in this event.

In 1937 Cleveland Jewry celebrated the 100th anniversary of its existence in the community, with a Hebrew Garden festivity tree planting program. Descendants of Simson Thorman, Cleveland's first Jewish settler, participated.

Set in a semi-circular niche just beyond the fountain and opposite the entrance to the Hebrew Garden is a bronze memorial plaque dedicated to the memory of Max E. Meisel by his B'nai B'rith associates.

Reliefs and plaques in the Hebrew Garden are the work of Cleveland artists of renown. The Musicians' and Gratz plaques are by Miriam E. Cramer, the Spinoza portrait by Max Kalish, the Szold plaque by Esther Samolar, the Emma Lazarus head by Walter Sinz. The three remaining philosophers' plaques are the work of Alexander Blazys.

Active in the establishment of the Hebrew Garden were Leo Weidenthal and Mrs. Jennie K. Zwick. Mr. Weidenthal, editor of the Jewish Independent, in 1936 received the Eisenman award of $1,000 for distinguished citizenship. Immediately upon the citation, Mr. Weidenthal turned over the $1,000 as a contribution toward the completion of the Hebrew Garden.

It was on March 5, 1927, that the Gan Ivri Women's League was organized at the home of Mrs. Jennie K. Zwick, for the purpose of developing the Hebrew Cultural Garden. At this meeting, plans were made for the planting of Cedars of Lebanon in the garden by Dr. Chaim Weizmann, then president of the World Zionist Organization, who was soon to visit Cleveland. Officers elected at this meeting were Mrs. Zwick, president; Mrs. Henry Frankel, treasurer; Mrs. O. Fink and Mrs. O. K. Greenberg, financial secretaries; Mrs. L. Dembo, recording secretary; Mrs. L. W. Phillips, publicity secretary.

On March 9, a committee representing the organization, called upon City Manager William R. Hopkins and presented plans for the embellishment and development of the garden. The committee consisted of Mrs. Zwick, Mrs. B. R. Brickner, Mrs. Henry Frankel, Mrs. L. W. Klusner, Mrs. D. Gara, Mrs. O. K. Greenberg, and Mrs. L. W. Phillips. The meeting was attended by Sculptor Max Kalish and Leo Weidenthal.

On Monday, April 11, Councilman Abner H. Goldman introduced an ordinance establishing the Cultural Garden and defining its units. The site chosen was diagonally across from the Shakespeare Garden, on the upper East Boulevard.

Among other pioneers in the Hebrew Garden cause were Edward J. Schweid, the late A. H. Friedland, the late Max E. Meisel, and the late Judge Lewis Drucker.

Present officers in the Hebrew Garden Association are Leo Weidenthal, president; Edward J. Schweid, vice-president; and Mrs. L. W. Phillips, secretary-treasurer.

The Hebrew Garden in its setting of tall old trees gleams "as a garden of abundance" reflecting teachings that have guided the way of myriads through the passing ages.

DAVID GURALNIK (1920–2000)

"The Yiddish Theater"

David Guralnik presents the story of Cleveland's Yiddish theater against its historical backdrop, which began in Romania in 1876 and in New York some fifteen years later. Clevelanders enjoyed Yiddish theater by 1910. A partial hiatus between the two world wars ended when the Jewish Community Center agreed to sponsor a theater program, with Mark Feder as its director. Guralnik contributed to expanding and diversifying the theater project, but he credited Feder with paving the way for later leaders to take Yiddish theater to new heights.

Source: "The Yiddish Theater, An Address Delivered by David Guralnik at the Jewish Community Center of Cleveland on January 10, 1993, in Memory of Mark Feder."

THE YIDDISH THEATER
An address delivered by David Guralnik at the Jewish Community Center of Cleveland on January 10, 1993, in memory of Mark Feder.

We're gathered here this afternoon, colleagues, co-workers, beneficiaries; but above all, friends of the remarkable man who was responsible for this very theater in which we are assembled—Mark Feder, whose memory we shall honor. But first let me stroll back down memory lane—given the constraints of time, it will more likely be a gallop—to see how Mark came to us. Nothing comes from nothing—everything has its antecedents, and so does this JCC theater program, now 44 years in existence.

53

Modern Yiddish theater, as we know it, began in Jassy, Rumania in 1876, when Avrom Goldfaden founded the first professional Yiddish theater and thereafter called himself the father of Yiddish theater, a title that no one has ever disputed. Yiddish theater quickly spread throughout Europe and by 1892, it had also moved to New York, where waves of Yiddish-speaking immigrants had begun to arrive. Soon the various professional New York theaters began to send out touring companies to the sticks, which included Cleveland, where such dramas and musicals were performed at the People's Theater, the Perry, the Globe, the Duchess, and finally the Manhattan, on Superior at East 105th Street.

Much of what they performed was classified as *shund,* strictly speaking, literary trash, but that may be an overly harsh judgment—it was truly pop culture, like today's soap operas and sitcoms. But in many American cities, there were literary groups who yearned for more artistic theatrical productions and so amateur groups were formed in a number of such cities to supply that quality theater.

Here in Cleveland, as early as 1910, there was already in existence a group of Yiddish theater-lovers who called themselves the Progressive Dramatic Club and who in that year presented a performance of Jacob Gordin's *Di Brider Luria.* By 1912, this amateur group had increased both in numbers and in activity to form a broad umbrella organization, the *Yiddish Kultur Gezelshaft,* whose theater arm was now called the *Literarish Dramatishe Gezelshaft,* the Literary Dramatic Society. The guiding lights of that group were Abel and Jane Rose, a couple who had recently moved to Cleveland from New York. Among the early leaders of the Cleveland group were Joseph Feder, the older brother of Mark; the Neshkin brothers, Fishel and Sam; Bertshi Vitkovich; Dr. Oscar Halpern, whose younger brother Moses, a well-known Cleveland architect, later designed and created a number of excellent expressionist sets for plays produced by the group; Max Scolnik; Sarah Leybovitch; among others. The group met regularly in the Labor Lyceum and prepared readings and sketches for performance before various Jewish organizations. From time to time they would produce fully-mounted, full-length plays in whatever auditorium was available. For example, in 1913 they presented Peretz Hirshbeyn's *Di Nevele* at the Council Education Alliance; in 1915, Hirshbeyn's *A Farvorfn Vinkl* at the Metropolitan Theater on Euclid at 50th Street; in 1917, Osip Dimov's play, *Yoshke Musikant.* In 1917, a national organization, the Literary Dramatic Societies of the United States and Canada, was founded and its first convention was held here in Cleveland at the Woodland Public Library.

World War I slowed down the activities of the Cleveland group and for a number of years they restricted their activities to cultural evenings of readings and monologues. But in 1930, largely under the impetus of the Plain Dealer, which seeking to celebrate the ethnic diversity of our city, proposed to sponsor a festival of international theater and invited the *Kultur Gezelshaft* to take part. They were fortunate to get the directional services of Chaim Ostrovsky, who was on leave of absence from the theater he managed in *Eretz Yisroel,* and on May 16 the group presented an elaborate production of H. Sekler's *Dem Tsadik's Nesiye* in the Little Theatre of the Public Auditorium. Thereafter, the group, now calling itself *Di Yidishe Teater Studyo,* continued to produce at least one play a year until the outbreak of World War II, with guest directors, among them Howard Da Silva, then a young actor at the Play House.

After the war, in 1947, the group sought to start up again and produced two evenings of one-act plays, one to celebrate Avrom Reyzn's 70th birthday and the other to celebrate Dovid Pinsky's 75th birthday. Those plays began my association with the group. In 1948, when the Jewish Community Center was founded, the *gezelshaft* petitioned the JCC founders to establish as part of its ongoing program, a theater that would regularly present plays both in English and Yiddish, and they recommended as the organizer and director of that program Mark Feder, the younger brother of the by-then deceased Joseph (Yosl) Feder, one of the original leaders of the *gezelshaft.* Mark seemed an ideal candidate for that job. Born in Europe, but brought to America as a lad, he was fluent in Yiddish, had had dramatic training at Carnegie Tech School of Drama and at NYU in New York City, where he was now working primarily as a Jewish humorist, doing monologues and stand-up comedy in the Catskills and in New York City. Early in 1948, he published a little volume of some of his monologues, titled *It's a Living,* and shortly we will hear excerpts from that book read by Sam Shane. The jacket copy of that book, telling about the author, is very revealing. Asked to explain his shift from the earlier part of his career as a serious student of play production to humor, he replied "*ich hob farblondzhet,*" but then went on to declare that all branches of show business are interrelated and to keep going one must be versatile. The final paragraph of the jacket copy is prophetic. It reads, "Though Mark Feder devotes all his time to humor, he still maintains a keen interest in the theatre and hopes some day to establish a community playhouse in which to experiment with plays of the American-Jewish scene."

Just a few months after the publication of that book in 1948, Mark came to a cocktail party for him in Cleveland—that was where I first met him—

where he and the leadership of the brand-new JCC could size each other up. We were impressed with how knowledgeable he was about both the current American theater scene and the classical Yiddish theater—and with his highly visible enthusiasm for such a formidable challenge. He, on the other hand, had an important decision to make along with Ethel, his wife. To leave New York City, the hub of the theater world and Ethel's home town, to come to the provinces to create a theater almost from the ground up—all he had here as a foundation was the *Yiddish Kultur Gezelshaft*—was not a decision to be lightly made. Fortunately for all of us, he made the right decision, and with the beginning of the program year in the fall of 1948, Mark and Ethel and their little daughter, Tova—she was then four, I believe—came to Cleveland to remain here for the next 24 years.

How does one begin from *aleph* to create a performing arts department? We had no physical theater, we had no theatrical staff, no technical experts, no set construction facility, and except for, as I mentioned earlier, a handful of Yiddishist theater lovers, among them a few skillful actors, no theater company as such. And yet Mark's first major production was an extravaganza titled *The Town of The Little People,* put on for two nights in December of 1948, in Severance Hall to large houses. It consisted of skits in English from Sholem Aleichem stories, with music, supplied by a full orchestra organized and directed by the late Elliot Morgenstern, dance ensembles choreographed by Lillian Weissberg, and with elaborate sets and costuming and a cast of dozens. I recall one small telling incident. Standing next to Mark in the wings, waiting to go on, I heard one of the actors step on a laugh, that is, begin to speak before the audience had stopped laughing, and then I heard Mark mutter, "Damn it, that's what you get when you work with amateurs." I tapped him on the shoulder and said, "And don't you forget it. That's the job you've assumed—to work with amateurs." He looked at me for a moment and said nothing. But I had misjudged him. Actually, one of Mark's greatest talents lay in his ability to bring out the best in his non-professional casts. In fact, he used to jest that in coming to the JCC to work, he not only continued his theatrical career, but he had also become a social worker. And there was truth in that jest, for Mark realized that as the head of a JCC theater, he not only had a responsibility to his audiences, to deliver the best theater possible, but that he also had a responsibility to those members of the community who wished to have a hand in theater work, and he creatively found ways to involve everyone who wanted to be involved, on the Performing Arts Advisory Committee, backstage in set construction and costuming, and on stage as well, where he somehow managed to integrate even those with lesser acting skills in smaller roles where they blended in unobtrusively and added positively to the production values.

From the very beginning, Mark surrounded himself with people who could help him fulfill his dream of a vibrant American-Jewish community playhouse. His faithful secretary through all those years was Lil Stamm. Also early on, Mark found Jerry Rose, a skilled electrician who had a love of theater and a very creative mind. Those early productions were mounted in some highly improbable places, including a stageless ballroom on the second floor of the quarters of the National Council of Jewish Women, Cleveland Section, on 105th Street, south of Euclid, where for such shows as *The Young and Fair, Morning Star,* and *An Enemy of The People,* Jerry had to improvise a stage, find ways to install spots that would illuminate it, and create a tiny backstage area where the actors could make quick costume changes. Other sites were also employed. The first full-length Yiddish play, Sholem Aleichem's *Shver Tsu Zayn a Yid,* opened in the little Chamber Music Hall at Severance Hall on May 14, 1950. It had glowing reviews in the local Yiddish press, which had eagerly been awaiting such a Yiddish production for nearly a decade. *Goldfaden's Kholem,* a Yiddish musical based on some of the operettas of the father of Yiddish theater, was presented in the Euclid Avenue Temple auditorium in 1951.

Early on, to give him guidance and help him build a cadre of theater enthusiasts, Mark had seen to it that a Drama Advisory Committee was organized, and the first chairperson of that committee was Lucy Wolpaw, who became one of the ardent supporters of the program and a frequent and talented performer in a number of plays. She was followed in the chair by Phil Steinberg, who was succeeded by Harry Wolpaw, and then I took over for nearly ten years. It was during my tenure that Mark's responsibilities were expanded and the committee became, as it is now, the Cultural Arts Advisory Committee.

By 1954, we had reached a point of strength that allowed us to plan for a permanent theater of our own. A committee, headed by Harry Wolpaw, raised the necessary funds to obtain a small storefront on Lee Road in Shaker Heights, and with much volunteer labor, a dandy little theater, seating about 150 people, was constructed. The dressing rooms were down in the basement, and during a performance there were constantly actors descending or climbing the narrow circular staircase. The theater was dedicated on November 14, 1954, and the first production there was *Skipper Next to God* by Jan de Hartog. The next was a fascinating production of Arthur Miller's *Death of a Salesman* in a Yiddish translation by Yakov Mestel.

Throughout Mark's tenure, Yiddish plays were presented whenever it was possible to assemble a cast—if not every year, at least every other year. Because of his earlier New York contacts, Mark began bringing to Cleveland stars of the Yiddish theater to appear in productions with our local Yiddish players. These included Leon Liebgold and Lil Liliana in *Greene Felder* by Peretz Hirshbeyn, a series of dance recitals by Felix Fibich, Maurice Schwartz in an English version of *Yoshe Kalb,* Max Bozyk in *Haketuba,* Eli Mintz in *Friends and Enemies,* Eliahu Goldenberg in *The Town of The Little People,* Pesach Borstein and Lillian Lux in *The Megilla of Itzik Manger,* Joseph Buloff on a number of occasions, including productions of *Seidman and Son* and *The Fifth Season.* Mark also brought us in one capacity or another Morris Carnovsky, Howard Da Silva, and others too numerous to mention.

Ethel Feder, who regrettably cannot be with us this afternoon, reminds us that in a profession marked by rivalries and jealousies, Mark displayed characteristic generosity toward members of the Jewish theatrical community, not only in bringing them here to star in our productions, but also in recommending jobs for them elsewhere. "I don't think," she adds, "they would have done the same for him."

With English language plays, Mark covered a broad spectrum, from fine dramas like *The Wall* and *The Visit* through musicals like *Lady in the Dark* and *Finian's Rainbow* through modern classics like *Our Town* and *The Iceman Cometh,* the latter guest-directed by Don Bianchi—his first directorial assignment, I believe, out of college. And there were many English productions of plays of specific Jewish interest—*The Burning Bush, The World of Sholem Aleichem, Cafe Crown, The Cold Wind and the Warm, The Tenth Man,* the musical *Milk and Honey, Unfair to Goliath*—and many, many more.

With the planning of this new JCC in the late 50's, Mark and his Drama Advisory Committee insisted that the plans include this marvelous theater, something that I believe no other JCC yet had. The theater was opened on December 10, 1960, with a spectacular production of *The Eternal Road,* guest-directed by Benno Frank of the Karamu Theater. Who could believe that a play by Franz Werfel with music by Kurt Weil, directed by a man who had worked with Max Reinhardt in Germany could bomb? Alas, it did.

In general, Mark had his finger on the pulse of the American Theater. When he produced Chekhov's *Ivanov,* guest-directed by Dorothy Silver, that play had not been done in America for decades, but the following year, it had a successful run on Broadway. The same thing with John Dos Passos' *U.S.A.,* and Mark's revival of *Finian's Rainbow,* guest-directed by Rhoda Payne, seemed to stimulate its appearance as a movie just two years later. Mark allowed himself the indulgence of appearing here in a play only twice—a cameo as Mendele Mokher Sforim, the book peddler in *The World of Sholem Aleichem*—who can forget that sparkling performance—just as who can forget Morris Baer as the poignant Bontshe Shvag in the same production. And then in his last year here, Mark starred in Arthur Miller's *The Price,* a stellar performance that he repeated in San Diego after he and Ethel had moved there.

But in addition to these so-called major productions—there were 72 in all—we cannot forget the splendid studio productions, staged readings of a wide range of plays, often with an accompanying lecture by some local academic, including an entire series on Bertold Brecht, a series on expressionist theater, from Elmer Rice's *The Adding Machine* through Ionesco's *The Bald Soprano,* a series on plays with themes from The Bible, a series on the plays of George Bernard Shaw, and the like. And then as far back as 1953, Mark and the *Yiddish Kultur Gezelshaft* sponsored an evening commemorating the uprising in the Warsaw Ghetto—and that later developed into an annual Warsaw Ghetto Commemoration, directed by Mark Feder, that in turn developed into our current annual *Yom Hashoah* Commemoration. And Mark began the annual Anniversary Celebration of Israel, beginning with the 10th in 1958.

And then there were the evenings of poetry readings, both in Yiddish and English, the concerts of the Jewish Singing Society, the various dance concerts, the lectures by noted scholars, both in English and Yiddish. And then there was the Suitcase Theater, a peripatetic group that went from organization to organization presenting playlets of social significance, and the playreading groups that studied and suggested plays for production.

All in all, a time of great excitement and vitality, for which the undeniable catalyst was Mark Feder. He left us a legacy upon which his successors in this JCC theater have been able to build, each in her own way, Rhoda Payne, Dorothy Silver, and now Elaine Rembrandt. They, and all the hundreds of people who had the privilege of working with Mark, at least those of us who are still around, owe him a debt of gratitude—and we owe it to him to see to it that the Cultural Arts remain a strong, vital part of the overall JCC program. And I'd like to ask all of you here to stand with me for a moment as we recall, in our own minds, this remarkable man.

JUDAH RUBINSTEIN (1921–2003)

"The Jewish Press in Cleveland"

A demographer and historian of Jewish life, Judah Rubinstein was a moving force in the creation of the Cleveland Jewish Archives at the Western Reserve Historical Society and served it with distinction for many years. A graduate of Western Reserve University, he devoted his early work to documenting local Jewish history at the Jewish Theological Seminary, a focus that led to his appointment as the first director of research at the Jewish Community Federation of Cleveland.

Rubinstein was especially interested in presenting primary artifacts such as photographs and original documents in a coherent telling of the story of Jews and their cultures, a commitment that resulted in two volumes, *Merging Traditions* (1978) and *Merging Traditions, Revised Edition* (published posthumously in 2004).

His passion for preserving the historical record of Cleveland Jewry inspired many to work with him on a variety of projects to advance that purpose and earned him the affectionate and apt sobriquet "Mr. Cleveland Jewish History."

In the following original piece, Rubinstein details the history of the Jewish press in Cleveland. The year 1889 saw the first of a long string of Cleveland Anglo-Jewish and Yiddish-language newspapers, family owned or publicly held, reflecting the variety of views espoused by Cleveland's Jews (see also the chapter on Leon Wiesenfeld in this volume). Rubinstein reviews the mergers and financial failures over the decades that produced lively realignments of the disparate elements comprising the Jewish press, with many papers battling one another in their pages. Increased coverage of Jewish affairs in other publications and a decline in the number of Yiddish readers contributed to a gradual diminution in the number of Anglo-Jewish and Yiddish papers.

Source: Judah Rubinstein, "The Jewish Press in Cleveland," Judah Rubinstein Papers, Western Reserve Historical Society, n.d.

THE JEWISH PRESS IN CLEVELAND

The first Anglo-Jewish newspaper in Cleveland, *The Hebrew Observer*, was established in July, 1889 by Hiram Straus and Sam Oppenheimer. Noting its appearance, *The Plain Dealer* reported that it "will be devoted to news and gossip of particular interest to Israelites" and added that the news would not be confined to Cleveland only. Oppenheimer, who had been the local correspondent for *The American Israelite*, severed his connection within two months after the paper started, and Albert Straus then joined his brother as publisher. A second Anglo-Jewish weekly, *The Jewish Review*, was established in 1893 by Oppenheimer and Jack Machol. The first issue was reported by its rival as presenting "a creditable appearance."

In 1896, Dan S. Wertheimer purchased the Review and in November, 1899, merged it with the Observer as the *Jewish Review and Observer*. Wertheimer was publisher and proprietor with offices in the Ajax Building on St. Clair. The masthead of the first issue listed Miss Jessie Cohen as editor, R. Rothe as associate editor, and M. Welfare as dramatic editor. The cost of announcements of betrothals, marriages, and births was one dollar each. Distribution was in 14 news stands including Herman Hexter's in the Arcade. *The Review and Observer* became a stock company in 1907, with Dan Wertheimer president and treasurer. Sam Oppenheimer was listed as his associate editor. The newspaper remained in the Wertheimer family until it ceased publication with the appearance of *The Cleveland Jewish News* in 1964.

The Jewish Review and Observer was the sole Anglo-Jewish newspaper in the community until 1906 when Maurice Weidenthal, a reporter and editor with several Cleveland newspapers, founded *The Jewish Independent*. When he died in 1917, his brother, Leo, continued its publication as editor and president until it, too, ceased publication in 1964.

The Cleveland Jewish News, the successor to the two family publications, first appeared on October 30, 1964 in a 32 page edition under the editorship of Arthur Weyne. Community leaders, recognizing the needs for an informed Jewish community, organized the Cleveland Jewish Publication, a non-profit corporation, to finance the newspaper. Lloyd S. Schwenger was president of its first board of trustees. The newspaper's offices were originally in the Film Building on East 21st and Payne Avenue until it moved to its present location in 1972 in the Cedar-Center area.

The beginnings of the Yiddish language press in Cleveland are less clear. Three early Yiddish language newspapers were *The Jewish Recorder, The Jewish Star,* and *The Daily Press.* The first was published in 1893 by M. Balogh and J. Wolf, who sold religious books and articles as the Jewish Publishing House at 236 Woodland Avenue. *The Daily Press* was founded in 1908 by Samuel Rocker, Adolph Haas, and Jonas Gross. Apparently Mr. Rocker had previously been editor and part owner of *The Jewish Star (Jewish Banner?),* which was published as a weekly. In 1906, he was referred to as "editor Rocker of the Jewish Banner ... still valiantly fighting the battle for Zionism." One source indicates that *The Jewish Daily Press* was sold in 1910, although the purchasers are not named. *Die Yiddishe Velt (The Jewish World)* first appeared in 1911 as a weekly and later became a daily. Samuel Rocker was its owner and editor until 1936. His son, Henry, succeeded him as publisher, and Leon Wiesenfeld was its editor for the next three years. Hyman Horowitz was its editor later for many years until it ceased publication in 1952. Toward the end, *Die Yiddishe Velt* became a weekly, incorporated more English, but with its readership largely gone, its demise was inevitable. In its last days it was published by Robert Herwald, who subsequently moved from Cleveland. Thereafter, Yiddish newspaper readers become wholly dependent on the New York press. In fact, *The Forward* for years carried a Cleveland section in its Chicago edition. For a number of years, the bound volumes of *Die Yiddishe Velt* were stored at Park Synagogue. When the storage space was needed, the newspaper was microfilmed, and the bound volumes were given away as scrap. This microfilm is now part of the American Jewish Archives collection in Cincinnati and constitutes a major source of local Jewish community history in this century.

About 1923, an effort was made to publish a second Yiddish-English language weekly. *The Jewish Guardian (Die Yiddishe Waechter)* appeared for a short while as a rival to *The Jewish World.* Dr. Charles Worstman and Rabbi Samuel Benjamin were listed as editor and managing editor respectively. The weekly had an Orthodox orientation and was partly an outgrowth of the earlier local Kehilla movement in which Rabbi Samuel Margolies was a key figure.

Possibly the last effort to establish a local newspaper was made by Leon Wiesenfeld in December, 1938 when *The Jewish Voice (Die Yiddishe Stimme)* appeared in English and Yiddish. President of the publishing company was

Ben Arsham. Mayer Atkin was vice-president and Elias Mantel, treasurer. Wiesenfeld had a falling out earlier that year with *Die Yiddishe Velt,* and in his newspaper attacked "the politicians of the Talmud Torah and the Zionist District" for what he described as their attempts to drive him out of Jewish public life. By mid-February, in a front page appeal in *The Jewish Voice,* Wiesenfeld admitted it was in grave danger without any financial reserves and scanty advertising revenue. Very likely it ceased publication several weeks later. Subsequently, Wiesenfeld issued periodically a slick paper, English language publication called *The Jewish Voice Pictorial,* which contained boiler plate articles plus his own features on aspects of Cleveland Jewish life.

With the demise of *The Jewish Voice,* the local Jewish newspaper scene stabilized. Interest and energy were directed outward to the plight of Europe's Jews and the war. The decline of the three local newspapers in the next two decades reflects the inevitable loss of a Yiddish speaking and reading generation, the Americanization of their children, and the extended coverage of Jewish affairs in the general press. *The Jewish World* and the two Anglo-Jewish weeklies however filled a need recognized when steps were taken immediately in 1964 to insure continuity of a Jewish press in Cleveland by establishing *The Cleveland Jewish News.*

Section Two

Civic Life

Flyer, 1943, for the Young Adult Division of the Jewish Welfare Fund (Jewish Community Federation).

Excerpt from *A Tale of Ten Cities*

Cleveland-born Sidney Z. Vincent attended Western Reserve University and spent his entire professional career in Cleveland, first as a teacher and later in Jewish communal service. He credited the Glenville Jewish Center with inspiring him to set his sights on a future of service in Jewish affairs, an interest he expressed in Zionist activities early in his student days.

He entered Jewish community work in 1945 at the Jewish Community Council, without the advantage of training in social work. He soon turned his attention to civil rights campaigns, fair housing efforts, community relations activities, and Jewish education and culture. He remained with the Jewish Community Federation, the result of a 1951 merger of the Jewish Community Council with the Jewish Welfare Federation (see also the chapter on The Jewish Community Federation of Cleveland in this volume), becoming its executive director in 1965, a position he held until retirement in 1975. (See also the chapter on Henry L. Zucker in this volume.) In 1959, he organized and led the first Cleveland community mission to Israel.

Vincent, in a long and distinguished career, helped found the International Conference for Jewish Communal Service, the National Foundation for Jewish Culture, the Institute for Jewish Life, and the Conference for Human Needs (in Israel). He also served as president of the Association for Jewish Communal Relations and the Conference for Jewish Communal Service.

Judah Rubinstein's abridgment of Vincent's chapter summarizes the migration of Cleveland Jewry from an early and strong core-city presence northward and eastward to create a solid but politically uninvolved Jewish presence living in definable areas in eight contiguous suburbs, creating a Cleveland nearly devoid of Jews. Vincent's description and analysis include the African American and non-Jewish segments of the new suburban constellation.

Source: Abridgment of Sidney Vincent's chapter, "Cleveland—City without Jews," excerpted from Eugene J. Lipman and Albert Vorspan, eds., *A Tale of Ten Cities* (New York: Union of American Hebrew Congregations, 1962). Reprinted with permission of Union for Reform Judaism Press, New York.

CLEVELAND — CITY WITHOUT JEWS

. . . [In Cleveland,] [t]he Jewish community is merely the most classic example of an almost universal tendency. Since the turn of the century, five neighborhoods have been centers of Jewish settlement—each progressively further east from the center of the city. (The western half of the city has never had more than 500 Jewish families.) When these neighborhoods have been left they have been totally abandoned, to the point where today, perhaps uniquely among American cities, Cleveland proper is almost literally a city without Jews. [. . .] Over 90 per cent of the Jews of Cuyahoga County, in which Cleveland is located, live in the suburbs and only two of the twenty-five synagogues are still in the city itself. Of the estimated 1000 Jewish graduates of public high schools of the county in June, 1961, a maximum of half a dozen received diplomas from Cleveland's schools—and the number will soon disappear almost entirely. Only some 250 of the 140,000 children attending Cleveland's public schools are Jewish. All but three of the Jewish service agencies are located in the suburbs.

Moreover, the concentration within certain specific suburbs is remarkably high, even though housing restrictions against Jews have all but disappeared everywhere. The Jewish density in a few middle and upper-middle class suburbs is probably just as high as it was fifty years ago in the downtown, rundown districts, when the Jewish community was overwhelmingly immigrant and first generation and had yet to be "accommodated" to the general culture. [. . .]

Although the "mother city" has completely disappeared, the line of Jewish settlement runs in an unbroken rough crescent, swinging north and then east through eight contiguous suburbs. One of the suburbs is primarily the home of newly-married or relatively young couples and another tends to have somewhat more status than the rest, but the similarities among the suburbs are far greater than their differences. Jews continue to think of themselves as a single community rather than as a series of separate neighborhoods. Attempts by national agencies to organize along distinctive suburban lines are frequently resisted.

[...]

Who then is left in the central city? The fact is that in the past twenty years, during a time of dynamic population growth, the central city has actually decreased in numbers. All the dramatic increase of population has been suburban. As a matter of fact, the white population of the city has in the past ten years dropped dramatically despite the recent markedly increased birth rate, the significant immigration of southern whites to help man Cleveland's heavy industry, and the fairly substantial migration from overseas following World War II, all tending to increase the white population of the city. The places of the whites have been taken by the Negro community which has grown during this period from approximately 85,000 to close to 250,000.

In summary, then, as contrasted with 1940, the central city has far more Negroes; it is almost completely emptied of Jews, and its white population is somewhat more Catholic since the out-migration of Protestants to the suburbs has been at an even more rapid rate than has been the case among Catholics.

[...]

The intense concentration of Jews in certain of the suburbs has led only slowly to the assumption of political responsibility. Although Jews constitute 70 per cent of the population in one of the eight suburbs in which most of them live, and form more than a majority in two others, there has never been a Jewish mayor in any community. With two exceptions, there is no more than a single Jew on any Board of Education. In the suburb where Jews have lived for the longest period of time—since before the First World War—there has never been a Jewish councilman who came to office originally through election. Both present representatives on city council [Cleveland Heights], as well as their few predecessors, were appointed to fill vacancies by the administration in power—and have subsequently been elected as "members of the team." The only real breakthrough has been in the past two years when the suburb with the highest Jewish density finally elected Jews to the majority of councilmanic posts. It may be significant that this community, as will be indicated below, subsequently almost split into two sections, with the non-Jewish section seeking through a long process to secede from the northern "Jewish" section.

In general, the "old settlers" retain a firm grip on the administration of suburban communities, and the incoming Jewish group makes inroads, if at all, slowly and fearfully, with a constant desire to include non-Jewish candidates on any slate that appears to be too strongly Jewish. The point of view of the newcomers (mostly Jewish) tends to be liberal and Democratic; the original group (mostly Protestant) tends to be conservative and Republican. No wonder tensions develop! The best symbol of the determination of the entrenched group to hold on to the machinery of power is to be found in the various appointive bodies which often remain almost completely Christian even in communities that are overwhelmingly Jewish. Not a single Jew serves on the Zoning Commission and only two of seven on the Library Board— both appointive—of the suburbs with the largest Jewish population[s], although, particularly in the former case, they make decisions which vitally affect Jewish institutions.

On the other hand, it is common to find Jews leaning over backward not to assume positions of responsibility too hastily. P.T.A. officers, for example, tend to remain overwhelmingly or predominantly Christian long after the school population has become mostly Jewish. In two instances, an unwritten rule is observed: one year a Christian president, the next year a Jewish one—and all without public discussion. It is simply understood that such topics are for the closed conference of top leadership, not the public platform of general debate.

[...]

Even within suburbs with strong Jewish or Catholic components, there is nearly always a clustering in certain areas rather than a general dispersal into the new neighborhood. A recent Yom Kippur survey of one of the suburbs [Cleveland Heights], for example, revealed that of its ten elementary schools, four had Jewish populations well in excess of 90 per cent while two had virtually no Jewish students. Real estate agents accept as a perfectly normal part of their daily operations that Catholics will want to settle only near new suburban parochial schools, Jews around the many new institutions they have built, and Protestants in "their" neighborhoods.

Certainly, the pattern of housing and voting, both in the suburbs and in the central city, makes any claim that Cleveland has solved its interreligious problems seem shallow and incomplete. Conflict is rare, but so is integration, no matter how one interprets that all-inclusive term.

THE NEGRO COMMUNITY

Increasingly, a kind of high level irritation with problems of Negro-white relationships breaks through the overlay of good feeling. [. . .]

Negro-Jewish relationships are particularly complicated. Every morning at the bus stops in the central city, there are knots of Negro women waiting for buses to transport them from their ghettos to suburban homes—often Jewish—where they spend the day making white homes clean and comfortable. At the same hour, dozens of Jewish businessmen will be passing them going the other way—from the suburbs to all sorts of business establishments in the city that serve the Negro trade. A substantial share of housing in the Negro area—with all the attendant irritations—is owned by Jews, partly because the neighborhoods are largely formerly Jewish.

Mistress and servant—storekeeper and client—landlord and tenant. Some of these relationships can be and are warm and creative. But the tendency is the other way. There are no peer relationships, few opportunities for meeting as equal to equal.

[. . .]

So the Negro-Jewish pattern is a strange mixture. Negro anti-Semitism co-exists with feelings of warmth toward Jews. The immediate symbol of the white hostile world too often happens to be a Jewish merchant or landlord, but at the same time, the opener of closed doors in employment or housing is also likely to be Jewish.

At least equally complicated is the feeling of Jews towards Negroes, compounded as it is of active support and understanding of a fellow minority, and uneasiness at the constant pressures on each successive neighborhood to which Jews move. The entire relationship presents a tremendous challenge to sober and objective social, economic, and psychological study.

INTERRELIGIOUS

What of religious relationships?

On the formal level a rather good report could be made despite such irritations as the exclusion of Jews from the higher Masonic degrees and a few other status organizations. The annual drives of the Catholic Charities, Jewish Welfare Fund, or the YMCA's attract contributions from individuals of all groups. Bequests are frequently reported designating as beneficiaries the charitable institutions of all three faiths.

There are projects on which the three religious communities—or more precisely, their leadership—work closely together. The Cleveland Committee on Immigration, for example, is primarily composed of representatives, official and semi-official, of the three religious faiths.

[. . .]

Hearings on civil rights proposals nearly always feature a Roman Catholic, Protestant, and Jewish spokesman, and some kind of secular instrument is usually formed for interreligious consultation. It is significant that such secular instrumentalities are necessary for this purpose.

[. . .]

Deeper than the contacts in the area of community relations are the relationships that have developed in the health and welfare field. Cleveland has a reputation for being a highly-organized (or over-organized) community. Certainly, the innumerable committees of the Community Chest and the Welfare Federation of Cleveland with its six councils (for hospitals, children's services, group work services, case work services, problems of the aged, and area councils) provide almost daily opportunities for staffs and lay leadership of various agencies, religious and non-sectarian, to work together on problems of services and finances in which they are all mutually involved.

The links between the Welfare Federation and the Jewish Federation are particularly close. The same building houses both agencies; the staffs hold joint meetings on regular occasion; Jewish health and welfare agencies place a high priority on work in their respective welfare federation councils. The immediate past president of the Community Fund was simultaneously a vice-president of the Jewish Community Federation.

[. . .]

Other formal interreligious contacts are moderately frequent. In addition to the program of the National Conference of Christians and Jews, which is of course based on equal formal representation from the three faiths, exchanges of pulpits between rabbis and Protestant ministers occasionally take place and neighborhood interreligious Thanksgiving celebrations have become more common. The annual Institute on Judaism sponsored by a local congregation results in a fine attendance of Protestant ministers. The Catholic university has in recent years become more of a center for consideration of intergroup relations problems.

There is considerable question, however, as to the depth of many of these contacts. The Ministerial Alliance is exclusively Protestant and there is no medium of any kind for regular exchange of views by the clergy. Indeed, except for the leading figures, rabbis and ministers scarcely know one another. On the lay level, however, the staffs of the Church Federation, the over-all Protestant group, and the Jewish Community Federation consult frequently and are part of an over-all clearing house in intergroup relations that meets monthly and involves all agencies in the community—except the Roman Catholic ones. [. . .]

On [. . .] two issues—censorship and Sunday closings—Jews officially tend to be on the sidelines about as completely as the Catholics are when civil rights are involved, with this difference: Jewish leaders feel strongly they should be in the battle opposing censorship and Sunday closings, but are often not prepared to pay the price of opposition. Catholics feel mildly they should be in the battle for civil rights but usually are not sufficiently interested to enlist with enthusiasm in the various campaigns.

The real drive behind recent activities aimed at enforcing the state law on Sunday closings that has for years been unobserved is, however, economic rather than religious. More and more places of business, particularly in the suburban areas, have opened on Sunday and have begun to cut seriously into the business of the large downtown stores. In retaliation, an organization has been formed called "Sunday, Inc.," which is an unusual combination of business and religious leadership. Its president has stated, "We have not approached this problem on religious lines. We have as our common bond a desire to keep merchants from doing unnecessary business on Sunday. The laws are on the books." But the same article announces the officers of the organization: a number of key businessmen, the executive director of the Cleveland Church Federation "representing Protestants," a leading Catholic official "representing Catholics," and a Jewish businessman "representing Jews." Here again almost all of the "offending" merchants are Jewish. Religious tension sometimes results, but as in the case of the art theaters, there would seem to be relatively little mass support by their constituencies of the official stands taken by the authoritative Christian groups, if one is to judge from the volume of Sunday sales in many neighborhoods that are certainly not Jewish.

EDUCATION

Problems of church-state relationships occur most frequently in the public schools. This is an issue that strikes home. Every Christmas season the irritations break out with renewed vigor—in Jewish neighborhoods.

On the one hand there is the organized Jewish community, committed to the separation of church and state. [...]

Jewish community organizations, unlike some Jewish parents, have consistently adhered to a strict separationist policy. As a result, school superintendents in the suburbs with significant Jewish enrollments have, in recent years, become sensitive to problems of Bible reading, prayers, grace before meals, and scheduling of school events on religious holidays. The rapid turnover of faculty in the elementary schools, and the need during the desperate shortage to import teachers from small communities where religion is accepted as an unquestioned part of the curriculum have, however, led to repeated classroom intrusions of religion despite official attitudes of the administration. [...]

All these issues, however, paled in 1961 in comparison to the struggle over federal aid to parochial schools. Here is a real "bread and butter" issue that the local Catholic diocese has begun to feature far more than any other. The Protestant church for once was united; every spokesman has vigorously opposed such aid. A number of Orthodox rabbis for the first time broke the solid Jewish "separation front" by endorsing government aid, but the Federation overwhelmingly repeated its traditional support of the separation principle. There can be little doubt that this will for years to come constitute the most controversial of interreligious issues.

OTHER ISSUES

[...]

Considerably greater emotional involvement is seen when the issues touch home directly, rather than being concerned with philosophical differences. Almost any Jewish institution seeking to build for the first time in a new suburb is likely to encounter resistance. Twice in the past decade, cases involving the right of synagogues to build in suburban areas had to be carried to the Ohio Supreme Court.

One of the cases had an ironic ending. For years, counsel for the suburb [Beachwood] fought through three courts with unprecedented tenacity to prevent the building of a synagogue. Despite all sorts of guarantees and assurances, it was alleged that the town would suffer from increased traffic problems, difficulties in providing services, and other similar situations. But the temple was hardly completed when the city fathers, faced by a desperate shortage of public school facilities, requested (and were granted) space in the new synagogue's school until a new public school could be built.

Religious exclusions practiced in a number of the suburbs by the company that developed the area were broken in the mid-fifties only after a bitter campaign and threats of taxpayer suits that would have depressed land values considerably. One suburb [Van Sweringen, Shaker Heights] enforces a complicated 25 per cent quota on Jews, and the northern section of a suburb [Forest Hills, Cleveland Heights] that is half-Jewish has developed a neighborhood compact that has succeeded so far in keeping out all but a single Jew. One community [Cleveland Heights] was almost torn apart by a campaign for a second high school, which many contended was motivated primarily by the desire of the northern half of the community (strongly Christian) to have "their" school, while resigning the original high school to the southern, "Jewish" section. In another suburb [Beachwood], an election was held on the question of dividing into two villages, one overwhelmingly Christian, the other just as strongly Jewish. Both efforts failed—but only after bitter campaigns. Permission to build a Jewish community center in a suburb [Cleveland Heights] was secured only after a long struggle, although a Lutheran high school was approved far more easily on an adjoining parcel of land.

In each of these cases there were more factors involved than religious differences. But no one who attended the various meetings of zoning commissions, city and village councils, or neighborhood town halls could escape the conclusion that, although problems of zoning and traffic and taxes were involved, religious hostility or unfriendliness were also powerful determinants of attitudes. Few situations present "clean" examples of bigotry; there is almost always a complicated intermingling of economic, sociological, psychological, and religious interests.

[...]

Sometimes neighborhoods change so completely as to create religious problems where there is no bigotry at all. One worried Christian mother, whose daughter attended a junior high school that is overwhelmingly Jewish, described in a thoroughly rational and unpunishing manner how her child was treated with perfect fairness and friendship during school hours, but was increasingly excluded from the social contacts that were becoming important to her. The family subsequently and regretfully moved from the neighborhood since dating possibilities had become virtually impossible for the daughter!

Despite the occasional highly dramatic cases where Jews have achieved top leadership in various civic roles, the community as a whole is, in a quiet and undramatic fashion, divided along religious lines. Cleveland has an FEPC, but evidence indicates that perhaps one out of every four job orders filed with private employment agencies is discriminatory against Jews. Perhaps equally significant is the increasing self-segregation in employment. A leading utility [Cleveland Electric Illuminating] in Cleveland, which had been closed to Jews for years, changed its policy and freely accepted Jewish clerical help. The local Jewish Vocational Service soon found itself encountering substantial difficulties in filling job orders, because the girls wanted to work in places "where they could meet Jewish fellows!"

Any observation that social life in Cleveland tends to follow rather closely along religious lines is often greeted with indignant instancing of various parties and gatherings of Jews and non-Jews. Nevertheless, these are overwhelmingly the exception and the so-called "5 o'clock shadow" is clearly visible in the community's social life. Jews socialize for the most part with Jews; Catholics with Catholics; Protestants with Protestants.

In 1958 the executives of two well-established women's civic organizations requested help in increasing Jewish participation in their work. The fact that these organizations contained few Jews could not be ascribed to discrimination; both have been eager for some time to expand their Jewish membership. Why, they asked, do Jewish women join so enthusiastically in the work of Hadassah, Council of Jewish Women, Sisterhoods, the Welfare Fund Appeal, and many other Jewish organizations, but are often so hard to interest in non-sectarian groups? Surely Jewish women are civic minded; surely they have much to contribute.

An easy—and truthful—answer would be that opportunities for advancement to top leadership are best in one's "own" organization. But like most easy answers, that explanation is only part of the truth. Over and over again, leaders of Jewish organizations described their impatience as they sat at meetings of a number of non-sectarian organizations, where the issues being discussed were "piddling"—a budget item of a few dollars or a minor, unexciting program detail. The really successful Jewish organizations, they claim, present far bolder challenges. What is to be avoided at all costs is dullness. And, they conclude, those non-sectarian organizations that are truly—not perfunctorily—open to all women and that grapple with basic community needs do attract Jewish women. Unspoken is what may well be the most important factor: Jewish women in Cleveland are more comfortable with Jewish women. But in any case, the fact remains unchallengeably true that the overwhelming majority of Jewish (or, for that matter, Catholic and Protestant) women are "club ladies" within their own religious groups.

Although the world of business necessarily involves more contact across religious lines, it is nevertheless true that the husbands, too, eat lunch (when there is no business appointment), play golf, and attend committee meetings most frequently with men who are of the same religious faith. If they are Jewish, they are very likely to have a Jewish insurance man, a Jewish lawyer, a Jewish doctor—except in the case of specialists. And, with variations, the same generalizations could be made about the other religious groups.

[...]

Is Cleveland, then, the best location in the nation? If the negative test of absence of conflict is applied, the boast can be very largely made good. But if the aim is a culturally diverse community where creative living of cultural groups is balanced by full and easy communications across religious lines, Cleveland, like most cities, still has a long road to travel.

Excerpt from *"I Belong to the Working Class"*

Polish-born Rose Pastor moved with her impoverished family to London's East End sometime between 1882 and 1886. She made cigarettes at a young age to augment the family's meager income before they moved to Cleveland in 1891, where Rose worked as a cigar maker while educating herself and writing articles for the student newspaper and New York's *Jewish Daily News*. She moved to New York in 1903 to work for that paper and, in 1905, married railroad magnate J. G. Phelps Stokes after working with him at his Lower East Side social service projects. She divorced Stokes in 1925 to marry Isaac Romaine, who shared her socialist views.

Rose was arrested and imprisoned for ten years under the Espionage Act for opposing the U.S. entry into World War I and for writing, in a letter to the *Kansas City Star,* "No government which is for the profiteers can also be for the people, and I am for the people while the government is for the profiteers." She was severely injured when clubbed by the police in 1929 during a demonstration for the removal of U.S. forces from Haiti.

A founder of the Communist Party in the United States, she lectured widely to promote her radical ideas and prominently supported the workers in the hotel, restaurant, and shirtwaist workers' strikes surrounding the turn of the twentieth century. She was a leader in the birth control movement. Rose counted Eugene Debs, Clarence Darrow, Upton Sinclair, Emma Goldman, and other liberal activists among her intellectual peers. Although a millionaire, she continued to be known as "Rose of the Ghetto" for her involvement in bettering the lives of the poor. Diagnosed with breast cancer in 1932, she went for treatment to Germany, where she died a year later.

Stokes recounts the grinding poverty of her early years and how she manipulated herself into her first job at age eleven. She recalls the cigar factory's overpowering smell, harsh work conditions, tenuous employment, and unfair salary: "Two weeks to learn . . . half pay for six weeks, then full pay."

The key to keeping her job was faster and better production. She was shocked to realize that the workers enriched the boss without equitable compensation. Desperation drove rebellion, and Rose experienced her first strike while working as a young woman in a cigar factory in Cleveland. She recalls the power the workers felt and writes that "the old timidity never again quite overcame any of us."

Source: An excerpt from Rose Pastor Stokes, *"I Belong to the Working Class": The Unfinished Autobiography of Rose Pastor Stokes,* Herbert Shapiro and David L. Sterling, eds. (Athens, GA, and London: University of Georgia Press, 1990).

CHAPTER II
Coming to America

The ship we sailed in was an unseaworthy tub.

The passengers were anxious. My mother mingled much with them.

She was always explaining to her fellow voyagers: "Our lives are risked to pile up riches for the company."

We had hardly got out to sea when a storm tore a great hole in the old vessel.

Deep down in the ship men and women walked in water to their knees. Men in blue coats and gold buttons came down to quiet the panic. But when the water rose still higher—when tables, benches, boxes, and trunks began to swirl about, a great wailing went up.

In the midst of it all, a woman in black knelt up to her armpits in the water, holding high above her head a black crucifix, and crying over and over again, "Bozshe moi! Bozshe moi! Bozshe moi!"

My mother sat quietly on a box with her baby, while we watched the crazed woman. I sat beside my mother, with a hand on her arm. I was not afraid. Perhaps because my mother had showed no sign of excitement. Perhaps because no one had ever taught me to be afraid.

An officer called down: "Stop your crying! We'll soon be safe in a port." Some would not believe it. But we really docked at Antwerp. For two days we were boarded in houses near the docks. When the ship was patched up, we were herded down into the bowels of her again, and once more set out on a rough voyage. Storms tossed us about. Sickness beset us down in steerage. Bodies were wrapped in canvas and buried at sea. Potatoes and herring, with bread and great chunks of salt butter (or what looked like butter) were the only food we were given. Men and women protested. They formed in groups and demanded a change, but none was made.

At the end of three weeks we steamed into New York harbor. It was early dawn. Every window on shore threw back at us bursts of golden sunlight; but the cold air, with steel fingers, gripped [the] body.

With both hands I clutched a thin little jacket close to my shivering frame, and stared at the flaming windows; thinking: "Somewhere in this city is Jacob the Learned Bootmaker."

Now there was confused running, hither and yon. My mother took me by the hand.

"Come Rosalie," she said, "we'll soon be in Castle Garden." [...]

Immigrants leaning against huge round bundles, exhausted with waiting, crying infants, restless children, men and women calling to each other across wide spaces. Iron pillars, iron gratings, stone walls—floors—all so cold and forbidding ... A gnawing hunger ... Children crying, "Bread, Mama!" Mothers slapping their children, pushing them away. "What can I give you!—I've got nothing!" "Is it my fault? Wait! Wait till we get out of here—wait!"

Waiting—still waiting. Complaints, protests. Men in uniform shoving bundles about; reading labels; pushing from them complaining men, women; hurling oaths at them; calling shameful names ... "Wait, can't you? you—! We've waited longer for you! Waddeye think America is, anyway—a banquet hall? Keep-your-shirt-on! ... " And I thinking, "How and why is it a garden?" The time seemed endless. When a large group of us were herded on a ferry boat for New Jersey, I was so weak from hunger that my legs refused to carry me. A man in a blue coat with gold buttons grudgingly lifted me in his arms and carried me to the boat. Here my mother counted out a number of coins. A peddler took them, and gave me my first taste of bananas.

My mother lacked the money to pay our fares to Cleveland, so an official gave us an address and put us on a train. At Philadelphia, in a boarding-house for immigrants, we waited for nearly a week before my stepfather sent us the money. He had a struggle raising it, and most of it was borrowed.

• • •

On the upper floor of a two-story frame structure in the rear of Number Four Liberal Street, my stepfather ushered us proudly and happily into a three-room flat.

There was a kitchen stove (invitingly warm!). There were tables, and beds, and chairs, and a clock; oilcloth on the kitchen table, and a gaily patterned linoleum on the kitchen floor.

My mother went from one room to another, her face shining.

My stepfather came after her, the baby on his arm, a happy light in his eyes.

"Oh, Israel!" my mother turned her glowing face to him. "You bought all this!"

"All this," he said, waving an arm at the new things.

"You must be earning good money."

"Not so bad," he remarked.

Something in his tone brought another question.

"Israel—is it all—paid for?"

"Well—" And seeing the shadows creep into my mother's eyes, he put an arm about her and kissed her.

"Never mind, Hindl, don't worry. I'll pay—in good time."

That evening, after I had rocked the baby to sleep and crept into my new cot, I heard two troubled voices talking from the kitchen. They were discussing me. What to do with me. Earnings were low, times were hard, and getting worse from day to day. Everywhere it was the same. All the neighbors were in debt. The grocer, the baker, the butcher, were beginning to shut down on credit. The Feinbergs downstairs were sending their daughter to get work in a cigar factory. Maybe I'd get work if I went along. If I got work where Jennie did, she could wait for me mornings and evenings, till I learned to find the way by myself . . .

Two days later Jennie, a tall dark raw-boned girl of thirteen, started out for the job in the cigar factory, and I went with her.

As we were leaving Jennie's kitchen in the cold and the dark, my mother kissed me, and my stepfather patted my head and gave me a dime.

They both laughed with forced gaiety:

"Look! Our little breadwinner," my mother chuckled, through tears.

And my stepfather too, with a catch in his voice: "Our Rosalie, already a working woman!"

• • •

We start out at dawn to be there before others fill the places.

The air is sharp with early frost. My thin jacket is like a sieve against the wind. I hold it tightly—with both hands to my chest and throat—as if the clutch of my hands could protect me.

Jennie too must be cold. She shivers.

"Come on, we must hurry!" She grips me by the hand. She is taller than I, and takes longer strides. Every few steps, I run to keep up with her.

The long way seems endless. Down the muddy unpaved street at right angles to Liberal Street. A turn to the right, then to the left down Orange Street. Down Broadway, on to the end of Ontario Street. Across the Public Square, dodging a confusing network of streetcars. Then left, for several blocks to the viaduct, and down—steeply, to a street under it. We've walked miles and miles, it seems.

Near the end of this street Jennie finds the number she has on a slip of paper. We enter the big loft building, our hearts pounding. We hold hands and climb two flights of stairs.

There are two doors: Maybe it's this one. Timidly, we push open a heavy metal door. The suffocating effluvium of tobacco dust strikes us in the face.

I want to run away from the unexpected offense. But I stand still beside Jennie, and continue to hold her hand.

There are many workers here—at work—benches all of new wood. A row each, facing the two long walls of the narrow loft; in the middle, two rows facing each other built as of one piece. The bodies of the workers move in short sharp rhythm as the hands roll dark brown sticks on a board, or cut dark brown leaves into patterned pieces, or chop the ends off the sticks with a small cutting-tool.

A man comes out of a newly-partitioned office near the door. A very comfortable-looking man. I have never before been talked-to by anyone so comfortable-looking—not even Mr. Cohen of the Princess Theatre.

"I'm Mr. Wertheim," he says. "Do you want work?"

"Yes, please."

Turning to Jennie: "How old are you?"

"Fourteen," and Jennie gets very red in the face.

"A fine big girl for fourteen," Mr. Wertheim says, placing a hand on her broad, square shoulders.

"And you?"

"Eleven."

"You're tall for your age, but—" he trails off.

Does he mean not to give me work? My heart beats! And something pounds in my throat and tightens it.

"What do you say to going right to work?"

He is including us both in his look! The blood that was pounding through my heart and clutching at my throat goes to my head.

We nod our yes, and at the same moment I think of the two troubled voices from the kitchen, and go dizzy with joy in the thought of being able to help.

"Oh, Jake, two more new ones," he calls to a large heavy-featured man.

The man leaves a bench where he is teaching a young worker, and comes to the door.

"The foreman," Mr. Wertheim explains. "He'll teach you stogie-rolling."

As we go with the foreman, Mr. Wertheim offers tersely:

"Two weeks to learn. After that half-pay for six weeks, then full pay. All right?"

Had he announced six months without pay we would have nodded our heads just the same.

At the end of the third week I get three silver quarters and two copper pennies—my first week's pay.

I run home with the treasure.

My mother takes it from me, looks long at the coins in the open palm of her hand, and with a bitter cry throws them on the table.

"The blood of a child! Look," she says, "look what it will bring!"

On a Friday morning, Mr. Wertheim came and stood behind my chair.

"Rose Pastor, how would you like to go home today, and help your mother? I'll bet she needs you. I'm sure she works very hard. You can come back Monday morning, and it will be all right."

Who would have thought a boss could be so kind! I thanked him and hurried home, glad to be of help to my mother.

She always had a burden of work to do, especially on Fridays. I scrubbed the kitchen floor, and ran errands to the grocer's, and filled the oil lamps, and brought up coal, and washed the baby's things down by the yard pump; and all the time I did my chores, I overflowed with gratitude toward the boss who spoke so feelingly of my poor overburdened mother.

On Monday morning, when I came to my work-bench, I said to the girl on my right—

"Wasn't Mr. Wertheim kind?"

"Kind?" The girl on my right chuckled, "It's a good thing you were sent home Friday morning. The factory inspector came in the afternoon. Some of the young ones can sit on two extra blocks, and look over fourteen. But not you."

Jennie too never told me till Monday:

"Oh, I passed. I look old. Mr. Wertheim didn't want to lose you, I guess, so he sent you home."

"Lose me?" I asked.

"Yeah!" said the girl on my right, "Lose ye, is what she said. The younger and quicker ye are, the more money the boss makes on ye—see?"

That evening, sitting at the kitchen table, eating supper, I regarded my kind stepfather. He was only a poor peddler. True he had a horse and wagon of his own, but he wasn't a boss: I could love and respect him.

My mother got acquainted with the neighbors, and they came in evenings, or Sunday afternoons. There was much talk, and my child's horizon again began to widen through the equal sorrows and bitter economic struggles of the little proletarian world about me. It was a hard winter. There was always someone losing a job, or hopelessly in search of one. Or the school children were without shoes or decent clothing. Or there was nothing to pay the grocer who refused further credit. Or someone came to borrow an egg for a sick child. Or the eternal Installment Plan Agent had been and threatened to take away everything unless something was paid on account—and with more than half already paid out! Or there was nothing toward the rent, most of the next month gone, and the landlord knocking daily at the door. Or there was an eviction threatened, and not a dollar to move with. Or a baby about to be born, and where will they get ten dollars for the midwife? Or someone suddenly taken ill, and which doctor will come and then wait for his money? Or a worker short-waged at the end of the week; exchange of experience with "docking" and other abuses in the shops. Or the bitter cold, and the problem of bed covers . . . No one had enough . . . Or coal; its price by the ton, and the big difference in cost to the poor who must buy by the sack. Or the advantage of one job over another. Or the disadvantage of working far from home; the cost in carfares; the loss in time; in sleep; in pay, through starting the day too tired. Or, we'd visit the neighbors; come, perhaps, when there was a quarrel— always over an economy; questions of nickels and dimes; of what to buy and what to save; of what should or should not have been done when there's so little money and one never sure of one's job.

Our lives were like our neighbors' lives. The Installment man came Monday mornings. There was not always the dollar to give him. We would take the money from the bread we needed, to pay for the blankets we needed as much. The same blankets, in the store, were half the price. All the neighbors knew it. My mother discovered it for herself. She raged against the Installment Robbers. "But how many poor workers are there who can buy for cash? Yes! That's why these leeches can drain our blood on the Installment Plan!"

"Father, don't buy any more on the Plan," I urged. "It's terrible. Mother cries when you're not here to see. We can go without things."

"Go without? No, daughter, we can't go without beds, and covers, and a stove, and tables, and chairs! And we get these things the best way we can. We can't just lie down and die!"

"We could buy *old* things, maybe," I said.

"The second-hand stuff you can pick up around here isn't fit to live with. Do you think I'd get such things—for Mother?"

He loved my mother. He would have given her the moon and stars for playthings had he been able. The least he could bear to let her have were the few cheap new things he was paying on. His work kept him driving his horse and wagon about the city—often, in the avenues of the wealthy. Sometimes he'd be called into the homes of the rich to cart away old magazines, or bottles, or rags, or old plumbing material, or discarded what-not. He knew the beautiful things the rich lived with. He saw the insides of their homes with his own eyes. And his lovely Hindl had to live with cheap, hideous things. Could he have borne to bring her to a home filled with stuff that was already broken down and worthless? Could he bear to have her work with a burnt-out, half-cracked kitchen stove, or rest in an old bumpy bed that left her broken in the morning, or give her the added agony of making shift with unsteady table, or half-broken chairs?

I sympathized with his eagerness to give my mother the best he could get, but I dreaded the Installment Plan Agent. My mother must have known the devotion, the passion that drove him into debt for her. "But Israel," she would plead, "don't buy anything more, this way. You see that we can't live, as it is."

My step-father's gains were uncertain. Some days he'd clear two or three or three and a half dollars. On other days there would be no gains at all. There would even be losses through a bad "buy." Or he would be cheated in the sale of his load. On such days the horse had to get his feed as when he salvaged two or three dollars from his labor. I brought home little enough, that first winter: between one and two dollars a week, at first. After that, from two and a half to three and a half dollars a week; and toward the end of the winter nearer four.

Food became so scarce in our cupboard that we almost measured out every square inch of bread. There was nothing left for clothing and shoes. I wore mine till the snow and slush came through. I had often to sit all day at my bench with icy feet in wet leather. My dress was worn to a threadbareness that brought me the jibes of some of my shopmates. I confided this to my mother. She looked about the barren rooms and wrung her hands, but said nothing. My mother knew my need for a frock—had known it for a long time. But how get me one? Well, that week she'd try. But that week was worse than the week before.

Something however must be got; anything—something that will make a dress!

Returning from work one evening, I found my mother at the kitchen table working on a bit of new checkered gingham. It was a frock for me. On a day when the sidewalks were solid ice under a blanket of new snow I first wore my gay little gingham dress. Over it was my thin jacket, clutched close with numb fingers. And I was working ten or eleven hours a day with swift, sure hands. Mr. Wertheim had said, one morning: "Rose Pastor, you're the quickest and best worker in the shop!" I didn't know or think how much I was earning for Mr. Wertheim, but I knew I was getting hunger and cold for my portion.

All winter long I wore the gingham dress and thin jacket. Every morning of that winter, when my mother tucked my lunch of bread and milk and an apple—or orange—or banana—newspaper-wrapped under my arm and opened the door to let me out into the icy dawn, I felt the agony that tugged at her mother-heart. "Walk fast," she would always say, "walk as fast as you can, Rosalie. Remember, it is better to walk fast in the cold."

After the long day in the stogie factory, and after supper and the chores for mother, there was my book—there were Lamb's *Tales*—the magic of words . . . Before the kitchen stove, when the house was asleep, I'd throw off my shoes, thaw out the icy tissues that bit all day into my consciousness, and lose myself in the loves and losses, the sorrows and joys, the gore-dripping tragedies and gay comedies of kings and queens, lords and ladies of olden times. I read and re-read the *Tales* with never-flagging interest. But (and this is perhaps a noteworthy fact) with complete detachment. Not then, nor later, when I read Shakespeare in the text did I ever, for even a fleeting moment identify myself with the people of Shakespeare's dramas. The rich lords and ladies, the ruling kings and queens of whom the supreme dramatist wrote in such noble strain, were alien to me. They moved in a different world. On the other hand, there lurked in my heart an undefined feeling of resentment over the fact that his clowns were always poor folk. He seemed never to draw a poor man save to make him an object of ridicule. Instinctively, I identified myself with his poor. Years later when I came in contact with the Baconian Theory I was naturally inclined to accept it. Lord Bacon could not have viewed the servants and slaves of his class and his period in any other light. But Shakespeare—"the lowly lad of Avon"—who was arrested for poaching on a rich man's preserves!—I held it against him in a vague, unformed way that he, poor too, could elect to make of his own kind, clouts and clowns, *Bobbees* and *Bottoms,* butts for the mirth of the wealthy patrons of the Elizabethan theatre.

During my first year in America I read nothing but Lamb's *Tales.* I had nothing else to read, looked for nothing else. It never occurred to me that there might be other books in the world. I had never heard of any. In the stillness of night I would read softly but audibly to myself from between the dull-red covers of my sole treasure.

• • •

At the end of winter I had quit the shop under the viaduct, and Spring found me in Mr. Brudno's "factory." Mr. Brudno ran what cigarmakers in Ohio called a "buckeye." A "buckeye" is a cigar "factory" in a private home. In other words, it was a sweat shop.

In the three small rooms that comprised Mr. Brudno's stogie "factory" were a dozen scattered benches. Of the dozen workers at the bench not counting strippers, bookers, and packers, six were Brudno's very own: four sons and two daughters. Several others were blood-relations—first cousins; and still another was a distant connection by marriage. The remaining few were "outsiders"; young girls and boys and—I—came to fill the last unoccupied bench.

Mr. Brudno was a picturesque patriarch, with his long black beard, and his tall black skull-cap. [. . .] He had come from the old country with a little money (not acquired through toil, rumor had it) and was determined to get rich quick in America. With money and six grown children, and the persuasive need of his poverty-stricken relatives and compatriots here and in the old world, he had an undoubted advantage over the rest of us. He put his children to work, and drew in his poor relations. In this godless America he would give them plenty of work in a shop where the Sabbath was kept holy! It was his strength, for they would work in no shop where the Sabbath was not kept holy. Their learner's period to be stretched out far beyond the usual time limit, thus adding much to his profits. The "outsiders" were young children. He hired them and drove them, and kept reducing their pay.

He would go about the "buckeye" dreaming aloud . . . This was his first sweatshop. By-and-bye he'd have a bigger place—a real stogie factory with dozens of new workers. His children would do all the work of foremen and watchers, and work at the bench too. Soon there would be a big factory building all his own. . . .

In the six years, off and on, that I worked for Mr. Brudno, his dream grew to reality. He did everything a boss could do to make his dream come true. Beginning in a little "buckeye," he soon moved to an enormous loft, where the dozen benches he started with, were many times multiplied. There his factory hummed with the industry of boys and girls, of men, women, and young children. The stripping and the bunch-making were concentrated in one end of the vast room where the rolling was done. The raw material was unpacked and sorted, the drying, storing, and other processes carried on in another room. Driven by Mr. Brudno and our own need, we piled up stogies rapidly. Brudno paid miserably little for our labor, and always complained that we were getting too much. But before long, he was able to rear a factory building of his own, on a very desirable site on Broadway. It was of red brick—and several stories high. There he drove us harder than ever, and in time added another story to his Broadway structure. Now he was a big "manufacturer"; he strutted about and watched us manufacture.

The Brudno family lived in a large house on Orange Street now. From their windows at a fork in the road where the street flowed into Broadway, they could see the factory—the source of all good things. . . .

Soon, his children underwent a remarkable change. They dressed differently from the rest of us, and looked with scorn upon our poor clothing, and our poor lives. They were getting culture. They discussed art, literature and the theatre with each other as they moved about the rest of us, and rarely deigned to draw any of us into their discussions. They were no longer tied to the work bench, but came and went as they liked. Their occupations were pleasant now, and varied. After all, were they not the sons and daughters of the boss? . . . The cleavage became sharper, from day to day.

One of Mr. Brudno's six children, a swarthy young son, was sent to college. [. . .] He attended Yale, and studied Greek and Latin among other marvelous things. Today his name graces the door to a successful lawyer's office somewhere in Cleveland.

At the age of twelve I had the good fortune to "fall in love" with this homely lad. I say "good fortune" because the circumstances were such as to provide me with a wholesome influence at a time when I was just awakening—and in need of a firm devotion. We were really strangers from start to finish. In those six years, and two beyond of my enchantment, we had three "conversations." The first—perhaps shortest, strangest speech in lovers' history—was when I rushed from my bench with other workers at the news of a street accident, and came to one of the windows. There stood Zelig! Of course, I was rooted to the spot! I could not go forward nor turn back and run. He had then been for a week or more the bright object of my deep devotion. But I could as soon have hoped to hitch my step-father's literal wagon to a literal star, as to have touched his hand. A young worker had remarked to me in the shop, one day: "Look at Zelig in that new hat. Becoming, isn't it?" At this, never before having looked at any being in any hat, I had promptly "fallen in love." It seemed to me that I had never beheld a being so glorious as that swarthy lugubrious youth! So, when the creature of my dreams turned from the window and looked at me I could move neither hand nor foot. Then—out of his four or five years greater maturity and riper wisdom, he shattered the spell of my embarrassment by making talk. As he addressed himself to me, an unbearable tightness gripped my throat. My idol placed one hand in his coat pocket, the other on his heart, thumb caught in vest, and murmured the unforgettable question:

"So you like noodle-pudding?"

"Yes," I blurted; and my tongue having at that moment released my legs, I turned and ran.

That was our first "conversation." Our second, a year-and-a-half or two years later, took place when he asked me the time of day from his cousin's work-bench at the far end of the loft on Broadway. Looking up at the clock on the wall—where I could see it and he couldn't—I told him. It was some minutes past two, I remember; and how thrilled I was that he had asked *me*!

A long time had again passed before we had our third and last "conversation." What it was I no longer recall. We passed each other on the stairs. He would have said "good morning," or something of equal importance, and I would have muttered some monosyllable and stumbled up- or downstairs, as the case would have been.

Until my twentieth year the dream held—a dream based upon ambition to learn: He loved books! He possessed and read books! And books were my passion too. . . . That was the secret of his hold on my imagination.

I steeped myself in books.

• • •

"Look," Brudno would say, "if she can do it, why can't you and you do it—and you? Earn more! You need to, don't you?"

Yes—*need!*—we understood that force well.

The workers at Brudno's would race with me, and gradually increase their speed. And I would race with the clock—and further increase my own . . .

By summer's end, I was the pride of Brudno's heart. I sped up the others, and turned out again as many stogies as the average slow ones. He was seeing results.

When the "buckeye" moved to the big loft and became a factory, Mr. Brudno announced a cut. The stogie-rollers were getting fourteen cents a hundred. Now it would be thirteen. We took the cut in silence. We were for the most part poor little child slaves, timid and unorganized. The thought of union never occurred to us. There was no strength in us or behind us. It was each one by his lone self. Not one of us would have ventured to pit his little self against the boss. We merely looked into one another's faces. No words. But each had the same thought in mind: Now there would be less of something that was already scarce: Bread, milk, or coal. Mr. Brudno owned the factory and we were his workers. Nothing could be done about it. So we raced some more . . . and still more, and more!

It never occurred to me that I was being used by the boss to set the pace in his stogie factory . . . And that one cut would follow another, as our speed increased . . .

A cut came the week that the new baby came.

"Rosalie!"

My step-father's voice, tense and unnatural with excitement, shook me out of sleep.

I heard my mother's shriek piercing the deep night, and rushed into the room next to mine.

"Mother! Oh, my mother!" What could be wrong with my mother?

My step-father rushed after me, and snatched me out of the room.

"Rosalie, run to the midwife! Say she's to come right away. Mother's giving birth. Quick!"

"Giving birth?" A new baby coming! . . . Out into the dark, chill, deserted streets I went, shoes unbuttoned, hair loose in the wind, feet flying . . .

It was hard enough to scrape together the ten dollars for the midwife. To get help for the two weeks of confinement was out of the question. For those two weeks, after shop, I did the work at home. There was no water in the flat on Liberal Street. I had to carry pails of water from the pump in the yard to fill the wash tubs upstairs and take the water down to spill. How heavy the sheets were, and how hard to rub clean! . . . Every day of the two weeks, I washed: Diapers, sheets, other "linens," carrying water up and down, up and down, till all was washed and rinsed, and the white things hanging out on the line in the yard.

There were meals to get and dishes to wash, my two-year-old brother to care for, and special things to prepare for my mother. Mornings, before daylight, my step-father would make the fire, and I would get the breakfast. He would stay to wash up the dishes and do a few chores before starting for his horse and wagon and the struggle with another day. By noon, the ailing Mrs. Feinberg would look in on my mother and babies and help out a bit. For those two weeks, I was given the privilege of leaving an hour earlier daily, on my own time of course, to help my mother.

At night, with tired feet and hands, and heaviness that hung on my eyelids and threatened to close them, I'd take up *Les Miserables* and shed a few hot tears of sympathy for poor little Cosette!

• • •

There were now five mouths to feed. My step-father tried desperately to supply bread for his growing family. He worked early and late. When winter came again, there were days when he'd climb down from his wagon with difficulty. The everlong exposure to frost and winter storm, and his attempt to save by taking no food during the day, began to tell on his splendid strength. He grew haggard and troubled. Deep lines ran like large new moons along the sides of his cheeks. There were lines like wires across his forehead. He was unable to understand why, with such hard trying, he could not keep hunger shut out; why he could not drive the stubborn wolf from the door!

I was then in my thirteenth year. Already I felt the staggering weight of the struggle upon my shoulders. I worked all day. My fingers flew! But what I got, together with what my hardworking step-father got, was not enough to keep us in the bare, needed things.

One day I had an idea. That evening after supper I slipped on my coat. My mother protested.

"Where are you going? And the dishes?"

"I'll do them when I get back."

My step-father protested. "Such a young child should not run around in the evenings." And my mother, musing on it, said, "Well, Israel, she's growing up. She'll be wanting some pleasure, poor child mine! She has little enough— nothing but her books! And these when she should sleep and rest. I suppose you're going over to Ida's house. . . . Let her go, Israel, let her go. It may be more cheerful there than here."

It was the same for several evenings, till I came home with the glad news.

"Mother! father! I've found one—where I didn't think to look: right here on Liberal Street, in the middle of the block!"

I had followed clues, night after night, but nothing had come of them. And here, on our very own street—by chance—in crossing to the other side, I discovered a "buckeye" tucked away in the rear of a yard. I had walked in, found the "boss" at his own bench, and asked for evening work. And he had said, "Come tomorrow, after supper."

How happy I was! At last I could help more.

But my mother drew me to her, kissed me and cried, and insisted that I must not go: "It is bad enough that you have to slave ten or eleven hours a day, and then do things about the house. How can I let you work all day and all night too! Was it to such a fate as this we were born?" My step-father went about the room beating his breast in silence. Then he broke into angry protest. "Damn such a life—damn, damn."

They threatened to lock me in, evenings. I threatened to take no supper and go from the factory direct to the "buckeye."

The following evening, my parents exchanged glances as we sat at table, so I rushed up from supper, bolted through the door, coatless, and ran down the street. I would have lost my chance to work had I failed to turn up as agreed.

All that winter, after the long day at Brudno's, I rolled stogies till midnight in the little "buckeye," lively as a sparrow because I was doing my utmost to help.

• • •

In the Spring that followed, Jennie's mother died, and the Feinberg family moved away.

"It is easier bringing water in and out on the ground floor," said my step-father. "A healthier place for the baby," thought my mother. So we moved into the rooms where the Feinbergs had lived. The thin floors with no cellar under them proved cold and damp. Spring brought much illness to our little world, and the baby took sick. Then too, my mother was nursing him at the breast, not knowing that she was with child again. The Doctor came and examined the infant. "You are poisoning him with your milk," he said. "Influenza is in the air."

For eight long months, without relief, my mother hovered over her baby. She barely slept, snatching an hour only when I was there to take her place at the side of the cradle. At first it was one lung, then double pneumonia. My step-father took a loan to pay the doctor; mortgaged his horse and wagon to bring him to the child. At the end of those eight grueling months, the third baby, my sister Lily, was born.

Pale and spent, with her dark head listless against the pillows, my mother lay with a child on each arm; the new-born infant and the newly-rescued infant. There was not a year between them, and both needed her every moment of the day and a good part of the disturbed night. Little Maurice, the eldest, not yet four, clung to a white hand on the coverlet, and gazed gravely at his mother and the two equally helpless infants . . .

We were now a family of six.

How to make ends meet?

My mother, my step-father, and I would figure to the minutest fraction the possible saving in this or that kind of food. Soup-bones, cabbage, stale bread—"a cent cheaper than the fresh, and better at that!" But no matter how we figured, we couldn't cover our need. Eggs and milk for the little ones, however, that we would have.

And again winter was coming. I must find another "buckeye"—must take evening work again. The boss was beginning to dismiss workers. More empty work-benches gaped ominously each morning at those of us who were still employed.

Something was in the air. Not only at Brudno's, but everywhere. Our little world of working fathers, dependent mothers, and young bread-winners was tense with an apprehension never felt before.

We were always hanging over a precipice. But now we felt that something was going to break; that the precarious bit of shale we called "life" to which we clung in such desperation would give way; and that we—all of us—with our poverty and our crust of bread, would go crashing down to disaster! This was the beginning of the crisis of 1893.

My step-father, though no worker in a factory, felt the effects of the crisis along with the rest of our class. His horse and wagon now carried fewer and fewer of the loads that gave a precarious living. At the week's end, after all was paid—feed and stall for the horse and shed-rent for the wagon—he would find only four or five dollars clear.

He worked harder now and cleared less. He would bring his diminishing loads to the warehouses, and get smaller return for them with every passing day. A deep depression settled upon him.

My own work too fell off. Most of the workers at Brudno's were sent home. A few were kept on part-time. These were the quickest and best workers—the most profitable to him in busy season—the boss preferred not to lose them. He pretended to be generous in keeping us on the payroll.

The three or three-and-a-half dollars I brought, when added to the miserable little that my poor step-father was able to bring in, spelled deeper need for us.

• • •

"Father, what's the matter? You're not eating *anything* these days."

"It's all right, Rosalie. I'll eat tomorrow."

He would go off into the bitter winter dawns without tasting food.

He seemed to be hurrying; now more than ever; always hurrying—as though trying to catch up with and overtake a rapidly vanishing hope of survival.

At night he would return and sit dejected at the table, never touching his supper.

"Israel, take a potato and a piece of herring," my mother would urge, placing a cheek against his cheek.

"Come, eat something. You can't starve yourself altogether because times are bitter. It will do none of us any good. You make it hard for the rest of us to eat our crust when you won't take a bite of it. Come!"

I see him in tears—see him break down and weep like a little child, his strong frame shaken with his sobbing.

"Take a quarter, every day, and buy yourself some good lunch, Israel," my mother begged.

But how could he spend a quarter—a whole quarter a day for lunch? His horse must have feed, his wife and children must have bread, and there was so little for his labor . . . And the crisis deepened.

One evening, some time later, my mother unburdened her troubled heart to me.

"I'm afraid, Rosalie, I'm afraid. Israel is going to the saloon for free lunches. He buys a beer to get a bite to eat. The bitterest days he goes in to get warm. He saves a few nickels on food, but where will it lead?"

I tried to quiet her fears.

"Soon father will be earning more. Then maybe he can buy lunches in a decent place."

But I was troubled. And again I began a long search for evening work. Finally, I found a "buckeye" some distance from home, where I was given work one or two evenings a week. It was not much, but it was something. I ran home with the hopeful tidings.

When I came to the door, I stopped. My heart beat violently. I saw my gentle, generous step-father, turned half brute with drink, struggling with my mother. My mother in agonized tones was pleading with him. I hurried in and slammed the door shut.

"Father," I called sharply. "You're drunk!"

He turned from my mother, and lurched toward me.

"So!—so you too call me names!"

Before I could escape, he had struck me a heavy blow across the face.

"That's all right, father, I won't call you names."

With quiet talk, I got him to his cot. I drew off his shoes and his coat, and covered him with a blanket. He muttered unintelligible things, and fell asleep . . . Soon the air was fetid with his breath.

Maurice, the eldest, cried and clung to his mother. The baby sister in the cradle was crying and little Emmanuel, the rescued one, wailed weakly. It was long before he could cry like any other child.

It took time to quiet them and get them to sleep.

Then my mother came and stood over the man she loved.

"Better to have died! Better to have died!" she moaned. She would not go to bed, but wailed and talked to herself far into the night. I sat beside her, filled with a great grief, but my eyes were dry. Endlessly there would be nights with scenes like this, but I did not foresee them. I felt only the tragedy of the moment.

"Go to sleep now, Mamele."

But she would not.

"What do you know, child, oh, what do you know!"

As we sat there and talked, however, a little I began to realize that, hereafter, added to poverty and hunger and the mad struggle to survive, would be the decay of that which was still sweet and sound at the kernel of life. A blind brute force, raging and relentless, had entered our home to stay. It would tear at the vitals of her children, at her love, and at the sound fabric of the man she loved.

But only a little of all this I comprehended. I was fourteen; not old enough to realize the full force of our disaster.

Now we went through that winter of crisis and tragedy—on what we subsisted; of the days of stark hunger; of the endless trudgings from one closed factory to another; of our struggle with my poor step-father giving himself over more to drink, the more his hope of livelihood vanished; of the nights without sleep because of hunger and despair; of the days in a frozen flat; of the children who cried for bread in the cold . . . I cannot tell of them now. There are some things in the lives of the workers that cannot be told. We have no words in which to tell them, even to each other in secret. These things, I feel, must lie buried in the hearts of our class, till they find expression in our deeds—on the great day of our self-emancipation.

• • •

We had a spell of temporary relief. Someone was willing to be a boarder.

How hard we tried to make shift in the already crowded quarters, the cheerless rooms whose cold air made grey mist of our warm breaths! How my mother struggled to serve him! I too, giving every spare moment of my time. Himself a poor worker he paid so very little, but we hoped it would help us to catch up a bit with the rent. Maybe then the landlord would not carry out his threat to dispossess us.

We didn't keep our boarder long. He was an unwholesome man, and I was glad when he was gone, though it meant the street for our few belongings. Where could we go with not a penny to advance on rent?

I went to Mr. Brudno with many misgivings and begged him for an advance in order to have a deposit on rent. He bargained much, cautioning me to remember when busy season came again, not to leave him for another boss. He advanced me ten dollars.

We moved in a blizzard. A tiny frame house stood vacant on the next lot, at Number Two Liberal Street. We gathered up the babies and moved into that tiny frame house, giving part payment on a month's rent. We lugged our few scattered belongings through a blinding, raging snow storm, sending the stove first—glad that we had found a way out so close at hand.

In the back of the new yard was an old shed. Here my step-father housed his horse and wagon and saved on shed-rent.

It gave him hope again.

"Look here, Mamele," he said with cheer, "it will help a lot. Now I shall be able to make a living."

He made a new start—tried to keep out of the saloon.

"Now we'll manage if I earn a little more—just a little more." How glad he was! But the force that held millions of the working class in a relentless grip of compulsory idleness and starvation was stronger than the strongest individual among us. A living was simply not to be made. Though a man threw his heart and his hands and his whole being into the battle for bread, those millions that were doomed were doomed! . . . A weaker man would have taken gas. He took alcohol.

"Father," I begged, "try! See if you can't keep away. If you tried hard enough, maybe . . . "

"I'll try, Rosalie. Did I hurt you yesterday? I'm sorry; you know I'm sorry. Mamele, come here." And he'd put an arm about my poor tormented mother; "You know what's in my heart. Do I want to hurt you, or her?"

My mother knew! He had a heart of gold. He would have had that heart cut up into little bits to feed his children. He was not to blame. Something else was to blame. He did not know what. My mother did not know what. Something without a name. It was stronger than the strongest man. No man could struggle against it when it had him in its grip. And men in the grip of this thing took their lives, or turned to crime, or to drink—because there seemed no other way out.

"Yes, Israel; yes, I know. Only, for the sake of the children . . . "

But the deepening crisis was too much for him. My mother saw the man she loved, the father of her children, descend to depths of misery and defeat from which there would be no returning.

• • •

The time came again when every bench was occupied—when the face of the clock was again the face of a foe.

Mr. Brudno was often in a genial mood now, but not too often. Frequently he was morose; at times, vindictive. His black skull-cap announced the mood. If he came through the swinging doors with the cap to his right or left ear we expected taciturnity or jest. If the cap sat against the back of his skull we looked for trouble. Then no work he examined was good enough for him. He would go from rack to rack; picking up handfuls of stogies. A mis-roll or two, a head or two badly sealed; a slight unevenness in length would call forth a violent fit of temper. He would hurl curses at the workers, break and twist the stogies out of shape, and throw them into the drawer of waste cuttings! A morning's work gone to the scrap-pile!

"You call this stogie-rolling? Get out of my shop. Get out, this minute, or I'll pitch you through the window."

Perhaps there were a couple of hundred stogies left in the rack. The worker was not always allowed to take them down, or count them. Cowed, pale with fear she would leave the loft in silence. The rest of us, bending our heads close to the work, were set to thinking—thoughts differing widely, feeling running from white fear to red rebellion—as after-mutterings revealed.

The most intolerable fines were inflicted upon us. For example, the leaf tobacco in which we rolled our "bunches" was often so rotted that we were forced to re-roll our stogies several times, each time removing the worthless piece to try another. Or, the leaf would be so badly worm-eaten we could not cover a third of the required number of stogies. This bad stock retarded the work. It meant rolling two or three hundred less in a day; it meant beside, unusual effort; increased care and anxiety; and a nervous strain that sent us home trembling from head to feet. Yet for this stock Mr. Brudno demanded the same standard of workmanship and the same number of stogies to the pound that was set for the finest leaf tobacco, and docked us heavily for the inescapable failure. When we opened our slim pay envelopes, we would often find from fifty cents to one dollar and fifty cents deducted, out of a possible five dollars. When driven too hard, some one of us would venture to complain in a timid voice: "But look at this stock, Mr. Brudno. How can you expect the same work out of such rotten leaf tobacco? See this and this and this!—and look at the holes in these . . . Look! look! I just brought this pound from the stripping room. We can't do the impossible!"

"Well, what's wrong with this stock anyway? A little hole, here and there— that's nothing. Rotten? That ain't rotten. You pull too hard, so it tears. Don't pull, or you'll go home."

"Ask your own sons and daughters; they'll tell you what sort of stock it is."

But if he ever asked them we were not told. The fines were taken out of our pay often without any previous warning; and those who complained too disrespectfully were "fired."

If a period of good stock followed, we would race madly. Now is the time to make up for the bad weeks! If then we succeeded—if we increased our speed and turned out a few hundred stogies more than usual at the week's end, Mr. Brudno would announce a reduction of a cent or two on the hundred. Before these attacks we were helpless sheep. We knew nothing of organizing protest. A few of us dreamed . . . But nothing came of our dreams.

Brudno's shop, however, was to have a strike—a curious strike confined to his relatives. One morning, at daybreak, I was roused by a sharp rap at our door. It was Lyoti, one of that group of blood relations whom Brudno drew from the old country with tales of work and freedom, in a shop that kept the Sabbath holy.

"I came to beg you please, not to go back to the shop, this morning!" he said. "We are on strike."

"We? Who?"

"The boss's relations," he explained. "We can't do the special work he gives us to do, and live on the pay. It is impossible."

I roused my sleeping mother. The children woke. They ran or toddled to the door of the tiny frame house on Orange Street where we now lived; half-naked; sleepy, yet curious.

I kissed my mother, kissed each child in turn, and forgot for the moment that our father, in despair, had left home the week before and had not been heard from since. A strike at Brudno's shop! Every outraged feeling in me broke into exultant rebellion.

"I'll stay out even if we starve altogether! Eh, Mamele?" My mother kissed me and nodded assent. There were shadows as we contemplated the children. "But a strike is a strike," said my mother. And Lyoti explained, "If we win you win too. If we win the boss will not dare to press you harder than he is already pressing you. He will not dare to take another cent off the hundred from anybody."

My first strike—a sympathy strike! I visited workers in their homes that early morning and got them to stay out. I picketed the shop. Lyoti turned to me for many strike activities. I did as directed and drew in others. At the end of some ten or twelve days the men returned in triumph. The boss had yielded to their demands, and the rest of us who appeared to have gained nothing, felt stronger—even a bit audacious in the presence of the boss. The old timidity never again quite overcame any of us—for was he not beaten in our sight?

Lyoti had a fine tenor voice, and knew many folk and art songs, as well as airs from the operas and complete movements from the works of great composers. Lyoti became my loyal friend, and taught me many of the songs he knew. When he asked me to marry him, I solemnly confessed to him that my heart was with his cousin Zelig. And though he proposed to me every six months or so over a period of seven years, each time forgetting his promise to be "just good friends," it did not spoil our friendship. We agreed to be hopelessly in love, each in his own way. He learned many new songs for my sake, and I read many books for Zelig's sake. We were happy in our misery and our company.

"Memorandum on Housing Situation, Lee-Harvard Area"

The Federation of Jewish Charities, later the Jewish Welfare Federation, was organized in 1903 to bring under one umbrella the diverse fund-raising needs of the growing Jewish community that had begun in 1839 when the first Jews arrived in Cleveland (see also the chapter on Lazarus Kohn in this volume). The federation in turn created the Jewish Community Council in the mid-1930s to respond to growing European anti-Semitism, establish relations with Cleveland's non-Jewish populations, and expand relations with national and overseas agencies. The 1951 merger of the two agencies created the Jewish Community Federation of Cleveland (see also the chapter on Henry L. Zucker in this volume).

The new organization quickly became immersed in social, welfare, and civic activities critical to the creative survival of Cleveland's Jewish community, working hand in hand with the synagogues, a network of federation-funded agencies, and partners in the general community. It has been a significant participant in ameliorating the plight of Jews in many lands, and it has close and productive ties with Israel. Its partnership with like-minded organizations enables it to help improve civic life for all Greater Cleveland residents through programs such as those designed to stabilize neighborhoods and address the needs of Cleveland's homeless and hungry.

In 1952, an African American couple bought a house in Cleveland's Lee-Harvard area, a white, middle-class neighborhood bordering an older, lower-class area into which African Americans had started to move. Demonstrations and protest meetings against the new owners and the Jewish businessman who sold the house followed. This document, reported by federation staff member Sidney Z. Vincent and written by Ralph A. Colbert, provides a firsthand account of the polarized community's efforts to resolve a situation that was common to many cities in the 1950s.

Source: Ralph A. Colbert, "Memorandum on Housing Situation, Lee-Harvard Area." A Report to the Jewish Community Federation's Community Relations Committee, July 23, 1953. Jewish Community Federation Records. Western Reserve Historical Society.

THE JEWISH COMMUNITY FEDERATION OF CLEVELAND, RALPH A. COLBERT, CHAIRMAN
Memorandum on Housing Situation, Lee-Harvard Area

A major and potentially explosive situation resulting from the sale of a house in an all white neighborhood to a Negro has arisen that may be of general interest.

Although the sale was consummated on *July 2, 1953* the report of the transaction did not become wide-spread for approximately a week. The area in question, located in the extreme southeastern section of the city (the Lee-Harvard section), is a new middle class neighborhood, composed largely of first and second generation Italians and Hungarians; religiously it is divided approximately 70% Catholic, 20% Jewish and 10% Protestant. The homes, in the $15,000 class, have almost all been built since the Second World War. The neighborhood of approximately a dozen streets forms a kind of island separated by only a block from a much older neighborhood of less social and economic standing into which Negroes have been moving. East 155th Street, at the extreme western edge of the island, is popularly referred to as the "38th parallel" and the home sold to the Negro, immediately east of East 155th Street, represents the first immigration into the island.

Feelings mounted quickly when the report of the sale became generally known and on *Friday night, July 10,* some 400 neighbors gathered seemingly without any official call, in the Sokol Hall, (Warrensville Heights Village) and there followed a series of bitter attacks and threats directed primarily at the seller of the house, a Jewish business man with a non-Jewish wife who, it was alleged, sold the home to Negroes out of spite against his neighbors with whom he had had considerable difficulties. Acting on the mistaken notion that the deal had not been consummated, the crowd appointed a delegation to visit the seller at his business to persuade him not to go through with the deal.

On *Saturday, July 11,* this delegation went to the store and demanded to see the owner and were told he was in Canada, a statement that subsequently proved to be without foundation. After demonstrating in the store for approximately one half hour, the crowd left. Over the weekend tension mounted and calls were received by the Jewish Community Federation staff from Jewish residents in the area who felt extremely threatened by the growing restlessness, since such great resentment was expressed against "Jews who pulled this dirty trick on us by selling to Negroes."

On *Monday, July 13,* the Director of the Community Relations Board, a city agency dealing with these problems, and the Secretary of the Community Relations Committee of the Jewish Community Federation toured the area and found considerable tension. Provision was made for 24 hour police duty at the home and a visit was held with the priests in St. Cecelia's parish to enlist their aid in helping to quiet the growing tension.

That evening, another indignation meeting was held at Gracemount School attended by approximately 400 people. The crowd was fairly evenly divided between those who wanted to explore legitimate legal steps and those who demanded "action" at once. Frequently, threats of violence were voiced by those who insisted that only by teaching the seller and the purchaser a lesson could further immigration of Negroes be prevented.

Cooler heads prevailed, however, to the extent that a committee of three was appointed to visit the new Negro owner in order to persuade him to sell his property to the assembled neighbors. At no point, then or subsequently, was any suggestion made by anyone present that the Negro had a right to live in the neighborhood and a statement by the councilman of that area that there was no legal way to make the Negro move was greeted with jeers and boos.

The director of the Community Relations Board and our staff member thereupon went at approximately 9:30 that evening to the home of the new owner, who had just moved in that day, and found him ironically just returning from the hospital where his wife was to undergo an operation. We found him to be a personable, good looking, soft spoken and highly articulate person about 40 years old, chief embalmer at the largest mortuary in the state. He expressed his determination to stay in the home that he had purchased in good faith and said further that since he had no children, with adequate police protection his family could make a go of the situation.

As we were talking, the delegation of three that had been appointed by the crowd arrived. One of the delegation happened to be a student some dozen years ago of the staff member and the resulting conversation therefore began in a somewhat unusually amicable tone. The delegation stated that they had no ill feelings and that they recognized the reasons motivating the owner to move. However, they added that extreme violence would result from his move into that area and if he wished to extricate himself from a difficult situation they were prepared to purchase his home at a profit to him.

The owner spoke at some length, thanking the delegation for their visit but pointing out that he had lived for 19 years in his previous house and that he intended to spend the rest of his life in his new home which precisely met his needs. He had thought his move over carefully over a period of some years and had entered into the contract in good faith. He was not a trail blazer, he said, nor had he any desire to act as a missionary to break into a new area. He had been in a position to purchase a better home than those in the already established Negro area and was unaware of how great a furor would ensue from his move. Once having moved in he saw no reason for moving out and was quite prepared to stand his ground no matter what might ensue. He concluded by stating that the group might want to delay their offer to purchase his house for three months during which time they would have an opportunity to know him better and he would have an opportunity to know them better, and if they still wished to make an offer at that time, he would consider it then, although he made no promises of any kind.

The delegation was obviously impressed by the sincerity of the presentation and the attractiveness of the personality of the owner. They stated that they would speak to the group that would assemble the next evening in favorable terms concerning the new owner but in all honesty they were hardly typical of the crowd that would assemble. One member of the delegation asked that the owner accompany them the next evening but it was agreed by all the rest that such a step would be premature. Instead, it was planned that the three members of the delegation would appear at the meeting the next night to state that negotiations were then under way with the owner and would be concluded by 9:00 o'clock that evening. They would then invite a delegation of 20 outstanding leaders from the crowd to accompany them to one of their homes to meet with the owner. It was also planned to have the Mayor of the city of Cleveland and a high ranking church official present at this gathering in order that all community forces could be brought to bear to win acceptance of the new neighbor. It was planned that after this smaller meeting, all those present would return to the large meeting to try to convince those there present of the wisdom of accepting an accomplished fact.

At the conclusion of this conference, after 11:00 o'clock at night, we found on leaving the house that over 100 people were assembled waiting for the results of the conference. It had been agreed that the delegation would limit their remarks that night to a statement that negotiations were still proceeding and the older members of the assembled crowd received the news fairly well. However, a large number of teen-agers, obviously out for a lark and not particularly interested in the real situation, raised a considerable fuss and were free with loud and repeated threats of violence. This younger group, it might be noted, conducted itself badly throughout all proceedings, despite all protestations to police authorities that they should not be allowed to congregate or loiter.

The next day, Tuesday, these plans were considerably changed. The Mayor, informed of the developments of the night before, called his Community Relations Board into emergency session and after considerable discussion, it was agreed that in place of the plan projected the night before, the assembled crowd should be invited to select 15 or 20 from among their number to visit with him, a church official and the Director of the Community Relations Board at City Hall.

The announcement of the Mayor's suggestion to the crowd that again gathered was greeted with a mingled reception. A number of those present expressed their feeling that this was merely a tactic of delay and that one well placed bomb would do more good than any visit to City Hall. Again, however, the gradualists won the day and some 20 volunteers set off for City Hall.

The Mayor and an important official of the Catholic Church who is a member of the Community Relations Board met with these members and listened to their arguments in considerable detail. At earlier conferences during the day, the Mayor had stressed the value of delay and the healing effects of time. Accordingly, he indicated to the group that the problem they had presented needed the attention of the full Community Relations Board and suggested that the group present meet the following evening with the entire Board and with the owner of the house and his attorney. Although the Mayor was extremely sympathetic to the representatives of the group and frequently said that "they had a problem," any indication of violence on the part of those present was met forthrightly by his statement that if anything of that sort were attempted, the proper police authority would end such activities with dispatch. The group agreed to the Mayor's suggestion and disbanded. It should be noted that after each of the meetings reported here at City Hall, crowds estimated at up to 100 waited at the home of the new owner until close to midnight to receive news of the meeting.

Throughout this period frequent meetings were held by representatives from the Catholic Diocese, the Protestant Church Federation, the Jewish Community Federation, and social agencies in the neighborhood at the call of the Community Relations Board in order to plan strategy. A number of constructive steps were projected including preparation of a statement by the three religious groups jointly urging calmness and the rights of all

Americans to fair and adequate housing. Newspaper support was secured in the form of editorials and calm and faithful news reporting. Lists of key individuals in the neighborhood were drawn up both of those most likely to resort to violence and those most amenable to pleas that they undertake positive leadership. Assignments for follow-up work for such individuals were made to those assembled.

On Wednesday night, the delegation of five met with the full Community Relations Board. Despite the objections of a minority of the Board who felt that there was no reason for providing a cloak of secrecy to what they felt were un-American expressions of opinion, the Board voted to go into closed session. Each of the five members of the delegation made statements stressing their own democratic feelings and respect for the owner of the property as a person. Each, however, went on to plead that their property would suffer severe economic damage from infiltration by even a single Negro, and disaster from a mass move of Negroes into the neighborhood. Each pleaded with the owner to sell his property.

In response, the new owner and his attorney stated that the property had been bought not for speculation but for permanent housing and that the intention was to remain. Members of the Community Relations Board tried to convince the delegation that they were mistaken on economic as well as human grounds. One of the members pointed out that a Negro had lived in his suburban, high status community for years without any adverse economic effects. Considerable discussion ensued during which it became apparent that the delegation was fairly friendly in attitude but adamant in its feeling that their economic rights had been violated, no matter what evidence to the contrary was offered. At one point, the attorney for the owner turned to the spokesman of the delegation and said, "Mister, you have never been a Negro."

After asking both sides to wait, the Board decided with some reluctance not to meet the issue head-on at this session but to defer to the Mayor's continued request for delay and it was agreed to invite the delegation to return again the following Monday night. Evidently relieved that the meeting had not concluded with a firm refusal to "help" and the consequent necessity to report back to the neighborhood that no relief could be expected from city officials, the delegation accepted the five day waiting period and promised to report to their constituents the following night.

On Thursday night, a crowd of some 400 again assembled at the school and heard a very moderate report from the delegation praising the efforts of the Community Relations Board and expressing the hope that "something would be worked out." Each of the five members of the delegation pleaded with the crowd not to indulge in violence and upbraided them for a few minor cases of violence that had occurred. Repeated assurances were given to the crowd that if they had confidence in their representatives, the situation could be worked out constructively. It should be stressed, however, that no speaker indicated that a constructive solution could be reached on the basis of an interracial neighborhood.

A lawyer was then introduced by the spokesman for the delegation with the statement that he might have the final solution of the difficulties. The lawyer spoke at length, stating that his plan represented the combined efforts of six attorneys and "the best legal minds in the county." Although further legal research was needed that would take until the following Monday night, he was certain that his plan provided a sound legal method of preventing in the future the difficulty they were presently going through. "Every nickel he owned" was tied up in his home, the attorney said, and his plan would prevent economic loss by making sure that further immigration into the area by a "certain" group could be stopped.

This solution consisted of getting all the neighbors to sign a covenant that they would not sell their homes without the consent of 10 neighbors. He was at pains to point out that the two recent Supreme Court decisions outlawing restrictive covenants did not apply in this case since no mention would be made in the covenant of race or religion. The covenant would keep out those of bad moral or financial standing or those who could not qualify "for one other reason." Great laughter greeted this final statement.

Tremendous enthusiasm was shown for this scheme which, the attorney stated, was "water tight" legally and volunteers were solicited to take the petitions around from house to house. This was the time, the speaker urged, for true neighborliness and only by real friendship and real sympathy could this constructive step be taken to make the neighborhood a model for all other neighborhoods in the city. This good fellowship was punctuated by such remarks as "Here is a pair of keys that someone lost last night. The cop that brought them to my house said that if it belongs to a Nigger to throw them down the sewer." Laughter and applause greeted this remark.

After considerable discussion the group was urged to go home and not to meet again until after the covenant had been prepared,—by Monday night. On this happy note the crowd dispersed, after agreeing that its next meeting would be held Monday at Eagle's Hall, since the school board had refused to issue a permit for a meeting within the school for this type of gathering.

No further meetings were held over the weekend. On Sunday, the St.

Cecilia's Church Bulletin contained the following featured notice which received wide publicity in the press the next day:

> "Christian principles of Justice and Charity have been seriously defied by participants in a neighborhood racial disturbance within the boundaries of St. Cecilia's parish. It is well to remember that: the very First Law of Christianity is to love our neighbor as ourself, regardless of language or color. That it is a serious sin to deny a colored family an opportunity to live in decent quarters. That to encourage prejudice; to help foster hatred; to deny another race the same opportunities we enjoy is not 'just politics,' it is acting against the primary laws of God."

Monday night, July 20, the committee of five and the Community Relations Board held their final meeting. The owner again reiterated his intention of staying on his property and another lengthy discussion ensued with the homeowners committee, during which the entire focus was on the economic effects of in-migration of Negroes.

Finally the Board and the mayor worked out the following statement representing their position:

> "Residents in the vicinity of 15508 Talford Avenue have expressed objection to the Community Relations Board concerning the purchase and occupancy of a home by Wendell Stewart on the ground that it will depreciate values in the neighborhood.
>
> "The Board appreciates the fine co-operative attitude of the committee expressing the views of the residents of that community. We appreciate their sense of leadership in bringing their problem before the Board.
>
> "The Board on the other hand is very proud of community relations in the city of Cleveland; the Board is very proud of the way different racial groups in our city have lived together.
>
> "The committee must realize that Wendell Stewart has purchased his property and has moved into this property with his family and that there is no power in the United States that can cause him to withdraw from that property.
>
> "He will be afforded the full protection of the law, and we urge this committee, and in turn the people whom they represent, to co-operate with us in maintaining good community relations, and in doing so we are confident that this problem will be solved."

Following the reading of the statement, the mayor volunteered to go out to the neighborhood the following evening to address a meeting inside Gracemount School to explain the statement and to answer questions. The committee expressed gratitude for the offer and asked that a Catholic church official, a member of the Board, also attend the meeting and address the crowd.

Meanwhile, in the neighborhood, a small but active group gathered at Eagle's Hall awaiting word from downtown. It was apparent that hopes for relief from that source were waning and that a mood of resentment was being engendered.

On *Tuesday evening, July 21,* the statement of the Board was printed, in all local papers together with an announcement of the evening's meeting.

That evening over 500 people gathered at the school, obviously in an ugly mood. None went inside the building, and a recreation department ball game in progress in the school yard involving a neighborhood team of schoolboys against those from a Negro playground was punctuated by cheers for the white boys and jeers for the colored boys.

When the Mayor arrived, (perhaps the most popular political figure in northern Ohio, having served as mayor longer than anyone else in Cleveland's history), the crowd burst out in boos and cat calls. Screams of "Don't go inside" came from all sections of the group, obviously as a result of schoolyard opinion that it was easier to break loose outside than in an orderly inside meeting.

The local councilman and members of the delegation pleaded with the crowd to go indoors and after considerable wrangling, a few started in, followed by an overwhelming surge by the rest. The tumultuous, packed meeting that followed can perhaps best be described in a highly digested description borrowing from the format used by playwrights.

The meeting opened with the councilman finally establishing order after considerable shouting from the crowd. After a very brief committee report, the Mayor was introduced. Then:

MAYOR: My fellow Americans—
    (Prolonged boos)
    If you want me to leave, I'll be glad to.
    (Diminishing boos)
    You face a difficult problem, one not to be solved by emotional outbursts.
    I am charged with the enforcement of the law, I am not unsympathetic
    with your situation, but I should like to pose one question: What would
    you do if you were Mayor and had sworn to enforce the law?

CRIES: *You* take him for your neighbor.

MAYOR: That's not the answer.

CRIES: In Georgia it is.

MAYOR: If you say "Get out" to this man, he can say "Get out" to you. If I can make him move, I can make you move. Would you move if I asked you to?

A SPEAKER: If I wasn't wanted here, I would. (Applause.)

A SPEAKER: What I can't make out is why these people don't keep to their own section? (Applause.) If we hang on to our homes and don't sell, they can't move in. Let's forget this one man and not sell. (Boos.)

MAYOR: I prefer to believe what I am hearing here tonight is economics, not bigotry. This country has had prejudice against my people, the Irish, against Jews, against your fathers and mothers. We're overcoming those prejudices. If you are not bigoted, and don't sell, you won't get hurt.

A SPEAKER: Will a covenant we draw up requiring consent of our neighbors to sell our property hold up in court?

MAYOR: Not if it is based on discrimination. (Boos.)
But it will if it is based on desire to preserve your property.
(Applause.)

A SPEAKER: The papers call us bigoted. But we are the ones discriminated against. This is all part of a well laid Communist plot, carefully worked out, to invade our neighborhood and take away our rights. (Violent and continued applause and whistling.)

A SPEAKER: Everybody here has missed the point. We came out of the slums and have built a fine neighborhood. We don't want another slum here for our sons. (Wild applause.)

A SPEAKER: When I worked in WPA the Negroes leaned on their shovels and said, "In 25 years you'll work for us, buddy." Now it's 25 years later, you're pampering them. (Applause.)

MAYOR: What would you do if you were Mayor?

ALL: Stop being a Mayor. Be a man. (Applause.)
There are many ways to skin a cat. Get him out.

A SPEAKER: I am an Italian. When I was not wanted in Shaker Heights, I was decent enough to get out. Why can't this man? Are 2,000 families to be sacrificed for one?

MAYOR: We cannot have second class citizens. How does discrimination against Negroes differ from discrimination against your people—Jews, Hungarians, Italians?

A SPEAKER: *We're* all white.

A SPEAKER: I don't think it's very nice after all I've done for my home to have to tell my friends and relatives there's a Negro in my neighborhood.

SPEAKERS: Get the colored cops out of our neighborhood . . . Quit wasting taxpayer's money on police protection for one family . . . Can't you use the right of eminent domain to buy the house? We need a library . . . If you can't help us, we'll lick you in the next election.

HEAD OF CIVIC LEAGUE: We are preparing signs, "Not for Sale" for our homes. That will stop the panic. Will you put them up on your house? (Mingled yells of "Yes" and "No.")

At this point, the priest spoke at length, urging calm and the rights of the Negro. He was received with complete discourtesy and lack of attention. Many left and there was considerable violent interruptions of his remarks.

At about 10:15 the councilman adjourned the meeting amid disorder and a general feeling of frustration on the part of all present. It seemed apparent that conferences with a few at a time were worthwhile, but that the mass meeting let loose irresponsible talk. Some felt, however, that the meeting had acted as a safety valve and was worthwhile.

It might be added finally that the Community Relations Committee of the Jewish Community Federation has sent letters of commendation to the Mayor and the Community Relations Board. A committee is to study further constructive steps to be taken, particularly through Jewish organizations in that area. Considerable question has been voiced, however, as to when such educational steps should best be undertaken and whether Jewish individuals should assume leadership in so heated an atmosphere, even if they were willing to do so. On the constructive side, hundreds of letters of support and congratulations have been received by the new owner, some from folks resident in the area. Many respectable groups have gone—or will soon go—on record supporting the rights of the Negro or any other American in such a situation.

The Negro community is tremendously concerned and interested in this entire problem, as best illustrated by the leading Negro minister's remark, "I would sooner have this Negro leave his house in an ambulance or a hearse than in a moving van."

Further conferences are also to be held on an interreligious basis.

REPORTED BY SIDNEY Z. VINCENT
July 23, 1953

"Oral History Interview"

Alfred Benesch, born of Bohemian immigrant parents, was an outstanding example of the achievements of many second-generation Cleveland Jews. Notwithstanding the demands of his busy legal practice, he pursued a career of service to the city and the state—and to the growing Jewish community, where he served on the boards of many organizations. A champion of humanitarian causes, the rising lawyer became counsel in 1910 to the newly formed Peddlers' Self Defense Association, which Jewish peddlers had created to protect themselves against police harassment.

Among many civic endeavors, Benesch served on the Cleveland City Council (1912) and was city safety director (1914–1915) and Ohio secretary of commerce (1935–1939). He provided exemplary leadership on Cleveland's Board of Education from 1925 to 1962, including two years as its president. He successfully opposed compulsory reserve military training in the high schools and became an acknowledged leader of liberal efforts following his 1922 fight against Harvard's Jewish admissions quota. In 1938, he argued in favor of Jewish assertiveness and against Jewish inferiority feelings when he spoke out forcefully for Hebrew-language instruction in Cleveland high schools.

Benesch's interview is wide ranging and significant in a number of areas. He provides important details regarding life in the lower Woodland Avenue community at the turn of the twentieth century and then chronicles his interactions as he rose to become one of the city's most noted public figures with politicians and power brokers, including Tom L. Johnson, Newton D. Baker, and Maurice Maschke. Importantly, the Benesch interview also touches upon his opposition to anti-Semitism in Cleveland and at Harvard. This autobiographical sketch of

Benesch's life is taken from "Alfred A. Benesch: Oral History Interview," and the interviewer was Rae C. Weil.

Source: "Alfred A. Benesch: Oral History Interview," interviewer Rae C. Weil, January 14, 1972, abridged and edited by Judah Rubinstein. Judah Rubinstein files, Jewish Federation of Cleveland Records, Western Reserve Historical Society.

ALFRED A. BENESCH
Oral History Interview
January 14, 1972
Interviewer: Mrs. Rae Weil [Abridged and edited by Judah Rubinstein]

I was born on March 7, 1879 in a house located in a little alley that ran between Case Avenue (now East 40th Street) and Wallingford Court (now East 45th Street). The street was so narrow that no wagon was able to go through; people had to walk whenever they wanted to go anywhere. This street was called Burwell Extension; it was an extension of Burwell Avenue and ran between East 34th Street and 40th Street.

My father's name, Isadore J. Benesch, appeared for the first time in the Cleveland Directory in 1876, which was the year he came over from Czechoslovakia where he was born. His occupation at that time was given as a porter in a saloon on Michigan Street. The street has now disappeared and is part of the Terminal Buildings. My father and mother were married in a hall on Croton Avenue, now part of the food terminal, by Rabbi Aaron Hahn. At that time, my father was making $7 a week and paying $4 a month rent.

We had no kindergartens in those days. My first school was Outhwaite School, which is located on Outhwaite Avenue just north of Woodland Avenue between Case Avenue (East 40th St.) and Wilson Avenue (East 55th Street). After my 37 years of service on the Board of Education, the members of the board honored me by naming the school the Alfred A. Benesch School, which was the first and only time a Cleveland school was named for a living person.

After graduation from Outhwaite School, I went to Central High School, a member of the Class of 1896. [During] four years [at] Central High School [. . .] Daniel Lothenman, my Latin teacher, took a personal interest in me and two other Jewish boys, August Grossman and Louis Stem. He persuaded us to take the entrance examinations for Harvard and kept us after school every evening in order that we might prepare for the entrance examinations. We succeeded in passing the examinations with one exception.

I was conditioned in my physics examination and was required to take a course in physics to make up the deficiency during my first year at college.

At college I was particularly interested in languages—Latin, French, German and Greek. I often wish that I had specialized in languages instead of in the law. My four years at college were uneventful. I got a scholarship every year which enabled me to go through the following year with some outside work to earn a little money. In those years, the total expense for my education for one year was less than $500. I finished three years of college and got my bachelor's degree and took a master's degree in my fourth year (1900) and then entered law school and graduated in 1903. My three years at college were very uneventful.

I returned to Cleveland and entered law office with Benjamin C. Starr, who was a member of the Class of 1878 at Harvard. In 1906 I formed a partnership with a former roommate at law school and a former Clevelander, Samuel J. Kornhauser. We were in partnership for several years until he joined a firm in Pittsburgh where his family lived. Then I practiced alone for a few years. We had a law office in Society for Savings, an ante-room and two private offices for which we paid $30 a month. A stenographer in those days cost $7 a week and unlimited telephone service was $3 a month.

I became interested in politics through Tom Johnson and was a very ardent follower of his tent meetings. During the first years of my friendship with Johnson, I was frequently appointed acting judge of the police court for which I received $10 for each sitting. Then in 1910 or 1911, I became a member of the City Council and was a member for four years. At that time the salary was $1200 a year. Tom Johnson took a particular interest in me during his administration, and during the time I was in Council, I defended the operations of the Cleveland City Hospital, which was then under attack by the Republicans.

Johnson was defeated by Herman Baer in 1909, and in 1912 Newton Baker became mayor. At that time I was still a member of the City Council, and Baker appointed me Director of Public Safety in charge of the police department, fire department, the building department and the department of smoke inspection. When Peter Witt ran for mayor in 1917, I ran again for Council and was defeated along with him and the other Democrats. I then practiced law alone for several years.

In 1934 I was appointed state director of commerce in charge of banks, buildings, and loan associations by Governor Martin L. Davey and was re-appointed when he was re-elected in 1936. In 1939 after Davey was defeated, Jerome Friedlander and Robert Morris asked me to form a partnership of which I was to be the principal member; I practiced law continuously after that time, from 1939 on. In the meantime, several things happened. I had become a member of the boards of the Hebrew Free Loan Association, the Hebrew Shelter Home, Council Education Alliance, Bellefaire, Federation, Highland View Hospital, and Mount Sinai Hospital.

I was a member of the Board of Trustees of the old Hebrew Relief Association (Jewish Family Service Association). I was the only member without a mustache or a beard. What has struck me with particular force is that during all these years that I have related, at least up to the 30's, the names then prominent in Cleveland Jewish history are unknown today. We didn't hear of the Ratners, the Glasses, the Myers. We knew of Martin Marks, who was the father of the Federation idea. [We heard of] Feis, the Josephs and the Goldsmiths, who were well known in the community but not particularly for their interest in public service or charitable efforts. If I may say so without disparagement, they were not willing to soil their hands with the result that they have been forgotten.

I think they succeeded in trying to prevent discrimination. I never encountered any discrimination in any effort that I undertook, never, any kind. I think men like Julius Feis and Charles Eisenman, who was the first president, or Sol Reinthal, were anxious to see that the Jews didn't get into trouble. It was their particular interest. I don't think they were particularly interested in preventing poverty or providing employment.

My grandfather was a strictly Orthodox Jew. So strict, in fact, that he used to cook his own meals rather than have my grandmother prepare them. He had a general Jewish education. When I went away to college he cried bitterly. I remember asking him, "Why are you crying Granpa, I'll be back in June for my vacation?" He said, "That's not why I'm crying; you're going to eat *trefe* food when you're away." I went to Sunday School in a little frame synagogue that stood on 40th Street opposite Orange Avenue. It was called the Bohemian Synagogue. The members were all Bohemian. One of the rabbis was Solomon Beckerman. I went there, I think, for three years until my father joined the Scovill Avenue Temple (Anshe Chesed), under Dr. Machol. I was confirmed there, but I was Bar Mitzvahed in this little Bohemian Synagogue on 40th Street.

The first Jewish social club in Cleveland was located at the corner of East 9th Street, then Erie Street, and a street called Sumner. It was located across Sumner Street and had a small frame club house located on the premises. I don't remember when the club was organized, but a few years after the organization, it moved to Halle's Hall, which was a large brick building at the corner of East 9th Street and Woodland Avenue. Perhaps it would have been better if the club had been left to die with the cemetery, because none of the Cleveland clubs is famous for any worthy undertaking. On the contrary, its standards of admission have generally been wealth, rather than participation in Jewish affairs. Not many of the members of the various clubs are affiliated with any temple, and very few club members are active in Jewish community affairs. Money has been the usual standard for admission. There was a time when the old Excelsior Club, now the Oakwood Club, consisted of representative Jews. It was difficult to become a member unless you measured up to a certain standard and that standard was participation in the Jewish community. Nowadays, money seems to be the only standard, the only requirement for admission.

I can't remember who the first Jewish judge was in Cleveland. But the Jewish judges, like the non-Jewish judges in the early days, were really elected on score of their ability and not for political reasons as they are today. There were no Jewish judges in the old days. On the other hand, the Jews have done well in the bar association. Eugene Freedheim was president of the bar association at one time, and now Sam Gaines (*geboren* Ginsberg) is now president. Eugene Freedheim made a good reputation as president. I think Maurie Bernon was president of the bar association at one time.

We haven't talked about our Jewish doctors. Jewish doctors have been generally highly regarded in Cleveland, and deservedly so. The earliest Jewish doctor I remember is Dr. [Marcus] Rosenwasser, who brought me into the world. He had a very high reputation; he was on the staff at Huron Road Hospital. Dr. Sam Friedlander has a very high reputation; I regarded him much less than I regarded his brothers. He has a brother in business in Wooster, Ohio and a brother in Dayton, whom I like much better than Sam. Sam was a czar. I had a fight with him on account of Jerry Gross. He thought that Jerry was a better violinist than a doctor. He may have been, but it was very poor grace for him to say so. The Jews have nothing to be ashamed of so far as the medical profession is concerned. They have done very well.

The best known Jewish businessman in my early days was Jacob Mandelbaum who operated a clothing store on the site of the old Forest City House where the Cleveland Hotel is now. That was Manny Mandelbaum's father. His father was the first Jewish merchant that I remember. Then there was Levy & Stern which is one of the oldest and most favorably known firm[s] in Cleveland. Then there was Strauss, who was in the dry goods business, and then there were Jewish brokers. The Jewish brokers have always been highly regarded.

The Halle brothers, of course were always very highly thought of. The names will occur to me later. Some of our best known pawnbrokers were Jews.

If I were in politics today, I would be a Democrat, I'm sure. I am sure that I'd favor those candidates who are more interested in the welfare of their country than they're in their own preferments; and that would be hard to find. I was a great admirer of the Kennedys. I'm beginning to lose faith. They're talking about the money that candidates are spending now, but look at the money he spent or his father spent, without which he could never have been nominated. Here's a man resigning from the cabinet, Maurice Stams, in order to raise money for Nixon's campaign. I don't think that happens in Europe.

If I were writing letters to the *Cleveland Press* like I used to, I would be writing about the lack of interest in vital matters. The average working man doesn't care whether other working men are getting more money, only if he is making more money. The average capitalist feels the same way about it. It took very little to anger me. I wish I could see some of those letters, to see what really mattered. The last letter I wrote was not published. It was on the subject of television: how putrid it is. Putrid is the only word I can use. Take an impressive, dramatic scene, for instance. They interrupt that in the middle to show a soap ad; or they'll introduce somebody whom everybody knows with a loud shout as though the audience can't hear. I don't know. Newspapers wouldn't publish it, I suppose it would interfere with their circulation.

I learned that there was anti-Semitism in Cleveland when at the suggestion of Newton Baker I applied for membership in the Union Club of which Baker was a prominent member. My application for membership was signed by Newton Baker and John H. Clark, who then was a United States judge in Cleveland, and I never heard anything more about the application. But, of course, I learned that Jews were not eligible for admission to the Union Club. And, since that time, I have refused to attend any function which took place at the Union Club. At one time, the Harvard Club was scheduled to hold its annual district meeting at the Union Club and to be addressed by Morry Seasongood who was my classmate. And when I informed him that the Union Club admits no Jews to membership, he refused to honor the engagement and the dinner was held at the then Manger Hotel.

Shortly after graduation, I wrote an article for the *New Era Magazine* on the subject of the Jew at Harvard. The purpose of the article was not to show there was anti-Semitism at Harvard but that members of the Phi Beta Kappa Society were guilty of anti-semitic tendencies. I learned that the man who should have been admitted to Phi Beta Kappa, who stood unquestionably at the head of the class, was not admitted to membership among the first eight; at that time Phi Beta Society members were elected on the basis of their standings. [An] Alpha Beta Kappa member had to be at least a *magna cum laude* member in order to be eligible. This man who was in the class of '99, the class ahead of mine, was not admitted, as I learned later because he was Jewish. I put up a fight for him. I don't know if the practice still obtains, but at that time the members of Phi Beta Kappa selected eight in their Junior year and the remaining 17 in their Senior year. When I learned that this man was not a member of the first eight because he was Jewish, several of us put up a fight for his admission; he was elected among the remaining 17, instead of among the first eight. I want to emphasize that anti-Semitism to which I have just referred was attributable not to Harvard authorities, but to the members of the Phi Beta Kappa.

In 1922, after I graduated, the president of Harvard set up a 10 per cent quota on Jews. There was correspondence that I had with President Cole which appeared in the *New York Times*. Well, as I recall, I was successful in having that 10 per cent quota dropped. President Cole didn't apologize in so many words, but the practice was never put into effect as a matter of fact. He was not adverse to accepting Jewish money though. Jacob Schiff was very liberal in his contributions to Harvard. I think that is all I can say on the subject of anti-Semitism.

I was elected in 1925 to the [Cleveland] school board and remained on. There were no questions regarding Jewish teachers or students in the school system. There was one period in which Norma Wulff and I were the only non-politicians on the board. The other five were Irish politicians, and we couldn't get anything over at all. Whatever they wanted, whatever appointments they wanted, they got. Fortunately, that lasted only a few years.

One of the first things I did was have ROTC eliminated from the school system. That's when I incurred the wrath of Newton Baker who was strongly for it and also for Davis, who was a classmate of mine and secretary of war. I don't think Baker ever forgave me for that. There was no really controversial decision I made. Of course, when the so-called majority bloc was on the Board, Mrs. Wulff and I didn't try to pass anything because it was unsuccessful. The major policy decisions technically were made by the board, but really on the advice and with the cooperation of the staff. The staff had real voice in many policy decisions.

I antagonized Superintendent [Robinson G.] Jones when I came on the Board. I forget what it was for. Mrs. Wulff and I often disagreed then, too.

But there were not what we call vital issues like today. Largely questions of appointment. The Board never got involved in curriculum at all.

There was no Black issue of any kind in my day. There were no attempts, like today, to get Black history and Black background materials into the school system. There was no attempt to do that for any other minority group. No Jewish issue.

If I were doing things over again, I would like to have been a teacher to build better understanding among whites and Blacks, among Republicans and Democrats. With respect to the educational system, I would like to see a more experienced and an abler superintendent than [Paul] Briggs. I think he is very weak; he doesn't compare with [Charles H.] Lake and [William B.] Levenson. I think he should be doing more for education and less for politics. Superintendents nowadays do what is calculated to enhance chances for retention. Education went right along on a rather routine way during my incumbency as president.

I haven't enough confidence in modern youth to give them a voice in education, on what they need to be taught. We would have discussion on what they wanted but generally speaking, I wouldn't want to adopt any of their theories. Of course, their attitude toward education is the same as their attitude toward politics. They think they deserve vocal prominence, and I don't agree with them because they haven't had enough experience. They look upon education solely as a matter for young people just as they would look upon politics as a matter for young people. I don't feel that media, television and radio have speeded up the education experience of young people to the point where they are so much more knowledgeable. Youth is trying to assume too much knowledge and too much authority.

In politics, I had an unusual background and opportunity. I had known so many important figures in politics; among them, Tom Johnson and Newton Baker, although Johnson was in a class all by himself. He was the greatest influence in my life. He influenced people because he knew how they felt. He knew how the ditch digger felt out on the street, and he knew how the president of [the] bank felt, and he was able to reconcile them. He had a remarkable faculty of drawing people together.

Baker never stopped being an aristocrat. Johnson would not have to command; he merely expressed a vague desire for something to be done, and it was done. People swore by him because they had confidence in his integrity, in his lack of prejudice and in his ability as a businessman. He was one man who went into politics a millionaire and died pennyless; his whole fortune was for the benefit of the public. You couldn't say that of Baker or of any of the other politicians who succeeded him. When we think of the kind of mayors we have had since then, we have to blush.

I got to know Tom Johnson at a barbershop at the corner of Woodland Avenue and East 40th Street, where my father and I used to go to have our haircuts. We met him there one night during a campaign, and he made an impression on me. My father knew him because he had met him at a single tax meeting then held in Dr. Cooley's church on Cedar Avenue. I just took a liking to him. I must have been impressed because he was the one who encouraged me to go into politics. I was elected to Council the year that Johnson died, 1911.

Newton Baker was mayor, and he appointed me safety director. I was in the Council at the time. He had some very good men surrounding him. He had a very strong cabinet—John Stockwell, Dr. [Harris Reid] Cooley, Peter Witt, Tom Kaufman, Tom Sidlo, Joe Hostetler. I was not the youngest member of the cabinet. I think Sidlo and Hostetler were both younger than I. But Sidlo and Hostetler immediately began to feather their nests immediately after they got into the Council.

Peter Witt was city clerk at the time I was in the mayor's cabinet. He was a very able man, a very strong admirer of Johnson. He probably did more to make Johnson prominent than any other individual. Witt was a very unusual character, very outspoken. He lost all respect for me because I accepted a position under [Martin L.] Davey. He didn't like Davey, but he didn't dislike me.

Governor Davey appointed me Ohio director of commerce. I served in that capacity for four years. It kept me away from Cleveland. I lived in Columbus and met some very interesting people. That's where attempts were made by our prominent industrialists to feather their nests. It was Davey's department. A lot of people thought that Davey was dishonest; I never found him so. When people went to him over my head and objected, he always upheld me.

When I came back to Cleveland in 1939, without my knowledge Jerry Friedlander and Bob Morris organized a firm and asked me to head it; I stayed in that firm up until now.

Before I leave the subject of politics, there is another well know[n] name—Maschke. The Maschke family lived on Woodland Avenue right near 45th Street. Their father had a grocery store at the corner of Case Avenue (40th Street) and Woodland Avenue. Maurice Maschke came into politics through a very minor position that he had in the County Clerk's office. Then when the Republican administration came in, he was made, I think, assistant county clerk. Herman Baehr was then county clerk. Baehr is the one who defeated

Johnson for mayor in 1912. I'll say for Maurice that he always kept his word; I think he tried to put good men into office. He wanted to build up the Republican party which suffered a good deal under the Democrats. Anybody in those days who [was] asked, "What do you think of Maurice Maschke?" would say that he was an honest man. I never denounced him. He was always willing to do a favor. I never had any public differences with Maschke. I had a great deal of respect for him, but didn't like some of his associates.

I was induced to go into politics because I came from a poor family. I told you what my father's first job was—a porter in a saloon on Michigan Avenue. But he became manager of the Singer Sewing Machine Company in time, and the highest salary he ever got was $3,000 a year. Of course, I had to work my way through college. He told me if I wanted to go to college, he had no objections but couldn't help me. There were four girls and two boys to support. Years after I was already practicing law, he came to my office bringing with him a cancelled note for $800 for money that he had borrowed from his bookkeeper. I don't know how many years it took him to pay it off.

The Bohemian Jews' little community did not expect me to do anything special for them when I was in politics. In fact, they never asked me to allow them to purchase land for their Bohemian cemetery on Baxter Avenue, which is still there. There is a Bohemian congregation who joined the Scovill Avenue Temple crowd, and there has been none since then.

When Federation was organized I had no participation. My first interest in what was then called charity was membership on the board of trustees of the Hebrew Relief Society which met in a little frame house on Woodland Avenue. And it was because of my interest in the community that I gradually developed a strong taste for participation in the various charities such as the Council of Education Alliance, the Hebrew Free Loan Association, and Bellefaire. I became a member of B'nai B'rith in the spring of 1904, and shortly was elected recording and financial secretary.

I can remember individuals more than I can remember institutions. I can go back to the original board of trustees of the Federation. The election of Charles Eisenman [as president] was not very popular because up to that time, Eisenman had done nothing in the line of social service. As a matter of fact, it was said that he wanted to become president of the Federation so that he could in a measure control the operation of the organizations, which of course he never did, nor did he ever try to do. He was not popular enough to be president. Martin Marks could have been that man. Martin Marks, although not a member of the original board of trustees, was the prime mover of the Federation and many of his ideas were carried into action. As a matter of fact, no other man who did form the original organization was as active except financial contributors to the operation of the organization.

The board consisted of members who had means and who had the ability to carry out the purpose of the organization in a financial way. Rabbi [Moses] Gries' first active participation outside of his own Temple, was as president of the Council of Jewish Women. He served only one term I think and then was succeeded by Mrs. Flora Schwab who served several terms. Sol Reinthal, I remember, was secretary for some years.

I knew the original men personally in the sense that I was able to say hello to them when I met them, although they didn't know me then up until I became active. Abraham Stearn I remember well from his connection with the orphan home. He was the only one of the original board who was interested in the orphan home; the others were not active participants in any Jewish organization outside of the Federation.

Of course, now every member of the Federation board is actively interested in some participating organization. It was not so in these days, when the original members were prominent members of the general community. Everybody knew Julius Feis and Sol Hexter because they were actively interested in the business of the community.

Today if the leaders of agencies they represent try not to interfere with the activities of other organizations, then I am in favor of professionalization. But, when Max Freedman tried to dominate the whole community just because he had money, I didn't agree. He was interested in the honor of being president of [a] big hospital, and he did not do a good job. Mike Glass and Dave Myers devoted just as much time to the hospital as he did and did a much better job. I think in many respects Dave Myers is the representative Jew of this community today. He has both the spirit and the means just as Mike Glass had.

Leonard Ratner is interested in all organizations and devotes a great deal more time than anybody else to charitable efforts. Of course, he hasn't the organization ability which is not needed nowadays. Max is the business part of the firm. I know Max, of course, but I never had anything to do with him as much as I have Leonard. I think that my family was the first family to meet the Ratners when they came to Cleveland and opened up a little butter and egg store on 105th Street right in back of where we lived.

The early agencies with which I was associated had no professional guidance at all. They were composed of laymen who did the best that they could and whose deciding factor was either money or lack of money. Those who had money were the givers and those that didn't were the recipients.

As for rabbis, the first rabbi that I remember was rabbi of a little building on 40th Street and Case Avenue, Solomon Beckerman. I don't know what training he had; he was Polish and was not a Hebrew scholar, I am sure of that. He would not be called a rabbi as you would classify our present rabbis who are students. The first Jewish rabbi that studied for the ministry in Europe was Dr. Aaron Hahn. He was rabbi of the first regular Jewish temple. I was confirmed at Dr. Michael Machol's temple [Anshe Chesed]. Today I am a member of Silver's temple.

There were no Hebrew schools outside of the Orthodox congregations. The most active members in the Orthodox community so far as the Sabbath schools were concerned were Rabbi Margolies who was at Harvard with me, and Solomon Goldman. But, they always laid much more emphasis on the instruction of their children than on their sermons; not so today. I am in favor of that emphasis if Judaism is to be perpetuated, yes.

I became a member of the board of the Bureau [of Jewish Education] because I thought that some member of the Reform Jewish community should take an active interest in Hebrew and Hebrew education; and that's where I met some real scholars.

We had laymen who were real scholars, men like Max Simon for instance. Max knew his Hebrew. Many of the members of Rabbi Cohen's temple were Hebrew scholars. I suppose my interest in Judaism may have sprung originally from my grandfather, who had no formal education; he had no trade as a matter of fact. He was so pious that he cooked his own meals; he wouldn't allow my grandmother to do this for him. That quality did not descend to any of his children or grandchildren, but his strong identification with Judaism and Jewry did descend to me.

Being Jewish has made a great deal of difference in my life. I'm sure that I could not have been interested in as many non-Jewish organizations even if I had been a Catholic, because there is a broader general interest among Jews in public welfare than there is among Gentiles. Whether that made any difference or not, I don't know.

I think the tradition of charity of giving for ours is stronger among Jews. It doesn't have anything to do with my Jewish education which was not so thorough. I think it was because I was born a Jew.

The real scholars of the Jewish community today are the members of the Orthodox congregations. If anybody were to ask who was the leading Jew in Cleveland, I would say [Rabbi Israel] Porath, and I would be condemned for it by members of the Oakwood Club. He had general respect as Jewish scholar and as Jew in the community. He was very highly regarded and quite loved by many.

I haven't talked very much about Israel and my interests. I read everything that I can lay my hands on which [a]ffects Israel, but I have never been anxious to go there. I think the reason is purely practical; I don't like traveling.

I don't think that the survival of Israel is important for Jews of the United States. I think that if all the Jews move to Israel, the migration would cause more anti-Semitism than exists today. The existence of Israel for Jews living in the United States has made a difference to Jews here, but has not made any difference with the Gentiles. It brought Jews of different shades of religious faith together.

But, I am not sure that the state of Israel is a good thing. On one hand it has created antagonism, and on the other hand it has created sympathy for the Jews. I don't know how they balance each other. I think that what is going to count in the end is physical strength, not ethical concepts. I didn't have any high regard for Ben-Gurion because he was a real czar; Golda Meir has some of his qualities.

Section Three

Work and Business

Workers at the Ology cigar factory on West 3rd Street, circa 1915 (Western Reserve Historical Society).

Excerpt from "Autobiography of Kaufman Hays"

Kaufman Hays turned his talents to finance, a field in which he had dabbled successfully as early as 1867, after he and his brother dissolved their clothing establishment (see also the chapter on Joseph Hays in this volume). He became one of the first Jews outside the East and West Coast financial centers to succeed in the fiscal services sector. In 1886, he helped found Euclid Avenue National Bank, which eventually became the First National Bank of Cleveland, the largest of the city's financial institutions. He served it as a lifelong director and as vice president, positions that brought him into close association with city and state figures and provided a seat of power that made him influential in Cleveland and Ohio affairs. In 1888, he served as vice president of the Cleveland City Council.

Kaufman became president of the Hebrew Benevolent Society in 1861. He was arguably the richest Jew in Cleveland in 1898 when his daughter, Fannie, was married to Rabbi Moses J. Gries, who served Congregation Tifereth Israel from 1892 to 1917 (see also the chapter on Abba Hillel Silver in this volume).

Kaufman's 1910 memoir reveals a self-sufficiency that served him well on the voyage to America, enabled him to navigate the pitfalls of immigration, and helped him become an entrepreneur at a young age. His sketches provide a glimpse into the inner workings of Cleveland's nineteenth-century retail economy and into the city's emerging importance in national banking and insurance ventures.

Source: An excerpt from Kaufman Hays, "Autobiography of Kaufman Hays," 1910, Western Reserve Historical Society, donated by Robert Gries.

AUTOBIOGRAPHY OF KAUFMAN HAYS.
March 9, 1910.

Was born March 9, 1835, in Stordorf by Alsfeld, Hessen Darmstadt, Germany.

At mother's death when I was nine years old, there were six children, four girls and two boys. The oldest girl was eighteen and kept house for father; two other girls, fourteen and sixteen years old, took places at Alsfeld. I helped in the house when not in school, but never passed up a chance to earn a little money in doing chores.

After leaving school, worked without pay for a cousin in the cattle business, and had to depend on drinkgelt which was very little.

About 1850 sister Rosa with several other girls went to America, and in due course of time sent me a small sum of money. With this money and what little I had managed to save, started for America, father and brother Joe going with me as far as Mainz. Took a boat for Rotterdam, thence by boat to London where I took a sailing vessel to New York, which made the trip in forty-five days. After being out about ten days, noticed the colored cook had killed a sheep and was trying to dress it but was making a bad mess of the work. Although but a midget beside this big, burly negro, I went over to him, took the knife and dressed the sheep. The captain had been watching the process, and when it was done took me into the cabin and served a bottle of wine. He said I should have fresh milk from the cow on board and any other necessities I should need, which made me happy during the balance of the trip and I gladly dressed a sheep every day.

We arrived in New York September 21, 1852. Had the address of Mrs. Alt who had worked for my mother when I was a baby, and she was delighted to see me. Visited there three days and then took an emigrant train to Buffalo, thence by boat to Cleveland. When we arrived at the dock, a lot of hotel runners took us—bundles and all—to a small hotel on River St., but did not like its looks, so left my bundles and started up the street; made inquiry for a Jewish hotel and was directed to the Moses Boarding House on St. Clair St. When I reached its door, some young man called, "Rosa, here is your brother." She came running and it was a happy meeting. She had come up for the holidays with the Hyman family who lived at Brimfield, Ohio. Although she knew I was on my way, did not expect me then. I had a twenty franc piece when I reached this city.

On Oct. 1st after being here three days, got a position with Mr. Sam Loeb, a clothier at $25.00 for the first year, $75.00 for the second, $150.00 for the third with board, clothes and spending money. On Thanksgiving Day Mr.

Loeb gave me 50¢, which was the first money earned in this country, and the first saved. I took my meals at his house, and as his wife and children only spoke English, it gave me an excellent opportunity to learn the language. To help me I carried a roll of ribbon paper in my pocket, and when I heard a word that I did not understand, put it down and when I met some of the young boys had them define it, which I put down opposite the word. In this way and by studying the roll when I was alone, in the course of three months I could speak English fairly well.

Mr. Loeb was a very careless man. Some mornings after breakfast Mrs. Loeb would give me a basket for groceries and when I got to the store would tell him what was wanted. He would tell me to put it in the corner and there it would stay. Then in the evenings Mrs. Loeb would ask me about the groceries, and one Saturday night she scolded severely. I told her had I the money the groceries would have been bought and brought home. This practice made me so angry that I told Mr. Loeb I would quit, but he would not listen. However, on Monday morning I carried out my resolution and went with Mr. L. Wolf, a grocer on Ontario St. at $4.00 per month, but did not like the way the business was conducted so left in about four months.

Got some goods and peddled in the country. Started out Euclid Avenue way for the country and travelled many miles in the course of the next six weeks. Then I sold my pack boxes and all, clearing about $100.00. Did not like the business but made lots of friends among the people I stopped with over night and they later traded where I was clerking. I would help with the chores wherever I stayed, help milk the cows or feed the stock, and go to church with them on Sundays. Where I stayed once over night, they were glad to have me come again, and I remember kindly a Mrs. Maps of Mayfield who would bring me in one of her first pumpkin pies every year.

Went to work for Mr. L. H. Schwarzenberg, a grocer, corner Orange and Broadway at $8.00 per month. In a few months sister Rosa was married to Mr. F. Loeb, who started a grocery. I helped him some to get started, but Mr. Schwarzenberg did not like it so I left.

One day I went with Mr. Loeb to the City Mills Store to buy sugar. Mr. Perry, the senior member of the firm, who waited on us, asked if I were in partnership with Mr. Loeb. When he found we were not, he asked if I would not come to him as there was a good opening, so I hired out at $250.00 for the first year, $400.00 the second and every year thereafter I got a raise for seven years. Was at the store but a few months until I was assigned to the calico and cotton cloth counter.

One day I discovered a large pile of Merimac calico, purple with white dots, the ends all faded. Took one piece to the entry clerk to make a memorandum as I was going to cut it up into remnants and wanted to make a report after it was sold, and if it was not all right I would stand the loss. After it was all gone, called Mr. Perry and told him what had been done. He patted me on the back and said, "Good boy, cut them all up fast as you can," which I did and they were quickly disposed of. And Mr. Perry thereafter made it a practice to supply me with remnants when he bought in the East. Every market day the women got in the habit of coming in the store looking for remnants.

Then I was given the silk and millinery departments until March 1, 1860, when I left to go in the hide and wool business with Mr. S. Thorman on Water St. Had saved every dollar I could while clerking and had made some very good investments in property.

On May 8, 1861, married Lizzie Thorman, with whom I had kept company for over six years.

After we were in business about six months, Mr. Thorman proposed to make his son Sam an equal partner. I asked, "On my capital?" "He has nothing to put in the business and your capital is considerably less than mine," but he would have it, so I submitted. About two years later Mr. E. Budwig married Esther Thorman. He was keeping books for Mr. S. Munn at $400.00 per year. Mr. Thorman came in the store one morning and said he was going to take Budwig in as an equal partner. I asked, "Have you any money to put in for him?" As he had not, I remonstrated, but he stated he expected to treat all the children alike, and I answered "On my capital?" "You don't know this man; give him a salary of say $800 to $1,000 for a year or two until you find out whether he is worthy." But he would not have it that way, so not to have any break up in the family I allowed it, but said I would get out of the business as soon as I could.

I kept on until February 1864, when I had a good chance to clean out the stock to very good advantage, and left them in good financial condition. There was a new lot of dry stock that came in having been bought by the buyers on the road, and in the meantime there was a large increase in the price, about $10,000 profit. Budwig said I was entitled to my share, but I would take none of it as things might change and it had better be held for a rainy day. They continued in business for a few years, and while others in the same line made money, they continued to lose.

In 1866 I went to Europe on account of my health, and Mr. and Mrs. Thorman decided to go also. Without success I advised Mr. Thorman to turn the business over to the boys and leave them plenty of capital, but to get out himself. By the time we got back at the end of six months, the business was in bad shape, and I had to endorse a large sum to keep then going. This continued for some time until I was notified by the bank that it must stop. Mr. Thorman was in St. Louis for a long time where I wrote him how things were going, but he paid no attention. Shortly before a Ten Thousand Dollar note became due, wrote I would not endorse any more, and if he wanted to save his name, he had better come home, which he did. He borrowed money and mortgaged his property, paid big interest until he could go no further. The good business went to ruin.

About that time my brother Joe was traveling with notions, and was anxious to get into business. As my health was not good, he proposed that I take care of the office. About March 1, 1864, we went to New York, bought the first stock, and opened on Water St. As fast as the stock came in it was sold, so I had to pack up and go again, and so the business started good. We continued until January 1, 1885, selling out to Klein & Lehman.

In 1867 was one of the organizers of the Teutonia Insurance Co. of Cleveland. We paid in 25%, the same as other insurance companies in Ohio, but I insisted in crediting the earnings every six months to capital until the stock was fully paid up. The Secretary of State was so pleased with that arrangement that he recommended the legislature pass such a law.

Mr. Luezkemayer was President of the company, Mr. Hessenmuller, Secretary and Kuney Krauss, Agent. One day Krauss went to Chicago and appointed a Herr Von Kern as our agent. He did a land office business but we got little or no money. The Directors sent Hessenmuller and Krauss to Chicago. Kern received them very nicely, wined them and dined them, and sent them back with notes, but no money. To save the company from serious loss, the directors insisted upon my going to Chicago to get rid of Kern. In July 1868, with full power to act, went to Chicago and worked with Kern for a week until I got what was outstanding, knowing full well what he had collected was spent. I then demanded the books. He claimed they were his. I showed him attachment papers, and if he preferred to make it public the constable was outside prepared to do his duty. Kern pulled out a drawer of his desk, grabbed a revolver and pointed it at me. I protected myself with a large book, but he thought better of the situation, put back the revolver and gave me the books, which I took to the office of Coulton & Sprague in the Chamber of Commerce. Policyholders that had not paid were notified not to pay Kern. It was my idea to quit Chicago as it was a losing game at best.

From Chicago I went to St. Louis on my own business, but before I returned our company had given Coulton & Sprague the right to write new business, to which I objected on my return.

A short time after, this firm wrote of a chance to buy out the Merchants Insurance Co. of Chicago. There was $54,000 cash in it which set them almost wild. Again they wanted me to go to Chicago, but told the Board I could make the report without going as I opposed it. They sent a committee which reported favorably to the seventeen directors all of whom were present at this particular meeting. I was the only Director to vote against the proposition, and insisted that my "No" be so recorded across the whole page of the minutes, and so it was done. They got about $1,500,000 of risks for that $54,000. The following day I went to Dr. Weber's office for treatment and he proceeded to tell me that surely sixteen directors knew better than one stubborn man, and I made a mistake not to make the vote unanimous.

The business in Chicago continued for a few years with little profit until the great fire, when the Teutonia Insurance Co. had a loss of about $2,500,000 which, of course, wiped out the whole concern. According to the laws of Ohio the stockholders were liable for the amount of their stock. The Directors held a meeting and insisted on my going to Chicago and getting them out of trouble. I went while the fire was still burning, established an office and notified the policyholders to come to the office. I laid the facts before them and settled with those I could, and in course of time all was settled.

Saturday afternoon I went to Milwaukee over Sunday to get out of the smoke and have a day of rest. Monday I went back to it again and worked until I could do no more, but got the stockholders free. A number of the old stockholders wanted to re-organize, but I opposed it so it did not go through.

In 1868 became a stockholder in the Citizens Savings & Loan Co., and in 1870 in the City National. From that time took quite an interest in banking.

In 1875 Mr. Stillman Witt, one of the directors of the Citizens, died and I was elected in his place, and later was put on the Finance Committee, which position I hold to this day. After retiring from active business, tried to have the City National Bank enlarge its capital and take on increased business, but John Whitelaw, the President, would not agree.

Mr. Myron T. Herrick and myself took initial steps toward starting a national bank on Euclid Avenue. We took a number of influential men in our confidence and started the Euclid Avenue National Bank. Both of us were made directors with Mr. J. L. Woods, President, C. F. Brush, Vice President and S. L. Severance, Cashier. In 1893 was elected Vice President, and held the position until we consolidated with the First National Bank in 1905, when we changed the name to First National. All the old officers retired and we elected younger men, but remained as Director and member of the Executive Board.

In 1886 was elected to the City Council and became Chairman of Finance of the City. Mr. Fred Green and myself formulated the depository law, which was passed by the Legislature in 1887. The City Treasurer, Thomas Axworthe, skipped with nearly all the City's money except a few thousand in the banks. Mayor Babcock, a Democrat, appointed me Acting Treasurer. I used to go over to the Euclid Avenue National Bank each morning and borrow Ten to Twenty Thousand Dollars, carry it to the City Treasurer's office in a newspaper, and after closing the office in the evening carry the amount on hand back to the bank. At last the City got the money in the banks released and I paid the Euclid Avenue National the amount borrowed, and in the course of six weeks, had everything straightened out when I asked Mayor Babcock to relieve me as I had no desire for the office as it took too much of my time.

Still I continued to devote considerable time to city affairs, being Chairman of a number of important committees, until 1892 when I refused nomination. This year H. M. Brown & Co. failed, owing the Euclid Avenue National Bank a large sum of money. I kept posted on all that was going on so when the stock was sold by the court, I bought it for the bank and was put in charge, clearing up a handsome sum for the bank after paying all expenses and salaries.

In 1893, The Turner Manufacturing Co. failed, owing the Euclid Avenue National Bank Forty-five Thousand Dollars. Mr. Turner was the assignee. The three banks, Euclid Avenue National, Broadway and Second National, Ravenna, insisted that the court appoint me as Trustee. Took hold of the matter in good earnest and the three banks put in more money. We bought in the mills, raw material and merchandise and organized The Turner Worsted Co. with a capital of Four Hundred Thousand Dollars, Two Hundred Thousand 8% cumulative preferred, Two Hundred Thousand common. We gave Mr. Turner Seventy-five Thousand common as a present to make him take interest. The preferred went to the banks in proportion to the amount due them. O. M. Stafford was elected President, C. A. Reed, Vice President and myself Secretary, Treasurer and General Manager.

In the course of eighteen months I found Mr. Turner was not working for the interest of the company and called him to account. He made a proposition to issue $200,000 gold bonds for the preferred stock and take over the mill. I told him that would never do as he ought to have at least $200,000 in cash to pay at least 50¢ on the dollar to the preferred stockholders and have at least $100,000 as working capital. He said he would not give $50,000 for the whole thing as nearly $24,000 was owed for dividends at that time, and the whole thing would sink and he did not want to go down with it. I said, if that be the case, he had better resign, which he did a few days later. A meeting of the Board was called, his resignation accepted and I was asked what I was going to do. As I had no manufacturing experience, I told them there was a man in the mill that could help me, and if they would excuse me a few moments would bring him in. Went to the weaving room and called Mr. Geo. H. Hodgson, telling him Mr. Turner had resigned and asked if he and I could run it and he expressed a willingness to try. Introduced him to the Board and we took things over, making a remarkable success. At this time it is one of the largest and best worsted mills in the country, with a capital of Three Million Dollars.

Excerpt from Oral "Autobiography of Mr. Joseph Hays"

The mid-1800s saw large numbers of German Jews migrate to America in pursuit of freedom and opportunities for personal advancement. Many went to Cleveland to reunite with family members or other compatriots or because they had heard about the thriving city east of the Mississippi that welcomed new residents, helped them settle, and provided many economic opportunities. Kaufman Hays's sisters arrived in 1850. Kaufman joined them in 1856 and brought his younger brother, Joseph, to Cleveland that same year.

In 1863, Joseph and Kaufman formed the Hays Brothers retail clothing business, a highly successful enterprise that lasted for twenty-five years and one of many Jewish-owned clothing firms that figured prominently in the mercantile trades, a major contributor to Cleveland's economic growth. In 1883, they sold Hays Brothers to H. F. Klein and S. J. Lichtenstadter, a firm that remained in business into the twentieth century. Joseph was also an ardent and successful fund-raiser for the Hebrew Benevolent Society, established in 1855 for local charitable purposes.

Source: An excerpt from oral "Autobiography of Mr. Joseph Hays" as told to Louis H. Hays, privately published January 1917, Western Historical Reserve Society, donated by Robert Gries.

PREFACE

The contents of this little book were dictated to me by my father during the Summer and Autumn of 1916. I have retained the exact wording of the dictation as far as possible. While this is a simple narrative of a comparatively uneventful life, it shows, nevertheless, the growth and developments from the simple start of an inexperienced immigrant, up through various stages; from farmer, peddler, on to retail traveling salesman, up to wholesaler and manufacturer. Each stage in the story indicates a logical development in my father's character and outlook on life, developing from the perspectives of a simple foreigner, to that of a staunch American of much force and character, accompanied by simplicity of habit and love for his fellow men.

It is the narrative of a quiet life, and if those who loved him will find these pages of interest, I shall feel amply rewarded for what has been a pleasant task.

—LOUIS H. HAYS
January, 1917

AUTOBIOGRAPHY OF MR. JOSEPH HAYS

I am taking this opportunity to relate many of the things that have happened to me during my lifetime, and which may be of interest to my children or children's children after I have passed away. I am 78 years old, and, in common with most people of advanced years, things that happened forty or fifty years ago are clearer to my mind than some that happened but yesterday.

I Am Born

I was born at midnight, between the 4th and 5th of July, 1838, in the little town of Storndorf, Oberhessen, near Alsfeld, Giessen and Frankfort, Germany. My father, Abraham Hays, was born in 1794, and died in Cleveland, 1877. My mother's name was Bertha Hexter. She died when I was 6 years old, in 1844, and is buried in Storndorf, Germany.

The family consisted of sisters, Betty, born in 1828; Rosa, in 1830; Fanny, in 1832, and Yetta, in 1842. Brother Kaufman was born in 1835, and I in 1838.

My Mother Died

After my mother died, my sister Betty, who was then a girl of 16 years of age did the best she could to keep house for us, and when Rosa and Fanny were 12 years old, they worked out for their board and lodging. Brother Kaufman and I also worked as soon as we were able to do anything at all. When I was 14 years old, I was put at regular farm work for two cousins of mine, and remained with them until I came to America, at eighteen.

I was always careful in keeping records of my business and not only balanced my cash daily, but very often between times, especially during the early years when money was hard to get.

I Prove My Honesty

One day when I was about 17 years old, I sold a farmer a calf, and after he had gone I found that I had given him the wrong change. The farmer had been away some hours, but I knew where he lived, and started on foot for his home. I traveled ten miles that same night in order to pay him the few cents which I unknowingly had short-changed him. This principle stood me in good stead throughout my entire business career, and I attribute much of my success to the integrity of my dealings, large and small. As a consequence, I obtained the confidence of those with whom I came in contact, and was always careful to be worthy of it.

First of Family to Go to America; Rosa Comes to Cleveland

My sister Rosa was employed at Alsfeld, and in 1850 she met a Mr. Wallach from New York, who came to Europe often to buy merchandise. He encouraged Rosa to go to America. The family all contributed their mite, and a friend in Alsfeld advanced twenty florins, which equalled $8.00, to help out. She worked in New York for a while, and made her headquarters with a former servant of our parents in Europe. A cousin of this woman persuaded Rosa to come out to Ohio, to Brimfield, a small village near Akron, Ohio. One day an old man came to Brimfield, from Cleveland, and he suggested to her to come to Cleveland, which she did, and got a position at Lowentritt's. After she was here two years, she saved up sufficient money to bring my brother Kaufman over. Rosa then went to work for Mr. Aaron Halle, who kept a grocery store [at the] corner [of] Wood and St. Clair Ave., now E. 4th and St. Clair Ave. Kaufman boarded at Halle's. After he was here two years, Rosa and Kaufman saved up enough to send money for Fanny and Yetta. Rosa in the meantime married a man by the name of Loeb, and with him started a grocery store at the corner of Cross and Woodland, which is now E. 9th and Woodland. Two years after Fanny and Yetta had arrived, the brothers and sisters sent money for Father Hays and myself. Two years after my arrival, we sent over for the last living member of our immediate family, Betty, who had married a Rabbi Moses Oppenheimer, who, with four children, arrived in Cleveland in 1858.

I Start for America

Father and I landed in New York City, Aug. 8th, 1856, on the Yeaberland, a three-masted sailing vessel, which took forty-nine days from Bremen to New York. The boat was so large that it could not come up to the docks at Bremen, and so we had to lighter out. I had never seen a boat before, and when I saw the people go into a little rowboat to reach the larger vessel, I did not think I could muster up courage enough to risk my precious self in so small a boat on such a great body of water. However, after standing there and watching boat load after boat load make the trip in safety, I finally concluded that my life was no more valuable to me than their lives were to them, and decided to make the try, so father and I got aboard the Yeaberland. I enjoyed the experience so thoroughly that the following day I went with the sailors in one of these same small boats gathering supplies at the various wharves for our trip across. I was so seasick that had anyone told me how long this trip was to be, I would surely have jumped overboard, as all the others of our family had made the trip in about thirty days, altho Yetta took sixty days to come over. It didn't take long tho for the seasickness to pass off, and we got used to the life on board the vessel. We played games and amused ourselves generally, but were overjoyed when land was sighted and we came into New York Harbor, Aug. 8th, 1856.

I Land in America

We were welcomed by some friends at the wharf upon our arrival, and remained in New York a week. One of my friends from Storndorf who met us, and who had been in America a great many years, said to me, "Joe, you are just ten years late in coming to this country." I answered that I didn't think that all the opportunities were gone even then.

My impression of New York was, naturally, one of great magnificence, as it was the first city of any great size that I had seen, but I had confidence in myself that some of the splendors would some day be mine.

I Arrive in Cleveland

Kaufman met us in New York and took us to Cleveland. We left New York one Friday night by Hudson River boat to Albany. It was the first steam vessel that I had ever seen, and the boat was much more magnificently equipped than the sailing vessel that we had previously traveled on. I remember as I went up the main stairway that I had never observed so large a mirror, and I thought as I looked into it that there goes a fellow that looks very much like Kaufman, when in truth it was I myself. We arrived in Albany Saturday morning, and left that evening over the Lake Shore & Michigan Southern Railroad for Cleveland, where we arrived Sunday morning, Aug. 16th, 1856. We went direct to my sister, Mrs. Loeb, and found the family well situated and prospering. My third sister, Fanny, was engaged to a Mr. Falk Klein, and they were married the Thursday following our arrival.

I Decide to Peddle

About two weeks after I had been in Cleveland, during which I had listened to tales of prosperity from people of our acquaintance—one said, "I own two houses," another said, "I own three," and a number of others said they owned one—I became impatient and was anxious to get out and earn money for myself. My brother Kaufman was then a clerk in the City Mills Store, and wanted me to go to school, but I told him I wanted to make my own way, and I had decided to peddle. He was satisfied, and the next day I went down to see him at the City Mills Store to get some goods to sell. When I got there he said, "Now, brother Joe, don't think that these goods are mine. I must pay for whatever goods you select that you don't pay for yourself." In other words, he guaranteed my account. He sent me out to a printing office to buy a large pasteboard box covered with black oilcloth and straps, and I returned with it to the store to pack my wares. Kaufman selected my first stock, which consisted of needles, pins, buttons, tape and various other notions, and I remember distinctly that he sold me some embroidered collars, the embroidery of which was made of starch and pressed on to the fabric. At the least bending of the material the embroidery cracked off. I remember that I took along some shirt-bosoms and handkerchiefs, etc., etc. The total value of the box, full, was $23.45.

I Start Out

Next morning, bright and early, my youngest sister Yetta, who had been in America then about two years, started off with me to show me the way out Euclid Ave. We started from Loeb's store, which, as I said before, was at the corner of what is now E. 9th St. and Woodland Ave. A week before I had made a trip into the country with my brother-in-law Klein on his butcher wagon, in order to get the lay of the land. I therefore knew something of what I was to encounter. Yetta left me at about Perry Street and Euclid Ave., which is now S. 22nd St. and Euclid Ave., and I continued east, but shortly turned in toward the south and tramped out Cedar Road.

Before starting, my brother Kaufman had given me a paper upon which was written the necessary questions and answers which I needed in selling goods, getting money changed and to obtain food and lodging. I remember some of the questions to this day: Do you wish to buy anything? I will sell you cheap. Is this money good? Can I have some dinner? Can I stay over night? How much is my bill? I would approach a farm house, and with this paper in hand I would rap at the door, and when I heard someone approaching I would stick the paper in my pocket, and the confusion ensuing on the opening of the door and the appearance of a strange person caused the desired words to escape from my memory, and I was many times forced to take out my paper anew and proceed with reading my cherished questions with the slip of paper in plain sight.

About noon I arrived at a home where I found a German-speaking maid. She went in to see the lady of the house, who came out and asked if I had hunger. This last word I understood from its resemblance to the German "Hünger." She asked me in, and I partook of a meal of sweet milk, bread and butter, all of which was a treat to me at that time. I offered this kind woman some goods in exchange for the meal, but she refused any pay.

I Am Directed to Lodgings; I Continue to Peddle

I then left and went on peddling from farm house to farm house until about 4 or 5 o'clock in the afternoon, when I found myself out at the first Shaker settlement, now Shaker Heights. Here men and women were sitting outside sewing and knitting. Among them I found a German-speaking woman, who was much pleased to converse with me. I asked if I could stay over night there, but was refused. This Quaker woman told me where I could find quarters for the night. She said, "After you leave here, you walk up a piece to a bush. After you get over the bush, to your left you will see a settlement like a German village, and there you will find a tavern." After I left that place, true enough, I came to a large thorn bush, and I said to myself, "I don't see any need of walking over it so long as I can walk around it." I turned to the right as directed and soon a boy came along in an empty wagon. He had been delivering wood in the neighborhood. I asked him for a ride, and he took me aboard. He couldn't understand me, nor I him, but we drove along, and finally came to the settlement the woman had told me about. There was a house that resembled a tavern at which I had stopped with my brother-in-law Klein the week before on my first trip into the country. I went in, and was told to go back to the kitchen where the proprietress was.

I went as directed, and asked for lodging. She said something that I did not understand and motioned toward the side door, and I thought she motioned me out. I went thru that door, but came back again thru the front one.

In an adjoining room I heard conversation, and soon some men came out from their evening meal. I found a German among them, and appealed to him to prevail on the woman to let me sleep there over night. He told me he had heard her tell me to put my pack over in the corner, when I thought she motioned me out. I slept there that night and was awakened at daybreak; had a good breakfast. I paid her 50¢ for supper, lodging and breakfast, which 50¢ she took out in trade, and I continued on my way to the next farm along the road.

I Meet the Sauters

As a general thing, the foregoing was a sample of my day's experiences on my first trip out. I was gone eight days, and was invariably treated in a courteous manner. I found good places to stop at along the line without much difficulty, and I tramped out as far as the Ridge Road, or that road just before going down into Gates Mill. Here I turned north, and on Friday night I stopped at the Sauter farm. This Mr. Sauter was a prosperous farmer. He had three sons, all farmers with families, living in the neighborhood, and another son, whose name was Seth, was a bachelor and school teacher, and I was thrown in contact with him on a number of my trips. Saturday morning I started from here for home, peddling as I went, and Saturday afternoon I found myself two and a half miles west of Willoughby.

My Honesty Again Proven

One day I was directed by one of my regular customers to a farm house several miles away, where they told me a woman lived who would like to buy some of my wares. I went there and showed her what I had to sell, and she picked out quite a nice lot of merchandise. She brought out a bag full of change and proceeded to count out my pay. There being so much change, I did not count it back until I was out of doors, and then to my surprise I found that she had mistaken a five-dollar gold piece for a nickel. This was one of the first times that I was sorely tempted, as I needed the money, and the chances are that the woman would never have known what she did, but my conscience would not permit me to go on. I went back into the house and asked the woman if she knew what she had done, and I showed her the handful of change which I had, and which we then counted over in the house, and, to her astonishment she found that she had actually made a mistake, and could not find words in which to thank me for having returned the money to her.

You may be sure that I had a steady and enthusiastic patron from that time on, and she told me at a later visit that she never had dealings with peddlers, but that she surely would make an exception in my case.

My First Sunday Out

Early in the day I began to make inquiry in order to find a good place to spend Sunday, as that was my day of rest as well, because I could do no business. In the small places I did not care to stop, and the large ones, as a rule, would not keep a peddler over Sunday. Finally I got to what I considered a very nice farm; the owner's name I later learned to be Wm. Taylor, whose son Henry was a baby then, and is now connected with the Wm. Bingham Co. I found there quite an old man, almost 80 years old, also an old lady and Mrs. Taylor. Besides, there were two nieces, two very attractive girls, who I learned were school teachers, there for a visit from their home in Columbus. As I applied for accommodation, Mrs. Taylor refused, saying that they never kept peddlers. The two young ladies, however, appealed to her, and from what I could understand, as the hired man was away, that she let me occupy his room.

Being a young man, 18 years old, small in stature and exposed to the dust and sun all week, I tried my best to make Mrs. Taylor understand that I had a home and sisters and a brother prominently known in Cleveland, and as evidence of my respectability I showed them that I had a clean shirt in the bottom of my pack. The young ladies both sympathized with me so much that tears ran down their cheeks. Mrs. Taylor finally consented to have me stay.

The old man that I mentioned before asked me where I came from— Germany? Bremen? When he said Bremen, I understood all, and explained that I came from Germany, and repeated the question over and over in my mind that night before falling off to sleep.

I Learn My A, B, C's

The following day, Sunday, the young ladies took turns teaching me my A, B, C's. One of these young ladies later married a jeweler in Painesville, and the other a Mr. Tillotson, the father of E. G. Tillotson, of Cleveland. It was a welcome day, that first Sunday of rest. I enjoyed every minute of it, and the next morning was up bright and early to proceed on my way toward home.

I Finish My First Trip and Get Scolded

I went tramping toward Cleveland, turning south and peddling along Mayfield Road. Wednesday night I stopped again at Sauter's, and tramped all the way in to Euclid Ave., corner [of] Mayfield Road, within one block of where I am now living. I could not find a place to stop over night. There was a toll-gate there, and I offered the toll-keeper 50¢ if he would let me sit on a chair all night, but he refused, and I had to continue on toward home. I wanted to stay out on the following day, as I was a trifle short of the amount that I had set for myself. However, I continued on home, which was at the corner of Cross and Woodland, where I arrived some time in the evening in a half-famished condition, not having had anything to eat since early morning. When I told my brother Kaufman about it, he scolded me, and said that in America one must work hard, but one must eat.

That night after my supper I emptied my money bag on the table, and sister Yetta helped me count it. She laughed and encouraged me as she stacked the money, and said, "Du wirdst noch ein Kotzen sein" ("You will be a very rich man some day"). The next day I went down to the City Mills Store and paid what I owed, $23.45. I purchased $8.00 worth more of goods for my next trip.

I Stop Peddling and Clerk in a Store

I kept on peddling that Fall until the weather became unsettled and roads were bad. I finally concluded to get a position to clerk in a store for the Winter. I got a position as clerk in a grocery store at $4.00 a month and board, working from 5 in the morning until 10 at night, except Sunday. The clerking gave me a good opportunity to learn English, but, in addition, I went to Spencerian College a few nights a week to learn English and penmanship. Anyone knowing my handwriting today would hardly believe that I took second honors in penmanship.

I Discontinue Peddling and Take Trains from Town to Town

As soon as Spring opened up I was ready again for the road. I had decided that in place of tramping thru the country I would take a train from one village to the other, and peddle in districts only where the homes were closer together, and that I would not go further than the sidewalk ran in a village, as the sidewalk meant people, and people were what I was after. My reasoning was that houses being closer and the demands of the town residents being greater than those in the country, the little expense of railroad fares would not be an important item. In this I was correct, and I found it as easy to obtain accommodations in some one house in any village as I had found it in the country, and as I returned to these towns periodically, I soon had a regular stopping place where I was welcome to stay over night.

I Help My Brother-in-Law and Sister Rosa

After I continued a few months successfully, it happened that a former partner of my brother-in-law Loeb, who had sold out to him, was going to start a competitive grocery store two doors below the Loeb grocery, and would certainly try to take our trade away. Some of my brother-in-law's best customers advised him to get me back, as they thought I could keep the customers together, and I must confess that my feelings toward this man for attempting to undermine my brother-in-law's business were as bitter as tho the problem was my own. It did not take me long to make up my mind what to do. After I came back I inquired as to what this competitor had done, and was told that he had forced them to reduce all prices. He had said that he was going to see Loeb make an assignment. I took hold immediately and stopped the reduction of prices at once, and called in our banker and had him figure out to a penny what a loaf of bread cost us. This he did, and I decided to put every item back to the old figure except bread, and that I reduced in price. At this time flour advanced in price, but we reduced our charge for a loaf of bread, and people came to us from great distances to buy this bread, which was a standard loaf for a lesser price. The other bakers in town naturally learned of this, and threatened to burn down our place if we didn't restore the price on bread, but we went right on doing a constantly increasing business, while our competitor did not last long.

I Manage a Clothing Store

After the business was in good running condition again, I had a position offered to me in a clothing store. I was a young man then about 19 years old, and I knew from experience that the girls in the town had more use for a clerk in a clothing store than they did for a peddler, and that naturally bothered me somewhat. I had heard also that some of these clerks later started their own stores and became wealthy, and this looked very encouraging to me also.

I took a position with Mr. S. Mann, who gave me the preference over an experienced clerk because he had confidence in me. He trusted me with his books, and I was able to find out first-hand from the books that some of these clerks who supposedly had gotten rich really did not own their stores at all. I found that they owed Mr. S. Mann for practically everything, and besides, when they came to stock up their wares they had to take what Mr. Mann would give them, and some of the stuff was none too good. I made up my mind then and there that if I ever intended to start a store I would do so with my own capital, and until I had my own capital I would not start a business. At the same time I made up my mind not to stay clerking longer than three months. My time was up in the Fall, and I had told Mr. Mann that I was going to leave, but he talked me out of it, and persuaded me to remain until Spring. I told him tho that in Spring I would positively leave, and no amount of talk would dissuade me from it.

I Loan Out My First Money

Up to this time I had been able to save up $250.00, which I loaned out at a high rate of interest on a mortgage to a farmer in Independence, Ohio. This farmer needed $200.00 more, and came to me for it. I was sorry not to have the money to loan him, and my brother offered to advance the $200.00, with the understanding that I could pay him off as I earned the money. This acted as a stimulus for me to get out and hustle in order to pay my brother and get possession of that second mortgage.

Kaufman Becomes Engaged

I then began to peddle in dead earnest from town to town. This I kept up for about two years. In the meantime my brother Kaufman became engaged, and was married in, I think, 1860. He was going to New York on his honeymoon.

I Plan to Go Into Wholesale Selling

There had been a family in Cleveland by the name of Engelhart, who moved to New York and were manufacturing rubber combs and like articles, in Orange, N.J. I asked my brother to bring back with him a gross each of the various articles which these Engelharts manufactured. This he did. My object was to develop into wholesale selling, provided I could make it pay.

This was at the beginning of the war, and during the years that I had been peddling, shirt bosoms and handkerchiefs were profitable and readily salable articles. When the war broke out, all things made of cotton took a very great advance, and with it other things as well, including my linen shirt bosoms and handkerchiefs. My trade could not understand why my wares should advance, as I had told them that they were linen, which they were, and the general cry was the advance in all things cotton on account of the war in the

South. Selling became difficult, so that I was on the lookout for new fields of operation which would yield profit.

I Learn About Watch Materials as a Business

One day shortly after this, I was in Plymouth, Ohio, and toward evening a man came along with a little box hanging at his side by a strap. He told me he was selling watch material, and asked how many jewelers there were in town. I told him only one, and he threw up his hands, saying if he couldn't see that man before 9 o'clock tomorrow morning, he would have to stay in this little place until tomorrow evening. I told him not to worry; that I knew the jeweler, who was a good man, and I would go with him and introduce him to Mr. Hoffman. This I did, and told Mr. Hoffman the conditions, and he at once agreed to meet the watch material man at 7 o'clock in the morning at his place of business and see to it that he got away to catch the 9 o'clock train, which I, too, had planned to take.

The next morning I was at the station early, waiting for the train, and as the leaving time approached, I looked around for my watch material friend, who came puffing in at the last minute. We greeted one another, and after we had settled down comfortably in a seat on the train, I asked if he had done any business, to which he replied, "Yes. About $10.00 worth." "Then," said I, "I suppose you made two or three dollars." "Oh, no," said he, "more than double that." I looked at that little box and said to myself if he can make so much profit with such a little box, which, after I was loaded down with my notions, I could still find room for, I should investigate this matter when I got home.

I Ask Advice

Cleveland's leading jeweler in those days was N. E. Crittenden, and I knew a Mr. Deitz who was a watchmaker for Crittenden's. Mr. Deitz lived near and patronized Loeb's grocery store. I called on him and inquired about watch material as a business, and he told me if I could get hold of the right line there was money in it. He gave me the name of various importers in New York, which I used later. Having decided to go down to New York to make my purchases, I told brother Kaufman about it. He discouraged me from doing it, saying that I had accumulated a little money and was now about to risk it in a business about which I knew practically nothing. I told him it was true that I knew nothing about the business, but I was sure I could learn. He said, in jest, "I suppose you are going to sell Crittenden." I replied, "Yes. That would be my first account."

I Go to New York

Before starting for New York, I went to my friend and former employer, Mr. S. Mann, and got a letter of recommendation and credit to a New York concern named Stettheimer, Altman & Co. Upon arriving in New York, I started out with Mr. Engelhart to call on those jewelry importers, thinking I could get the goods on consignment. It being war-time, this proved impossible on account of the general rise in gold of which most of the watch material was made. Of the four or five concerns called on, I next day selected one to have my dealings with. I picked out a man by the name of Dinkelspeil, and put my case in his hands. I acknowledged to him that I had no experience in that business, and that he seemed to be an honorable man in good circumstances, to whom the profit he could make on the sale would not induce him to give me bad advice. I asked him if he thought I could make a success of the watch material business. He looked me all over quizzically, and with a smile he said, "I can guarantee nothing, but greater fools than you appear to have made a success of the line." That was all the encouragement I ever received. I asked him how much it would take to fit me out, and he told me anything from $200.00 to $5,000 or more. I asked him then to get up an assortment of proper quality for good jewelers, the outfit to stand me $500.00. This he did for me, and did well. I remember my buying a case to hold these supplies. It was small, but beautifully made, with trays, catches and trimmings, and cost me $16.00.

I Learn What Discount Is

After making my arrangements with Mr. Dinkelspeil, I referred him to Stettheimer, Altman & Co., to whom I had my letter of credit. He told me to come back on Friday and he would be ready for me. I returned Friday, as agreed, expecting to find everything in good shape, but he did not act just right. I asked him if he had looked up my references and what they had to say about me. He said, yes, they said they would not guarantee my account, but if Mr. Dinkelspeil would give them the discount they would pay the bill in full. This was a new one on me, as I had never heard about discount, so I asked him what that meant, and Mr. Dinkelspeil explained that there was a 6 per cent discount for cash on the $500.00, which equaled $30.00. I told him that I would pay cash and take the discount myself. I then went over to Stettheimer, Altman & Co. and asked for $500.00. They did not hesitate, but wrote out a check for that amount and handed it to me. I did not mention before that I always had moneys to my credit with Mr. S. Mann, who acted

much as my banker. I took the check back to Mr. Dinkelspeil and got my
$30.00 discount and my box of watch material.

I Make Good My Promise

I came back to Cleveland, and, true to my statement to brother Kaufman, I
sold my first bill to Crittenden's, some forty-odd dollars worth, and then called
on different jewelers, and succeeded in selling all of them something.

I Sell Wholesale

I then discontinued retail peddling, and traveled over the state of Ohio,
selling wholesale only to retail stores. I proceeded in this way for about two
or three years, and made considerable financial headway. From the time
that I began selling wholesale, I had considered going into business for myself, owing to the fact that there was only one wholesale notion business in
Cleveland, called Stilson, Leek & Price, who themselves had been wholesale
notion peddlers with wagons.

I Plan to Go Into Business

I took a liking to a young man in a New York notion house, and had
several talks with him, and thought perhaps to take him in as a partner. As
I intended to continue on the road, I needed some one to take care of the
business at home, the shipping, and ordering of stock as needed.

Kaufman Joins Me

After I had concluded to go into business, I talked the matter over with
brother Kaufman, as he was older than I and had considerable experience in
business. He said he would join us in business if that young man measured
up to my claims for him. My reply to Kaufman was that one partner was
three-quarters more than I wanted, and if he wanted to join me I would drop
the other fellow, as I had no definite arrangements with him and he talked of
making a trip to Europe to consult an uncle, who would furnish some capital. I heard nothing from this young man, so with brother Kaufman started
the firm of Hays Brothers in 1862, and continued in business until 1884. We
rented a store on Water Street, now West 9th. This store was wedge-shaped,
12 feet in the front, 17 in the rear, and 65 feet deep. It ran from Union Lane to
Water Street. It had been used previously for a retail clothing store, and we
agreed to pay $800.00 a year rent for it. The reason that I liked it was that it
would not take much merchandise to fill it full.

Beginning of Hays Brothers

We started equal partners, Kaufman and I, and both of us went to New York to buy our opening stock. This consisted of general notions, furnishing goods and watch material.

Our First Bookkeeper

When we came home we opened up our business, and I went out on the road. We did a very satisfactory business right from the start. We hired a bookkeeper, taking a young student from business college, and agreed to give him $350.00 per year. He was to make himself generally useful in the store. We then hired another young man to help out, and I brought from Milan, O., a young man by the name of Hopkinson, whose father kept a drug store down there. I had seen considerable of the druggist during my periodical visits to Milan. He was a good, honest, hard-working fellow, but unfortunately was in the clutches of tuberculosis. I thought a great deal of the son, and tried to help him get on his feet.

After I made two or three trips thru the country, I found, when I came home, we were always short of goods, so I had to go to New York again and again. We kept on for a while this way, the home end of the business being largely in the hands of the bookkeeper and the boys above mentioned, as my brother Kaufman was seriously ill with rheumatism, and continued so for a number of years.

I Am Held Up

One day the father of our bookkeeper came to me and suggested that we raise his son's wage, as he said his son was offered a job at much better pay. He well knew that I could not afford to let him go, but I did not feel right about this forced raise. This young man was practically under contract with us, and it showed pretty poor principle for him, with the backing of his father, to break an agreement, perhaps the first or second in his business career. I was forced to even up with the offer, but did so in the belief that there was a day of reckoning coming.

We Go Into the Toy Business

With the idea of going into toys for the holiday trade, I had a talk with a man from Cleveland whom I met in New York, and who had been in the retail toy business for years. I asked him if he knew of a good house where I could buy a stock of toys and where I would get proper treatment. He assured me that he would give me the name of just such a concern, Meisel, Lampy & Co., one of the best in America. I went there and saw these people. They treated me very well; in fact, they were too nice to last, but they had a beautiful lay-out, and very good to select from. I made a very careful selection there. Being perfectly green in that line, when I came home, I spread out the goods and called in some friends who had been retailing toys for years. They almost all assured me that I had nice goods, but my prices were too high. I felt consoled that the selection was good. As I had bought only $150.00 worth, I felt I was not stung very badly, and as this was only May or June, I had plenty of time to look about and get better prices elsewhere.

Being acquainted with one of the men at the head of the notion department of H. B. Claflin & Co., by the name of Jones, I one day complained to him and spoke about my little toy experience. He smiled all over and said he did not blame me, and thought we could remedy that, and recommended me to what he thought the best house in the country for toys—Althof, Bergman & Co. The other concern—Meisel, Lampy & Co.—were jobbers themselves.

I Am Over-charged 100%

I went to see Althof, Bergman & Co., and it did not take me long to find that Meisel, Lampy & Co. had over-charged me just about 100 per cent. I bought a bill of $2,000.00 from Althof, Bergman & Co., took the goods home, and our business started, and we did very well with the line and intended to lay in a bigger stock next year. We bought a great many domestic toys direct from the manufacturers, which we worked in with our imported line.

Next July and August I went down and bought from Althof, Bergman & Co. a bill between $4,000.00 and $5,000.00, and they "wined and dined me." I made up my mind that those would be the last toys I would buy in New York; that either we would go out of the toy business, or buy direct from the people the importers bought from.

I Have Experience With Thieves

One day I was in the store and two men came in. One said he wanted to look at tablecloths, which he supposed were kept in the basement, evidently having our store confused with M. & M. Halle's. We, however, kept our table-cloths in the rear of the first floor. The other fellow who came in with this supposed customer asked if he could sit in front by the stove, as it was cold out, it being along in December toward inventory time. I said, "All right."

My man did not buy very quickly, and after a while the one sitting by the stove said he was going back to the hotel, and left. I did not think there was anything they could steal, but got suspicious and worked my man toward the front of the store. I noticed at once that there were some pearl buttons under the shelf near where this one fellow had sat, and the boxes seemed empty, or nearly so. I called one of our stock clerks to count the pearl buttons, as it was stock-taking time. This made my man nervous, and as I noticed this I told one of my stock men to call a policeman, and I told this man to tell us where his hotel was, and that I would not release him until he did. The policeman arrived, and he went with us up to Eagle Ave. We found the other man when we got there, and demanded the buttons. He turned to the woman of the house and asked where she put the buttons that he brought in. She went to the back yard and returned with them. We then took both men to the police station. The one who stole the buttons was arrested and was finally sent to the work-house for thirty or sixty days. He pleaded with me to let him off, as he said he had a wife and children to support, but I told him that if my entire fortune had been where the pearl buttons were, he would not have given my wife and five children a thought, nor could I, under the circumstances, let him off. The other one we let go.

Kaufman Goes to Europe

As my brother Kaufman had been suffering from rheumatism, I suggested that he go to Europe for a cure, and while there to buy our stock of toys. This he did. It was at the time of the Franco-Prussian war, and Kaufman ordered our goods shipped by sailing vessel. They were ten weeks on the way, and I was very anxious and worried until the goods arrived in Cleveland, just in the nick of time for Christmas trade. We had a very successful season, but because we wanted our goods in time, I sent my orders to Europe in January for the following Christmas trade.

We Move to Larger Quarters

We remained in this little store five years, and then moved north on the same side of the street, to 143 Water Street. We paid a man $500.00 for his option on the store as we needed more room. The new building was 21 feet front by 165 feet deep, five stories high, with basement. When we moved in the neighbors wanted to know if we had been East already, as we moved so much merchandise from the old to the new place. They wondered if we could fill the basement and first floor of this five-story building, and Kaufman suggested that we rent out the upper three stories. I objected, and said we will first move in, and if we find we have too much room, we can then consider renting. We moved into our new quarters January 1st, 1865. We filled the new building from roof to cellar, and it wasn't long before we were pinched for additional place, and rented lofts adjoining from Alcott, Horton & Co., for woodenware. On the first floor we had notions, on the second, furnishing goods, on the third, toys, etc. The fourth and fifth floors and basement were used for storage.

A Confidence Game

One morning a tall, lean man, carrying an empty grain bag on his arm, stopped in at the store and addressed me as Mr. Hays. He said if we handled any sacks such as those, he could do a large business with us, as he claimed to be a commission merchant by the name of Clark down at Clark & Rockefeller's place at 136 River Street. As an ambitious young man, I was interested and asked if we did not have something he could use. He went thru the stock with me and selected a lot of staples, and said if I made the prices right he would continue to do business with us. This I did. He ordered the stuff to be sent to Clark & Rockefeller's place at 136 River Street, but did not say anything about paying the bill. The goods were packed up, and I made out the bill, which I receipted, and told our young man Hopkinson to hand over the receipted bill only in the event of his getting the money. In due time Hopkinson came back, having left the goods, but Mr. Clark had torn off the receipted part of the bill, which Hopkinson brought back. He also said that Mr. Clark would stop on his way past in the afternoon and pay the bill. I was busily waiting on trade, and suggested to Kaufman to go over to Adams, Jewett & Co., where Mr. Clark said he had been buying, and who were a young house like ourselves, and find out about this new concern. I then proceeded to forget all about the whole transaction.

That evening I went to the theatre at the Academy of Music, Bank Street, now West 6th, and enjoyed myself very much, but just as I was getting into bed, this whole Clark matter came back to me, and I could not sleep. It was not the $173.00 that concerned me nearly so much as the idea that a young man, supposedly up-to-date, should permit himself to be swindled. The line of talk this man Clark gave me, the conspicuous way in which he wore his heavy gold watch chain—in fact, his whole make-up and the circumstances surrounding his introduction, did not seem just right to me. At daybreak I got up and left a note at Mrs. Loeb's, where I boarded, saying that I would not be in to breakfast, and went down town. I went directly to 136 River Street, but as it was then only 4 A. M., no one was about. I then walked over to the Union Depot and spoke to my friend, Van Dusen, the depot master, about this affair. He said he knew Mr. Clark, and was quite sure he had not left town, but would look for him this morning, as all trains in all directions at that time left Cleveland in the morning. The last train out, and no Mr. Clark, so I went back to 136 River Street. One door of the store was open, and I went in. There was a porter rolling barrels, and I asked him if there was a package of goods delivered the previous evening. He said he used to work for Clark & Rockefeller, but he did not work for the people who had just moved in. He pointed up at a shelf and asked if those were my goods, and I thanked him, as they were. I then knew that I would have my money or the goods, and decided to sit down and wait for Mr. Clark's arrival.

About 8 o'clock a thin, tall fellow came in. He was the bookkeeper. I never remembered having seen him before, but he said, "Good morning, Mr. Hays. What brings you out so early? Mr. Clark and I stopped at your place last night on our way by, but the store was closed as it was late, but Mr. Clark said he would stop on his way down this morning." I said that was all right, but I would wait. Nine o'clock came, and no Mr. Clark. I had sent word up to the store where I was, and continued my wait. The young bookkeeper came to me again, saying that my time could not be very valuable to wait so long, but I told him I had plenty of time to wait, and I did, until about 10 A. M., when Mr. Clark came in all in a hurry. He said, "I had intended to stop on the way down, but it was late, and I had some things to do, so did not." However, he said he would stop on his way to lunch, so we would have our money to bank before noon. I told him I was there, and wanted either my money or my goods. He said he was too busy then, but if I felt that way about it, he was satisfied. He took the goods from the shelf, packed them in a barrel, which I had an expressman haul up to the store. When I arrived there, Kaufman wanted to know where I got my information about these people. I told him the whole thing did not look good to me after we were once in.

Well, this whole matter was a big swindle, which cost the merchants of Cleveland over $23,000.00. After Clark & Rockefeller moved out of 136 River Street, these swindlers moved in and used the name of Clark as a disguise. They would get in merchandise and ship same to confederates all over the country, and never paid a cent.

Our business prospered in our new location, and continued for a number of years. Our main business was men's furnishing goods, but finally the clothing men, our principal customers, did not want to buy furnishing goods from concerns selling notions, and this proved a great drawback to our business. The question then arose what was the best thing to do. We finally concluded to drop notions and toys and go into the gent's furnishing business exclusively.

We Move Again to Still Larger Quarters

One morning Mr. Edward Bingham came in. He owned a double store north of St. Clair Street on the east side of Water Street. He wanted us to take his store, which had been occupied by a clothing house—Adams, Goodwillie & Co. I agreed to take the store at the same rental that we were paying, which was $1,800.00 per year. He had previously received $4,500.00, but he gave us the store at our price because he wanted to chase the hoodoo from it if possible, as several concerns that had previously occupied the property had failed, and he felt that we would continue to make good. This was at 82 and 84 Water Street, now West 9th Street. We moved to this location in January, 1873, and remained there until we wound up our business in 1884.

Jos. Elsinger Comes Into the Business

About 1866 I hired two young men for the business. One was Jos. Elsinger, who was working with A. & G. Redberg, a notion house, and the other was Albert W. Hammer, who was then traveling for some concern in town. About 1870 Elsinger's salary became quite an item, and brother Kaufman thought the best thing to do was to give him an interest in the business, which we did, and changed the firm name to Hays Bros. & Co. This went along for about five years, when Elsinger left us to take a position with Morgan, Root & Co., wholesale dry goods, now Root & McBride Co.

I Get Married

January 16th, 1866, I married Rosette, eldest child of Louis Henry and Phoebe Schwarzenberg, who had been residents of Cleveland since 1849. We were engaged to be married in January, 1865, and five days later I bought the first house I ever owned, next to the corner of Huron St. and Central Place, which is now Huron Rd. and Sheriff St. In this house, which stood where the Sheriff St. Market and Storage Co. now stands, all of our children were born. Bertha, now Mrs. Chas Eisenman, was born August 17th, 1867, and was our only daughter. Four sons followed her. Hiram was born September 25th, 1869; Eugene, January 3rd, 1872; Louis, January 24th, 1874, and Clarence, February 4th, 1876. This property on Sheriff Street was 40 × 132 feet, with a house and barn on it. I paid $3,800.00 cash for it, which was quite a sum in those days, even for a property in what was then considered a desirable residence district. The house was frame, but of modern construction. It had high ceilings, and a considerable yard between the house and barn. I put in plumbing and gas. We had a good well for our water supply, as this was before the days of city water.

We Decide to Wind Up the Business

From the day I started business, I had built with the thought of its continuing forever. I had hopes that my sons would some day come into the business and continue it, and hand it on to the next generation, so I built honorably and was square in all my transactions, but as the profits grew smaller and the expense larger, I could not see a future in the business for either myself or my sons, and I made up my mind that this was no business for them to follow, and desired to discontinue it. My oldest son, Hiram, was then about of the age to take a part in the business, but having decided upon this course, we closed out our business, and the firm name of Hays Bros., which had stood for something in those days, passed out.

Political

When I came to Cleveland, Loeb's baker was a German, and in 1856 practically all Germans were Democrats, because in 1854, two years before I came to this country, the "know nothing party," which was the forerunner of the Republican party and later merged with it, was against all foreigners, and to combat this, practically all foreigners were Democrats. On account of my associations, I naturally drifted into the Democratic party.

Civil War broke out in 1861, and at that time I was peddling wholesale, and was prospering. Not yet being an American citizen, I could not be drafted, but because of the loyalty I felt, and the appreciation for the opportunities which this country offered me, I wanted to show this appreciation by sending a substitute to the front. I agreed to pay a man $600.00 for enlisting in my place. This was common practice in those days, and if you were drafted you could furnish a substitute. This I did without being drafted. In 1866 I took out my citizen papers and marriage license at the same time. I also bought my house on Miami Street, now Sheriff Street, and upon our marriage we went to live there, in what was then the old first ward.

The boss of the ward in those days was Cyrus Merchant, who was also councilman. I became active in politics.

About this time Myron T. Herrick and L. Weed came up from Wellington, Ohio, and lived in the first ward, and we three joined forces to oust Mr.

Merchant from his position. In this we succeeded. At this time they wanted me to run for councilman, but I was so tied up in my business that I could not accept.

I Go Into the Iron Business; I Retire From Active Business

After I had made up my mind to get out of the furnishing goods business, I was then about 46 years old, too young to retire, so I looked about for some business to get into. I had some friends who were in the scrap iron business, who spent more in living than I had ever been able to earn. I thought if I could only save what they wasted, it would be enough for me. About this time my brothers-in-law, Henry and Ephraim Schwarzenberg, were in the scrap iron business on Merwin Street. They had not made much progress up to this time, but wanted to move to larger and better quarters on Scranton Ave. They decided to put up a building there, and I was the financial means of their doing so. This led me into a business association with them under the name of Schwarzenberg, Hays & Co., which lasted only three years, when I went into the business for myself under the firm name of Joseph Hays & Co., which was conducted without interruption until July 1st, 1916, when I retired.

Western Lands

When I was in this country about eight months, a man came here who was handling Western lands. A number of my friends bought a section in Missouri, and I took one also. I paid $8.00 per month for eight months for this land, at the rate of about 12½¢ per acre. I had a great deal of trouble with this property, as it was sold for taxes a number of times, even tho I held the receipt from the proper authorities in my own hands, and it always cost me from $75.00 to $100.00 in lawyers' fees and expenses to regain title to the property.

I still hold this land. It is in Oregon County, one of the southern tiers of counties in Missouri. It is near the Zinc Belt, and I visited it once, in 1898, with my son Louis.

My Mother

I do not remember much about my mother, who died when I was 6 years old, but the women of our village, after I grew up, would tell me about her and how she often acted as peacemaker when they went to her with their troubles.

We all must have inherited our thrifty qualities from her, because my father never was able to make any real progress in business. He was handicapped thru having asthma in a very severe form. He did what he could to support his family, and Kaufman and I supported him in retirement from the time he landed in America in 1856 until he died of old age in 1877, in his eighty-fourth year. He lived with our sister, Mrs. Oppenheimer, on Orange Avenue, in a house which brother Kaufman owned, and in which the family lived, rent free, for many years.

Father was buried in the old Willett Street cemetery, but later his body was exhumed and transferred to Mayfield cemetery, where we erected a stone bearing his name and also bearing the name of my mother, who died in 1844 and is buried in the little Jewish cemetery in Storndorf, Germany.

Ideas of Economy

I always had fixed ideas about economy, and my late wife and partner worked and saved with me for that "rainy day." Our ambition was to get to the point where our income, outside of our business, was sufficient to support us when we grew old. It was a great comfort and satisfaction to us that we arrived at this position before her death.

We were often much concerned by the standard of living of our children, and we often sent for them and called their attention to some of our axioms: "The time to save is when you make"; "Take care of the pennies, and the dollars will take care of themselves." I came to realize, in later years, however, that there are two sides to that question, as there is to every other. Nature provides the capacity for enjoyment for the various periods of our lives. If we partake in a reasonable way, as the years go on, we will get the most out of life and living. If, however, we restrain ourselves too much, the years pass on and with them our appetite for these pleasures, and we are left with only the memory of unsatisfied desires, but with no capacity for the enjoyment of same.

To illustrate this point, during my young manhood I spent much of my time in the New York market buying merchandise for our rapidly growing business. I was passionately fond of fruit. Anyone who knew New York in those early days will recollect the stands laden with the finest fruit at almost every turn in the market. In the morning I started out bright and early, and at almost the first stand I would stop and for a few cents buy an apple, or pear, or peach, or whatever fruit was then in season. This I would eat with great relish, and then, passing these stands all day long, I would hold myself in check, saying, "No, you have had your fruit for today," when for a few cents a day I could have enjoyed the blessing of a reasonable appetite.

During the last ten years of my life I had my office on the second floor of the Sheriff Street Market & Storage Company, and as I came in and went out each day, I passed stands laden with fruit as fine as ever graced the stands in New York in the olden days. I could afford to buy a carload, but the desire to enjoy the taste of the fruit was gone with my young manhood, and I was conscious of a loss so that I was inclined to agree with the philosophy which says "Enjoy what you can while you may."

I Join the Excelsior Club

I was not a charter member of the Excelsior Club, but joined it several years after its organization.

During most of my active business career I was unalterably opposed to the playing of poker at our club, and fought it with all my might. Around me centered the opposition, and it was not until we moved into the clubhouse now occupied by the Education Alliance that I refrained from my opposition. First, because in a club of the kind that we wanted we needed all kinds of people, and secondly, because I became convinced that if men must play poker, it would be better that they played at their own club rather than to have them go thru back alleys to get into a game. I was then able to see, and I made it my business whenever at the club, to know who the players were.

One holiday afternoon I came up to the club and found a game in progress in one of the card rooms. The door was open, evidently for ventilation, but some one had put a screen in front of the table so I could not see who was playing. I was not slow in knocking the screen over, and to this day I do not know if it was put there for my benefit or not; all I know is that it was not put up again to my knowledge.

I Am Active in the Relief Society

In 1857, the Fall after I came here, we started the Hebrew Relief Association. Every member was to pay $4.00 per year. We started with 120 members, and at the annual meeting the year following, we found we only had 20 members left. I realized that we not only needed more members, but more money also. I began to solicit funds, and called on people to pay into the fund. It gave me considerable trouble, however, to get them to give. When we had 120 members and were getting from each $4.00 a year, we gave an annual ball to help the fund along. I was much opposed to this ball, as I did not believe that we should dance at the expense of the poor. I suggested that everyone give as much as they felt able, and that we discontinue having a ball. This brought in considerable more money. I continued to collect for the Association for many years, and only gave it up when my eldest son, Hiram, took my place.

I was such a persistent collector that after a while when they saw me coming they would not argue, but reached for their pocket-books.

[These last sections were not, of course, written or dictated by Joseph Hays; their authorship is uncertain.]

Death

Joseph Hays died suddenly as was his wish, Thursday afternoon, December 14th, 1916, at about 5 P.M. He never fully recovered from the loss of his dear wife and life companion. He often expressed himself as being ready, when the call should come, and he was.

During the last summer of his life he spent much time dictating his biography, and he worked almost up to the last minute on his personal books. He intended to spend the winter in Miami, Fla., as he had done the previous year, and had made reservation for his companion, Miss Diederick, and himself for January 6th, 1917. At his death we found that he had completed his inventory for January 1st, 1917. He had worked at his desk so that he would have everything up to the handle before he left for the south.

Wife Dies

Fortunately for him, his death was sudden and painless as he was dead before he fell, just opposite his home which he loved so well. He had made a compact with his late wife that whichever one buried the other, the house was to be kept up to the end. At the time of this agreement, little did they suspect that it would be the dear wife who would go first. She died almost as suddenly as he. May 1st, 1914, Rosetta Hays had a stroke of paralysis, and lived only forty-eight hours thereafter. She, too, felt that her life was complete, and was satisfied to go, dying May 3rd, 1914.

I Make My Last Will

If one can conceive of taking pleasure in the making of a will, it was so in the case of Joseph Hays, for several months prior to his death he kept adding clauses and increasing the amounts of his gifts, until finally he had given away considerably in excess of the tithe mentioned in the Bible.

Both parents had often spoken about what should be done in the future when the time for dividing the estate came. Both agreed, and with them all the children, that the one who needed the most should receive the greater share of the estate. While the eldest son had been far from unsuccessful, he had not, up to the time of the making of the last will of Joseph Hays, attained the degree of success of the other members of the immediate family, and received only his due as all had been brought up to see it.

One View of Death

To show that there was little that Joseph Hays did not think about, in his desk after his death we found a clipping which he had signed, and which read as follows:

"When I die I hope my children will wear as little black for mourning as possible. White and mauve I like, but not black, and I hope they will not shut themselves up, but go out among their friends and to places of amusement. I am not afraid of them forgetting me, but I want them to be happy." (Signed) Joseph Hays.

Excerpt from *Smoke Dreams*

Jewish entrepreneurship was a significant factor in the growth of many American communities, including Cleveland. Julius Caesar "J. C." Newman was one adventuresome immigrant who contributed to that heritage.

When Newman, at age fourteen, arrived in Cleveland from Hungary with his mother in about 1890, she paid $3.00 a month to apprentice him to a cigar maker. He became a journeyman at the end of his apprenticeship, fully expecting to earn his living in the cigar industry. A recession three years later, however, ended his employment. Driven by what he understood to be the American dream, Newman began his own cigar company in a barn behind the family home. He was employing seventy-five workers five years later. By 1916, J. C. had factories in Marion and Lorain, Ohio.

The J. C. Newman Cigar Company merged with the only other remaining cigar maker in Cleveland, the Grover Mendelsohn Company, in 1927. J. C. purchased the Mendelsohn shares in 1938 to become sole owner. With his encouragement, the Newman family moved the business to Tampa, Florida, in 1954. As J. C. had predicted, the company successfully retrained the local cigar workers, transitioning from hand rolling to the use of machinery. The company currently employs seven hundred workers.

This selection from Newman's book encompasses a number of topics, including his own immigration experience and his rise in the cigar industry. The latter topic provides details on the production and marketing of cigars in the 1890s and early 1900s, with several vignettes relating to the neighborhood bars and stores that served as outlets for this quintessentially masculine product.

Source: Julius C. Newman, *Smoke Dreams: An Autobiography by a True Pioneer in the Cigar Industry* (Tampa: Florida Grower Press, 1957).

FIFTEEN DAYS OF HERRING . . . THEN AMERICA

I was born in May of 1875 in Koronch, Austria-Hungary, a small village consisting of about twenty peasant families, located between the two towns of Rusko and Terebash. My earliest recollection of life in this suburb was the small parcel of ground upon which stood an imposing brick house, the only brick house in the village. This was not only our home, but also the village tavern. It was surrounded by a few acres of land and about fifty acres of woods. We raised chickens, ducks and geese on the land and grazed several cows over its pasture. We grew our own vegetables and most of our food supplies. My mother, also, was born and raised in this same house, her father being the original tavern keeper.

This entire suburb was owned by one Count Andrashy, the Prime Minister of Hungary, who lived in Budapest. Rusko, a town of about one hundred families, was about a half an hour's walk to the west of our village. The other town, Terebash, where I attended school, consisted of about one thousand families. Here, also, was the palace of Count Andrashy and Countess Katherine, his wife.

The Countess's birthday was celebrated each January, when all the school children marched to the palace to sing the National Anthem, "God Bless All Hungarians," in her honor. We would stand and shiver in the cold while the Countess came out on the veranda to acknowledge the serenade, smoking a long black cigar and bestowing a small gift to each child. This occasion I celebrated all through the primary grades.

At fourteen, I graduated. Just a year before I completed the graduation, my father left for the United States, a long and tedious journey, to join my three older brothers, who had already settled in Cleveland, Ohio. A year later, a brother near my age, my two younger sisters, my mother and I bade farewell to the family home and also launched forth on the adventurous trip to America.

How well I recall the week of waiting for the ship's sailing from Bremen, Germany. The October voyage in 1889 was long and stormy, with our family going steerage. A 15-day diet of herring on the trip left a memory that prevented me from eating it again for many years. And, oh, that rock and roll of the ship!

We landed at Baltimore, and when I got off the boat, I was impressed by the slenderness of the people and their fine clothing. Early Saturday evening, we left by train for Cleveland, sitting up all night, but made happy by the purchase of sweet rolls and bananas, neither of which I had ever seen before.

MY FIRST PAY, MINUS $20 TO LEARN THE BUSINESS

To us Cleveland was a bewildering, big city, and this was to be our home. We were met by many relatives, who gazed at us with great curiosity. Our first home was small—very small. Crowded together within its walls and longing for our old peasant friends, the familiar smell of woods and country, we were an unhappy group. When we could stand it no longer, a family council was held. It was decided to pool whatever money we had and buy a home on a large lot, which also supported, of all wonderful things—a barn!

My next plan was to get a job. However, I couldn't speak the language, had no training of any kind and was not acquainted with the ways of the new land. But, I had to have employment, so out I went seeking work. I soon learned to recognize the sign, "Help Wanted," and wherever I saw it, I went hopefully in. Finally, my brothers made arrangements with a buckeye cigar shop employing eight people. By paying the sum of twenty dollars, I could work four months for the privilege of learning the business, receiving no salary. I found that my main job was hauling in buckets of coal to keep the place warm and going out for beer for the cigar makers, but in the meantime, I learned my trade. I considered myself fortunate that at fourteen my career in life was already launched.

Finally, the four months of apprenticeship were completed, and I thought that I was a finished product. I was paid now on a piece work basis and earned $3.60 the first week. This sum I turned over to my mother, who generously returned a quarter for my personal expenses. Once a week I allowed myself the luxury of an ice cream soda, priced at 5¢, at a place where they gave two scoops of ice cream.

• • •

The first week following my arrival in Cleveland, I enrolled in a night school, which, to my great surprise, employed a woman teacher. I never dreamed that a woman could teach school, but my respect for her grew as she applied the wonders of teaching to my education. I continued to attend school for several years, while at the same time continuing my work as a cigar maker. I was with a new company now and was earning from six to eight dollars per week. Still, I was not content with the cigar business as my life's work.

By the time I was seventeen, I decided to make a move. I discussed the possibility of employment in New York with one of my friends and co-workers, also seventeen. We had little money, just enough for our fares, but, luckily, I got a job the second day I was there, also in a cigar factory. I worked there only two months, since my parents wrote me long letters which were filled with grief over my absence. So, I returned home to my old job.

I continued working until the early part of 1894, at which time William Jennings Bryan took the country by storm with his famous "16 to 1" speech. It presented a plan by which one gold dollar would be converted to sixteen silver dollars. Few people understood the plan of changing the country from a gold to a silver standard, but many newspapers picked up the cry and advocated Bryan's nomination for president.

FROM HOME CIGAR PRODUCTION TO MY FIRST FACTORY

The economic crisis of 1895 resulted in a financial panic. The factories gradually closed, throwing thousands of workers out of employment, including me. Jobs were impossible to get, money scarce. Realizing that I must contribute my share to the support of my family, I decided to make my own cigar table out of some old boards and to turn the family barn into a one-man factory.

I had to get orders first, as I had no capital; so I went to the neighborhood saloon, explaining that I was about to launch into the cigar manufacturing business. I asked for and received an order for the colossal amount of 500 cigars. The family grocer then gave me an order for 500 cigars, and with a few more successful prospects on my list, I had total orders for about 2,500 cigars. I figured that this would require about $50.00 worth of tobacco, and, since my total capitalization was $65.00, I was in business.

I paid my three-cent carfare to West Ninth Street, and there I bought two bundles of tobacco from a tobacco jobber. I carried it by the same means of transportation to my barn factory.

I decided at this time to invest $15.00 of my total wealth in a savings account at the Society for Savings bank, which at that time paid a handsome 6% interest. I now felt that I had a back-log and would never be completely broke. Some fifty years later, the bank called to inform me that my original $15.00 deposit had compounded itself to over $250.00 and wanted to know what to do with my savings. I had completely forgotten, but decided that my money was in safe hands and left it where it was as a security fund.

Work involved in making my opening production of 2,500 cigars would take about two weeks. I cased the tobacco, stripped and dried the filler, and after about four days' preparation, I began to manufacture. Neatly boxed, my first order was proudly delivered exactly one week after I opened business. Luckily, cash was paid on delivery.

Whoever came to visit our house was invited to help strip tobacco in the barn. Finally, I was ready for more production. I canvassed the city and found a wholesale grocery house named William Edwards Company who gave me an unbelievable order for 10,000 cigars. I nearly fell over! I explained to the company that I would prefer to deliver the orders in lots of 2,500, and I was informed that this arrangement would be satisfactory. Was I happy!

I immediately engaged another cigar maker and with his help made another table. It took us about three weeks to complete delivery. Payment had been received for each lot of 2,500 as they were delivered. I was always grateful to this company, which remained my customer for 55 years, until it went out of business. John D. Rockefeller was one of its bookkeepers at one time.

I was still single, so there was no one to object to my working from 60 to 70 hours per week. While making my rounds in the evenings, I became acquainted with some precinct and ward politicians, and I gradually learned a little bit about politics.

It was a problem to sell enough cigars to keep me and the other cigar maker busy. Soon another difficulty developed. The barn was unheated, and it was impossible to work there in the winter. So, I moved into the house and stored the tobacco in the basement, where the family canned goods was [sic] also stored. This turned out to be rather impractical since my mother discovered that her home-made canned goods and jellies were acquiring a strong tobacco flavor. The family was disconcerted and decided that I must move out or stop manufacturing cigars in the house.

Thus, my next stage of growth was rather automatically determined. I rented a store in a new building for $20.00 per month and moved in. By this time, I had about five cigar makers working for me.

After about a year, my landlord gave me notice to move, as the tenants in the apartments above complained that they, too, were being saturated with tobacco perfume. I appealed my case to the realty company officials who had rented the store to me and told them I wouldn't move. They asked me why, and I answered that, according to contemporary law, since I had occupied the store for more than a year, my lease automatically renewed itself. They were quite surprised to find that I was familiar with realty law. We finally reached a compromise; I would not have to move if I kept the tobacco stems under cover. So, I stayed two more years, until I again needed more space. I then moved to larger quarters consisting of a retail store, factory space in the rear and one floor above.

• • •

In 1898, the Spanish-American War was declared. I was a great admirer of Teddy Roosevelt, so I wrote to Washington to offer my services to the Roosevelt Rough Riders. I advertised my store for sale, but by the time a deal had been consummated, the war was over. So was my retail cigar business. My thought had been to continue the manufacturing business while the war lasted, as we all thought it wouldn't last too long.

I then moved into a new factory building on West Ninth, where I had room enough for from 75 to 100 workers. In the meantime, I had to work harder than ever to keep the factory in production. I would spend every afternoon visiting saloons trying to obtain orders, saloons being large retailers of cigars in those days. I spent two or three nights a week collecting accounts; the other nights I devoted to school and to a correspondence course, in which I had enrolled with enthusiasm.

About the time I moved from the home production factory into the store, I engaged my first salesman, a man about my age. I found him to be a sincere fellow, so I proposed that he begin work at 7:00 A.M., wrap his own orders, make out the delivery book for the cartage company, copy the orders in the journal and do other clerical work. His official multiple title was Clerk-Bookkeeper and Salesman; his salary, $18.00 per week. He worked for me for two years, after which time he left to accept a job selling candy and tobacco for another firm for $22.00 a week. I could not compete with this vast sum!

In 1902, as business gradually increased, I advertised for a combination bookkeeper and stenographer. Among the many applicants was a young woman of about twenty, from Zanesville, Ohio, named Katherine White. She told me that she had been a school teacher for two years. She was single and thought life would be more attractive in a big city. I hired her at the rate of $10.00 per week and told her I would give her a raise in two-weeks time, if she could do the work and liked her job. Two weeks passed and I made her manager of the office, as well as financial secretary—really the boss. If anyone wanted money, including me, they had to get her official sanction.

Miss White was a red-haired, Scotch-Irish, straight-laced woman, and she carried a gun for protection when she took our funds to the bank. The longer she stayed, the more efficient she became, and she soon took over many of my problems and worries. I sometimes wondered which one of us was really the boss, since I always had to report to her. She stayed with our firm for fifteen years, a faithful and trusted person who did much to further our progress. To this day, I owe much of our success to her pioneer effort and ability.

• • •

The first brand of cigars I manufactured, I named "A-B-C." The label was plain and showed a streetcar bearing the names Akron, Bedford and Cleveland, Akron and Bedford being neighboring suburbs of Cleveland. This was really the ABC of our business, our first recognized brand of cigars.

About three years later, we introduced a brand called "Dr. Nichol." A photograph of a dignified, white-bearded doctor appeared on the label, and the caption, "One after each meal, or oftener, if desired," was signed "A. Nichol, M.D." The name, Dr. Nichol, became identified with our company, and soon I was nick-named Dr. Nichol. Many of our business friends came to the factory, asking for Dr. Nichol, and expecting to find a man with a white beard.

The new cigar contained a combination of domestic and imported tobaccos. The wrapper was imported Sumatra, which grew in the East Indies, then controlled by Holland. This cigar was fine, light and "good burning."

Five cents was the popular price for a cigar, a loaf of bread, a quart of milk or a bottle of beer with a free lunch and a floor show thrown in. Those are often called "the good old days."

Our operations continued for a few years, and then the tariff on the Sumatra wrapper jumped from 50¢ to $1.85 per pound. This cut out most of the profit on a 5¢ cigar, bringing about another problem. During the Spanish-American War, it was impossible for the cigar factories to obtain Havana wrappers, which were used on the higher priced, 10 and 15¢ cigars. So, a wrapper grown in Connecticut called Connecticut Broadleaf was substituted. Only the tip of this large leaf was used as a substitute for the Havana wrapper, the balance being used as a binder. This made a fine tasting and fine burning cigar.

I began experimenting by using the whole leaf, cutting it into three wrappers to cover three cigars. Out of this I made a new 5¢ cigar, which I called "Judge Wright." The cigar label bore a picture of an astute judge with the small imprint, "Judge Wright is always right." Incidentally, this cigar showed more of a profit than did the Dr. Nichol, so I began to promote the sale of both.

To my surprise, the Judge Wright took such a lead that we put our best efforts behind it. As a result, we couldn't supply the demand; it had become Cleveland's leading 5¢ cigar. Many manufacturers tried to copy us, but I held the edge, since I already had the knowledge of processing this type of tobacco.

I found that we had now outgrown our factory and that there was not enough labor in Cleveland to make our new product, so we opened a small factory in Lorain, Ohio, a town not far from Cleveland.

Up to that time, there were many factories in Cleveland, and in spite of the shortage of workers and demands from other plants, we had always been able to round up a sufficient number of cigar workers for our needs. One evening the superintendent of one of the large cigar companies with a branch in Cleveland came to see me at my home. He inquired how it was possible for a small company to pay its superintendent more money than his company, which had millions of dollars worth of capital. I explained to him that my key employees were viewed as associates and that, since I had no partners, it was my wish that they share proportionately in the progress which we were making.

In one way I was fortunate, for most of the men whom I selected as prospective department managers proved to be sincere and able to accept responsibility. This may have been due to the fact that I began my cigar making career at about the age of fourteen, carried my dinner pail like all other laborers and was well aware of what constituted a day's work. I was about nineteen when I started my own little business, and when I began hiring help, I could always see the point of view of the employee, as well as that of the employer. This fact set the pattern of friendliness with my organization that I have followed throughout my business life. I was also fortunate to secure good supervisors, one of whom was later made superintendent. Most of them were connected with us for many years. One man was with us for over forty years, until his death.

This policy with employees has worked out well to our mutual advantage. Once a year, the firm gave a party for our employees. The executives participated, and all were called the Newman Family.

• • •

At the beginning of the First World War, many strange things happened. Most commodities, such as potatoes, disappeared from the market. President Wilson appealed to all citizens who owned any land, even if only a back or front lawn, to plant, as war gardens. Food was badly needed. Everyone carried food cards to meet this emergency.

I leased a sixty-acre farm not far from Cleveland and made arrangements with the government to supply one hundred bushels of seed potatoes for the purpose of establishing a war garden for our two hundred employees. I secured a tenant farmer and his family to help supervise the farm and to look after the two cows, one Holstein and one Jersey, the horse and the farm equipment. The cows were to supply milk for the wives and children of our employees who had been called to the service. It proved to be an expensive experiment, but I was glad to do this as a security measure. Anyone who wanted potatoes was given ground, free seed and the opportunity to plant a crop. Many availed themselves, but half of the employees were not interested.

The food shortage lasted all during the war, but when the war ended and normalcy was restored, food was plentiful again. Food cards were recalled. We no longer had need for the farm experiment. It proved to be too expensive a luxury for me to be a gentleman farmer.

During World War I, my thoughts returned to my birthplace and the plight of European refugees. I signed affidavits for a family and accepted the responsibility for bringing them to this country and guaranteeing their support.

During World War II, I brought three families to America. They all became citizens of this country and are now well established here.

• • •

One peculiar incident of my early days in the business stands out in my memory. I went into a saloon run by an Irishman, "Little Patsy Riley." His friends in Irishtown looked upon him as a super man and what he said, went. There were a number of rough looking sailors in his place one day, when I was showing him my samples of cigars, and they thought they would have some fun with me. I heard one of them say, "Let's stand him on his head!" So, I stepped bravely up and said, "Come on, boys, let's all have a drink." They looked at me with amazement, but they all accepted a drink of whiskey and a big beer for a chaser.

My profits for a month were gone, but Riley seemed to think that I was a good sport. He said, "I'll give you an order for 1,000 ten cent cigars, and when you deliver them, you'll get the cash." That called for another round for the sailors, who wanted to know when I was coming back. I told them I would be back on Monday, and they were waiting, this time with friendly, smiling faces. They were all interested in how I was getting along and how business was. In the meantime, they all gathered at the bar and helped hoist the bundle of cigars to hand to Mr. Riley. Nothing was too much for them. I, in turn, bought the whiskies and beer washes. This was a new thing for me.

After a couple of rounds, several of the men offered to accompany me. They were well acquainted with many good saloon keepers, so I took along a couple of sponsors to introduce me to the higher-ups in the field. Every introduction was accompanied by a round of drinks. I found that, in spite of their becoming good friends, this was too costly a proposition. It cost me more than the total profits, so I had to change my course and call on wholesalers, drug and cigar stores.

From that time, I began to make greater progress, and when I was twenty-eight, I had the largest cigar factory in the city of Cleveland.

HOWARD W. BRODY (1916-)

"The Life and Times of a Jewish Farm Boy"

Howard Brody's father, Morris, emigrated from Lvov, Russia, to escape re-cruitment into the czar's army, going first to Buffalo, New York, and thence to Cleveland. There, he met and married Anna Goldman, who had immigrated with her family from Austria-Hungary. Encouraged by the Jewish Agricultural Society, the Brody family moved to a fruit farm in Geneva, Ohio, in 1924.

Brody's memoir is a compelling window on the world of the 1920s and 1930s when the Jewish farming movement tried to get Jews to "return" to the land. Brody's family learned farming on the job, struggling to maintain a cohesive life even though Morris Brody commuted to Cleveland to augment their income. The harsh life did not interfere with the family's commitment to Judaism, shared with the other families in the farming settlement.

Source: Howard W. Brody, "The Life and Times of a Jewish Farm Boy," Geneva Jewish Farmers Reunion Records, 1990–1992, Western Reserve Historical Society.

PROLOGUE

You had to be there. To appreciate what my generation of boys and girls— especially farm boys and girls—have lived through, you had to be there, then and now. From buggy or sleigh transportation on unimproved roads to 550 air-conditioned miles per hour at 35,000 feet; from ground-return telephone and day-old newspapers to satellite communications; from pencil and paper to word processors; two world wars and a world-wide depression. Never in the history of human endeavor has change, some for the better and some not, occurred at such a rate, and an increasing rate, at that.

You have to sit down to a multi-course dinner with a selection of wines and remember your mother shooing away a bevy of hungry cats, muttering, "Go away, cats, I don't have enough for my kids." You have to remember a burning home at night and only the pajamas on your back the next morning, when you stand before a long closet rod hung with suits, and the slacks and shirts on another rod in another closet. You have to catch a horse, and harness it and hitch it to a buggy if you want to go somewhere, and you have to turn the ignition key in a luxury car, to know where we have come from. I do not know if I would want my children and/or my grandchildren to live through those experiences, but somehow I believe my generation appreciates what we have now more than they do.

THE BEGINNING

If Morris and Anna Brody were alive today, we would be preparing to celebrate their 100th birthdays. In fact, Morris' eldest sister, Ethel, has just gone to her reward at 100. If her longevity has been bestowed upon this nephew, I may live long enough to put on paper everything that I think needs to be recorded. If no-one but my children and grandchildren ever read this, I hope at least it will give them a sense of their own history and heritage.

When John F. Kennedy was being briefed on the destructive capacity of the world's armies and armaments, he muttered, "And we call ourselves human beings." The truth is that a good portion of the world's civilized people find themselves living in places they or their ancestors fled to because of religious, economic, or political persecution. So if the Czar had been less enthusiastic about recruiting young men for his armies, and young Morris Brody and his peers less unwilling to serve, there might have been no concentration of Jewish farmers around Geneva, Ohio, and I would not be writing this. More accurately, I would not be.

The record is not clear on how he made his way out of Lvov and to Buffalo, N.Y. It must have been a much more desperate solo dash for that teenager than for Anna Goldman, who traveled from Austria-Hungary with her parents and siblings in a more deliberate, organized pilgrimage.

They met and married in Cleveland, Ohio, and he settled down at a bench in a ladies' garment factory, hoping to live and raise a family in peace. He fled the Czar's military only to be called by Uncle Sam, but I was born in 1916, and he was classified 4A (I still have his draft card, and mine) so he was not a soldier in World War I.

By the time he was in his early thirties he was suffering from ulcers, and the family doctor (dear old Dr. Levenberg, I can still picture him the better part of seventy years later) had no cure. In those days if a city dweller had something incurable the fashion was to send him "to the country," to a healthier environment. Already the Medical Profession was beginning to be aware of urban pollution, but the only remedy available was to flee the city, and flee he did.

In those days an organization called The Jewish Agricultural Society was trying, especially via low interest loans, to help Jews "return to the land." For Morris and Anna, it was not a return; aside from backyard poultry in Austria-Hungary, it is doubtful if either of them had ever been on a farm, much less worked on one in their lives.

In 1923 Morris' mother Freda and I spent two weeks as boarders on the "Atkin Farm" south of Geneva, Ohio, and over the years I have often wondered what connection that might have had with our family moving to a fruit farm close by in February, 1924. I never found out.

Morris could probably not have picked a less propitious time of the year to move. February 4, 1924 was what February usually is in Northeastern Ohio, and I have a brilliantly clear recollection of standing at a window with "Mom" and "Daddy" looking out over that snow covered landscape, at the nearest neighbor's house, a quarter of a mile away. "Their name is Brrrick-holder," I remember him saying, and in my seven-year-old mind there was, and remains, a vision of a man carrying bricks. It was a long time before I learned that the name was Burkholder, and two of the Burkholder brothers (there were four) were to become Morris Brody's best friends and closest associates of all the "Gentiles" in the area.

One of the Burkholder brothers, bachelor Norman, was the strongest man I ever knew. I once watched him lay on his back with his feet against the spokes of the rear wheel of a Fordson tractor and raise it off the ground.

Thus began thirty years of terribly hard work, some eventual gratification, and a life that would make an indelible stamp on all of us. He knew absolutely nothing about farming, or fruit growing, but that unfamiliar ground for him paled by comparison to what faced his wife—mother of three, the youngest not yet a year old.

The creature comforts she had known all her life were utterly lacking. There was no running water. There wasn't even a source of water in the kitchen. There was no electricity. The nearest thing to "Household Appliances" as we know them was a wood-burning stove. There was no central heating. There was no paved road. There was no automobile. The nearest store of any kind was six horse-drawn miles away, when the road was open. Her parents and siblings were 50 (read that a million) miles away in Cleveland, accessible only via an eight-party ground-return telephone system—the umbilical cord that tied her to civilization. We did have regular mail service. I doubt if she had ever built a fire or pumped water or lit a kerosene lamp in her life. In the face of this, dear reader, know that she kept four sets of dishes and tableware—one "Milchedik" and one "Fleischedik," both sets duplicated for Passover.

(I have just read what I just wrote. Sitting here in an air-conditioned study in the sub-tropics, more than sixty-six years later, surrounded by creature comforts she could not have dreamed of in 1924, I am struck, as never before, by the enormity of what she faced.

And her situation was not that unique; too many farm family wives in those times shared her lot, although I suppose compared to the mothers that took their families west in covered wagons, they had it easy.)

The original farmstead that we occupied consisted of roughly a semi-circle of thirteen buildings, all of wooden construction. At one end stood a huge two-story barn, made of rough-hewn foot-square timber, with not a piece of metal of any kind in the frame. Some said the frame had been erected in 1813, and from what I have been able to learn of the history of the Connecticut Western Reserve, that could have been true. On Friday evening, August 10, 1928, two days after my twelfth birthday, lightning struck that building, and in less than an hour it was gone. The only animal inside was my pet Beagle, Nellie, and I found the buckle from her collar when the ashes had cooled. The frame had collapsed, but inside those huge timbers the wood was intact.

The emergency ring on the party line telephone roused the neighborhood, and heroic efforts saved the other buildings. Little did we know.

That building had just been replaced when "Daddy," while gassing up his truck to take the first load of grapes to market on October 8, somehow ignited the fuel supply with his kerosene lantern, and the entire semi-circle, except for the new barn, was wiped out. Morris Brody, however, was not.

On the morning of October 9, 1928, there he was. A family of five without a home, a few sticks of rescued furniture and almost no clothes, an apple and grape crop ready to be harvested, all his equipment except the truck gone, the only building a 20 × 40 foot barn, already home to several horses and cows, and winter a month away. One of his sisters told me years later "That was the only time I ever saw the man cry."

I can't fathom what he, and she, must have gone through. I was there, but only twelve years old, and maybe my mind just refuses to remember how tough it was. He was a volatile, emotional man; how would you like to have been on the scene when his distraught wife, living with her mother and nursing a five-year-old son through a bout of influenza that nearly killed him, accidentally burned, mixed up with other trash, an insurance check for $7,000.00?

I look back, and try to appreciate the strength of character, the dedication, the love, the sheer determination that pulled them through. I don't know if I can.

He had learned to read and write English at "Night School" in Cleveland before moving to the farm, and he put that skill to immediate practical use. He read voraciously, devouring publications from the Agricultural Extension Services, the Cleveland Plain Dealer, the Ohio Farmer, the American Fruit Grower, and last but not least, the Jewish Farmer.

That unique publication, $2.00 for three years, was printed in English from the front, and in Yiddish from the back, and was in circulation monthly from 1908 to 1939. Due primarily to the efforts of a man named Miller, who was a Field Agent for the Jewish Agricultural Society, every issue is bound and preserved in the Library of Congress, in Washington, D.C. I think it was printed in New York City, and its advertising was strongly oriented toward Connecticut, New York, and New Jersey, but its editorial content, and the "technical" writing ("Tzu Plantzen a Veingarten," in the Yiddish alphabet) had national appeal. I have had some enjoyable times in that Reading Room, with those publications.

THE SCHOOLS

The only recollection that I have of school in Cleveland, Ohio, is of one of my mother's sisters walking me to Hazeldell School kindergarden [sic], but the four-room rural school building in South Harpersfield (Cork) Township made a lasting impression. It's still there, and has been enlarged. This was a typical rural school building in those days, and as a matter of fact it was only shortly before we arrived that the community "graduated" out of a one-room facility. There were four teachers, and each one handled two grades; the 7–8th grade teacher was Principal.

Having "skipped" a half-grade at Miles Standish Elementary on Parkgate Avenue in Cleveland, I had just finished Grade 2 at mid-year when we moved, and at Anna Brody's insistence, I was enrolled in the third grade at Cork. In order to complete Grade 3 in the remaining 12 weeks (rural schools let out very early in the year), I had to learn the "Multiplication Tables," from 1×1 to 12×12. She saw to it that I did.

School was 2 miles from home, via horse-drawn wagon or sleigh or Model T Ford "Kid Hack," and in very cold weather the girls (never the boys) carried hot bricks or flat-irons in their laps to keep their hands warm. We all carried our lunch, usually in a tin lunch box with a thermos bottle in the lid, except for the rare times when the PTA would come to the school basement and prepare a hot meal. To this day the sight of a scoop of mashed potatoes drowning in brown gravy puts me right back at my desk in that classroom.

I have always been a stickler for proper grammar, spelling, and sentence structure, and I am sure that the teachers I had in those impressionable years are responsible. They were all women and most of them I loved. One of the meanest women I can ever recall was my Grade 5 teacher, followed by—Oh, joy! Pearl Cutshall, who I adored from afar for two years. I know I worked to excel because it would please her; a smile or a pat on the back or cheek (!) from her was an angel's caress. That's how it was—Miss Delameter in High School French, Miss Fisher in Music, Miss Philips in Physics, how well I remember their faces and voices after all these years! They were young, and eager, and wonderful, and the only academic qualification they had was two years of "Normal School." The love I had for those young women, and the love of learning they instilled in me are in me still. They were all in my heart and mind, a half-century later, when I served as President of the Cleveland Hill School Board in Buffalo, New York, and when I negotiated labor contracts with the teachers of my own children.

There weren't many Jewish children in those schools; there were three of us in a High School graduating class of forty-two. And while I never knew of anything overt, Anti-semitism was always there, and we felt it.

(I still get a knot in my stomach when I recall walking along a country road, a frightened ten-year old boy with an eight-year old sister, and seeing the huge white letters, K K K, painted on the red brick road, with an arrow pointing in the direction we were walking.)

The fact that we Jewish farm children were among the better students, with higher aspirations, didn't do much to increase our popularity. We were rarely, if ever, part of the "In" group. We were farm kids at a mixed urban-rural High

School, and we had to take the School Bus home after school because it was too far to walk and we had to get home to "do chores," so we found it very difficult to take part in after-school activities, including athletics. The Kauvar family lived in Geneva with their three sons, but otherwise every Jewish student that I can recall lived on a farm.

And we kept reminding the other students—and teachers—of the difference by taking off from school on Jewish Holidays and having Matzohs in our lunch boxes during Passover. I managed, anyhow, to be Treasurer of my class, take part in several school drama presentations, win second place in a model plane endurance (flying) contest, and graduate with the highest boy's average in my class. Top honors were won by a girl!

Brother Stanley and I went on to Ohio State University, but there wasn't enough money to send three children to College, so sister Shirley went to work in Cleveland. I am not even sure there was enough money to send two; it wasn't until a long time later that I learned that when "Daddy" would press a dollar or two in my hands as I got on the "Big Four" train for Columbus that he kept less than that in his own pocket.

ON BEING A BOY ON A FARM

In the 1920's, -30's, and -40's, in the days of the family farm as my generation knew it, growing up on a farm was a totally different life than that enjoyed by our city cousins. Living on a farm meant swimming in the nude, (on horseback!), tinkering with machinery, hunting, sledding behind a dog and skiing behind a horse, exploring in the woods, watching the change of seasons, migrating birds, baby animals being born, caring for animals, and working with horses. And hard work. When I was in High School I could start to run in the morning and run all day; when I was inducted into the Army at age 25 the most strenuous exercises they could turn up did not increase my pulse by a measurable amount.

As a young man I took part in a joint effort by men, machines, horses, and dynamite in a land-clearing project, from six acres of virgin forest to an actual field of corn. Stanley, then a small boy, witnessed the proceedings from a safe distance, but the whole effort made a deep impression on him, showing what could be accomplished with sufficient sweat and determination. He reminded me just recently how absorbed he was by watching me from a sick-bed as I plowed the whole piece. He would watch me follow the two-horse plow over a hill and out of sight, and after a time would see the horse's heads coming back over the hill. Each round trip made the plowed area a little wider, and after five days the job was finished. It wasn't until 1990 that I was aware that he had even been watching, and only then did I learn how he had learned a lesson by observing.

Horses remained important on those farms, even as tractors began to make their appearance, partly because change is hard to accept, and partly because you didn't have to put kerosene into a horse! On the other hand, you couldn't stop a tractor by yelling "WHOA!," although some reportedly tried. I think I loved horses even more than dogs; if I were to have one or the other now, I know which it would be.

The ubiquitous all-steel Fordson tractor was so powerful and so poorly designed that, given a too-heavy load to pull, it would rear up and over backwards, frequently with serious consequences to the driver. Fenders over the rear wheels helped, but all that was needed to correct the problem was a longer hitch; apparently nobody realized that, and the noisy steel contraptions were disappearing rapidly by the late '30's. In August, 1988, I encountered one of the old beasts in a lumber camp on Vancouver Island, British Columbia. It was like meeting someone from the past.

Someone owed Morris Brody $10.00, and in lieu of cash gave him a tired old Model-T Ford truck of 1926 vintage, and that vehicle became our steed, toy, teacher, work-horse, and hobby. Brother Stanley and I furthered our understanding of things mechanical keeping that contraption running. With a flat bed it hauled fruit in from vineyard and orchard, with one rear wheel jacked up and a belt around the tire it drove a saw to cut firewood, stripped down to the bare chassis and gas tank (seat) it took us to the swimming hole in the summer and pulled us on skis in the winter. One front wheel was larger than the other, and the front end had a permanent list to starboard. There was NEVER a time, day or night, summer or winter, that that truck failed to start and run. We also had a '31 Chevrolet pick-up truck, but it never occupied the place in our hearts that the "Model-T" did. I even wrote an "Epic Poem" about it that started out—

"Three leagues south of Erie's breakers,
Ten times ten and eighteen acres
Rise up high on a bluff above the brown Grand River's shore,
In the center stands a building,

Low tile walls and green roof shielding
From the elements the remnants of a '26 "T-Ford" . . . "

and went on for two dozen verses!

I still have, on my work-bench, several of the very hand tools and special "Model-T" wrenches we worked with then, and with my car keys I carry a "Model-T" ignition key, but I don't recall if it was from that truck or not.

A big part of our day was allocated to "doing chores." In the summer that meant little more than twice-a-day milking, but usually in cold weather the animals were kept indoors, and tending horses and cows became a labor-intensive project. Stalls had to be cleaned, and water pumped, and feed carried, and cows milked, and you could not put it off till tomorrow! The water came from a well drilled by a well-drilling machine on a spot pin-pointed by a "Diviner." For those who don't know what that means, a Diviner locates underground water by walking slowly about with a forked (Y-shaped) pencil-thick branch of a peach tree, held in two hands, horizontally, by the top of the "Y." When over a spot suitable for drilling a well, the branch bends and the stem of the "Y" points to the ground, as if to say, "This is the place, drill here." The truth is, I suppose, water would have been found at the 80-foot depth anywhere in the yard!

For a long time Anna Brody refused to learn to milk. She said if she did it would become her job. But she did, and it did, and she and I milked from two to four cows (twice a day) for years. But I am hard-pressed now to say why we bothered. I always felt that unless you had a commercial dairy enterprise it was not worth it. Cows were a real burden. Somebody had to be home to do the milking twice every day, and there was no such thing as a farm family taking a day off and not caring what time they got home. Tradition!

We brought the warm milk in from the barn and immediately ran it through the Daisy Cream Separator, a mechanical marvel that accepted the milk in its wide maw at the top, and delivered a stream of yellow cream out of a tube on the side. Skim milk poured from the bottom, and the tremendous centrifugal force required was generated by a boy or his mother turning a long crank. The cream was allowed to become slightly sour, and then hand-churned into butter; the skim milk either became cheese or was laced with "Calf Meal" and returned to the barn to be fed to calves.

When I had gone off to college, and "Daddy" and Shirley were working in Cleveland, all of those duties of mine were inherited by Stanley, and he and "Mom" spent a lot of time on the farm, alone together.

Our poultry flock was either destroyed by the October 1928 fire or disposed of, but prior to that we maintained a substantial flock of chickens, who shared the "chicken yard" with a collection of noisy, ill-tempered geese and ducks. There was a mean old gander who especially hated small boys and was big enough to make his point. I shall never forget the thrill of taking him fairly across the side of his head with a small green apple, well-aimed and fired (from a safe distance) by a rubber "sling-shot." I never told a soul.

We did generate a little cash selling butter and eggs, but if anyone had kept accurate books I think I know what they would have found. Mom used to periodically ship a large metal box, compartmentalized to carefully hold a gross of eggs, to her family in Cleveland. I remember the rural mail carrier picking it up, and bringing it back empty a few days later.

At regular intervals we were visited by a "Schechet" who traveled from Cleveland and stopped at two or three farms where we would gather with poultry and animals for kosher "Schechting." The trauma of watching him in motion faded quickly at the sight of what Mom put on the table for dinner (lunch) and supper (dinner). What can you know about the enjoyment of food if you haven't spent a bitter cold winter morning in the woods and come home to a steaming bowl of Anna Brody's barley soup, made from one of those geese.

In those days there were all too-frequent stories of upset tractors, fire-related injuries, and the like, but as I think back on it, we Brodys were remarkably free from the usual farm accidents. I don't recall any of us being seriously injured: the worst that happened to us was Stanley's broken rib, courtesy of a spirited heifer with inch-long horns, and a broken leg suffered when sledding in the woods, by himself.

Four of us were slightly injured, and Stanley more seriously, in an automobile accident in Cleveland in 1930, but our rural luck held out when we were all, plus an Aunt and a cousin, in a Model-T Ford coupe that upset one night on "Clyde Hill," very gently. We all walked away from it, and walked home, but when "Daddy" and I went back to get it with a team of horses the next morning, we found it burned to a crisp.

I have vivid memories of the bedroom that I shared with my brother in the house that still stands there now. There were summer nights with the windows open, listening to accordion music coming in on the breeze from celebrants at our neighbors a quarter-mile west. There were bitter cold clear winter nights, and sometimes a glass of water on a bed-side table frozen solid in the morning. Stanley had a technique of jumping out of bed in the morning, grabbing his clothes, diving back under the covers, and emerging fully dressed!

The covers, of course, were heavenly large, soft, white sheets, sewn together sandwich-like, with mountains of goose- or duck-down feathers in between, home-made, of course, and providing insulation better than any "store-bought" quilt ever made!

And crystal-clear, biting cold winter nights, when AM radio reception in those days of uncluttered airwaves was clean and crisp, lying in a darkened room with the only lights the red and green dial of a small portable radio, bringing in KDKA, Pittsburgh, or KMOX, St. Louis, or—wonder of wonders—a French accented voice—"Ici rahdio Cahnahda"! How far away that was! Best of all, WLW, Cincinnati, at mid-night—

"Moon River, a lazy stream of dreams,
Where vain desires forget themselves,
In the loveliness of sleep,
Float on, drift on, Moon River, to the sea . . . "

Love poems and organ music, and, sometimes, loneliness that stabbed like a knife. Bitter sweet.

AGRICULTURAL ECONOMICS

I was a teen-ager during the depths of the Depression, and I can recall wondering, during those times, as we witnessed farms all over the country going bankrupt, why the economics of family farms resulted in the loss of the home when the farm failed economically. I wondered why we farmers lived on our farms. Why not have a house "in town" and go to the farm each day to work it like other people went to their offices and factories. Modern day agribusiness does work that way, doesn't it? Little did I know about collateral, personal loan guarantees and the like. I do recall Morris Brody making a trip to the Jewish Agricultural Society's Chicago office to suggest a moratorium on the interest, unless they wanted to wind up owning a bunch of farms!

The pooling of a few dollars by friends and neighbors to buy up a bankrupt farm at auction or a "Sheriff Sale" and handing it back to the former owner (debt free) is a phenomenon unknown in modern times; in those days who ever heard of "Chapter 11"?

Everything that Morris Brody and his fellow growers learned from reading, experimenting, the Extension Service, the JAS, and any and all other sources of information concentrated on how to grow high yields of high

quality fruit, or poultry, or milk, or eggs, but no one, and I include my years
in the College of Agriculture at Ohio State University, paid enough attention
to marketing. Rural "Co-ops" were in vogue at that time, it is true, but they
were usually oriented toward pooling buying power in order to get the best
possible prices for equipment and supplies, but I don't recall that they placed
much emphasis on marketing.

It took a Russian immigrant, with less than perfect command of the
language but burning desire, to organize those grape growers, Jewish and
non-Jewish, into a cooperative marketing group to present a united front to
the processors, and get started on the road to prosperity.

They even tried to present a united front to the Ohio Legislature. I had the
unbridled thrill, as a student at Ohio State, of sitting in the spectators' gallery
and hearing my "Daddy" exhort the Ohio Legislature to put a tax on wines being
"imported" into Ohio from California. Guess how far he got with that one!

It took the same immigrant to cajole and browbeat his tight-fisted neighbors into pooling sufficient dollars to induce the Cleveland Electric Illuminating Company to increase its customer base and run an electric line down
the South River Road.

Each farmer had to pay $150.00 (in 1931!) for each pole on his property.
"Old Man Washburn" refused to pay his share—"My father and grandfather
farmed this place without electric power, and so can I"—so the others had to
pay for his poles, and when the line was run and paid for he tapped in anyhow.
Electric power meant electric motors and stoves, forced air heating, HOT
AND COLD RUNNING WATER, a big, beautiful "console" model Philco
radio (brother Stanley still has that Philco, and it still operates), electric lights
and fans, and no more dangerous kerosene lamps or lanterns.

But Morris was expert in these matters with those people; who do you
think did the same thing with 1927 dollars to get the South River Road paved?
The paving contractor hired draft-horse owners from far and wide to spend
the summer with their teams on our farms, pulling scoop-shovels six days a
week, widening and grading the road so it could be paved. The two brothers
who stayed [with] us, with their four magnificent Belgians, had a RADIO,
and it was on that battery-operated instrument that we heard of Charles
Lindbergh's historic flight.

I am not sure where he came by his ability to get all those farmers, Jew
and Gentile, some of whom had little to do with or respect for each other,
to act in concert. I recall an old photograph of Morris as a young man, part
of a collection of wild-eyed self-styled socialist revolutionaries in front of a

garment factory, probably in Cleveland. Who they were or what they called themselves I don't recall; the words "Workers of the World" come to mind.

Maybe someone at that time inspired him; maybe he heard a speaker galvanize a disparate group to pull together. Whatever it was he had, it was sufficient to knit together a mixed bag of farmers to get a road paved, run an electric line, and join forces to market their crops instead of competing with one another.

We had regular, eagerly anticipated visits from a Field Agent from the "JAS," one Samson Liph, who traveled around his territory, dispensing technical and financial counsel and moral support. I think my parents were favorites of his, and I recall him taking meals at our home frequently. When, on one occasion "Mom" apologized for the meager fare she was able to put on the table, boiled beef, he took her strongly to task. He reminded her that in England boiled beef was considered a delicacy, and, furthermore, when Anna Brody served it to him, it was no less than that in the United States, too!

It was all too commonly supposed that fruit growers had idle time during the winter, but in truth there was much to do, although without pressure. It was a time for repairing buildings and equipment, and for pruning. Fruit trees and grape vines must be cut back annually to prevent them from growing too large and producing small fruit, and all of the cut-off "brush" must be disposed of, either by filling gullies to control erosion, or by burning.

The first springtime activity on a grape farm is driving the posts that support the wires (that support the vines) back into their holes from which they had been raised by alternate freezing and thawing. The wires had to be repaired and stretched taut, and then the "canes" tied to the wires, arranged so the new growth would get light and ventilation.

In those years we rather indiscriminately threw large amounts of deadly insecticides and fungicides on all kinds of trees and vines, with little regard to environmental consequences. The College of Agriculture at Cornell University was among the first to begin to become concerned, and I was fortunate enough to have one of their graduates, Dr. Norman Childers, as a Faculty Advisor when I was in Graduate School at Ohio State University from 1937 to 1941. My research was funded by the Sherwin Williams Co., and Tobacco By-Products Co. (Lucky Strike), and I gained Master of Science and Doctor of Philosophy Degrees by showing that these chemicals were, in fact, also harmful to the plants they were meant to protect, not to mention the residual and cumulative effect on other plants, and animals. You can imagine that this information was not kindly received by the chemical industry. I am proud to have been in on the cutting edge of that kind of thinking, and as a matter of fact, improvements in these and other procedures in viticulture tripled the yields by the 1980's on the same vines that we tended in the 1920's!

Then as the season wore on we sprayed and cultivated; in the spring hoped we wouldn't suffer frost, that could ruin a year in one windless night, and in the summer hail storms, that could accomplish the same thing in a few minutes on a summer afternoon. Grapes in bloom are nothing spectacular, but peach and apple blossoms are a sight to behold, and smell!

We began to pick Transparent apples in mid-summer, followed by Wealthies, then Macintosh, Jonathan, Baldwin, Stayman-Winesap, and last of all, Rome Beauties. Peaches came along about the time of the "Wealthies" and "Macs," and the Concord grapes along with the Baldwins. It was a busy time. As I have visited that area in recent years I have noted that the "tree fruits" are virtually gone; the apple and peach orchards that I knew no longer exist, and I am not sure why. I can take you to a Howard Johnson Motel and Restaurant that stands where once an apple orchard stood.

Prosperity among the grape growers along the Fruit Belt on the southern shores of the Great Lakes in those years was dependent, as I remember, on $80.00 a ton for "Concords"; land values, loans, and budgets were based on that figure. It shouldn't be hard, even for the uninitiated, to calculate the effect of a drop to $16.00 in the course of one harvest, 1929. The $64.00 short-fall is immediately obvious; what takes a little thought to appreciate is the effect on the morale of the growers. The Stock Market crash was part of the story, but the fact that a large number of growers were competing for the dollars of a few smart buyers was what really made it a disaster, and the lesson wasn't lost on Morris Brody. (See the entry of November 19 from Anna Brody's diary below.)

We set up a roadside stand, as most others did, and I invite you, dear reader, to consider selling freshly picked glorious Alberta or Hale Haven peaches for 15 cents a half-bushel, in a basket that cost 5 cents. And even that was a better deal than loading your truck with peaches at midnight, to drive it to the Farmers Market in Cleveland early enough in the morning to gain a curb-side stall, only to have the day slip away with no buyers, head for home, and dump your peaches off a bridge on the way because you needed the baskets to pick more (unsalable) peaches. Frustration? Is there any wonder so many gave up? This was the life that was thrust on Morris Brody because he had ulcers!

The bitter irony of his career, of course, was that he had to go back to work in Cleveland, when farm work was not too pressing, to support the farm that he bought to escape working in Cleveland. He made the round trip twice a week, and lived with his mother while working in a garment factory. For a brief period there was a garment factory in a loft in Geneva, set up there by a Cleveland manufacturer to make it easier to get rural, part time help, and Morris put in time there, too.

Aside from the emotional trauma endured during the harvest season at the time of the two fires in 1928, or watching the prices fall at the onset of the Great Depression in 1929, I think the most difficult grape harvest of all was in 1933, when the weather broke before the crop was "in."

I had graduated from Geneva High School early that summer, and stayed home the rest of the year to help with the summer work and harvest before enrolling at Ohio State University in January 1934.

More pointedly than I am able to describe, the heart-breaking physically—and emotionally—exhausting succession of the November days of that fall season is vividly recorded in Anna Brody's daily Journal (the italics are mine):

> Monday, October 30, (1933) . . . Fair-Warm. Picked (grapes) all day. Sold 1 ton to Kosic . . . 1 . . . ton to Trumbull woman.

The picking season had started a few days earlier; when I wasn't picking, it was my job first to spread empty half-bushel baskets ahead of the pickers, and I took pride in my ability to judge the crop on the vine, and to know just how many baskets to drop. They were nested together in bundles of four or six, and I was able to throw them accurately several rows to either side. Then I hauled the fruit in from the vineyard, and spread out the full baskets in the yard or in a shed, to wait for buyers to come by and bid. I had a wagon and two horses, I was 17, and proud of my responsibility. It was actually more labor efficient to do this work with horses rather than a tractor, which required a driver; a good team of horses could navigate the vineyard and orchard rows by themselves, responding to verbal commands.

> Tuesday, October 31, . . . Fair–Very warm. *No sale.* Stopped pickers from picking—ran short of baskets.
> Wednesday, November 1, . . . Fair–very warm. *No sale.* Picked all day.

Now the weather started to turn—

> Saturday, November 4, . . . Fair–very cold. *Pickers . . . would not stay.* Morris, Shirley and I picked all day.

Monday, November 6, 1933 . . . Grapes very wet. *Pickers did not work.* Morris and I picked all day.

For the most part the "pickers" were temporary hired hands, with little pride in their work, who really didn't care if the grapes got picked or not, as long as they were paid in cash at the end of each shift.

Tuesday, November 7, . . . Started snowing. Grapes sold for 30.00 (sic). Wednesday, November 8, . . . *pickers did not come. No sale.* Thursday, November 9, . . . very heavy snowfall in late P.M. *No sale.* Brought big stove up.

The snow was now over two feet deep, and grapes in baskets on the ground were in danger of being overlooked and lost. (In spite of my best efforts, some were.)

While all of this was going on, Anna Brody was keeping house for a family of five, preparing school lunches and three hot meals a day on a kerosene stove until cold weather made it necessary to set up the huge wood-burning stove in place of the "oil stove" in the kitchen. That meant starting a wood fire, and re-starting it for each meal if you were out in the vineyard all day.

Friday, November 10, . . . Snow all day. Picked in P.M. in heavy blizzard. *Will remember this for a good many years to come, hundreds of baskets of grapes standing in vineyard covered over with snow. No sale.* Saturday, November 11 . . . Heavy snow all morning, rain at noon, grapes frozen solid, . . . ice on vines. Still have a few rows to pick. *No sale.*

As I write this I can still hear frozen grapes bouncing like marbles on the wagon bed, I am aware of the smell of sweating horses in the bitter cold air, gloves frozen half-clenched, to grasp a basket handle, and the fear that all of this will go for naught if no-one comes to buy the grapes.

Sunday, November 12 . . . Krzic boys finished picking, thank goodness! Sold 6½ ton at 30.00 . . . Tuesday, November 14 . . . Very heavy snowfall . . . lots of grapes still in vineyard. *No Sale.* Wednesday, November 15 . . . Very cold–snow. *No Sale.*

Thursday, November 16 . . . Howard finished hauling grapes in from vineyard, all covered with snow. *No sale.*

The snow was too soft and deep for a bob-sled, so I had borrowed a high wheeled wagon from a neighbor in order to negotiate the 2–3 foot deep snow in the vineyard, and it was real work to retrieve the full baskets from under that snow, load them on the wagon, and haul them home, all the while wondering if any buyers would ever show up. The pickers left the full baskets under the bottom wire of the trellis, and you knew just about how far apart they should be, so it was not purely hit and miss to go down through the snow to locate them. Nevertheless, Stanley still reminds me that he found 21 scattered baskets of grapes that I had missed when the snow melted in the spring!

Friday, November 17 . . . Water frozen in basement. *No sale.*
Saturday, November 18 . . . Snow still on grapes. *No sale.*
Sunday, November 19 . . . *No sale all morning. Very . . . worried expected to sell today sure.* Finally 2 trucks loaded at about 3 P.M. Still about 4 ton left but heavy load off our minds. *Wonder if this lesson will help any for next year's picking and selling.*
Monday, November 20 . . . Cohodas took last load of grapes at 29.00 per ton.

Elsewhere in this narrative I have mentioned the qualities of determination and strength in the face of adversity that we children were exposed to by our parents in those difficult years. The harvest seasons of 1928, 1929, and 1933 were the ultimate test; I can only hope we were observant and aware enough to appreciate what we witnessed.

SUMMER CAMP

I don't recall the first time I heard the expression "summer Camp," but it surely was not a household word with us in the 1920s and 1930s, when friends and relatives in Cleveland "discovered" all of us on the farms. Every summer week-end they descended on Ashtabula, Lake, and Geauga Counties, and it was a considerable journey. I recall a family friend—I think his name was Unger—climbing down out of his tired old touring car in our farmyard, and bragging that he had made the 50-mile trip from Cleveland, and only had "two flat tires"! And "Uncle Joe" Klein was trapped on the farm when a Sunday afternoon storm made our unimproved (mud) road impassable for several days. He would go out every morning and touch the road to see if it was dry enough to drive on.

On those fun summer week-ends the men and children played baseball and pitched horseshoes, and went for walks and picked fruit, and went swimming, and the women were engaged in an endless round of cooking one meal and cleaning up in time to cook the next one, and how they loved it!

One or more cousins at a time would spend weeks at a stretch on "Uncle Morris' farm" and it really was great fun for the children, if in fact it meant extra work for an already overworked "Aunt Anna." We always felt that it was much more of a thrill for them to spend time "in the country," than it was for us to go to the city.

We all looked forward to and enjoyed those visits a great deal, and the winters were longer without them.

ON BEING JEWISH

All of the Jewish farm families that I remember tried very hard to maintain their Jewishness in that little corner of the diaspora and I doubt seriously that many of us have such a serious commitment to our religion, and its ritual, today. At one point, for a short while, we actually had a resident Rabbi in Geneva, but it couldn't last—there just weren't enough members and money to maintain a full-time Rabbi and congregation.

The High Holidays, however, were deserving of special consideration. Arrangements were made every fall to have a Rabbi come to Geneva and full-blown Orthodox services were conducted in some-one's home that had the capacity. This usually occurred during the height of the picking season, and many the Rosh Hashonah morning was spent in prayer, and the afternoon in the orchard.

Both sets of Grandparents were alive and well in Cleveland, and we visited them frequently. I attended many Saturday morning services in a little Schul on 149th Street, and remember well my father's father engaged in serious, joyous debate with his cronies over the nuances of meaning of passages in the "Siddur" (Prayer Book).

Little heed was paid to Bat Mitzvahs, but Bar Mitzvahs were another matter! Accordingly, a Lehrer (teacher) was brought out (once a week, as I recall) and we gathered in someone's home for Hebrew School. I also studied briefly in Cleveland under a marvelous old man, whom I knew only as "Simcha," who not only taught me to read Hebrew, but to translate. I regret that I have forgotten most of it, but to this day I take great delight in reading the Hebrew text in the prayer books and trying to translate as I go along.

Morris had a younger brother, Herman, who passed away around 1927 while a student at Hebrew Union in Cincinnati, and two of his classmates married two of Morris' sisters. I recall the two young men courting my aunts; they would come to the farm to visit, and they were so polished, and romantic, and suave, and intellectual!

I was Bar Mitzvah in the living room of our farm home, and still remember the songs (Shamray Shabboth!) led by the two uncles, now ordained. My mother bought a set of exquisite little wine goblets for the occasion, and I still have one. They cost her ten cents each, the equivalent of a half bushel of peaches, less the basket. In later years we joined Tifereth Israel in Ashtabula, and the last time I celebrated the High Holidays in Ohio was there, in 1941, sitting next to one of Rabbi Kleinberg's sons, who was already in uniform, on Military leave.

Now, in 1990, Sam Simon, grandson of the founder of that congregation, is my good friend and neighbor in Florida.

Morris and Anna were still on the farm when I returned from the Service in January 1946, and they still had some hope that I would take it over. I had been injured twice in the Philippine Islands, and the medical advice was that my damaged knee would not stand the rigors of farming for very long. It was suggested I find another career, and I did.

The span of the Twentieth Century seems almost to parallel the span of that Jewish experience in Northeastern Ohio and those that still live to remember it. It was around the turn of this century that Morris and Anna and their peers found their way through Ellis Island into the New World, (I think without exception their contemporaries that I knew were Eastern European or Russian born) and there won't be many of us left with first-hand experience or recollections of those days around Geneva when the century ends. There are a few grandchildren who will hear distant voices, and faintly recall sights, and sounds, and smells, but the memories won't be as vivid, or poignant, or meaningful.

As far as I know, the Ornstein property near Chardon, Ohio is the only one of those farms still owned by the family. Son Jacob (Professor of Language and Linguistics at the University of Texas in El Paso) and daughter Frances (Falls

Church, VA) still own it, and have a tenant farmer. Leonard Kroner lives in Geneva, and owns a farm "south of town."

In 1953 "Brody's Fruit Farm" on the South River Road was sold, and by now the original 118 Acres have been divided, and comprise two farms. Morris and Anna moved back to Cleveland for a short time, and then to Ft. Lauderdale, Florida, where he passed away on July 4, 1962. She moved back North, to Youngstown, Ohio, to be near Shirley, and succumbed to a failing heart in February, 1964. They lie at rest in suburban Cleveland, next to his sister Ethel and brother-in law William Goldberg. Their children, grandchildren, and great-grandchildren are scattered from Florida to Ontario, and from California to Massachusetts.

REUNION

For several years starting around 1926 the Jewish farmers of that area maintained a primarily social "Society" (as I recall they referred to themselves as the "Jewish Farmers Association of Geneva, Ohio") and they met periodically at one home or another for business and recreational reasons. I remember how the spirited conversations (arguments) that went on frightened us children. But now, of course, we reminisce and laugh!

The highlight of those gatherings that we best remember was the three-day "Picnic" on the Flock farm in 1928. Some of us still have copies of a huge photograph that was taken of the entire gathering, featuring the honored guest, Rabbi Abba Hillel Silver of Cleveland, Ohio. Sixty-one years later Norman Cohodas provided a copy to the Cleveland Jewish News, and it was reproduced in the August 11, 1989 issue, with Norm's suggestion that we have a re-union.

Norman and I had similar travel plans at that time, and we met at the home of his son (Art teacher at the University of British Columbia) in Surrey, British Columbia, having not seen each other in close to fifty years. There, in a lush green valley in suburban Vancouver we two Jewish farm boys from Geneva, Ohio got serious about bringing together as many of our former friends as we could. On July 7, 1990 about a hundred of us had dinner together at Quail Hollow, not far from Geneva, and a picnic July 8 at Geneva-on-the-Lake.

Dr. Sanford Rikoon, Professor of Rural Sociology, University of Missouri, Columbia, was the honored guest this time. He addressed our dinner meeting and attended our picnic the next day with photographic mind and tape recorder always at the ready. He has indicated that our experiences in Ohio will be included in a treatise he is writing about Jewish farmers all over America, and I am pleased to know a permanent record of those lives and times will still exist when all of us are gone. If all of our parents could only know it, they would be pleased, as well.

EPILOGUE

All things considered, it was a hard way to live and make a living, but there wasn't much in those days that was easy. I am sure that Morris and Anna Brody, and all the other parents would be proud of what has become of their progeny. The desire to make a better life for themselves brought them to these shores and the desire to make a better life for their children catalyzed them after they arrived. Those were not the "Good old days," these are, and they gave us the start, the "platform," as brother Stanley so aptly calls it, to make it so.

> "A boy on a farm looks up at a plane, and dreams of far-away places; a man on a plane looks down and dreams of home." (Anon.)

And finally, I do consider myself fortunate that I have spent my life as a farm boy, student, laboratory researcher, soldier, public servant, world traveler, businessman. There may be some who have lived more varied, exciting lives; I wouldn't trade. I have looked up at that plane, and I have looked down.

HOWARD W. BRODY
Palm Harbor, FL
November 1990

Section Four

Jewish Continuity

Protest, 1975, at Cleveland City Hall in support of Vladimir Slepak, a Soviet Jewish scientist (Jewish Community Federation).

Alsbacher Document: Ethical Testament, 1839

Moses Alsbacher did not write the so-called Alsbacher document, although he was the acknowledged leader of the band of nineteen young emigrés who left Unsleben, Bavaria, in 1839 in search of a new life. Rabbi Lazarus Kohn, the teacher in their village, composed the letter as a parting gift.

Although we know little about Kohn, we know much about teachers in the Jewish tradition. They are far more than conveyors of knowledge: they are the moral conscience of their pupils. As much as they teach the Hebrew language, essential in the life of a learned Jew, they teach the content and the interpretation of the texts, as well as the *musar,* the ethical import of Jewish instruction. Kohn committed himself to Jewish teaching out of a deep religiosity and a profound concern with perpetuating the received tradition by imbuing the next generation with its obligations, the worthiness of the enterprise, and the knowledge of the historical journey their ancestors took. The document survives to this day as testimony to the power of a revered teacher to affect the lives of his charges.

Kohn's message, to which a list of signatures of more than 230 Unsleben friends and neighbors was appended, follows in the tradition of ethical wills, normally presented to sons by fathers to remind them of their obligations to the Jewish heritage and the moral demands of Judaism. Kohn emphasizes safeguarding the memory of previous generations, invokes God's blessing on the expedition, warns against the seductive power of the "tempting freedom" of the new land, and admonishes them to place the spiritual above the material and to remain good Jews always—all comprising a typical rehearsal of the values that help assure Jewish survival.

Source: Letter from Lazarus Kohn to Moses and Jetta Alsbacher, May 5, 1839, Western Reserve Historical Society.

My dear friends Moses and Jetta Alsbacher:

I give you by way of saying goodbye a list of names of the people of your faith with the dearest wish that you may present these names to your future heirs yes, even to your great-grandchildren, of which may you have many, under the best family relationship and under pleasant economic circumstances.

I further wish and hope that the Almighty, who reigns over the ocean as well as over dry land, to whom thunder and storms must pay heed, shall give you good angels as travel companions, so that you, my dear friends, may arrive undisturbed and healthy in body and soul at the place of your destiny, in the land of freedom,

But I must also, as a friend, ask a favor of you.

Friends! You are traveling to a land of freedom where the opportunity will be presented to live without compulsory religious education.

Resist and withstand this tempting freedom and do not turn away from the religion of our fathers. Do not throw away your holy religion for quickly lost earthly pleasures, because your religion brings you consolation and quiet in this life and it will bring you happiness for certain in the other life.

Don't tear yourself away from the laws in which your fathers and mothers searched for assurance and found it.

The promise to remain good Jews may never and should never be broken during the trip, not in your homelife, nor when you go to sleep, nor when you rise again, nor in the raising of your children.

And now, my dear friends, have a pleasant trip and forgive me for these honest words to which the undersigned will forever remain true.

Your friend
Lazarus Kohn
Teacher

Unsleben near Neustadt on the Saale
in Lower Franconia
in the Kingdom of Bavaria
the 5th of March 1839.

[Spellings of names that follow are transliterated from the German, e.g., "Jetta" as in the German, rather than "Yetta."]

(1)
Mayer Rosenberg
Hinele, wife
Aron Hayum, farmhand
Besle from Weisbach, maid

(2)
Loeb Kalb, rabbi
Huebchele, wife
Estherle, daughter

(3)
Gerschon Brandus
Guedel, wife

Jakob Brandus
Mariana, wife
Merle, daughter
Abraham, son

(4)
Hirsch Adler, rabbi
Deile, wife
Aberle, son
Hinle, daughter
Lazarus Adler, doctor and rabbi, son

(5)
Moses Adler
Besle, wife
Weirle, daughter
Abraham Toch
Sarle of Eichenhausen, maid

(6)
Simon Lilienfeld, widower

Moses Lilienfeld
Bule, wife
Hirsch, son

(7)
Eisig Lustig
Rifka, wife
Menke, son
Abraham, "
Seligmann, "
Kallmann, "
Hinn, daughter

(8)
Simson Rosenbaum
Rifke, wife
Moses, son
Jakob, "
Tendel, daughter
Hanna, "
Abraham, son, is already in America

(9)
Heinemann Liebenthal, widower
Moses, son
Issak, "
Estherle of Schweinshaupten, maid

(10)
Israel Lamm
Idel, wife
Deile, daughter
Kallmann, son

(11)
Loeb Mussliner
Terz, wife
Seligmann, son
Jokel, "
Schlome, "
Besle, daughter
Bela, "

(12)
Hirsch Dinkel, widower
Schmule, son
Hayum, "
Jakob, "
Schenle, daughter
Sara, "
Gulde, "

(13)
Kaufman Rosenbaum
Rachel, wife
Abraham, son
Kuselloeb, "
Liebman, "
Isaak, "
Golde, daughter
Frumet, "
Roes, "

(14)
Hirsch Klein
Rifkele, wife
Abrahamloeb, son
Juedle, "
Aberle, "
Falk, "
Reichel, daughter
Golde, "

(15)
Baruch Lustig
Mamel, wife
Loeb, son
Kallmann, "
Mayer, "
Eisig, "
Miriam, daughter
Bela, "
Lea, "
Sara, "

(16)
Sander Bein
Tarz, wife
Joesel, son
Solomon, "
Zerle, daughter
Juettle, "
Mariana, "

(17)
Abraham Engel
Klerle, wife
Isaakloeb, son
Roes, daughter
Miriam, "

(18)
Nathan Apfel
Guedele, wife
Seligmann, son
Aber, "
Feibel, "
Rachel, daughter

(19)
Samuel Bach
Heffel, wife
Hanna, daughter
Mayer, son
Simchel, "

(20)
Maennle Donnerstag
Rifka, wife
Seligmann, son
Aber, "
Guedel, daughter
Fradel, "
Geller, "
Esther, "
Voegel, "

(21)
Samuel Sachsenheimer
Serle, wife
Roes, daughter
Zerle, "
Hanna, "
Guedel, "
Breinle, "

(22)
Moses Gaertner
Rechle, wife
Besle, daughter
Perle, "
Eva, "

(23)
David Gaertner
Sara, wife
Abraham, son
Moses, "
Berla, daughter
Voegel, "
Gudel, "

(24)
Abraham Kuhl
Maedel, wife
Golde, daughter
Bela, "
Zerle, "
Hayum, son
Gabriel, "

(25)
Moses Tuch
Zipar, wife
Fradel, daughter
Jochevet, "
Beierle, "
Jakob, son

Simchel, son
Hayum, "

(26)
Assar Loeb Alsbacher, Barnass
Babet, wife
Jetta, daughter
Hanna, "
Sara, "
David, son
Isaak, "

(27)
Falk Rose
Jendel, wife
Mariana, daughter
Heinemann, son
Reichel, sister
Joseph Saalman of Neuhaus, apprentice

(28)
Falk Lamm
Schenle, wife
Hinele, daughter
Isarias, son
Loeb Lamm, brother

(29)
Hienle, widow of Loeb Rosenberg
Marmias, son
Levi, "
Cheske, "
Bunle, daughter

(30)
Joseph Mittel
Hanna, wife

(31)
Reiz, widow of Simon Mittel
Simchele, son

Nathan, son
Isaak, "

(32)
Weinle, widow of Loeb Rosenbaum
Natle, son
Esther, daughter
Wolf Brandis of Massbach, apprentice

(33)
Esther, widow of Heidenbach/
    Friedenbad
Schmule, son
Hinnle, daughter

(34)
Estherle, widow of Simson Tuch
Seligman and Nathan are in America

(35)
Madel, widow of Rabbi Isaak Alsbacher
Jachet, daughter
Jittel, "
Fradel Dienstag, sister

(36)
Hitzel, widow of Moses Langem/Langer
Hinle, daughter

(37)
Sara, widow of Abraham Mutter
Samuel, son
Feibel, "
Voegel, daughter
Perl, "

(38)
Jittle, widow of Kallmann Sommer
Baruch, son
Schmule, "
Bess, daughter

Gella, daughter of Bess

(39)
Fleischhauer's children
Mendel
Ruben
Mosche
Fradel

(40)
    CHASEN
Seligmann Lubliner, single
Sara Lubliner, neice

(41)
Teacher
Lazarus Kohn, single
Rifkele Kohn, sister

(42)
Simon Kuhl, single
Joseph Kuhl, "
Michael Gaertner, "
Hayum Gaertner, "
Rifkele Lilienfeld, "
Idel Gottgetreu, "
Jetta Gottgetreu, "
Miriam Gottgetreu, "

(43)
Israel Frey, saddlemaker from
    Eichenhausen
Sara, wife
Berle, son
David, "
Fradel, daughter

(44)
Baruch Lustig, the younger from
    Schweinshaupten
Debora, wife

Mesche, son
Miriam, daughter

(45)
The company of the emigrants:
Moses Alsbacher
Jetta, wife
Jittle, daughter
Simson Hopfermann
Sara, wife
Seckle, son
Voegele, daughter
Zerle, daughter
Mayer, children of Thormann

Simmle, children of Thormann
Ramle, "   "   "
N. B. Simson Thormann is already in
    America

(46)
Moses Rosenbaum
Hanna Rosenbaum
Ruben Fleischhauer
Sara Lubliner
Schenle Dinkel
Reichel Klein
Breinle Salb and child
All from here

Handwritten Account, May 2, 1975

Laura Porath, granddaughter of the prominent rabbi Israel Porath, provided a handwritten account of her reflections as she accompanied her grandfather's coffin on its trip aboard American Airlines to its final resting place in Israel, where Rabbi Porath had been born.

The account is lovingly written and reflects the caring and admiration that Laura Porath feels for the "Dean of the Orthodox Rabbinate in Cleveland." The reader is exposed to his ideas and his life story, told in a narrative style by one member of his loving family.

Source: Laura Porath, handwritten account, May 2, 1975, Western Reserve Historical Society. Reprinted with permission of Laura Steinberg (née Porath).

[SCHOOL ESSAY ON RABBI ISRAEL PORATH, MY GRANDFATHER]
Laura Porath, May 2, 1975

"Handle with care and dignity"—that was the label that was required by American Airlines to be on the carton to cover the coffin of my grandfather.

A dismal rain beat down as the last of the funeral procession left the airport. The body of my grandfather, Rabbi Israel Porath, was on a plane to Israel where his life had begun. Within a few hours he would be back in the native land he loved . . . forever.

My grandfather was the Dean of the Orthodox Rabbinate in Cleveland. He was looked up to by all members of the Jewish community whether Orthodox, Conservative or Reform. I recall walking with him at a city-wide function at Fairmont Temple. As we walked, people turned their heads and said, "There is Rabbi Porath." I felt proud standing next to him. He was a distinguished looking man. He was of medium height with a medium frame. He had a white beard and white hair, upon which he always wore a skullcap or hat. He wore glasses behind which he had blue eyes that twinkled. Other people would walk over to him and say, "Rabbi Porath, do you remember me, you married my wife and me twenty years ago?" My grandfather would then reply in his own witty way. "I hope you won't hold that against me."

Abba (as I and all my other cousins called my grandfather) was born in the Old City of Jerusalem in 1886. At the age of three he began his Hebrew studies and at the age of eleven he graduated from a prominent school in Jerusalem. He then went on to study with Rabbi Kook, the Chief Rabbi of Israel, who ordained him.

In 1905 Abba married Peshe Miriam Tiktin in Jerusalem. I remember the story my grandmother would tell. She was walking in the park with her girlfriends, and my grandfather with his boyfriends. When my grandmother first saw my grandfather she knew he would be her husband. They had been married sixty-eight years at the time of his death. A true love story in its self.

After World War I, my grandparents came to America and first settled in Plainfield, New Jersey, where he had a pulpit in a synagogue. In 1925, my grandfather came to Cleveland for a convention and was offered a position as a Rabbi here. He accepted and remained in Cleveland for the rest of his life.

One evening we had a family get together at my house. One of my cousins said to Abba, "Is it true that you speak four different languages?" Abba, who was a modest man, just nodded his head. However, my grandmother spoke up and said, "He knows seven different languages in addition to English he knows Turkish, German, Yiddish, Arabic and Hebrew."

Abba would always clear his throat before he spoke, and when he did speak all would listen. His speeches had beautiful vocabulary filled with alliterations and humor. He could capture an audience in seven minutes while it took others a half hour to say. He read many different newspapers and magazines to know what was going on in the world. Therefore, in his speeches he would relate to world situations.

Abba has this power about him. Whereby he was respected and asked questions of by all. He knew how to interpret Jewish law. When David Berger was killed in Munich during the Olympics, his funeral was to be on the second day of Rosh Hashana (which is not observed by Reform Jews). The prominent Reform Rabbi who was to officiate at the funeral asked my grandfather if it could be held on Rosh Hashana. Abba's reply was since there is a matter of time that body has to be buried it would be permissible. However, he also pointed out that television cameras would be covering the funeral, and the car procession would pass by almost every synagogue in Cleveland on its way to the cemetery. The funeral was held on the day after Rosh Hashana.

The Jewish National Fund of Cleveland honored my grandfather by dedicating a forest to him in the Kennedy Memorial in Israel. He was the first Clevelander to be honored there. I had the privilege to visit the forest in December while visiting in Israel. I was very much impressed to see the names of other dignitaries next to my grandfather's forest, such names as Hubert Humphrey.

With Abba there was no generation gap between his children, grand-children, and great-grandchildren. I remember sitting in the rocking chair when my grandfather would come up behind me and pull the chair all the way back. He played with all of us in one way or another.

In addition to being a Rabbi, he was a lecturer, scholar, and author. He wrote the book *Mavo Hatalmud—Outline of the Talmud* (Jewish Law) which is an eight volume set, and is used by students, laymen, scholars, and authorities of Jewish law. Prior to his death he made arrangements to have his book revised and reprinted with over one thousand additional questions and answers.

Excerpt from *Portrait of a Rabbi*

Rabbi Samuel Silver, ordained by Hebrew Union College in 1940, served Reform congregations in Wilmington, Delaware, Cleveland, Ohio, and Stamford, Connecticut, and in several Florida communities. He has published a number of volumes in the fields of interfaith relations and Jewish humor, in addition to *Portrait of a Rabbi,* his biography of Rabbi Barnett R. Brickner. He resides in Boca Raton, Florida.

As the following excerpt relates, Brickner was called from Toronto in 1925 to lead Cleveland's Anshe Chesed congregation, founded in 1837 as the city's first Jewish organization. He had an "electrifying" impact on the congregation and the community from the outset. He was an exemplary teacher, a gifted orator and debater, and a celebrated radio personality, and his sermons and lectures filled the sanctuary to overflowing. He pleaded for a liberal Judaism true to its commitment to the possibility of change. His innovative synagogue programs attracted renowned guest lecturers. He earned national recognition for his labor arbitration skills. First and foremost an educator, he transformed the synagogue's school into an educational laboratory.

Source: An excerpt from Samuel M. Silver, *Portrait of a Rabbi* (Cleveland, OH: Barnett R. Brickner Memorial Foundation, 1959). Reprinted with permission of the Barnett R. Brickner Memorial Foundation, Ketchum, OH.

PORTRAIT OF A RABBI
By Samuel M. Silver

[. . .]The move to Cleveland meant living in a larger city, but it meant up-rooting home and family. It also probably meant less scope for one's efforts, for in the United States there were many Reform rabbis, whereas in Canada he was one of but two: the other, in Montreal.

When Brickner finally said yes and the word got out to the congregation and was then relayed to the rest of Canada, there was a nation-wide chorus of regret. Almost at once, invitations came to the Rabbi, from all parts of Canada, plead-ing with him to address their groups before he left for the "States." The result was that the Rabbi embarked on what friends called a "farewell tour." As on previous trips to the "provinces," Brickner was greeted by large crowds, includ-ing many from small and isolated towns where no rabbi had ever penetrated. A farewell address was carried coast-to-coast over Canadian stations.

The Cleveland congregation asked their new Rabbi to come to them during the summer. To comply, he hastened the winding up of his affairs in Toronto.

From London came a congratulatory note from Israel Zangwill who said, "I was sure you would soon be discovered." Brickner had wrought well in Toronto. He had vitalized and liberalized the congregation. He had created institutions and organizations that would serve the community for a long time. To thousands he had brought the message of liberal Judaism. He had made friends he would never lose. Throughout the rest of his lifetime he would be called back again and again to renew friendships and to deliver addresses. He was prepared for new challenges.

VIII

The Cleveland community to which Rabbi Barnett R. Brickner was called in 1925 was, in many ways, one of the most advanced, culturally and civically, in the nation. The congregation he was to serve was one of American Reform Judaism's most prominent. Like Holy Blossom, Anshe Chesed was the pioneer Jewish organization of the city, having been founded in 1837 and chartered in 1846. It had begun as an Orthodox congregation and had gradually liberalized itself under the leadership of a number of rabbis, including some outstanding Reform pioneers such as Gustavus Cohen and Michaelis Machol.

Rabbi Machol had retired from the active leadership in 1908 and served as rabbi emeritus until his death in 1912. He was succeeded by Louis A. Wolsey, among the first graduates of Hebrew Union College to serve the congregation. During the ministry of Wolsey, the congregation had made important forward strides. A gifted orator and administrator, he had led the congregation in the building of a beautiful edifice on Euclid Avenue at E. 82nd Street in 1910 and then, still not satisfied, in the erection of a huge annex, complete with religious-school classes in 1924, the year before he announced his departure. His friends were legion in the community, his accomplishments numerous, his reputation glistening. He was not, in the parlance of the living room, "an easy man to succeed."

That Brickner did succeed in "succeeding" Wolsey was attested to by many, including Wolsey himself. Brickner's effect on Cleveland was nothing less than electrifying. Even before his induction, in April, 1925, an announcement that he was to occupy the pulpit was coupled with a newspaper notice in which the congregation pleaded with nonmembers not to come for lack of space. And when he spoke, a crowded sanctuary thrilled to his words spoken in a voice which was to become so familiar to thousands of Clevelanders.

In July, 1925, the religious editor of the *Cleveland Plain Dealer* stopped the new Rabbi long enough for an interview. As seen by the reporter, "Rabbi Brickner is a young man (33). He is heavily built, weighing 195; his head is crowned with bushy, dark hair, framing features in which a flashing smile often appears."

Asked for his views; Brickner told the reporter, "I look upon religion as a mountain up which men are climbing towards the peak to God . . . My concern is that every man shall find a road, and as long as he is in ascent I am not going to quarrel with him about who has the right road. Let the ascent be the test."

The temple bulletin was abrim with announcements and innovations and new programs that were introduced with the arrival of the new Rabbi. The Men's Club decided on a bi-weekly downtown luncheon meeting with the Rabbi; the Sisterhood made it known that they were inaugurating a current events course with him. The Alumni Association, a club of post-confirmants, and their friends, also claimed the Rabbi as theirs for a series of meetings.

The ceremony of installation for the Rabbi was a banner event of the year 1925. It occurred on a Sunday evening, October 9, and long before the announced time the large sanctuary was full. Special police looked after the throngs round about the temple and fire officials put a stop to the stream of standees admitted by the ushers. Hundreds milling about had to be denied access to the proceedings.

Rabbi Abba Hillel Silver, Brickner's one-time Herzl Club confrere, preached the installation sermon. "We must walk the road of unpopular causes," he declared, "the hard road of frustration and defeat, if we wish to arrive at the only victory which matters, the victory of the spirit."

Also on hand at the service to welcome the Rabbi were: City Manager William R. Hopkins; Rabbi Solomon Goldman of one of Cleveland's Conservative synagogues, The Jewish Center; Dr. Dilworth Lupton, of the First Unitarian Church, later to become the *Cleveland Plain Dealer's* religious editor; and the president of Holy Blossom who publicly expressed regret at Toronto's loss and envy for the people of Cleveland over the annexation of "his" Rabbi. David Kohn, president of Anshe Chesed Congregation, presented the new rabbi.

In his response Brickner blended the amenities with a theme which he was to use quite often in Cleveland. He warned against the congealment of Reform into another Orthodoxy. True, in Toronto he had helped transform a Conservative congregation into a Reform one. Yet, he held no brief for a Reform which fell into one, unchanging mold. "Keep Liberal Judaism liberal," he pleaded in his inaugural address. Another highlight of the service was specially composed music by James H. Rogers, the celebrated organist and musical director whose association with the temple endured for half a century.

In August, 1925, the congregation had voted to shift its major service from Friday night to Sunday morning. Friday vesper services and Saturday morning services were also scheduled. When the Brickner Sunday morning lectures began, the Euclid Avenue Temple became the mecca of thousands of Clevelanders. The Rabbi's discourses took the town by storm. He dealt with the issues of the day, personal problems, and intellectual questions. The press provided elaborate coverage of the talks, and members of the congregation beamed with pride over the popularity of their Rabbi.

Extra pride was induced in 1926 when an announcement reached Cleveland from Toronto. The University of Toronto disclosed that a "Rabbi Brickner Scholarship Fund" had been established in perpetuity by the local Federation of Jewish Philanthropies "as a fitting tribute to his devotion to the service, not only of his office, but the whole community." The scholarship was to be given to the student who excelled in the social sciences, regardless of race, color, or creed. A reunion with his erstwhile congregation also took place that year when Brickner returned to install his successor, Rabbi Ferdinand Isserman. The trips to Toronto and Canada never ceased. As late as 1957, thousands of delegates and observers attending a Biennial Convention of the Union of American Hebrew Congregations in Toronto heard the city's mayor, Nathan Phillips, a member of Holy Blossom, acknowledge the influence which Brickner had exerted upon him, and then add, in a facetious style typical of him, that it was Toronto which had made Brickner great and then contributed him to the spiritual enrichment of the United States. Sitting in the audience, Brickner joined in the laughter.

Within a year the Brickner Sunday discourses were attracting such huge audiences that the bulletin was regularly printing apologies to those who could not be admitted, especially temple members. Long before the service was to begin people would enter the sanctuary to get seats.

Under these circumstances, it was natural that local radio stations should see in the Brickner lectures a public service opportunity. Radio was still in its early years, and the broadcasting companies were on the alert for good programs. Both the contents of the Brickner messages and the quality of his voice lent themselves admirably to radio broadcasts.

One station essayed to air the Brickner talks directly from the pulpit, and the idea was an instant success. It did not solve the seating problem, because the larger number of listeners only whetted public curiosity for a look at the Rabbi and the temple from which he spoke.

From 1926 on, Brickner became a radio personality of the first magnitude. Over the years, various radio stations secured his services, under different arrangements. For a time he brought the microphone to the pulpit, but this hampered his delivery. Afterwards, he was engaged by one station to do a weekly series of talks. On another broadcast he answered questions submitted to him. There were intervals when he was regularly broadcasting over two stations. The local station managers told their national officials about him and, in time, he was invited to make frequent network broadcasts. On the "Message of Israel," the largest religious program on the air, he was for decades one of the most popular of speakers. Each broadcast would stimulate an avalanche of letters upon the Union of American Hebrew Congregations, the program's sponsors.

His local programs also yielded hundreds of letters. For years he was confronted with the prodigious task of trying to keep up with the "fan mail," and could scarcely accomplish it, inasmuch as the broadcasting was, after all, but an ancillary part of his regular duties.

The saga of the Brickner broadcasts had many aspects. In the first place, they brought the voice of a rabbi, the views of Judaism, and a clear, prophetic approach to social and civic problems to thousands who would not otherwise have been exposed to them. Many an individual had his prejudices laundered, his incipient xenophobia corrected and his spiritual outlook broadened by virtue of the Brickner broadcasts. Secondly, the radio ministry of Rabbi Brickner brought to a synagogue many who would otherwise never have an occasion to witness a Jewish religious service. Thirdly, his broadcasting obligations stimulated the Rabbi, too. They kept him on the *qui vive* with regard to communal, national, and international problems, and compelled constant research.

In addition, the radio work encouraged other ministers to emulate Brickner. At rabbinical conventions, Brickner was quizzed by his contemporaries about his broadcasts. He shared his experiences with colleagues and thus was instrumental in expanding the scope of this vehicle for the interpretation of Judaism.

It might here be added that, a few years later, the established popularity of Brickner as a radio "star" helped immunize Greater Cleveland against some of the mind-poisoning inflicted upon the nation by the Reverend Charles Coughlin. When that Michigan "radioracle" began his career by preaching a mild form of New Dealism, with utterances favorable to President Franklin Roosevelt, he won applause from Brickner, himself a liberal. But when Coughlinism took a sharp turn to the fanatical right, Brickner struck out against him. His program followed Coughlin's. Scarcely had the echoes of the blasts out of Royal Oak died down than they were refuted by the Cleveland Rabbi. The radio duel between the two clergymen captured the attention of Cleveland and also Detroit, which, sharing a lake with Cleveland, listens to Cleveland's radio stations. The sharp rejoinders of Brickner probably also helped move church officials ultimately to put the quietus on their errant subordinate. Another extremist whose fulminations Brickner succeeded in offsetting, at least in the Cleveland area, was the late, flamboyant Senator Huey Long. In one broadcast, Brickner referred to Coughlin and Long as the "Amos and Andy" of native fascism.

Index and insight to the enormous effect of Brickner's radio career, which made his voice familiar to so many Clevelanders, is the fervor of the letters he received. Not untypical but most revealing is this one which came from a University professor, who said of his radio sermons, "They were eloquent, moving, uplifting, altogether beautiful." He continued, "It seems to me that besides possessing great talents as an orator, and scholarship of a high order, you have the right conception of the moral and religious needs of a modern congregation. For years I have kept away from all church services, because I felt in them nothing inspiring, nothing that might be construed as fit mental food for a man or woman of culture, because in a word, they bored me. I fear that many thousands of people in this and in other countries are in my predicament. They might go to religious services if they were made the beautiful thing they ought to be. Your congregation is to be congratulated on having as their leader a man of your accomplishments and on having Sunday morning services which are, from every point of view, artistic, cultural, ethical and religious and of a distinctly high order."

From Toronto, where Cleveland radio stations sometimes penetrate, a woman wrote in 1927: "Please accept my written applause for last night's sermon on Happiness. It certainly was a pleasure to listen to such a sermon, and, believe me, when I say that it must have brought happiness to many. While I was a little late tuning in and did not hear your name announced at first, I knew that it must be only Rabbi Brickner. Toronto misses you!"

And here is what a Jewish listener wrote once: "I have heard two sermons by you today and I still don't say *dayyenu* (enough)!"

While on a Presidential mission overseas for President Roosevelt, to visit military installations and to bring a religious message to our fighting forces, Brickner's plane was once forced down in Central Africa on the grounds of a hospital. Not being expected, the Rabbi handed his credentials to the doctor in charge. Before the Rabbi could introduce himself, the doctor said, "You are Rabbi Brickner. I recognized your voice. I'm from Toledo and my wife and I never failed to listen to you on Sundays."

Many of Brickner's radio addresses were printed in the *Cleveland Jewish Review and Observer* whose editors, notably Howard Wertheimer, were among the strongest admirers of the Rabbi.

IX

Besides his broadcasts, Brickner came strikingly to the attention of Cleveland's general public through another enterprise initiated shortly after his arrival in the Ohio metropolis. This was a forum, or lecture course, which brought to the Euclid Avenue Temple the leading lecturers and news-making celebrities of the day—and also multitudes representing every faith and walk of life.

The "Course," as it came to be known, was one of the most successful of its kind in the United States. Managed by Mrs. Emil Brudno, it was a success from the outset and soon became "the talk of the town."

The best-known names in public and cultural life found their way to the temple through the instrumentality of the course. The great lecture bureaus, who "book" the speakers and artists, came to look to the Cleveland temple as a major promontory of the platform picture. It was taken for granted, in those days before television, that as soon as a person became famous or as soon as some illustrious or newsworthy European came to these shores, he or she would be on display in the "course."

Princess Alexandra Kropotkin, Channing Pollock, Max Eastman, Dr. Alfred Adler, Bertrand Russell, Ezio Pinza, and Gregor Piatagorsky were some of the attractions one year. Stephen Wise, Aaron Sapiro (whose legal suit brought an end to the anti-Semitic career of Henry Ford), John Haynes Holmes, Chaim Weizmann, John Erskine, Michael Strange, John Cowper Powys, and John Watson were on the roster another year. These great and near-great were given the opportunity to voice their views at the temple and each of them gained something in return: exposure to the opinions and personality of the host-rabbi. For many of them it was the first and only contact with a rabbi, and it can readily be imagined that preconceived notions about rabbis, Jews, and temples underwent considerable illumination.

Most of these celebrities were the recipients of the hospitality of the Brickners. They would spend varying amounts of time in the Brickner home, would discover the Brickner charm, and would, in informal discussions, learn what the Rabbi had to say about matters political or belletristic, as the case might be. The results were incalculable, and they touched both Jews and non-Jews. In Toronto, Brickner had so strongly stirred Pierre van Paassen, that the Dutch-born writer thought of becoming Jewish. As he told the story to a Euclid Avenue Temple audience years later, Brickner had discouraged him from converting to Judaism, asserting that Judaism could greatly benefit from good *Christian* friends. Van Paassen abstained from adopting Brickner's faith, but not from many of his views. Ultimately, van Paassen, still imbued with enthusiasm for Brickner's advanced theological views, did become a Unitarian minister.

One of the Jews who felt the Brickner touch was Max Lerner, whom Brickner "introduced" to Cleveland. Once aloof from Jewish organizational life, Lerner underwent a transformation in his outlook, partially at least due to the influence which Brickner had upon him. The Rabbi won Lerner over by pointing out that the Jewish intelligentsia are needed by organized Judaism, and, furthermore, he proved that Reform Judaism, at least, is a natural ally of the liberalism espoused by Lerner and men like him.

Of Brickner, Lerner wrote: "His was one of the first temples at which I lectured quite regularly, and he was one of the first men with whom I found I could discuss the question of anti-Semitism, Israel-Zionism and, in the very same spirit, the questions of American liberalism and the American promise. We met frequently, at Cleveland or New York, or crisscrossing each other in our trips around the country or abroad. There was never any need for us to waste words of explanation to each other. The political and human empathy between us was complete, so that we could start our conversations knowing that each was starting from the same premise."

The "Course" was responsible also, as indicated, for causing many people who would ordinarily never see a rabbi to do so. Brickner's introductions of the speakers, his conduct of the question period, his casual observations about the presentations left a deep impression on the audiences. Often Brickner, in what was ostensibly the subordinate position of chairman of the evening, would outshine the guest speakers in eloquence and profundity, for, as most of us discover, a famous person is not always a good speaker. The "big names," therefore, would sometimes fail to appeal, but Brickner, the local favorite, would, on such occasions, invariably "save the night."

IX [SIC, SHOULD BE X]

In addition to the broadcasts and the lecture course, one other "extra-curricular" activity brought Brickner considerable note and notice. Beginning in 1926, the Rabbi was called upon often to serve as an arbitrator in labor disputes. It is a measure of the confidence which the Rabbi inspired in all segments of the city that, albeit an avowed liberal, he was persona grata with management as well as with labor in a number of vexing disputes. It was during his second year in Cleveland that he became the impartial chairman for the city's clothing industry. For several years, he undertook the delicate and time-consuming task of trying to settle the differences between the Amalgamated Clothing Workers of America and its employers.

In the Thirties the dry cleaning industry of Cleveland was shaken by charges and counod,ercharges involving "racketeering" and kindred ills. A "Wholesale Cleaners Club" was abolished by court injunction and the air was full of suspicion and mutual distrust. Although the two sides were ferociously at odds, they could agree on the wisdom of securing the services of Rabbi Brickner as an impartial arbitrator. An appeal was made to him and once again he stepped into a difficult situation, with powers described by the industry attorneys as "supreme." It required much time and tedious negotiations on the part of the Rabbi to bring "cleanliness" to the cleaning industry. In similar fashion the Rabbi helped put an end to strife in Cleveland's baking industry.

Again in 1934, the Rabbi was called in to help solve a critical industrial altercation. This time it was a dispute between the employees of the city-owned Cleveland Railway Company and the operators of trolleys and buses. The ominous prospect was the paralysis of the city's transportation system. Summoned again to function as an arbitrator, Brickner and others were able to stave off a strike, to the immense relief of the city and to the satisfaction of both sides.

Lest anyone believe that the congregation was anything but proud over the public service performed by its popular and versatile Rabbi (even though many hours went into the assignment), it would be well to turn to the temple minutes of 1934 and observe that the president of the congregation, Irwin Loeser, referred thus in his annual report to Brickner's role as arbitrator: "It afforded an opportunity for service in a worthwhile cause, and it is gratifying to note that the work of the arbitrators resulted in a peaceful settlement of what threatened to be a serious industrial controversy fraught with possibilities of great losses to the participants and the public."

X [SIC, SHOULD BE XI]

Despite the plethora of "outside" activities, Brickner's major preoccupation, of course, was the welfare of his own temple and congregation. From the moment he set foot in Cleveland, his primary concern was the building up of the temple program, its expansion, and its deepening.

His success was profound both in tangible and intangible realms. One of the most palpable changes he instituted was in the curriculum and program of the religious school.

He was basically an educator. While still a youngster in knee pants, he had exhibited a great flair for communicating information to audiences. He believed that classes ought to be interesting as well as instructive. A product of Teachers' College, Columbia University, he was an adherent of the principles of progressive education, as expounded by John Dewey. In recent years progressive education has been the target of many attacks, and some august periodicals have attributed many of the nation's woes to the doctrines of Dewey and his "dewy-eyed" apostles. This is not the place to examine the indictment against the progressivists, but it is germane to point out that the basic premises laid down by Dewey and advanced by such disciples of his as Brickner have not been successfully refuted. Cardinal elements in the Brickner approach to education were respect for the distinctive nature of each child, the need to find the proper motivation to make him want to absorb the data at hand, and the further need to embody in the classroom process all of the insights about children gleaned from the findings of modern educational psychology. Brickner was hospitable to any device which would make the subject matter more arresting to his students. With the help of such educational aides as David Pearlman (a Herzl Club alumnus, who went on to become a rabbi), Nathan Brilliant, Mrs. Sigmund Braverman, and, later, Rabbi Philip Horowitz, he created a religious school which was often hailed as one of the finest in the land.

He gave the school content. Hebrew became a staple of the curriculum for all children, the rationale being that the language linked the Jew to his past, to his contemporaries in Palestine-Israel, and prepared the child for intelligent participation in religious services.

He gave the school standards. Children were expected to meet certain levels of achievement, so that they would be discouraged from taking spiritual training lightly and would be stimulated to derive as much benefit from their schooling as could be afforded in the relatively short time given to it. By making the expectations of the religious school match those of the public school, the children's own respect for the temple school was substantially lifted.

He gave the school color. To induce children to give more of their time to religion, he introduced the club-system, with weekday afternoon sessions during which more data was often imbibed than was the case in formal sessions. Plays, carnivals, pageants, contests, original worship services, special services geared to the mental grasp of the child, story sessions,—a vast array of methods designed to lend enchantment and glamour to studies were initiated and authorized by the Rabbi.

The Brickner religious school became a sprightly and vital institution. Brickner himself helped train teachers and indoctrinate them both with methodology and Jewish information.

In the Brickner school, two generations were given a solid background of Jewish learning. Thousands of alumni trace their lifelong interest in Judaism to the training they received in that school. A large number of the graduates themselves went on to become temple educators; many became teachers of religious schools; several became rabbis.

For three decades the school was the object of visits by temple educators who wanted to see the famed institution at firsthand and acquire ideas for the improvement of their own schools. A formidable share of the Rabbi's correspondence reflected the same admiration and curiosity, as Brickner was incessantly supplying information about the school to interested parties.

XI [SIC, SHOULD BE XII]

The Brickner impact on the temple program might be summed up in the very words used by the Rabbi at his installation service, "Keep Liberal Judaism liberal." The Rabbi was concerned over the possibility that Reform itself might freeze into another Orthodoxy if it did not regularly reconsider its form and norms.

In Toronto, we recall, the Rabbi sought to "liberalize" the congregation. In Cleveland, on the other hand, he might be said to have "traditionalized" the congregation. The two achievements were not inconsistent.

Reform Judaism, it must be remembered, does not call for the elimination of old customs and ceremonies as such. It does advocate the elimination of rites which no longer have meaning or relevance. Reform asserts that traditions are not to be preserved just because they are traditions. Indeed, Reform goes further and maintains that the traditional pattern of Judaism is not blind obeisance to the past but continuous change to satisfy current religious needs.

With this concept often elaborated upon by Rabbi Brickner from pulpit and platform, he brought Reform up to date in his Cleveland congregation by restoring some ceremonies which had assumed fresh meaning and significance to the temple-goers of his day, among them the sounding of the real shofar instead of a cornet at the High Holy Day services; the recitation of the *Yizkor*, the memorial prayer, on the last day of some of the holidays; the singing of the *Kiddush*, or blessing over the wine, and the lighting of the Shabbos candles at the Friday night services.

These and other rituals were not merely restored in their older guise. In each case the ceremony was modified to satisfy the aesthetic sensibilities of the modern worshipper and the canons of Reform Judaism. These characteristics also applied to the Brickner policy with regard to the Bar Mitzvah service. Bar Mitzvah a la Brickner was a far cry from the ceremony of old. It was not obligatory, nor done in a perfunctory manner. No one could become Bar Mitzvah without at least three years of preliminary study of Hebrew. It became a privilege, not a chore for a boy to become Bar Mitzvah. Eliminated from the ceremony was the long chant, which is still meaningless to many a youngster. Instead, the boy had to master the Hebrew of his Torah reading, and he demonstrated that it made sense to him by translating the passage, line by line. Gone was the notorious Bar Mitzvah talk, with its banalities. Instead, the Rabbi delivered a charge to the lad and then blessed him. Nor did the temple suffer from that Bar Mitzvah problem which troubles many a congregation: the unwillingness of the boy to continue his studies for Confirmation. Confirmation had a strong hold on the children at the Cleveland temple. To make that appeal even more graphic, Rabbi Brickner would meet with the parents of the Confirmation Class and convey to them the significance of the event and its profound implications. The Confirmation services at the temple were deeply moving events, even for those whose families were not directly involved in the proceedings.

The best way to describe what Brickner did to "traditionalize" the temple is to say that he invested it with a "more" Jewish style and flavor. Transcending the actual changes in rite was the atmosphere which the Rabbi breathed into the temple. Reform had grown cold and austere in its liturgical style and in its outlook. Today, the entire Reform movement has undergone a marked change in tone. That tone may be heard in the actual strains of the music sung in choirs; more of it is traditional than was the case in years gone by. The tone may be caught in the greater use of Hebrew at services. Reform rabbis today are not afraid of Yiddish, introducing it into their conversations and even into their sermons. The modern Reform rabbi recognizes his community of interest and objective with the rabbis of other Jewish groups.

All of these "reforms" were highlights of the Brickner ministry in Cleveland. Indeed, he helped to lead the national Reform movement as well as his own congregation in these directions. In 1932, when he was given the honor of delivering the sermon at the convention of the Central Conference of American Rabbis, he spoke on the topic of "The Reform of Reform Judaism," and made the point that continuous renewal was the rhythm of Judaism. "Every page of the Talmud," he pointed out, "reveals Israel's ability to grow."

His advocacy of a "reformed" Reform was also in evidence at biennial assemblies of the Union of American Hebrew Congregations, parent body of the nation's liberal temples. In this generation-long effort he was to find an ally in the man who was to spearhead the move to synthesize the teachings of Isaac M. Wise and Stephen S. Wise: Rabbi Maurice N. Eisendrath, who was to succeed Brickner's successor as rabbi of Holy Blossom Temple in Toronto and then go on to become the president of the Union. Often a member of the national board of the U.A.H.C., Brickner ever and anon raised his voice most effectively to plead for a more positive brand of Reform Judaism, one more closely attuned to the past and more hospitable to other Jewish groups in America. Brickner's role in fashioning Reform's new *anschauung* was a considerable one, and mention should be made here of a soldier-in-arms who joined Brickner in many of these ideological engagements: Rabbi James G. Heller, his closest friend in the rabbinate.

XII [*SIC, SHOULD BE* XIII]

The immense popularity of Brickner as orator and interpreter of religion led, in 1928, to one of the highlights in his life and in the history of Cleveland, a full-dress debate with Clarence Darrow, the famous agnostic lawyer.

Darrow was at the crest of his fame in the mid-twenties. He had become a front-page figure in the Leopold-Loeb case in 1923–1924. In 1926, he had bested William Jennings Bryan in the Scopes trial; although he had technically lost the notorious "monkey" case he was regarded as the victor, and Bryan's death was widely attributed to the mortification he had suffered at Darrow's hands. Other trials had also lifted Darrow to dazzling prominence, and soon he became a prize of the lecture bureaus who sent him up and down the land to voice his unorthodox views and make fresh headlines wherever he went.

Brickner had on a number of occasions paid his respects to Darrow's opinions about the Bible and religion, taking exception to his cynicism and mechanistic point of view. He had done this from the pulpit and on the radio.

Brickner was also called upon to comment on Darrow in a question-and-answer period which had been instituted in connection with the temple's Sunday morning services. This unique feature, whereby Brickner answered questions from members of the congregation, intrigued his listeners and often called forth minor oratorical gems which displayed the Brickner eloquence at its best.

The widespread attention accorded to Brickner's strictures against Darrow prompted the Advertising Club of Cleveland to propose a formal debate between the Rabbi and the attorney. The subject was to be "Is Man a Machine?"

Both principals agreed, and before long interest in the encounter rose mountain-high. Place of the event was to be the downtown Masonic Auditorium. Tickets, at various prices, sold briskly. A radio station pre-empted the broadcasting rights. Before long, all tickets were gone and the Advertising Club and the Rabbi were besieged for seats by those who wanted to attend but couldn't.

On the night of the debate, hundreds were gathered outside the auditorium. The debaters had to share the stage with 200 people who were seated on it, and many others stood for the two hours of the debate.

The debate proved to be a spectacular, although friendly clash, engrossing the attention of the audience, and according to a banner headline in the morning newspaper, 500,000 radio listeners. A reading of the text of the talks, three by each of the speakers, reveals that Darrow had met his forensic and logical match. This was the conclusion of most of the audience which roared its reactions to the extraordinary encounter. It was also the "verdict" of a number of civic and university groups who voted on the question. According to former Judge Ben B. Lindsey, the Denverite who was noted for his "companionate marriage proposals, "Rabbi Brickner was the most brilliant opponent Darrow ever faced."

In the treasure house of his mind, many a Clevelander stored the memory of that night on February 9, 1928, when an intellectual contest ignited the kind of frenzied enthusiasm usually bestowed upon exciting sports events. In 1928, radios were still not universally owned, so many living rooms were crowded the night of the debate with visitors who wanted to "listen in." In public places, amplifiers had been set up, of the type which were used for broadcasts of the World Series baseball games, and crowds huddled around them, wildly cheering the arguments about theology, physiology, and philosophy.

Although Darrow had conducted many debates with clergymen before, he was at a disadvantage when he faced Brickner, for the latter represented a kind of religion with which he was not familiar. Darrow was accustomed to dealing with fundamentalists, the protagonists of a faith which accepted the words of the Bible with absolute literalness, which took exception to the findings of physics, chemistry, physiology, geology, and anthropology, and which clung to extreme theological positions. Darrow had developed ways of puncturing the claims of the literalists, and he counted on those devices to help his case and cause in Cleveland.

But for all his reading and research, Darrow had failed to discover religious liberalism which had reconciled the discoveries of science with the belief in a God of spirit Who was real to its adherents without the literal acceptance of the Bible. Darrow never understood that, in a very important sense, he and Bryan were not really on opposite sides of the fence. Both of them were actually in agreement that if you could prove Biblical passages inaccurate or contradictory, you thereby invalidated the theses of religion per se. The liberal religionist is not so easily discomfited. He interprets many Biblical stories figuratively; he readily admits that the scientific portions of the Bible reflect the limited knowledge of those who wrote it, but he stoutly maintains that the Bible's value is not weakened by these concessions since the ethical ideals in Holy Writ are still inspiring. He furthermore believes that the teachings of science do not eliminate, but rather heighten, the need for a God idea to provide a rational explanation for the authorship of the marvels of earth and sky.

In his presentation, Darrow unleashed the weapons that had so often served him well in routing his pietistic opponents. But Brickner easily parried these sallies by pointing out that they did not apply to his position. Nor, Brickner made it clear, did assaults upon the Book of Genesis make the belief in God any less tenable.

Nettled by a liberalism he did not quite grasp, Darrow cried out in the debate, "He (Brickner) cannot be an evolutionist and a theologian although some people try to straddle that far." Here Darrow admitted his own limited knowledge about modern religionists who have no trouble harmonizing theology and Darwinism.

Sensing his own quandary but unable to understand it fully, Darrow declared, "The only man who can debate the other side of this question and give you anything for your money is the fundamentalist." This was followed by laughter, but Darrow could not laugh off the feeling that his forensic blows were not landing on an opponent who bewildered him. "I insist," he continued, "that between that theory (the creation story in Genesis) and mechanism there isn't a place to rest." Darrow was simply not aware of the fact that between Genesis and Darwin there is a place to rest: theological rationalism.

With remarkable adroitness, courtesy, and good taste, Brickner used Darrow himself to disprove what Darrow said. The lawyer insisted on denying the existence of a soul, of idealism; he went so far as to say that there was no essential difference between Lincoln and a chimpanzee (Brickner, remembering that Lincoln's Birthday was a few days off had asked Darrow whether he saw any distinction between the Emancipator and a chimp). Brickner cited as proof that something in man goes beyond the chemical, the very impulses which actuated the great criminal lawyer to plead for his clients. That extra-mechanical ingredient, said the rabbi, is "the consciousness, it is the unity, it is the ego, that we call, thank God, Clarence Darrow, that says to society, 'Society, you ought not to do this inhumane thing to a criminal!'" The large crowd roared its approval.

The full savor of the exciting event is graphically conveyed in the account which appeared in the *Cleveland Plain Dealer* Friday morning, February 10: The banner headline read: "DEBATE IS HEARD BY 500,000; Darrow and Brickner Wrestle Over Problem of Man and Universe: Throngs Listen at Radio Dials; Record Crowd Jams Masonic Auditorium and Cheers Verbal Hits with Fervor of Fight Fans; Arguments Sweep from Chimpanzee's Forest to Homes of Artist and Poet: Handclasp Brings Two-Hour Contest to Harmonious and Friendly Close."

The Masonic Auditorium verbal bout was not the last between Brickner and Darrow. They met again in Cleveland and in several other cities as well, each time attracting great crowds and arousing great interest. The idea went so well that one enterprising impresario arranged for Brickner to break a verbal lance with another noted agnostic of the time, Dr. Harry Elmer Barnes. Their debate topic: "Is God a Myth?"

An arresting aftermath of the debate with Darrow occurred in 1956, on Broadway. The great contest made so profound an impression on a young Clevelander, then enrolled in the Euclid Avenue Temple religious school, that he developed an unshakable interest in Darrow and his views. That youngster grew up to be the playwright, Jerome Lawrence, who, with Robert E. Lee, created the play, "Inherit the Wind," a dramatization of the Scopes trial. A reading of the play, which featured Paul Muni in the role of Darrow, reveals that its real theme is the statement that Darrow was a religious man despite his ostensible deprecation of religion—a replay of what Brickner had said in Masonic Auditorium, wrote Jerome Lawrence:

"Rabbi Brickner had a tremendous influence on my life and growth as he did on thousands of his other students and friends who came within the orbit of his towering brilliance and magnetic personality.

"His debate in Cleveland with Clarence Darrow on 'Is Man a Machine?' first whetted my interest in Darrow and his work. It thus had a direct bearing on our decision to write 'Inherit the Wind,' many years later.

"But his warmth and intellectual guidance throughout the years has [*sic*] been a stimulus and an inspiration. The last time we were together, we sat before an open fire in his living room (I had spoken at the Fairmount Temple that day) and discussed until long past midnight the place of the writer and the minister in our society today: the necessity to be angry (at the right mo-ments), the ways of combatting complacency, conformity, the ways of waking up the dozing Miltown generation.

"I was proud that he considered me his son. To all of us who try to deal with the fascinating fire of ideas, he was a father whose like we shall not see again."

XIII [SIC, SHOULD BE XIV]

Before Darrow there had been Europe. In the summer of 1927 Brickner spent three and a half months abroad. The trip was part vacation, part work; he was an American representative at two important gatherings: a Conference on Jewish Rights, in Zurich, to discuss the status of Jewish minorities in Europe; and a conference of the World Zionist Congress, in Basle. His travels took him to Poland and Russia, Turkey and Greece, Egypt, Palestine and Italy, as well as Switzerland. This was one of a succession of overseas trips which helped to broaden his horizons and keep him *au courant* with the feelings and conditions of people in Europe, information which was always reflected in his lectures.

In letters home to his wife, Brickner told what moved him.

He was moved by a group of young boys and girls in Poland who were readying themselves for the hard life on a farm in Palestine. "I saw men and women at work on their fields, stables, etc., inuring themselves for a two-year course in preparation for life as *chalutzim,*" he wrote. "The idealism was contagious. You could kiss them. There were girls from fine homes who had run away and were contented to toil in pathetic circumstances. The boys sleep on the hay in the barn. The cattle have it better than these boys. Do they complain? No. They sing and ask only when they will get to Palestine. Enclosed you will find a flower plucked from their soil soaked with the sweat of Jewish selflessness. Here is a movement that can inspire love that is truly religious. Oh, darling, how you would have loved it!"

"What I Would Say . . ."

The Lithuanian-born son of a Hebrew teacher, Abba Hillel Silver emigrated with his family to New York's Lower East Side in 1902. He early immersed himself in Hebrew cultural activities in the cause of Theodor Herzl's political Zionism—to which he devoted the major part of his life. Ordained a rabbi at Hebrew Union College in Cincinnati in 1915, he first served a congregation in Wheeling, West Virginia. Officials of Cleveland's The Temple–Tifereth Israel—invited Silver to become its rabbi in 1917 partly because they hoped that he would be able to attract Eastern European Jewish emigrés to the synagogue, which had been founded and was run by Jews of German origin.

Silver was outspoken in his support of many liberal causes. He was especially ardent about and lectured widely on Zionism and Hebrew. He considered the building of a Jewish homeland in Israel the "historically inescapable task of Jewry." He believed deeply in the concept of Jewish peoplehood and wrote compellingly about religious messianism.

An early critic of Nazism, he was an organizer of the 1938 anti-Nazi boycott. In 1943, as head of the American Zionist Emergency Council, he mobilized Jewish and non-Jewish opinion on behalf of Zionism. Many consider his address before the United Nations on May 8, 1947, in which he presented the case for an independent Jewish state in what was then Palestine, to be his crowning achievement. Silver also served as president of the Central Conference of American Rabbis (Reform) and the Zionist Organization of America.

One hundred German high school students visited Cleveland in 1937, part of Nazi Germany's exchange program with many nations. Profoundly attuned to Nazi strategy and methods, Rabbi Silver seized that occasion to expose the dangers of Germany's propaganda department, headed by master propagandist Josef Goebbels.

Noting that such exchanges include Germans from all occupations, Rabbi Silver sounds a clarion warning about the pro-Nazi propaganda purposes of the campaign on American soil and among the academics brought to visit German universities. He closes with a challenge to the visiting youth to observe carefully the "mood and quality of democratic life."

Source: Rabbi Abba Hillel Silver, "What I Would Say to the German Students Arriving in Cleveland," address delivered at The Temple–Tifereth Israel, Sunday, May 2, 1937, Abba Hillel Silver Papers, Western Reserve Historical Society.

What I Would Say to the German Students Arriving in Cleveland
By Rabbi Abba Hillel Silver
At The Temple on Sunday, May 2, 1937

This evening there will arrive in our city one hundred students from the high schools in Germany to spend six weeks in our city and to attend our high schools. In their return to Germany, they will take with them presumably one hundred Cleveland high school students to spend a similar period of time in Germany. The students who came across—this student exchange—on the face of it, is a very innocent and commendable enterprise. It is highly desirable, of course, for the sake of better understanding between nations today that there exist the freest, greatest degree of neighborliness between the student bodies, faculties and school systems generally of all countries.

No one, leastwise the liberals and the friends of international good will and cooperation will therefore object to students from foreign countries coming to our schools and students from our shores visiting schools on other shores.

But we are dealing here not at all with an innocent enterprise of a well-intentioned government bent upon international good will. We are dealing with a very shrewd piece of propaganda on the part of a very unscrupulous government which in its own land has trampled under foot those very ideals of tolerance and good will, freedom of thought and free education which their student emissaries presumably are to acquaint themselves with in Cleveland and in free America.

The purpose which prompted the German propaganda department which is headed by that malevolent Goebbels to send those students here is not educational but political. There have been streams of such contact groups coming from Germany in the last few years, especially engineers, bakers, clothiers, chemists, even brewers to learn the art of beer-making.

And now high school students. Their purpose is not to learn from America. The Nazis are convinced that they have nothing to learn from anybody. They are omnipotent. They are perfect. They are so perfect, that they feel they ought to rule the world. These contact groups are being sent in order to persuade the American people, and similar groups by the way are being sent to the other countries which the Nazi Regime would like to cultivate, these contact groups are being sent in order to persuade the American people that in Germany all is sunshine and roses, that the German people today is just one big happy family and that all the criticism that exists and which has been launched against the Third Reich is lies made by the Jews and Communists; that Hitler is above all things interested in world peace and that the rearmament of Germany which he has stimulated and which in turn has stimulated a mad rearmament race of the whole world is simply intended to save the world from communism and from Jewish domination. And so, whatever land the Nazi government would like to cultivate is being subjected to a systematic campaign, carefully planned and outlined by its public relation experts. These groups who come to this country from Germany are coached, trained. Their missions are purely fictitious. The real purpose is propaganda.

In the same way the German government is spending huge sums of money to bring over to Germany American students, American professors, presidents of American colleges and universities in order to subject them to an intensive course of pro-Nazi propaganda and in order to counteract that natural resentment which exists in American academic circles of the shameless trampling under foot of the sanctities of free education.

Every few months the Nazis discover some new occasion to send out invitations to the universities of the United States and England and other countries to solicit delegates to come to Germany. Last year it was Heidelberg. This year it is Gottingen. Next year some other excuse will be discovered to invite institutions of the great intellectual centers of the world to come to Germany. Fortunately, our great institutions have not permitted themselves to be beguiled. Oxford, Cambridge, Yale, in our own land, have refused because they know what it is about. They are not naive and they wish to utilize this opportunity to demonstrate their resentment of what has happened to culture and learning in Germany. Those professors who did go to Heidelberg were subject to a veritable barrage of pro-Nazi propaganda which nauseated them.

So that the liberals in our city of Cleveland who have gotten up on the high horse of broad-mindedness and who insisted upon the coming of those German high school students to Cleveland as an act of international good will of happy augury are simply as naive as the Nazis would like them to be.

The Fascists of the world haven't money to spend to finance a three thousand mile jaunt for one hundred high school students just to acquaint their young darlings with American democracy. The Fascists and the Nazis haven't any money as they themselves say for butter nor have they any money for trans-Atlantic picnics. They need their money as they say for cannons and for propaganda.

I should like to have you know that their students did not wait upon being invited. They were on the high seas long before your Cleveland Board of Education had an opportunity even to invite them as visitors in the classrooms. Their youths—please do not speak of them as children—they are not nine, ten or eleven year old children who are coming over here. They [sic] talk about children is to win sympathy. These young men and women are hand-picked, carefully trained youths of seventeen, eighteen, nineteen, twenty. They are the backbone of Mussolini's and Hitler's followers. They are not children. They are serving here as the nuclei around which will rally pro-Nazi sentiment in the community.

Cleveland will experience, in the next six weeks a whole series of receptions, the first of which takes place this evening in the Public Hall, and meetings and demonstrations, the singing of the Nazi songs and perhaps the Nazi salute. The schoolwork of these one hundred pupils is purely incidental and the commonplace in all this business. Most of these students are inadequately prepared either by their knowledge of English or the duration of their stay here to learn anything substantial in the schools of the city. And the one hundred students from Cleveland who will go with them for six weeks to Germany will be subjected as any organized group of visitors is subjected in Germany to a very skillful and very subtle campaign of propaganda so that they will come back home at the end of the summer full of enthusiasm about the loveliness of Germany. Perhaps also inoculated also [sic] with the virus of anti-Semitism because you can readily understand that Mr. Goebbels is not going to take these young people to the concentration camps, the prison camps nor to the ghetto schools to which Jewish students have been consigned. They will not see with their own eyes when they go to Germany what has actually happened to that regime—to tolerance and decency.

In a hundred homes in Cleveland, upon the return of these students—these homes will become centers from which will radiate good will, friendship, appreciation of the marvelous Germany of Hitler. That is the purpose of this coming to Cleveland of these German students.

Their coming here ought to be utilized by us to call the attention of the American people to what has actually been done in Germany to education, to the havoc which has been wrought in the academic life of the country.

There is a popular saying that when a man is going mad it begins in the head. And that is where the madness began in Germany—in the head—in the high schools, in the universities. One of the first places of Nazi propaganda, of anti-Semitic propaganda were the high schools and the universities in Germany. They were the first when the Nazis came into power to submit themselves to the dragooning of the Nazis. Every professor, Jew or non-Jew who had been liberal, who had advocated peace, was thrown out of the classroom, driven either into exile or to suicide.

The ship which carried these hundred students must have passed on the Atlantic the ship which was carrying back to Europe Thomas Mann, crown and glory of German literature who was not only deprived of his citizenship but the university of [Bonn] which had honored him with an honorary degree—that university had the meanness to notify him that it had now decided to reject his degree—non-Jew—the very glory and pride of German literature. That is what is happening in Germany, the land of culture, the land which is now inviting our students to come and to learn culture in the ways of civilized life. There all education is regimented. It is all a part of the Nazi conformity. Any difference leads to the concentration camp or worse. The whole aim of German education has been revamped. The whole of the German people is to be educated for war.

In "Mein Kampf," Hitler writes: "It will be the task of the Nationalist State to see to it that an adequate education is given to youth in order to provide for a generation prepared for the final and greatest decisions on this earth. The nation which will take this road first will be the victorious one."

The purpose of education in Germany is not to train young people into the ways of civilization, cooperation, culture so that they will have a free mind so as to be enabled to revere truth. Not at all! The purpose of the new education is "werhaftigkeit." The whole spirit of the new education is the "wergeist." Any group of schools in Germany which is still independent like the Catholic and refuses to be dominated by means fair or foul into this spirit of the state schools—that is why you have this campaign today against the Catholic priests, monks and the most infamous and indecent trials—not to clean up the moral life of Germany but simply to discredit the Catholic church and its educational institutions in Germany.

And of course what happened to the Jewish teachers and students is a well know [sic] fact unfortunately. That is why when these students arrive in Cleveland, we are opening our Jewish Welfare Fund Drive in Cleveland. That is why we appeal to people to give money to German Jews. German people did not need our help four or five years ago or any time before that. What has happened that we must now go from door to door to ask for alms to support the lives of men, women and children in Germany who years before were the most munificent supporters of other people? What has happened is that this iniquitous regime who has the effrontery to send us their one hundred students as "Exhibit A" has forced scientists such as Albert Einstein out of Germany, has taken a community of six hundred thousand men, women and children and has crushed them under the wheels of barbarism. That is why tonight we open our campaign to keep these unfortunates alive.

And what happened to the Jewish children in Germany is, of course, the most indecent chapter in the record of indecencies of this regime. It began first with separating Jewish children in the classroom, sending them off from their friends with whom they had played up until this time, branding them with the mark of shame, warning non-Jewish people against playing with them, walking with them or talking with them.

The following letter was received from a boy thirteen years old, the son of a Jewish father and a Christian mother who had been brought up in the Christian faith. The letter was written from Paris where the family fled. This is the letter from a thirteen year old Jewish lad who had been raised from birth as a Protestant.

"I was the only Jew in my class. Until Easter I was a Protestant, and then they found out that my father was a Jew and so I became one. After that everything was different. No one would be friends with me. No one would answer me. In school no one would sit next to me. They all used to want to before, as I was the best in the class and they all wanted to crib. Now I had to sit all alone on the back bench. At first I was frightfully unhappy—more so as the masters who always used to like me could not stand the sight of [me] any more. When they came into the classroom everyone had to jump up and with their right hand outstretched, shout 'Heil Hitler.' I did too—or I didn't. I don't know. If I did, then the whole class would shout 'The Jew is profaning our greeting!' And if I didn't the master shouted 'You wait, you Marxist bastard!' Then I was ordered to shout 'Heil Hitler!' alone three times. The whole class laughed. I was

so afraid, I wanted to cry. And then I used often to be late so that I shouldn't
have to shout 'Heil Hitler!' The master used to give me extra work to do as a
punishment. He wrote in the class book, 'For Jewish slovenliness.'

"Once I did not know the answer—I used always to know before—so
he [asked] me if the only think [*sic*] I could do was 'Fires and murders like
my father.' Once when I could not answer, the history master said I should
be slaughtered like father. I tried to pull myself together, but tears used to
sometimes come and then they used to say I was a dirty coward like the rest
of the Marxists. The worst thing of all was in the 'Breaks' in the courtyard.
We children of Jewish and Marxist parents had to go into the corner of the
courtyard by ourselves. Then there was always trouble. The others shouted
nasty things at us and threw stones. Once I defended myself, so they hit me
and bullied me fearfully. Those in charge didn't even come near.

"At singing it was worse still. I had to learn the text of the Horst Wessel
Lied and the other songs and then I had to say them alone. Again they used
to laugh and shout horrid things.

"In drawing I had to do nothing but swastikas. Once I got detention because I drew a crooked one. Then the master wrote in his book, 'For ridiculing
the German symbol.'

"Before I used to be the best pupil. Now I was the worst. Whether I got
something right or wrong, I always got the worst marks. I was the scapegoat
for everything."

That, of course, was not an isolated incident as you may well imagine.
Those things took place by the hundreds and thousands. Jewish children were
at first allowed to attend public schools but since last Easter they have been
driven out of the German schools and forced into ghetto schools. Recently,
a friend of mine turned over to me a letter which she received from a little
Jewish girl. This is the letter:

"My dear Aunt:
    "Hoping you are very well. I am writing today myself and you will imagine
I have a peculiar motive. Two days before we go Eastern-holidays and in
receiving my testimony, I was told that I have to leave the school. Now I have
no other chance than to go to the single Jewish primary school. But I have
no mind for that because it is limited relating to space and not an agreeable
stay, also no possibility neither for swimming nor for gymnastics.
    "Dear Aunt, nearly all my friends are . . . abroad, the majority in Amer-
ica. Perhaps you can arrange for me that I will be claimed by somebody

of your acquaintances who is ready to take me. Please do me the favour [of] taking care for it. I would be very obliged to you for always.
"With many thanks and all love, I remain,
    Yours"

In the Aryan schools—the high schools from which these hundred emissaries are now coming to Cleveland—it is compulsory to give instruction in the theory of race, and MacDonald, whom you will recall, was the former High Commissioner for Refugees, in submitting his final report to the League of Nations said this:

"According to a decree of Reichminister Rust, no 'non-Aryan' pupils may be admitted to German elementary public schools. 'Racial science,' teaching that the 'non-Aryan' is a perverse and traitorous creature has been made a fundamental part of the school curricula by order of the Prussian Minister of Education. The Instructions issued by the Prussian Minister for Economy and Labour, for example, in March 1934, setting forth the subjects recommended for 'civic education' in professional and technical schools, contained suggestions for the study of 'the new structure of the family and nation on a racial basis, and in this regard the Jewish question.'

"Among the official school texts chosen by Reichminister Rust for this racial study are the following: Adolf Hitler's Mein Kampf; Theodore Fritsch's Handbook of the Jewish Questions; H.F.R. Gunther's Racial Science of the Jewish People; and A. Rosenberg's Protocols of the Elders of Zion and Jewish World Politics. The instructions given to German school teachers on methods of lecturing schoolgirls on the Jewish question advise that 'when raising the Jewish question with the girls, steps should be taken by the teachers to bring out the fact that Jews are of Asiatic descent and cannot mix with 'Aryans,' and that intermarriage with Jews is out of the Question.' In the schools of Bavaria a text-book by van Fikenscher, Aufbruch der Nation, is used with the approval of the Minister of Education and is particularly devoted to reconstructing German history so as to portray the Jew as a villain. The Handbook of the Hitler Jugend teaches the same doctrine."

And then, there is that new book of nursery rhymes which has been printed for four and five year olds—pictures and poems and in each one the Jew is represented as the devil or some horrible person to be shunned and avoided as the enemy of little children.

And it is this regime, an organized state of 65 millions which has poisoned the whole educational system with infamous lies—it is this regime which has asked American citizens of Cleveland to send their children to their schools and which is now sending its young people as its emissaries to us.

I wish I had these hundred people before me. I assure you I won't get a chance. I would like to say a few things to them if their ears have not been stopped and their eyes not covered by blinkers. I should like to say to them: Try, if possible to utilize these few free weeks, the freest weeks which you have had in your lives and which you are likely to have for many years to come, to learn what a free people really does, how a free people really lives, how a civilized nation tries to solve its problems without resorting to tyranny, blood purges, how a great nation can grow, as this nation has grown, in spite of the fact or perhaps because of the fact that it is built up by the labor and sacrifice and enterprise of peoples of all races, creeds and color. Here we try to make not ancestry and blood, but character and ability and loyalty the measuring rod of human worth. I should like to take them into our schools and libraries and show them how we try to learn more, how we try to advance more in knowledge not by stifling opposition but by trying to learn from the opposition what of truth may be in it. Here we don't burn books. We don't lie. I should like to tell them that here, too, we train our children into the love of country—patriotism. We don't try to [fill] them with egoism, belligerency. We don't romanticize here about soldiers or war. We try to cooperate as friends and neighbors with other countries. I should like to tell them that here, too, we have our fanatics and zealots of all kinds. But we don't turn our government over to them, or our institutions. I should like to tell them, finally, that during the next few weeks that they will be here, that they will be able to catch something of the mood and the spirit of free America. They will go back home not happier but wiser and it is this wisdom wedded to some discontent which will be in their souls that may some day bring about the unhappy regeneration of their unhappy Fatherland.

LEON WIESENFELD (1885–1971)

Excerpt from *Jewish Life in Cleveland in the 1920s and 1930s*

Polish-born Leon Wiesenfeld continued a career in journalism after arriving in the United States near the start of the twentieth century, working first in New York City for the legendary Abraham Cahan's *Jewish Daily Forward*. He moved to Cleveland in 1924, where he significantly influenced Jewish journalism for the next three decades (see also the chapter on Judah Rubinstein in this volume). He was associate editor of Cleveland's *Die Yiddishe Velt* (*The Jewish World*) for ten years before becoming its editor in 1934. Striking out on his own four years later, he founded an English-Yiddish weekly, *Die Yiddishe Stimme* (*The Jewish Voice*), which folded a year later. Undaunted, Wiesenfeld created *The Jewish Voice Pictorial,* an English-language annual that lasted into the 1950s. He also published a novel, two plays that were widely performed on the Yiddish stage (see also the chapter on David Guralnik in this volume), and an account of Jewish life in Cleveland in the 1920s and 1930s. Among his other Jewish activities, Wiesenfeld was an organizer of the Cleveland Zionist Society and a director of the Jewish Orphan Home.

Wiesenthal moved to Cleveland to head the newspaper *Der Yiddisher Waechter* (*The Jewish Guardian*), which survived for six weeks and appears to have been created solely to enable publisher Rabbi Samuel Benjamin to attack Rabbi Solomon Goldman, his successor as rabbi of the large Jewish Center–Synagogue complex Benjamin had built. Wiesenfeld's chronicle of the struggle between Orthodox Judaism and modern Orthodox-Conservative Judaism is an insider's view of synagogue and rabbi as seen in the interaction among Rabbis Benjamin, Goldman, Barnett Brickner, and Abba Hillel

Silver and their congregations—a Cleveland saga closely monitored by the American and Canadian Jewish press.

Source: An excerpt from Leon Wiesenfeld, *Jewish Life in Cleveland in the 1920s and 1930s: The Memoirs of a Jewish Journalist* (Cleveland, OH: *The Jewish Voice Pictorial,* ca. 1965). Reprinted with permission of University of Georgia Press and Ellen Fishman.

CHAPTER 8

The Rabbis Goldman–Benjamin Fight over the Jewish Center

As I have already mentioned in several passages in the present series, I came to Cleveland early in January in 1925 in order to start on my duties as co-editor of the Yiddish daily of the time, *The Jewish World.* But I failed to mention that that was my second arrival in Cleveland on similar business. The first one was in February of 1923, when a new daily was to make its appearance under the name of *Der Yiddisher Waechter.* I was engaged as Managing Editor.

The *Waechter* had had a previous existence as a bi-lingual weekly in Yiddish and English. Now its publishers, consisting of Rabbi Samuel Benjamin and two well-to-do orthodox Jews—M. A. Katz and Abraham Sachs—decided to convert it into a daily. The Editor-in-Chief was the well-known writer Dr. Ezekiel Wortsman.

Dr. Wortsman, whom I knew quite well, came to New York to find a suitable staff of writers. When he saw me in Cafe Royal, the meeting place in those days of Jewish writers, he offered me the position of Managing Editor on the new daily. I was at that time the editor of a Yiddish weekly in Brooklyn, *The Brooklyn New Journal,* which was also a bi-lingual. I was quite reluctant to get away from New York.

Wortsman offered me a relatively large salary and told me the publishers had invested 100,000 dollars in the new paper and its existence was completely assured. I accepted the offer.

But on arrival in Cleveland three weeks later I realized I had made a serious blunder. In the first place I found out Cleveland had for years had a daily Yiddish paper, *The Jewish World,* and there was hardly room for another one. In the second place, Wortsman was either misinformed or had misled me, there was no money invested to guarantee the continued existence of the new publication. Besides, I saw that neither Wortsman nor his publishers had the slightest idea of what it took to run a daily paper. Furthermore, the purpose of the new publication was not to serve Cleveland Jewry but to fight Rabbi Solomon Goldman of the Jewish Center and *The Jewish World.*

It became quite clear to me that I was not going to stay in Cleveland very long. But it was too late to pull back immediately. The first issue of *Der Yiddisher Waechter* was published. It was rich in content, well put together and it put *The Jewish World* into the shadow. The only thing I did not like about the first issue was that its editors in Yiddish and in English, Dr. Wortsman and Rabbi Benjamin, had fired most of their shots in it.

Now that the reader has an idea about the new daily, it may be worthwhile to acquaint him with the struggle that went on day by day during the six weeks of the existence of that daily.

The name has been mentioned of Rabbi Samuel Benjamin. Older readers will certainly recall the good name of that rabbi, who was then a young man. The younger readers probably never heard of him. Let me, then, tell the whole story.

Rabbi Samuel Benjamin, a native of Palestine, came to this country at an early age and studied at Brown University and at the N.Y.U. Later he took a full course at the Jewish Theological Seminary in New York and was ordained as rabbi. He was thus—or was supposed to be—a Conservative rabbi.

He came to Cleveland to occupy the pulpit in the outspokenly Orthodox congregation of *Anshe Emeth Beth Tfilo,* the so-called "Polish" synagogue, where his predecessor had been Rabbi Samuel Margulies, the son of the well-known Orthodox rabbi in New York. Rabbi Margulies, an extremely able man, who was also a partner in the *Jewish World* publication, was killed in an automobile accident. As he was what is called a "progressive," or "enlightened," rabbi, the representatives of the congregation, which was recognized as the leading Orthodox congregation in the city, sought a successor of the same type. Despite the fact he was a Conservative, Rabbi Benjamin was chosen.

Rabbi Benjamin quickly adapted himself to the new atmosphere, began to feel at home with the members of the congregation and slowly but surely made himself popular in the community. Like his predecessor, Rabbi Margulies, Rabbi Benjamin was an able man and an ambitious man, anxious to make further progress. The synagogue became too small to hold its growing membership and Rabbi Benjamin, together with the leaders of the congregation, began to think of a new large structure. It was then that the plan was born to put up a Jewish Center. The plan met with general approval. The father of the idea was Rabbi Benjamin.

The young rabbi devoted himself heart and soul to the task of building the new Center. He worked out the details of the plan, he raised the funds and did everything else connected with assuming the successful consummation of the project. Finally the edifice was completed—at the cost of a million dollars, which in those days was a tremendous sum of money.

But as soon as the complex of buildings were ready to function, the membership was rocked by a controversy which in time reverberated throughout the whole of American Jewry. The new large and beautiful synagogue was to remain, according to the old constitution, forever and forever strictly Orthodox. But many of the members were by now inclined to a more progressive approach. This was especially the case with those members whose grown up children had been subjected to the influence of Reform Judaism and were not ready to follow exactly the practices of their parents. These members demanded certain liberal reforms in the synagogue and in the Center. The die-hard Orthodox element refused to compromise and the struggle between the two factions grew more and more acrimonious.

Rabbi Benjamin, though, as already mentioned, himself a Conservative, stood fast by the Orthodox element and refused to bend. At the same time the membership increased steadily and the newcomers were mostly of the more liberal element. Ultimately the latter won out. Rabbi Benjamin was relieved of his position and his place was taken by Rabbi Solomon Goldman, the Conservative rabbi of the *B'nai Jeshurun* Temple of East 55th Street. Rabbi Goldman, though a scion of a long line of pious rabbis and Orthodox *hassidim,* was himself an outspoken Conservative. He encouraged the liberals. Moreover, he undertook to convert the *Anshe Emeth Beth Tfilo* congregation into a Conservative temple.

Rabbi Benjamin, embittered, humiliated and without a pulpit, had a substantial following in the community. The Orthodox members in the Center were with him and were ready to back him in every possible way. He was not a coward, not one who gives up a fight after a reverse. He established the weekly publication, *Der Yiddisher Waechter* and with the help of his Orthodox friends, carried on a vigorous fight against the new leadership of the synagogue and the Center, against Rabbi Goldman and against *The Jewish World,* which supported Goldman.

When the new daily was discontinued, after the "large sum of money" Dr. Wortsman had told me about ran out in six weeks, the embittered Rabbi Benjamin with Wortsman's help, returned to his attacks, now even more virulent, in the old weekly. I naturally left Cleveland as soon as the new daily closed up, but I continued receiving the weekly while in New York and followed the developments. To tell the truth, I had very little interest in the whole business.

One fine day, when I received the paper, I became greatly agitated. I found a report in it that a week earlier, Rabbi Benjamin, on returning from a Friday night service at the synagogue, was attacked in front of his house. Two policemen with a warrant in their hands, seized him and threw him into the police patrol wagon as if he were a common criminal. He was taken to police headquarters downtown and was subjected to a strict investigation. He was soon released and had to walk because of the Sabbath all the way from downtown to his home. As he reached it, all tired out and exhausted, he was confronted with something even worse.

Near his house was Philip Rocker, son of Samuel Rocker of *The Jewish World*. He waited for the rabbi and when he saw him he attacked him and beat him up quite severely.

During the six weeks of my stay in Cleveland I had very little to do with Rabbi Benjamin. I had a few discussions with him, mostly about matters relating to the publication, and found him to be a fine, decent, affable person. I took no part in his campaign, although I often thought that if I were in his place I would act just that way. After all, it was he who built up that beautiful Center and enriched Cleveland Jewry with an important communal institution. When I now read how he was rewarded for his troubles, I had a feeling of genuine indignation. I felt strongly enough to want to write an article expressing my sentiments, but just then I noticed a statement by Dr. Wortsman that this was the weekly's last issue.

This man who brought about the arrest of Rabbi Benjamin was one by the name of Herman Stein. He came to the United States from Rumania as a very young boy, working, among other jobs, as a newspaper vendor, distributing *The Jewish World* to subscribers early in the morning and selling it to casual buyers later in the day. In time he rose to become the Advertising Manager of the paper, where a wide field was opened for his genius. He later became the owner of an advertising agency and grew rich.

Since Mr. Stein has now been dead for some years, it is not proper to tell too many unfavorable things about the dead. Let it be said that the Jews of Cleveland had no reason to find pride and joy in his causing the arrest of a spiritual leader or in many other acts of his.

The Struggle against the Center Continues

Two years later, when I came to Cleveland again, Rabbi Benjamin and Dr. Wortsman had long been gone from the city. But the struggle against the Center went on with full vigor, perhaps even in a more acrimonious spirit than two years earlier. Most of Rabbi Goldman's opponents had been driven out of the Center and were now carrying on their Holy War from outside. The Orthodox brought in law suits in the court against the Rabbi and the congregation, claiming that they were violating the constitution of the congregation, according to which it was to remain Orthodox in perpetuity.

But that alone was not enough. They carried on a propaganda campaign in the form of handbills and paid advertisements in *The Jewish World,* leveling against Goldman some pretty strong charges. Naturally, Goldman replied. He wrote his own advertising copy, in which he showed even less moderation in tone than his adversaries. When I arrived to take up my duties in *The Jewish World,* the publication had taken no editorial position on the struggle. Mr. Rocker for certain reasons saw no need to be anything but neutral. Mr. Rocker was fond of Goldman and admired him for his great scholarship. Besides, he had no reason to love the Orthodox crowd who had tried to ruin him by founding a rival publication. During its whole career the *Waechter* pictured Mr. Rocker as a monster and besmirched him. Such things are not easily forgotten. Mr. Rocker remembered it.

Mr. Rocker figured in Cleveland as an Orthodox Jew, even as a leader of the Orthodox Jews of the city. His publication, too, was considered to be an Orthodox organ. But he did not think the new reforms in the Center constituted a menace to Orthodox Judaism. His attitude aroused a good deal of antagonism in many Orthodox circles. Still, when Rabbi Goldman first proposed to introduce mixed seating in the synagogue, Mr. Rocker published an editorial opposing it, which forced the rabbi, for a time, at least, to postpone the innovation. It did not last long, though.

Rabbi Goldman was not a man to be easily frightened and was a much better fighter than his Orthodox opponents. One fine day he carried out his program and converted the synagogue and the Center into a full-fledged Conservative institution. The result was a storm of protest not only in Cleveland but almost in all of the United States and even Canada. But Goldman was little affected by it and went on with his plans. As time went on, more and more reforms were introduced until the institution was as far removed from Orthodoxy as East is from West. His congregation stood by him and backed him in all his undertakings.

There were new lawsuits and new public debates of a stormy nature. They led nowhere. In court, the Orthodox won one suit, lost another. A lower court ruled in their favor, a higher court granted the appeal. Later the lower courts took a different position and the Orthodox kept on losing their case. But they kept on fighting, even though the fight swallowed a lot of money and never gave up.

On their side the Orthodox element had the support of articulate public opinion. The two widely circulated Orthodox Yiddish dailies of New York, *The Morning Journal* and the *Tageblatt,* as well as the Orthodox *Jewish Courier* of Chicago (a Yiddish daily), backed the champions of Cleveland Orthodoxy. Reporters from the Jewish press, including the Jewish news agencies of those days, often visited Cleveland. They collected enough material to file lengthy reports and stories, to which Goldman replied by paid advertisements in *The Jewish World.* The Orthodox counter-advertised and the Jewish community of Cleveland was in a fever. People argued, quarrelled and even fought physically. It was one continuous public scandal.

Rabbi Goldman was a virulent foe of Orthodoxy. I don't know whether his hatred was the result of accumulated resentment because of the fight that was waged on him or he had been carrying it in his heart for a long time. But I know that if he had the power, he would have exiled all Orthodox Jews to Siberia, as long as not to have them in Cleveland. I tried to convince him that his hatred was unreasonable and that he was going too far, but to no effect. Any such attempt to bring him to reason only kindled his hatred more.

Rabbi Goldman was what is usually known as a "likeable fellow." He was, on the surface anyway, a friendly, pleasant, always smiling man. True, the Orthodox element hated him, but others, even if they did not agree with him respected him and rather liked him. I was one of such people. I first met him the third week I was in Cleveland and we became friendly from the very first meeting. He could be a good friend.

But he could also be an enemy. He bore a deep implacable hatred for the Orthodox leaders. Once he asked me to come to a luncheon at the Hollenden Hotel where he was to lecture on religion. I was not in a good mood that day and felt no desire to go. Fifteen minutes later a taxi stopped at the office of *The Jewish World* and I was practically coerced into going with him downtown to the luncheon. I had no choice.

In his lecture, which was highly interesting and informative at the outset, he poured out venom on Orthodox Judaism, and particularly the Orthodox leaders in Cleveland. Even I, who had no particular interest in the whole controversy, blushed to hear him talk. There was a large crowd, including some non-Jews and a few judges who were to decide on the merits of the lawsuit Rabbi Goldman was engaged in. I was not the only one who felt Goldman had gone too far. Some Reform Jews present felt that way, too. A well-known Christian lawyer in Cleveland told me after the lecture: "The rabbi spoke as if he were an anti-Semite."

As we rode back together in a taxi on the way to my editorial offices I wanted to discuss his lecture with him and point out that he had gone too far. But he refused to discuss the subject. I wondered if he himself realized that a man in his position must not lose control over himself or he simply did not want to talk about the subject.

But time heals all wounds and settles all problems. I am not sure Goldman's wounds were healed, but the excitement slowly died down. The paid advertisements in the paper were discontinued. One of the leaders of the Orthodox opposition, the above-mentioned Mr. Katz, died and the anti-Goldman movement gradually gave up the ghost. Orthodox Jews, including even Orthodox rabbis, drew closer to Goldman and some became his friends, although a lawsuit against him was still pending.

Rabbi Goldman's popularity grew and his adversaries were entirely forgotten. That was the end of the long-drawn-out fight.

CHAPTER 9
Rabbi Goldman Leaves Cleveland for Pulpit in Chicago

One Friday morning, as I sat working in my editorial office, Rabbi Goldman telephoned me and asked me to be his guest for lunch at his home. I asked what the invitation signified and he replied it had no particular significance, he merely felt like having a chat. I knew him well enough by then to take his statements and assurances with a grain of salt, but I accepted the invitation nevertheless.

In his house I found him almost buried under an avalanche of books, among which were some I knew he could not read—Greek and Latin volumes. When I inquired why this book exhibition, he suggested we first eat. After our repast, we went into his sizeable library, where he told me the following story:

The University of Chicago, he said, was about to establish a chair for Hebrew and he was trying to get it. This reminded me of the story of the Hebrew Chair in Cleveland. "Another Chair?" I asked. "Are you looking for new troubles?"

Goldman answered that this time it was the real thing and that he needed help, and that I could be of help.

I was amazed. Of what use could I be to him in such matters? I was curious. He told me all the books I saw piled up were there with a purpose. He was collecting material for a new brief history of the Jewish people. I had no doubt Goldman was capable of writing a good history. For one thing, he was a very fine scholar. Still I asked facetiously what the Greek and Latin books were doing there. He laughed out loud and that was the end of it.

To make a long story short, the rabbi finally let the cat out of the bag and told me he wanted me to write an article about him for the Yiddish daily in Chicago, *The Jewish Courier*. The article was to dwell on his project to write a new Jewish history. I could not understand why that article should be printed in the Chicago paper and not in our own local Cleveland Yiddish daily, in which I worked. His explanation was that the editor of the Chicago paper, the late Dr. S. M. Melamed, one of the foremost scholars of his day, was the intermediary in negotiating the establishment of the Hebrew Chair. Melamed it was, Goldman told me, who suggested that I write the article for him. But why could not Melamed himself write such an article? I inquired. The answer was that Melamed felt it would look better if the article was written by a Cleveland man rather than by one in Chicago. I had my doubts, but, as I have already said, I was fond of Goldman and could not refuse him. The piece was written and appeared in the Chicago *Jewish Courier*.

It did not take me long to discover that my doubts were justified. The whole story about the Hebrew Chair at the University of Chicago was a hoax. True, Melamed acted as Goldman's intermediary, but not about a Chair at the University. He sought to get him appointed to the pulpit of the largest and wealthiest Conservative temple in Chicago. The deal was consummated and Goldman himself announced his resignation from the Center in Cleveland, and he was leaving the city. That was in 1929.

Goldman's resignation evoked a sensation in Cleveland among the Christians as well as among the Jews. His adherents at the Center, who worshipped him, were shocked. They did not wish to lose him and did everything they could to induce him to change his mind. But Goldman was determined.

Goldman's answer to all the entreaties was that he would be happy to remain in Cleveland but that he could not because Rabbi Silver made it impossible for him to remain. Silver, according to Goldman, kept him down, made his life miserable. I was so close to Silver in those days as I was to Goldman and I knew Goldman was not telling the truth. The two men did not like each other very much, both of them important personalities and great scholars, but I never heard Silver say anything in disparagement of Goldman. Anyway, Goldman's claim that "Silver is driving me from Cleveland," was greatly exaggerated.

The real reason why Goldman left Cleveland for Chicago lay elsewhere: in the first place, a much larger salary and better prospects for additional income; in the second place, the ambition to become, in Chicago, the equivalent of Silver in Cleveland. In fact, in time he admitted as much to me himself. (Goldman's salary in Cleveland before he left was $11,000 annually and he was offered $12,000 to remain. His salary in Chicago was $18,000.)

Ten years later, when I left *The Jewish World* and founded the present publication, I did a good deal of traveling in the Middle West to get subscribers for the magazine. Nearly everywhere I heard the same story repeated to me by local rabbis about Silver forcing Goldman out of Cleveland. Nobody knew better than I did how unfounded that story was.

Court Favors the Orthodox Again

It did not lake long for Rabbi Goldman to turn out a great success in Chicago. The Chicago Zionists, who, unlike the Zionists of Cleveland, were united, helped him a great deal. They received him with open arms, pampered him and boosted him. There were in Chicago other rabbis who were known for their scholarship, but no one could match his driving ambition to become, as he told me himself, "the Abba Hillel Silver of Chicago." His popularity grew day by day and he soon attained his set goal. He did become, thanks to his talents, the Silver of Chicago.

Here, in Cleveland, his loss was felt for a time. But days, weeks and months passed and he was well-nigh forgotten. People remembered him only when a court of non-Cleveland judges passed a verdict on the latest suit of the Orthodox members against the Jewish Center. The three judges ruled in favor of the Orthodox. They strongly rebuked the former rabbi for changing the character of the congregation and demanded the restoration of the Orthodox status.

The verdict evoked joy among the still remaining Orthodox warriors and caused a sensation in Cleveland Jewry. In the Center itself, where Rabbi Harry Dawidowitz officiated, the verdict caused consternation. It was like a thunder out of the blue sky.

Good or bad, justified or not, the sensational verdict could not be ignored by the local newspaper. I naturally gave it proper space. The policy of the publication was still the same as that introduced by Mr. Rocker years earlier:

editorial neutrality. The paper could, however, not do less than print a full report. But, honest and impartial as the report might have been, there were people in Cleveland, friends of Rabbi Goldman's, who were unhappy. The most dissatisfied person was the late Rabbi Barnett R. Brickner, who did not like the tone of the report.

I was at that time the Cleveland correspondent of the Jewish Telegraphic Agency and the Middle West correspondent of the widely read New York daily *The Jewish Day.* Naturally, I filed my dispatches to them about the verdict. My article to *The Day* was written two days after the event and was rather exhaustive, giving the full story and its background in as objective and impartial a spirit as I was capable of. When the paper arrived in Cleveland, Rabbi Brickner, who had already accumulated a store of grievances against me, sounded an alarm.

Rabbi Brickner objected not so much to the body of my article as to its title. The then Managing Editor of *The Day,* the late Z. H. Rubinstein, who was fond of sensational headlines, printed my article under the headline he made up, saying "Cleveland Court Finds Goldman Insufficiently Pious." Rabbi Brickner, who was not familiar with the techniques of making up a newspaper, blamed me for that "heinous crime."

He wrote a long very angry letter to Dr. S. Margoshes, who was then Editor-in-Chief of *The Day,* expressing his "sharpest protest" against my "irresponsibility."

"Rabbi Goldman," said Brickner in his letter, "is still as greatly beloved by the Jews of Cleveland as he was when serving here as spiritual leader of the Jewish Center. People swear by him and adore him. And now comes one . . . who dares to write about him in this manner."

Dr. Margoshes and Brickner were old friends, but Margoshes was in no hurry to publish the protest. Instead he sent me Brickner's letter, inviting me to write a reply which would be published together with the letter. I wrote a reply, using much more moderate language than Rabbi Brickner, but I did ask him some pertinent questions.

First of all, I wished to know when his friendship for Rabbi Goldman had become so great and sacred that he felt it his duty to take up the cudgels on his behalf and abuse me in that way. I reminded him that in his numerous conversations with me he expressed an altogether different opinion about his "friend." I pointed out that in writing the letter to Dr. Margoshes, protesting against my article which was in no way offensive to Goldman, he was motivated by personal considerations which were not germane to the subject.

In those days friendship between the rabbis—real, genuine friendship—was inconceivable, no matter whether it concerned Orthodox, Conservative or Reform rabbis, rabbis of the same denomination or rabbis of different denominations. Below the surface of amiability the clerics were possessed of such a morbid deep jealousy which actually poisoned the air. This was known not only to most Jews but also to many non-Jews.

I think I knew better than anybody else what went on among the rabbis behind the scenes. Each one of them, in his anxiety to enlist my help in getting his favorable publicity, confided in me. No sooner did Rabbi X get a play in the paper than Rabbi Y telephoned to complain. The rabbi who was lucky enough to have his name in print that day—or the previous day—was declared to be unworthy of it; the complaining rabbi was the overlooked hero. There were exceptions—rabbis who were not interested in publicity. Those I did not know too well and seldom heard from. Rabbi Brickner was not one of the exceptions.

The friendship between Brickner and Goldman was never as close as Brickner made it out to be in his letter to Dr. Margoshes. Before I go on to explain what made Rabbi Brickner write his letter, let me say a few words about Rabbi Brickner's personality.

When Rabbi Brickner Arrived in Cleveland

Rabbi Brickner, as is still well known to many people, arrived in Cleveland late in 1925 to take over the pulpit of the Euclid Avenue Temple. He came here from Toronto, Canada, where he had been Rabbi of the *Holy Blossom Congregation*—a Reform Temple. He had made himself popular and well-liked not only in Toronto among Jews and non-Jews but in all of Canada. He was a friendly man, not given to putting on airs, as some other rabbis do, folksy and truly democratic in his dealings with people.

About two weeks before Rabbi Brickner was ready to leave Toronto I received a letter from Dr. Margoshes, who then was Director of the Toronto Zionist Office, and a day or two later another letter from the late Abraham Rhinewine, editor of the *Toronto Hebrew Journal*—a Yiddish daily. Both letters from men who were friends of mine introduced Rabbi Brickner as a man worth cultivating, as one of the finest personalities in American Jewry. Both Margoshes and Rhinewine depicted Brickner in the brightest colors and urged me to accord him a favorable reception, assuring me that he is a real man of the people, a fine Jew, who was sure to enrich the communal life of Cleveland Jewry.

When the rabbi came to Cleveland I was preparing to go to see him and interview him for the paper. But he forestalled me and called on the editorial offices of *The Jewish World* on Woodland Avenue the day after his arrival. He inquired about me and was shown into my office. He came in, smiling amiably, introduced himself and addressed me very warmly, telling me that in a certain sense he was my countryman. His mother, he said, was born in Galicia, where I was born. He spoke a very fine literary Yiddish, unusual among American-born Jews, which evoked my admiration.

He spent two hours in my office, during which time my impression of him passed from favorable to enthusiastic. It was unusual to find among American rabbis such a man. I had not met one until Rabbi Brickner walked into my office. I wrote so in my article about him in *The Jewish World*. A few days later I went to his installation at the Temple. Rabbi Silver, who installed him, spoke about him with great warmth and praised him to the sky. My admiration for the new rabbi increased.

To my amazement, Brickner came to the office again a few days later. He came to thank me for my warm articles and, besides, he wanted to meet Mr. Rocker, whom he had missed on his first visit. He also told me he was anxious to meet Cleveland Jews from all walks of life, rich or poor, educated or simple, workers and employers. I was greatly impressed by this attitude. His predecessor at the Euclid Avenue Temple, the late Rabbi Louis Wolsey, used to keep aloof from the Jews of the East Side for whom he felt a deep contempt. He was a bitter anti-Zionist. Here, on the other hand, was a rabbi who was altogether different. What more could one expect?

During our conversation, Mr. Rocker came in and I introduced the Rabbi to him. Mr. Rocker also became enthusiastic, and as a result wrote a warm editorial, commending the new Rabbi to Cleveland Jewry. I did everything in my power to make Brickner popular among the Yiddish speaking masses. In time he did win the favor of all classes of Jews, including even the strict Orthodox.

But, in the meantime the Cleveland Zionist District became the scene of an ever-growing unlovely strife between its leaders and Rabbi Silver. A similar strife was carried on also in the Jewish Educational Bureau where Silver was president. Brickner, being a member in both, was in quiet sympathy with Silver's opponents though he did not participate directly in the quarrels. Silver, in spite of all the quarrels, was still the most respected Rabbi in Cleveland. His personal popularity far exceeded that of any other rabbi. In time Brickner also fell into the net of rabbinical jealousies. I tried a few times to persuade Brickner from injecting himself into a controversy whose results could only be harmful, but to no avail.

The fight in both, the Zionist District and the Jewish Educational Bureau, grew worse and worse and often reached the stage of an ugly scandal. Silver left the Educational Bureau and Brickner was elected in his place as president. In the District the situation, far from improving, deteriorated even further. Presidents came and Presidents went. Some of them like Max Simon, David Ralph Herz and the late Municipal Judge Louis Drucker, honestly tried to bring about peace in the Zionist District, but the quarrels went on forever. This situation reached its climax when the late Rabbi Goldman and later the late H. A. Friedland assumed the Presidency of the District.

During most of these years I took the side of Rabbi Silver in spite of the many friends I had in the District. This was not to the liking of many of those friends and least of all to the liking of Rabbi Brickner.

Rabbi Brickner was jealous of the publicity I found necessary to give Rabbi Silver in the controversy in the Zionist District and the Bureau of Jewish Education. Our friendship began to cool off. Soon afterwards another incident, which I would not like to recall, reached to the point when I felt forced to break with him altogether. The rabbi then became my enemy as a result.

Now that Brickner felt I had wronged his friend, Rabbi Goldman took up the cudgels for him and wrote his very angry letter to Dr. Margoshes. Goldman himself laughed at the whole business.

Soon a Cleveland Court of Appeals annulled the verdict of the three out-of-town Judges. The Orthodox, however, still had a chance to take the cause to the Ohio Supreme Court. But they were already tired of the litigation, of the long and bitter struggle, and did nothing further. This was the final end of the bitter struggle. The Jewish Center remained Conservative and after World War II disappeared from 105th Street altogether. Under the leadership of Henry A. Rocker and Rabbi Armond E. Cohen a new and beautiful conservative Temple was erected at Euclid Heights Boulevard which is now known as the Park Synagogue.

Many years later, when Rabbi Brickner tragically lost his life in Spain, I mourned him from my heart and went to his funeral carrying in my heart the same feeling as all his friends.

CONTROVERSIES IN OTHER CONGREGATIONS

The so-called "war" around the Jewish Center was not the only . . . Congregational [battle] in the history of Cleveland Jewry. There were others which preceded it. Already as early as 1845, when Cleveland was a city of about six thousand people and only a handful of Jews, differences with regard to rituals caused the split of the small Jewish community. Some years later similar splits took place in other Congregations, the last one of which was the split some thirty years ago in the *B'nai Jeshurun* Congregation, now known as The Temple On The Heights.

This last split was not for the cause of rituals. It was caused as a result of the decision of the Temple's leadership not to renew its contract with its spiritual leader, Rabbi Abraham Novak, after the new Temple was built. The present Rabbi Rudolph Rosenthal was engaged in his place and that was not to the liking of a small group of dissenting and indignant members. They took up a fight against the leadership and for a time it looked that another Goldman-like struggle was in the making. Fortunately, however, Rabbi Novak was not just another Benjamin and Rabbi Rosenthal another Goldman. The dissenting members left the Temple deciding to form another Temple with Rabbi Novak as its spiritual leader. This was not an easy-going matter. It took quite a long time before the new Temple came into being. After a few years of struggle Rabbi Novak quietly left Cleveland to occupy the pulpit of the conservative synagogue in Rochester.

The splinters, however, did finally succeed to enrich Cleveland Jewry with another conservative synagogue. They purchased a small church on Washington Boulevard which they converted into a Temple. Rabbi Jack Herman was brought from New York and entrusted with the spiritual leadership. Under his capable and very energetic leadership the small Temple was soon greatly expanded and is now the third largest Conservative Temple in Cleveland. It is known as The Community Temple.

There were many splits also among the Orthodox Jews and new synagogues kept on being built until they were out of proportion. But this is a story by itself. Today, however, there are quite a few less Orthodox congregations in Cleveland. Instead of building new homes of worship the Orthodox found a much better way. They joined together and built instead a few large Congregations among which the Taylor Road Synagogue is the largest. Rabbi Louis Engelberg is its spiritual leader. Also the former Tetiever Synagogue was joined with other synagogues and is now one of the largest Orthodox synagogues in the city. It is known as the Warrensville-Center Synagogue with Rabbi Jacob Muskin as spiritual leader. The second largest Orthodox Synagogue is that of the Heights Jewish Center where the eminent Rabbi Israel Porath is its spiritual leader.

Excerpt from *Libbie*

Libbie L. Braverman was a teacher of teachers, an innovative educator, and a sought-after lecturer on education and the state of Israel. She was born in Boston, Massachusetts, the daughter and granddaughter of rabbis. She earned a bachelor's degree at Western Reserve University and did graduate work at the University of Pittsburgh and Harvard University. She left public and Hebrew school teaching to devote herself to Jewish education. She had taught at Euclid Avenue Temple while still in high school and served as its education director from the late 1930s to 1951. (See also the chapter on Samuel M. Silver in this volume.)

Braverman wrote textbooks, pageants, Hebrew-language instruction materials, and three books about Israel. She was the first woman to lecture under the auspices of the Jewish Chautauqua Society, and she participated in the work of Hadassah, Israel's Technion, Israel Bonds, the Jewish National Fund, and the Council for Jewish Education. She taught at the College of Jewish Studies in Cleveland and served on the boards of many Jewish agencies and organizations.

In this excerpt, Braverman rehearses the familiar yet always new story of a family's migration to America and acknowledges her family's formative influence on her commitment to Jewish learning and choice of career. Her discussion of her pioneer work in Reform Jewish education reveals much about its status in the early twentieth century. She considers as well the work of Cleveland's Jewish educators of that period.

Source: An excerpt from Libbie Braverman, *Libbie: Teacher, Counselor, Lecturer, Author, Education Director, Consultant, and What Happens along the Way* (New York: Bloch, 1986).

"LIBBIE DEBORAH LEVIN"

Libbie Deborah Levin born in Boston, Massachussets. That is recorded in the annals of Boston history. Other than that my birth didn't cause a ripple.

My father, an Orthodox Rabbi, didn't receive much of a salary and, as is the custom, had to depend upon the generosity of the membership of the synagogue for a livelihood. So, we find him moving from one community to another in search of a fairly decent paying position.

This accounts for my being born in Boston, my brother Jack in Hoboken, New Jersey and my youngest brother, Harry in Montreal, Canada.

My father did ultimately settle in Pittsburgh, Pennsylvania where he served his congregation for 25 years. At the end of that time he was named Rabbi Emeritus. He then retired to Venice, California where he became spiritual leader of a congregation whose Youth Group started with sixty-year-olds.

Sometime before Pittsburgh, my father was head of the Talmud Torah Hebrew Schools in Montreal. My grandfather was the Orthodox Rabbi of the community. When I went back to Montreal, many years later, to address the Women's Welfare Organization, I mentioned my grandfather's name, Rabbi Eleazer Drucker. A number of women came up after the lecture to tell me that he had officiated at their weddings.

My father also earned recognition. One of the women said that he had been her son's inspiration to study for the rabbinate. She was grateful to Rabbi Morris A. Levin, my father, who had urged him to become a Rabbi. He is now one of the outstanding Rabbis in the United States. His name is Rabbi Louis Levitsky.

I recall a very beautiful family life when we lived in Montreal. At school I took turns at being either a terror or an angel. I think of the rhyme we used to recite:

There was a little girl who had a little curl
Right in the middle of her forehead
When she was good, she was very, very good,
But when she was bad, she was horrid.

We used to receive report cards each month and were ranked according to our grades. What would you think of a girl who ranked first one month and thirty-first the next? I had so much energy (they didn't call it kinetic in those days) that I would often get into mischief. How the teachers tolerated me I still don't understand. Perhaps their forebearance is why I was so tolerant of students who later came under my care. It was a right approach, for those youngsters who were troublesome turned out to be leaders in the community.

When I was in high school, Miss Dayton found a way to keep me quiet and under control. She put me in charge of the study hall. She was able to do her own work as I kept the study hall in order. In Montreal, I was head of the class. Sarah Berland, a conscientious, steady and reliable student, was competing with me for a college scholarship. She was conscious of the rivalry but, stupid me, I didn't even recognize it as such. So what happened? My family decided to leave Montreal and Sarah lost her rival. I will never know if I might have won.

My father was a great scholar, interested in Jewish education. He wrote a book in Yiddish called *"Pedagogy Among The Jews."* My father had been one of the first in his family to come to America. He was responsible for bringing his brothers and sisters to the United States.

My mother, one of six children, two girls and four boys, was a member of the Drucker family. She had the Drucker nose, as I have. She had a tendency to be heavy, and so do I. It was a Drucker trait, but we kept our weight down. My mother was pretty, with brown eyes and black hair. She was kind, tender and solicitous. When I came home from teaching Hebrew after school, (I was still in high school), I would find my meal hot and ready. But, the one she especially catered to was my brother, Harry. No matter when he came home, he was fed with the best of everything. Whatever he especially liked, he found on his plate. When we lived in Cleveland, our main meal was served at noon because my father, who was principal of the Hebrew Schools, began his work day in the late afternoon. Thus, poor mother was forced to run a mini-restaurant.

Aunt Anna was a college graduate, rare for a female in those days. Each of the brothers would help the next one through school. Uncle Aaron, the oldest, studied for the rabbinate at the Jewish Theological Seminary. Just before his ordination he fell in love with a non-Jewess and eloped with her. That ended his rabbinical career. The couple moved to Chicago. He did post graduate studies there and later became a Professor of Economics at Colorado Springs University.

My Uncle Saul, the next oldest brother, was always interested in children. He was superintendent of an orphan home in Chicago. He next headed a larger and more prestigious orphanage in Baltimore. From there he moved to Boston where he had greater opportunities to pioneer in work with retarded children. He wrote a book called *"Children Astray,"* filled with case histories of children he treated. The work was well received and remains on library shelves to this day.

Uncle Harvey was my mother's second youngest brother. Because he lived in Cleveland, most of the Drucker family eventually settled there, but we had to make some stops along the way.

My grandparents left Montreal in the early nineteen hundreds. They opened a store in the Jewish section of Harlem near 110th Street, where they sold Hebrew books, taleysim (prayer shawls) and phylactories. They also sold wine and matso for Passover. I remember the kegs of wine that were fermenting through the year to be ready for the holiday. I also recall my mother's youngest brother, Uncle Lewis, delivering the matsos on a go-cart when he came home from school. He received his law degree at the City College of New York which he called the "Heder on the Hill."

My grandmother was truly the business woman. She prepared the wine and ordered the matsos. She and Uncle Lew ran the business. My grandfather was the proud scholar who rarely left his books or the House of Worship.

When my grandmother died, my mother brought our family to New York from Montreal to take care of Grandpa and Uncle Lew. When grandfather passed away, Uncle Lew left for Cleveland to join Uncle Harvey, who by this time had become interested in politics. Lew became a successful lawyer, ran for office and became a Judge.

Aunt Anna married Dr. Wilfred Kotkov, Professor of Homiletics at the Jewish Theological Seminary in New York. One night, while coming home from a lecture, he was assaulted by two thugs. They thought he had money in his briefcase and struck him on the head causing a severe concussion. He suffered for two days and died at the height of his career. This tragedy wrecked the lives of my aunt and her two children, Lester and Debby.

When my grandfather passed away, my father took us from New York to Chicago, where he became head of the Moses Montefiore Hebrew Schools. I was a student at the school and won a gold medal, a Jewish star which I cherish to this very day. When I graduated from the Talmud Torah, my father registered me in a Talmud class in a private school, conducted by Doctor Hershel Sweden, a great educator who was head of the Chicago Home for the Aged. As the only girl in the class I felt isolated, but many years later I enjoyed the distinction of being the only female on the Board of the National Council for Jewish Education, the upper echelon of Jewish Educators.

While in Chicago in my first year at John Marshall High School, I was invited to teach in one of the local Hebrew Schools. The children were as big as I was, but that didn't daunt me. Here's where I got into the habit of working after school. In the same year I became a Sunday School teacher in a Reform Temple. The rabbi was Samuel Cohon, who later became a professor at the Hebrew Union College in Cincinnati, Ohio.

During this time, my father received a call to lead the Community Hebrew Schools in Cleveland. My parents left me behind to complete my semester at school. When I graduated, I received a letter of recommendation from Rabbi Cohon to Rabbi Louis Wolsey of Cleveland. Little did I dream that at the Euclid Avenue Temple I would start a career of long standing. In Rabbi Cohon's letter of recommendation he wrote to Rabbi Wolsey, "Our loss is your gain." Rabbi Wolsey engaged me at once. I also taught Hebrew after school at the B'nai Jeshurun Temple on East 55th and Scovill, later named the Heights Temple. Even in those days I was self-supporting. I had just graduated from high school when I accepted a summer position at Camp Ten-Rab, located on one of the Finger Lakes of New York, where I was to be a drama counselor.

By the next summer, Uncle Saul had organized Camp Pinegrove. He invited me to be Head Counselor of the Girls' Camp. After all, I did have experience as a drama counselor at Camp Ten-Rab. At Pinegrove I received my early training as a Head Counselor. I brought along a few counselors and a number of children from Cleveland.

In addition to heading the Hebrew Schools, father was Rabbi of the Anshe Grodno Congregation, located on East 55th Street, near our home, where he sermonized on weekends. We lived in the Majestic Apartments on East 55th Street and Central Avenue, right across from The Temple. Often from my window, I would see Rabbi Abba Hillel Silver drive up to the side entrance with a great big dog. Then he was tall, lean and handsome and still a bachelor.

By this time I had graduated from Central High School, just a block north on 55th Street. I had just entered the Cleveland School of Education to become a teacher. Occasionally my schoolmates and I would get into trouble with Miss Pope, our Dean. We would come back late from lunch hour because we had hiked all around the area. She would gaze sternly at us. Despite these transgressions we were good students and the teachers thought well of us. I made friends with one of the Professors, Mr. Lemuel Brown, teacher of literature, who influenced me in my choice of courses.

Fate changed a carefree teenager into one with heavy responsibilities. My education almost came to an abrupt end.

One day before going to school, I helped my mother prepare for a marriage ceremony my father was going to perform at home. The couple needed a place to get married. My mother, always helpful, had offered our apartment. She had no help so she had to do everything herself. On this particular morning she wanted to stretch our precious Cluny lace tablecloth on the carpet in the dining room. I got down on the floor to help her. We had to pin down each edge of the lace. It was quite a task. We completed our work and I went off to school. In mid-morning I was called out of class. There had been a telephone call. My mother was in the hospital on Carnegie Avenue, east of 55th Street. How I made it there I'll never know. I took a street car to East 55th Street and ran the rest of the way. I found her in agony. She had been washing windows earlier that morning. In those days we had iceboxes, but in addition we would use a box outside the kitchen window, to keep foods cold in winter. The window box gave way when she leaned on it and she fell three stories to the courtyard below. She broke her back.

When I entered the hospital room I heard her moaning. She had been given a pain killer, but she was in agony. It was horrible to watch her. Two nurses were standing over her. She kept asking for something to ease the pain. One of the nurses said to me, "She may open her eyes and when she does, she should see you smiling." The other nurse looked at her angrily. She knew it was hopeless. When I came out of the room I said to my father, "She must live! If she has to be in a wheelchair we'll take care of her. We'll do everything. Oh God, just let her live!" My mother never regained consciousness.

She was laid out in the apartment. The Hevrah Kadisha (Holy men whose task it was) washed her and prepared her for burial. They needed some cloths so my father gave them our most beautiful linen napkins. We were up all night. I remember standing near the wall and banging my head against it. I wasn't conscious of what I was doing. They probably thought I was losing my mind. It was such a shock, I wasn't able to absorb the tragedy. Carrying the plain pine coffin, the pallbearers walked from the house to the synagogue. There were many eulogies, so many that I finally said to my father, "Isn't it enough?" I was in a state of shock. I was numb. I couldn't eat. I didn't sleep. I would wake up screaming. Fortunately there were people around who took care of everything. All my uncles came except Uncle Aaron who was way out in Colorado. My Aunt Anna came with Debby who was about five years old. She was adorable. Having her around helped ease the pain.

After a few days, a discussion took place as to what I was going to do. My father thought I should leave teacher training and go to business school. My Aunt Anna responded with a great big NO. I must continue to study to become a teacher. That was the way of life of the Druckers . . . education, study, leading toward a dignified career. How different my life might have been if I had followed his advice.

I went back to school. Since my brothers came home from school at noon and my father was in the habit of having his big meal at noon, it was my responsibility to come home and serve them. I learned how to cook. For the Sabbath I would make the gefilte fish. My neighbors taught me how. I would prepare the meals the night before. Fortunately the lunch hour followed a study period. I would use the time to rush home by street car, serve the food, and hurry back in time for the next class.

But I couldn't study. I just couldn't concentrate. Though, I found that the classroom was a good place to lose one's self.

I would get home around six, serve supper, do the cooking and cleaning. After a while my father found a housekeeper to do the work.

Once I baked a cake. I went to my room to study. Suddenly I smelled something burning. I opened the oven, the cake was burned to a crisp. Weeping, I took it out of the oven and began to take bites of the cake. What a traumatic experience that was!

As far as school was concerned, gone were the days of carefree fun. Gone were our noonday adventures. All I know is that I didn't fail that year, although I really should have. They took into account the work I had done the previous semester and gave me good grades. I made up for their confidence by doing better the following year. That summer I took a course at the Cleveland School of Art. I made some batiks which I still have and earned six credits for the course.

The following year my father decided to marry again. He chose a woman who owned a small general store in Collinwood with a spacious apartment behind the store. We all moved out there. She was a friendly person who was flattered to become the wife of a rabbi. She had two children of her own and we became a family unit.

Soon afterwards, though, I went to live with my Uncle Lew on Empire Avenue. I had already graduated from the School of Education and was a cadet teacher at Gladstone School, along with the other girls who were in our group. Anna Krutchkoff lived across the street from the school and her mother insisted we bring our lunches there and she would provide the tea. By this time, I had recovered some of my former pep and was again the leader. We were conscientious and as a result were considered good teachers. One of the girls became a supervisor and two others became principals.

Evenings I was able to take some courses at Western Reserve University.

All of these came in very handy in later life, especially a course in Elizabethan Shakespeare and one in theater.

I continued to teach Hebrew daily at the B'nai Jeshurun Congregation near my home after school and at the Euclid Avenue Temple on weekends. To complete my degree requirements in those days, I had to appear before a panel of teachers of the school in order to get a degree. They asked some pretty difficult questions. I had majored in education and literature.

They asked me a question about education, and I said I could best present my point of view by showing them how I taught Hebrew in our school. They were interested. I stepped up to the blackboard, took a piece of chalk in my hand and demonstrated some of the devices I had created at Euclid Avenue Temple. I wrote out the Hebrew words; presented the prayers. The prayers demonstrated the Hebrew words . . . thus the deductive method of teaching which fascinated the Board. I passed with high honors.

After passing, we were assigned teaching positions in various parts of the city. I went to Memorial School. Miss Norris was the principal. I was teaching youngsters in the second grade. These were bright children who probably had learned to read on their own. But, when it came to arithmetic or spelling, they knew very little. It was my job to teach these subjects. I set up a grocery store. I involved the children in real-life experiences. Toy telephones on each desk were the "mothers" who ordered, the "clerks" would take the orders and book-keepers would okay the cost and the change for a ten dollar bill and thus the entire class learned. Preparing shopping lists helped improve their spelling.

"THE HEBREW LANGUAGE NO LONGER GREEK"

Rabbi Louis Wolsey was the popular spiritual leader of the Euclid Avenue Temple. He had been there for eighteen years and had a life contract.

Rabbi Wolsey was a classical Reform rabbi, part of a group that was responsible for divesting our religion of many of its colorful ceremonials which gave animation to Judaism. To his credit, however, it was he who introduced the teaching of prayer Hebrew into the curriculum of the one-day-a-week school.

He asked me to demonstrate the teaching of Hebrew before a meeting of the Sisterhood. The lesson was received with mixed feelings. Some of the women were impressed but there were a number who were resentful. We were told that, as parents, they didn't know Hebrew and yet were good Jews. Why did we have to burden the children with this foreign language? They were satisfied to let the rabbi read the Hebrew which was "all Greek" to them.

This antagonism didn't stop the rabbi. We introduced Hebrew in the lower grades, planning gradually to continue its teaching as the children moved up from grade to grade.

I divided my time on Sunday mornings between the temple and my father's synagogue. Part of Sunday morning I spent at the Temple then I took a streetcar to the synagogue.

I would conduct the assembly in my father's school, in addition to preparing the holiday programs. The children would come to our home after school during the week for rehearsals to be ready for each performance. How I was able to work at both schools continues to puzzle me.

When Rabbi Wolsey left the Euclid Avenue Temple, Rabbi Barnett Brickner came from Toronto, Canada. David Pearlman was the Education Director. He did a fine but pedestrian job. He went on to the Hebrew Union College to become a rabbi. When he left Euclid Avenue Temple, Nathan Brilliant was brought to Cleveland to become our Education Director. It was a good choice. He received his B.S. degree from the City College of New York and his M.S. from Columbia University. He taught Mathematics and English in the Junior High School and was also principal of the Uptown Talmud Torah in Harlem. He was well qualified for the temple position. He had a positive attitude toward Judaism and Jewish education. He was determined to "Judaize" our program.

He gave me a title, which kept changing periodically as I accepted more responsibility. When he left I became Education Director. If I did well in any of these capacities it was due to his sympathy, his training and his encouragement.

Together, we undertook the task of enriching our program, involving our young people and many of the parents. Gradually, our creative efforts made ours an enviable school which new members sought to join just so their children could benefit from our special kind of Jewish education.

Soon, Brilliant and Braverman were writing pageants together. Nineteenth century rationalism had stripped Reform Judaism of a great deal of ceremony, leaving the service wordy and cold. We were not the only ones who were striving to reinstate ritual, ceremony and pageantry. The churches were also aware of the need for change. We decided to appeal to the heart and to the eye. Combining the eye and the ear, we began experimenting at our Children's Services, presenting pageants which made the Bible and history come alive.

Rabbi Brickner agreed to our plan. It took the membership longer. We were all conscious of the fact that whenever we introduced something new for enrichment purposes, we were accused of bringing orthodoxy into the temple. These people had misgivings about the presentation of pageants in the Temple. Gradually we converted many of them.

After all, the use of pageantry in religious services is as old as religion itself. It was part of the ancient temple service and, in modified form, is a vital part of the Orthodox Jewish religion. The reading of the Torah on the Sabbath, the procession of the Torahs on Simhat Torah, and the Megillah reading on Purim are all forms of pageantry.

Each service centered around a theme. My theory was to have a minimum of preparation and a maximum of participation, using large groups of children both as readers and as dramatis personae. With this approach, the children remembered the lesson and the pageants had a deep and lasting effect.

Dr. Emanuel Gamoran, Education Director of the Union of American Hebrew Congregations, discovered our work and felt it was innovative and exciting. He asked us to collect the pageants after a goodly number had been performed, thus *Religious Pageants for the Jewish School* by Nathan Brilliant and Libbie Braverman was published in 1941. A landmark in our history! Then in 1951 he asked us to collect our educational material and to put it into a book . . . he felt our work was important enough to be published for all educators to use. And so, *Activities in the Religious School* was born. This included the Consecration Service, also an innovative concept. We decided that bringing the child into the school needed a ceremony. We recommended that we consecrate children who entered the first grade. We prepared them in advance. Addie Rosewater, our dedicated and creative first grade teacher, volunteered to write some verses for a few of the children. The teachers prepared the class to recite the Shma and Torah Tsiva Lanu Moshe (the Torah commanded us by Moses) for this was the theme of the ceremony. The girls were dressed in white and the boys in dark trousers, white shirts with bow ties.

The day came. The children lined up outside the temple. Each one held a miniature Torah over the heart. Then they marched down the aisles to the pulpit. They stood on the platform, facing the Ark. Six children who had the verses stood close to the Ark. They recited their verses, the last one leading into the pledge of the Shma. There wasn't a dry eye in the house. Many temples over the country used our Consecration Ceremony and began accepting the pageants and Children's Services we wrote.

We prepared Children's Services which were produced by the Euclid

Avenue Temple. Both the pageants and the services were mimeographed in the beginning but later they were published.

It was a holiday that was instrumental in forcing me to make a decision that would affect my entire career. Purim was approaching. We were planning a Purim Carnival. I took a day off from public school and went to purchase items we needed. I was hurrying from place to place. Of all people, I bumped into the chairman of the religious school. When he realized I was downtown shopping on school time, he became concerned. When he recognized that duties at the temple were so demanding he suggested that I resign and give full time to the temple. I was reluctant. After all, I had chosen teaching as my life work. After weighing the matter back and forth, I decided not to resign but to take a leave of absence for study. This was by way of protection. In the event I wasn't happy with the change, I could always return. In the course of the year I registered for a few courses at Western Reserve University, and assumed more responsibility at the temple. I enjoyed the work, I found it stimulating. At the end of the school year I made my decision. I agreed to leave public school teaching and take the position of Director of Activities. I was put in charge of the Special Hebrew School. There were six teachers, capable teachers, most of whom had been trained by the great Chet Alef Friedland.

Now Nate and I went to work in earnest. We initiated the idea of AD-LO-YADAH, the name the Israelis gave it in Israel. That name is taken from the Bible—three words that mean "until he didn't know." The phrase refers to someone who drinks so much that he does not know the difference between cursing Haman and praising Mordecai.

We involved teachers, students and parents. It became a huge undertaking. The Art Club painted enormous panels on brown wrapping paper, depicting scenes from life in Israel and significant events in the Purim story. Each class assumed responsibility for a booth in the carnival. The booth started with a table. Lathes were attached to give it height. These were covered with colored crepe paper to reflect the nature of the booth. The colorful awning helped unify the structure. Some of the classes built booths to represent the architecture of the land of Israel. They built modern buildings like those in Tel Aviv. They created domes to reflect the architecture of Jerusalem. What a busy place this became! Thousands of people came and went. There were attractions for everyone. The games often were named after the characters in the Purim story—Crown Esther, Shoot Haman, Feed Mordecai and a Shushan Tea Room. There were signs with the names of the streets of Tel Aviv and Jerusalem in Hebrew. There were streamers strung across the entire hall saying HAPPY PURIM. Every conceivable space in the hall and adjoining rooms was used. Of course we had a Costume Parade. Another landmark.

Another year we added a Miniature Floats Parade. We've watched the Tournament of Roses and other Float Parades, why not a Parade of the E.A.T. Ad-Lo-Yadah? Ours had to be in miniature. What a rare opportunity for creativity and involvement! None of this was done in school time. We held those hours as too precious. All came in after school or in the evening to work. Everyone, parents and students alike, was caught up in this exciting activity. They built the floats, placed them on coaster wagons and used puppets or dolls for characters.

A list of rules was posted when the Floats Parade was announced. There was also a list of suggested subjects. It generated a month of activity, outside of school time. The excitement took over.

The long tables were lined up the day of the parade. This huge runway reached from one end of the recreation hall to the other. There were more than forty floats. Each had a number so that the audience and the judges could identify them. And, of course, the school band made itself heard.

The judges had the unenviable responsibility of rendering a verdict. That year they were Isaac Van Grove, director of *A Romance of a People,* an enormous production at Public Hall; Dr. Thomas Munro, Director of Education at the Cleveland Art Museum; and Judge Maurice Bernon, chairman of our Temple Religious School Committee.

Another activity we initiated involving students, teachers and parents was the Social Service Project for Hanukah. After all, we were in the mood of gift-giving and gift-receiving. We were the fortunate ones. Let us think of those less fortunate. This was one of the eight steps of charity described by Maimonides.

We contacted the Social Service Organization. We asked for the names (not necessarily the right names) of families in need. We asked for the ages of the parents as well as the age and sex of each of the children. When we received the names of some fifty families, the entire school went to work. The class analyzed the needs of each case. After much discussion they decided on the most appropriate gift. Then volunteers assumed responsibility for their particular undertaking. If they needed to collect money, that was one job; if they promised to donate a doll, that was another; if they wanted a sweater, perhaps someone in the group would offer his own services or that of the mother to do the knitting. All of this produced excitement, participation, enthusiasm. The holiday became alive for them as they attached themselves to our history and contributed to the idea of Shalah Manot (gift giving), a tradition in Jewish life.

There were many such opportunities to involve our children and make the holidays come alive. They became events in Jewish history, not just something to read about. It was something vital, striking roots in our history as they felt an integral part of Jewish life and the continuity of our people.

Another landmark! We produced a musical! It was a colossal undertaking, or so we thought. *Jews in Egypt,* a Passover play by Shlomo Grossman who wrote the words and Samuel Goldfarb, who created the music had just appeared.

This was no pageant. It included over a hundred of our children. It was presented on the stage of our auditorium. We painted the scenery. We produced colorful costumes. We created lighting effects. We trained a chorus. It was a big production. We didn't use school time. The children came to Temple after school for rehearsals.

Jews in Egypt had a profound impact on the entire school. The songs we sang in the show became favorites in the school. "To the Red Sea" sung throughout the year, became number one when the children voted for their favorite songs to sing in our Songs Parade at Assembly at the end of the year.

The assembly, we felt, was the mirror of the school. Our assembly programs were carefully planned. They included a short service, which included the Hebrew they learned and was made meaningful in the classroom. There was always a report on Keren Ami and anything of importance that was taking place. For example, when we were preparing for Hamishah Osor B'Shvat (the New Year of the Trees) there would be an additional report, indicating progress made and the children's involvement in helping Israel. And then there were meaningful songs relating to the approaching holiday and Israeli songs and Jewish folk songs. We believed that a singing school is a happy school. There were special programs, a skit, a song, a puzzle, a game, a challenge between two classes, all relating to what was being learned in the classroom and showcased at assembly. All these programs served to identify our children with their Judaism and to give them ample opportunity to tie them to Jewish tradition.

Another innovation: In order to make Hanukah a part of living tradition, we placed a sign in the lobby that was changed each day of the week. Sigmund Braverman had designed a four-foot Menorah that today is on exhibit at the Jewish Historical Museum. Each year we placed it in the lobby a week or two before the holiday, with a sign which read: "Light the first Hanukah candle on December 20th." Each day the sign would indicate the number of candles to light. Every day of the Hanukah holiday we would gather around the Menorah. Who were there? The students who attended Hebrew School, club members and parents who had come to call for their children.

We would gather late afternoon after sessions and the right number of candles would be lit. Students from the Hebrew classes and from the clubs would have the responsibility of leading the service and the Hanukah songs. The Junior Choir stood on the steps leading into the lobby. They introduced the ceremony by singing:

On this night
We will light
__ little candle fires
They shine so bright
On this night
These little candle fires.

We all chanted the prayers and the choir would lead in the Hanukah Songs.

It was a glorious ceremony, as we gathered in the dusk. No other light—just the reflection of the Hanukah lights on the faces of the children. It was moving—parents, children, teachers, office staff and the rabbi all participated.

Our one problem was to persuade parents to cooperate with the school. No matter how much we taught about the holiday, the story of the Maccabees, the prayers, the idea of gift-giving, we were only going through empty motions, if there were no carryover into the home.

We called holiday workshops to explain to the parents what the school was teaching. We tried to indicate that with all the preparation, with all the study, all the excitement that was generated in the school, if nothing was done in the home to give the holiday reality, it was unfortunate. If the house was dark on Hanukah, if there were no festivities, our work was futile. We succeeded in persuading many parents to cooperate. So many were grateful to us for making the holiday live for their children, but unfortunately, there were those parents (perhaps the same ones who objected to the study of Hebrew) who remained stubborn, even to the extent of having Christmas trees ("a small one, doesn't mean anything"). Fortunately, the number of recalcitrants did decrease as our school spirit penetrated the community.

Another landmark! We brought the fathers to the temple before the Passover holiday. We were aware that many of the men could read Hebrew but were embarrassed to conduct the Seder. Some came. We went through the Seder, step by step, indicating how important it was for the family to identify with life in Egypt in those days. Thus, they gave meaning to the dipping in the salt water, the tasting of the bitter herb and even the Haroset.

We pointed out that our sages were wise when they made the child the star of the evening by involving the children in the entire procedure.

We recited the prayers together. We talked about the Afikomen which kept the children's interest to the end of the Seder. The men were grateful. They told us afterwards how delighted they and their families were for a Seder that was meaningful to the entire family.

I choose these few holidays to illustrate what we were able to accomplish. There were many more fruitful activities that made Jewish history come alive in our school. We received calls from other congregations asking for our innovative projects . . . the landmarks of our history.

This is the material Dr. Emanuel Gamoran asked us to gather for publication in the books called "*Activities In The Religious School*" and the supplement which included samples of assembly programs.

Excerpt from *Involvement in the Soviet Jewry Movement*

This monograph is Dr. Louis Rosenblum's personal account of the beginnings and growth of the Soviet Jewry movement in America. This version, authored in 2007 for this volume, was published in expanded form online in 2008 as *Involvement in the Soviet Jewry Movement: A Personal Journey, 1961–1978* and highlights Cleveland's contributions to the movement. The author, a retired scientist and member of the Senior Executive Service, directed the Solar and Electrochemistry Division at the Glenn (formerly Lewis) Research Center of the National Aeronautics and Space Administration (NASA) in Cleveland. He fought in the battle for Okinawa in World War II, was awarded the Bronze Star, and served in the army of occupation in Japan after the war. He earned a PhD in organic chemistry at Ohio State University and subsequently was employed by NASA until his retirement in 1981.

Source: Louis Rosenblum, *Involvement in the Soviet Jewry Movement: A Personal Journey, 1961–1978*, published online in May 2008, with additions in October 2008 and February 2010, available at www.clevelandjewishhistory.net/sj/index.htm.

FROM THESE BEGINNINGS

It began innocently enough in a discussion group. In the fall of 1961, a few of us at Beth Israel—The West Temple, in Cleveland, Ohio, formed a social action committee. As chairman we selected Mort Epstein, a soft-spoken, deliberate individual who headed a graphic design firm. Mort was recognized in the Cleveland community as a long-standing advocate for fair housing.

Two others who sparked the group were Herb Caron and Dan Litt. Herb was an assistant professor of psychology at Western Reserve University and a researcher at Crile Hospital. Dan Litt, our rabbi, felt it important that the congregation reach out beyond the confines of Beth Israel, to the larger Jewish world. The remaining members were Don Bogart, a NASA nuclear physicist, a gentle man and ardent advocate for social justice; Dave Gitlin, an allergist, an outspoken political activist who took over the committee chair in October 1962; and lastly, me, a thirty-eight-year-old NASA research manager and president of our small congregation.

The Holocaust figured prominently in our studies and deliberations. Not surprisingly, we returned to it again and again; after all, it was the central Jewish tragedy in our lives as teenagers or young adults. What particularly struck us was the poverty of response to the dire predicament of European Jews from the U.S. government and—most distressingly—from the American Jewish leadership. Chaim Greenberg, in his angry, anguished essay "Bankrupt," published in the February 1943 issue of the *Yiddishe Kemfer,* bared the sin of Jewish leaders. He castigated them for continuing their "normal behavior of in-fighting and advantage-seeking," one organization over the other, rather than unifying to create a political force to save a greater number of European Jews from the Nazis.

By 1963, we concluded our studies of the Holocaust period. Clearly, the next question was, is there, nowadays, a major Jewish population at risk? That led us quickly to the plight of 3 million Soviet Jews, well over a quarter of world Jewry. Anti-Semitism was widespread in the Soviet Union, much of it promoted by the government. To boot, the government actively suppressed Jewish cultural and religious expression. It was not much of a stretch to foresee—given the tragic fate of tens of millions of Soviet citizens during Stalin's reign—two possible dire outcomes: denied cultural and religious opportunities, Jews would, in a generation or two, disappear as a distinct people; alternatively, a campaign of anti-Semitic pogroms and forced resettlement to camps in Siberia would result in physical decimation and incalculable misery.

Our sources of information were manifold. We collected a small library of articles and books by academics, as well as by Western observers in the Soviet Union. Among the latter were some by Israeli diplomats who had spent considerable time in the Soviet Union. Recall that in 1948, the Soviet Union had voted in the United Nations to recognize the state of Israel and had established formal diplomatic relations. Consequently, there were Israeli diplomatic observers in Moscow up until the infamous 1953 "Doctors' Plot," when they were expelled by Stalin. Following Stalin's death, political relations with Israel resumed.

Jews in Eastern Europe, a quarterly published in London, England, beginning in 1962, provided detailed information about general anti-Semitic campaigns by the Soviet government. There were reproductions of Soviet cartoons that depicted Jews in like fashion to the Nazi portrayals. In many instances, the Soviet authors merely lifted and recycled old Nazi cartoons, only changing the caption to suit Soviet purposes. Books and newspapers from Soviet publishing houses regularly characterized Jews as alien and inimical to Soviet society. Here was a major state blatantly peddling rank hatred.

Additionally, there was cultural deprivation. From Stalin's time on, the Jews were essentially denied access to Jewish culture, including religious expression. Jewish theaters, publications, and newspapers were forbidden. And members of the Jewish intelligentsia—a large and talented group of individuals—were effectively wiped out, executed or imprisoned by Stalin, between 1948 and 1952. In areas of large Jewish concentration, many synagogues were forcibly closed; the remaining few functioned under control of state-vetted officials. *Minyanim,* private prayer meetings in homes, were banned. No Hebrew bibles or prayer books had been published since 1917.

FIRST CONTACT WITH THE JEWISH COMMUNITY FEDERATION OF CLEVELAND

In mid-1963, we contacted the Jewish Community Federation of Cleveland (JCFC) to ascertain if any national Jewish organization was providing guidance on the Soviet Jewry issue and if a committee had been set up locally to address the matter. We were surprised to learn that nothing was afoot nationally or locally. Herb Caron appealed to the JCFC to establish a committee to look into the issue and make recommendations for appropriate action. And subsequently, a subcommittee on Soviet Jewry was set up under the Community Relations Committee of the federation. After a few meetings, it was apparent to us that the pace was pedestrian and that little of practical value was forthcoming. For example, the subcommittee did agree to establish a speakers' bureau—good. Yet when push came to shove, it was the efforts of Don Bogart and Dave Gitlin of Beth Israel that produced a slide lecture on Soviet Jewry. And when speakers were needed to fill requests, members of our little Beth Israel group ended up doing the entire job.

In October 1963, we formally organized the Cleveland Committee on Soviet Anti-Semitism (CCSA), a nonsectarian, interracial, interreligious entity. Herb and Dan were instrumental in lining up the board of directors. As honorary chairman, they enlisted Ralph Locher, the mayor of Cleveland. Other members were Msgr. Cahill, president of St. John College; Bruce Whittemore, director of the Cleveland Area Church Federation; Leo Jackson, a prominent African American and a member of the Cleveland City Council; and Rabbi Phil Horowitz, the associate rabbi at Fairmount Temple. Herb took on the job of executive secretary to the board. With a letterhead and an honorary board, the committee was off and running. In November, we distributed our first publication, *Soviet Terror against Jews: How Cleveland Initiated an Interfaith Protest,* containing a description of the Soviet Jewish problem and the *Appeal to Conscience to Soviet Leaders* that we requested the reader sign and return to us. About the same time, we placed a large ad in the Cleveland newspapers with the *Appeal to Conscience* and a clip-out return coupon to sign. In April 1964, a second publication, *To the Leaders of the Soviet Union,* was distributed containing a letter to Soviet premier Nikita Khrushchev and the names and addresses of over six hundred signers of the *Appeal to Conscience.*

These and later publications brought us attention from the press and from Clevelanders and individuals elsewhere in the United States who asked to receive our mailings. Within a few years, we had amassed a significant mailing list (which, in time, grew to include international correspondents). Strange as it seems, our small operation was in contact with people across America who sought information and advice or wanted to exchange experiences. (In retrospect, this was a measure of the latent enthusiasm to succor Soviet Jews that later would be called "the Soviet Jewry movement.") We had no central office; rather, we worked out of our individual homes. Periodically, we met to confer at Herb's house. We were committed to doing whatever we could.

ON THE NATIONAL SCENE

In September 1963, Supreme Court Justice Arthur Goldberg, after reading accounts about Soviet Jewry, invited Senators Abraham Ribicoff and Jacob Javits to meet with him to discuss what might be done. This was followed by a meeting with Secretary of State Dean Rusk and subsequently, at the end of October, with President John F. Kennedy. Goldberg reported that the president had considerable prior knowledge of the issue of Soviet Jewry. Kennedy suggested, as a first step, that Goldberg and the senators meet with Soviet ambassador Anatoly Dobrynin. Kennedy personally arranged for the meeting. As one might expect, Dobrynin denied any problem existed for Jews in the Soviet Union. Kennedy's assassination on November 22 closed the door for the time being on further help from the administration. Then, on December 19, at Goldberg's suggestion, a meeting to discuss the matter of Soviet Jewry was held with representatives of leading American Jewish organizations. The justice informed them of his concerns and filled them in on his earlier meetings with the president and others. Goldberg presented his conclusion that silence in the matter of Soviet Jewry was not desirable; on the contrary, responsible action was very much in order.[1]

Apparently, Goldberg's meeting with the Jewish establishment reinforced their resolve to get moving on the Soviet Jewry issue. Only a few weeks earlier, prodded by Rabbi Uri Miller and Rabbi Abraham Heschel, the leaders of several American Jewish organizations had met and agreed to bring together resources for public action and education. This, then, was the lead-up to a conference on Soviet Jewry convened in April 1964.

The establishment's difficulties in getting off the dime had to do mainly with organizational prerogatives and jealousies. It would appear that the natural leader of a Soviet Jewry campaign would have been one of the defense organizations that proclaimed their mission "to defend Jewish interests at home and abroad." The rub was that in the United States, there were three independent Jewish defense organizations: the American Jewish Committee (AJ Committee), founded in 1906; the American Jewish Congress (AJ Congress), founded in 1918; and the Anti-defamation League of the B'nai B'rith (ADL), founded in 1913. Each may have seen the Soviet Jewry issue as an opportunity to expand its agenda, its fund-raising, and its importance—if it had an exclusive lock on the issue. But as for sharing an issue, forget it; for over half a century, these organizations had eschewed cooperation, parceling out responsibility, or eliminating replication of effort. Other potential leaders—the several Zionist organizations—wanted the Soviet Jewry issue addressed, in the hope that Jews might be permitted to leave the Soviet Union for Israel eventually. But in general, they were waiting for others to take the lead. Among the religious organizations, Agudas Israel and the Lubavitcher Hasidic movement were deeply concerned about Soviet Jews but were adamant in holding to *shtadlonus*—quiet diplomacy.

Lastly, there was the National Jewish Community Relations Advisory Council (NJCRAC), the umbrella organization that supported local Community Relations Councils (CRCs) found in major U.S. cities. Local CRCs were independent community organizations in earlier times. Eventually, however, most were subsumed within their local Jewish community federation, as in Cleveland. The NJCRAC had a "natural" interest in the Soviet Jewry issue, and it was a potentially important player, particularly in coordinating activity at the community level.

Among the national Jewish organizations, there was no absence of knowledge about the plight of Soviet Jewry; what was lacking was consensus on who should lead and what should be done—and the result was a stalemate.

AN AMERICAN JEWISH CONFERENCE ON SOVIET JEWRY

Yet there seemed to be a glimmer of hope. The Conference of Presidents of Major Jewish Organizations (CoP) announced a pro tem conference to be held April 5–6, 1964, in Washington, D.C. The NJCRAC was assigned to organize the American Jewish Conference on Soviet Jewry (AJCSJ). It appeared to us a golden opportunity: first, a chance to learn more (there were plans to have major speakers, experts on the issue, as well as political figures) and then, a chance to meet others with an interest in Soviet Jewry. We applied through the Union of American Hebrew Congregations to be appointed delegates from Cleveland. A few weeks in advance of the conference, a mailing went out to the delegates providing the agenda and the text of fourteen resolutions to be voted on at the close of the meeting. Among the resolutions were the expected ones on programs and actions, such as establishing a national day of prayer. What caught our attention was the final resolution. It stated that after adjournment of the conference, "the presidents of the national Jewish organizations would meet to consider how to implement plans set out by the Conference." To us, this was a red flag. What confidence could one have that this same group of "leaders"—deadlocked for several months on the organization of a national Soviet Jewry effort—would now break with past behavior? With this in mind, Herb, Dan, and I discussed ideas for a new resolution, a resolution to create a national Soviet Jewry organization to continue the work of the conference. We undertook to write to a number of other delegates about our trepidations and thoughts of what might be done at the conference.

At the hotel on the first day of the conference, the three of us quickly separated to buttonhole delegates. Our two talking points were the need to jump-start local activities and the need to create a national organization, adequately staffed and financed, to support and coordinate local efforts. That afternoon, we caucused with delegates from several cities. In short order, we agreed on wording for a resolution for conference follow-on and arranged with the hotel to have copies mimeographed. That evening, members of the caucus passed out copies of the resolution to the delegates. It proved to be the spark that ignited the delegates: here was *tachlis* (purpose).

To make a long story short, on the second day of the conference, after the "official" resolutions were passed, our resolution for conference follow-on was offered from the floor. At that, the conference chairman, Isaiah Minkoff, executive director of NJCRAC, lost his cool. He denounced "these unspeakable Bundists from Cleveland, who circulated among the delegates this destructive resolution" and ruled our resolution irresponsible and non-admissible. A great commotion followed, with shouting from the floor: "Is this a democratic meeting or not?" Pandemonium ensued. Finally, the chair relented and agreed to entertain the resolution. It was seconded and passed by an overwhelming vote.

The final result was that our resolution was folded into resolution 14, which then read, "Immediately upon the adjournment of this Conference, the Presidents of the co-sponsoring national Jewish organizations will meet for the purpose of considering how best to assure that the plans set out herein will be systematically implemented. It is our further proposal that the Presidents develop the means of continuing this Conference on an ongoing basis, adequately staffed and financed, to coordinate and implement the resolutions of this Conference." We felt elated. We had pushed through, almost unanimously, a resolution we believed would provide us with a national organization that would be a force in promoting Soviet Jewry activities throughout the United States. Very soon, though, we discovered that was not to be. What the CoP did do was continue the AJCSJ as an ongoing entity—without funding. And for staff, an NJCRAC employee, Al Chernin, was assigned on a part-time basis as AJCSJ's one and only staff member. In short, it was a sham. They had taken a page out of Grigori Aleksandrovich Potemkin's playbook. (On and off over the next five years, we and other local Soviet Jewry councils expended time and energy fighting for the AJCSJ to be given the resources needed to make it an effective organization, without success. It was like pounding sand.)

TRANSFORMING THE CLEVELAND COMMITTEE
ON SOVIET ANTI-SEMITISM

By the end of 1964, it became evident that the CCSA, as constituted, had serious limitations. It was a letterhead organization, riding on the credibility provided by the names of our prominent board members; it lacked a substantial membership and roots in the larger Jewish community. All told, we were a handful from Beth Israel with a sprinkling of Eastsiders. We had made a splash both locally and nationally, but to become an effective force, we needed to re-create ourselves. So, in January 1965, we did a makeover. I recruited Abe Silverstein, director of the NASA Lewis Research Center (LeRC), as chairman of our board and expanded the board to include well-known Jews from various sectors of the Cleveland community. Also, we changed our name from the Cleveland Committee (suggesting a temporary entity) to the Cleveland Council on Soviet Anti-Semitism. We incorporated as a nonprofit organization with the state of Ohio. Then, thanks to a single event, we markedly increased our membership.

The event was a community rally, a joint effort by the JCFC and the CCSA. The federation provided the financing, and they and we shared in organizing the program and arranging for speakers. The federation engaged Heights High School auditorium, a large hall that was centrally located in the area of major Jewish population—a great choice. The event, billed as "A Community-Wide Rally to Protest Soviet Anti-Semitism," was held March 7, 1965. The attendance was overwhelming—a crowd of 2,200 plus—more than filling the 2,000-seat auditorium. The overflow was moved into the hallways in the building, and portable speakers were quickly put in place. This display of interest was a revelation: concern about Soviet Jews was latent among ordinary American Jews. The program went well. The principal speaker, Rabbi George Lieberman from New York, gave an impressive account of life for Jews in the USSR. Prominent Protestant and Catholic religious leaders provided expressions of concern, and a number of local, county, and state political figures offered support.

The rally was a major step forward in the education of the Cleveland Jewish community about Soviet Jewry, and it was a step forward in informing the public about the CCSA. For the CCSA, the immediate outcome was impressive—over five hundred new members! Here again, we had an instructive demonstration of the impulse to help a threatened Jewish population.

GOING FACE TO FACE WITH VISITING SOVIET CULTURAL GROUPS

A membership base gave us the opportunity to consider ambitious new action projects. One such project involved touring Soviet cultural groups, such as ballet companies and orchestras. The idea was to present to a group a petition of concern for Soviet Jews, a petition addressed to the leaders of the Soviet Union. We saw such an encounter having two major effects. First, a report of the encounter would assuredly get back to the Soviet government, via the KGB minders accompanying the group. Second, reports of the encounter in the local newspapers and on radio news would publicize the Soviet Jewry issue. As it evolved, the project encompassed a large number of CCSA members and others. In front of the theater would be a few dozen of our people who offered to the entering theatergoers a printed piece with a cover resembling a playbill. Inside was a concise summary of the situation of Soviet Jews and a copy of the petition to the Soviet government to be presented to the Soviet group that evening. Then, a delegation of six or seven would go backstage after the performance to present the petition. Of course, our public relations committee notified the press ahead of time about our plans. All in all, we received excellent media coverage and supportive editorials.

The first of these encounters on May 9, 1965, with the Moiseyev Folk Dancers, was an unqualified success. From then on for a decade, this action was repeated with each visiting Soviet cultural group. In November 1969, the JCFC Community Relations Committee joined with us in an encounter with the Osipov Balalaika Orchestra, and in later years, the JCFC took on the organization and execution of the encounters. This was a success of another kind—helping the federation move to a greater level of involvement (particularly in those times, when staid organizations eschewed public demonstrations).

AGREEMENT BETWEEN THE JCFC AND THE CCSA

Thanks to our projects, publications, and national involvement, we had established the CCSA as a significant presence in the community by 1966. As a result, we were not at all surprised when, in May, Sid Vincent, executive director of JCFC, suggested that we discuss our discrete roles in the community. Shortly after, Abe Silverstein and I met with Sid and a few of his staff. Out of that meeting came a draft of a three-point agreement, which we concluded in July. I will quote from the final agreement:

1. The JCF recognizes both the urgency of the problems of Soviet Jewry and the value of helping the work of the CCSA. 2. CCSA is concerned with a single problem and its work is of both local and national scope. The JCF, through its Community Relations Committee, has had, and will continue to have, programs in this area. Techniques appropriate to the CCSA are not necessarily so for the JCF. Our aim should be to preserve autonomy and full freedom of responsible action for both organizations, while achieving maximum cooperation. 3. It is suggested that the JCF undertake to support specific projects of the CCSA.

Both organizations were well served in this accord, which was the first of its kind anywhere in the United States. And over the following years, cooperation in projects and events was the rule rather than the exception. I might add it was also an explicit acknowledgment of the national scope and reach of our efforts by an establishment organization.

The federation was open to our requests for funding, with the proviso that any funds granted be for specific projects and not for operating purposes. This suited us. We had a number of projects in mind but lacked the money. From 1966 through 1971, we submitted to the federation, annually, a list of projects and associated budgets. Over that period, we received an average of about $3,000 a year for approved projects, which gave a substantial boost to our efforts. And because we operated with volunteer help, we were able to leverage the federation's contribution.

CCSA PROJECTS

A sampling of the many projects designed and carried out by the CCSA, presented in rough chronological order, follows.

Spotlight

The CCSA newsletter was appropriately called *Spotlight*. The first issue came off the press in 1965, and it was published sporadically through 1969. (It is important to note that in that period, no other widely disseminated newsletter on Soviet Jewry was published in America.) Herb, who is a fine writer, was the editor. He also drew the cartoons and line art that embellished each issue—a wonderful talent. I contributed an editorial or two, and I was responsible for a page on action programs and another on material available from the CCSA. By 1969, *Spotlight* had a distribution of over eighteen thousand copies.

A Handbook for Community Action

Early in my involvement, I became acutely aware of the need for a resource book on Soviet Jewry. So in 1965, I cobbled together my first *Handbook for Community Action on Soviet Jewry*. The handbook was republished in two later editions—in 1966 and 1970—each with more and updated content and a larger press run than the one before. Designed with a broad range of users in mind, it contained suggestions for action programs; material for talks and sermons; dramatic readings, songs, and plays; teacher guides and teaching units for use in schools; and reports, articles, and other factual material on Soviet Jewry.

Organizations, libraries, and individuals throughout North America purchased the handbook. The Cleveland Federation provided a special grant that enabled us to mail a free copy of the third edition to all Hillel Foundations on campuses throughout the United States and Canada.

Protest Seals

Early in 1967, I asked Mort Epstein to design a postage stamp–sized seal that would succinctly impart our message. It seemed that such items were part of the ephemera that no self-respecting mass movement or political campaign could do without. Mort came up with a powerful graphic design of a fractured star of David frame containing a multitude of faces with onion-domed towers in the background; beneath the graphic were the words "Protest the Oppression of Soviet Jewry," all on a deep-red background. Over the years, the protest seals were of exceptional value in two ways. First, they raised visibility of the plight of Soviet Jews: placed on mailings, these seals carried our message far and wide. Second, the seals proved to be a supplemental source of income for struggling grassroots Soviet Jewry groups. The CCSA records show that from 1967 through 1978, we sold 415,000 sheets, 50 seals to a sheet. Soviet Jewry groups in the United States and Canada purchased them from us in bulk. We billed them at a little over our cost, and typically, they retailed a sheet of seals for fifty cents or a dollar. Mort's design became an icon of the Soviet Jewry movement.

Movie

In the fall of 1966, we set out to create an up-to-date film on the historical and present-day problems of Jews in the USSR, a film that could be used as a springboard for public discussion, an educational aid in schools, or a television feature. Our project was completed in the summer of 1968. The professional production team—all but one being volunteers—consisted of Mort Epstein, artistic director; Art Laufman (head of the Motion Picture Section, NASA Lewis Research Center), camera and sound; and Ernie Walker (also from NASA LeRC), camera, and to complete the roster, I (a nonpro) took on the job of producer. I was able to enlist the help of Rabbi Abraham Joshua Heschel to provide comments on Soviet Jewry. Rabbi Heschel, one of the most significant thinkers of our time and a civil rights activist, was then professor of ethics at the Jewish Theological Seminary in New York. We filmed Heschel's section of the movie on location at the seminary. Finally, Dorothy Silver, a distinguished Cleveland actor, lent her voice for the voice-over sections of the film. The JCFC provided a grant of funds to cover the cost of film, processing, and travel.

We titled the 13-minute, 16mm, color and sound film *Before Our Eyes,* after Rabbi Heschel's remark in the movie, "Before our eyes a people and a culture are being made to vanish." The CCSA rented—or sold outright—copies of the movie. Organizations or individuals overwhelmingly chose to rent; between 1968 and 1978, there were about 450 rentals. Several copies were sold: a half dozen to the South African Jewish community and a couple each to Jewish organizations in Canada and England.

Leadership Conferences

As part of an effort to develop local leadership, we cosponsored two training conferences with the JCFC. The first was held in August 1966. As major speaker we brought in Dr. David Weiss, an immunologist from Berkeley, California, who had recently visited the Soviet Union and written a perceptive account of Jewish life there, published in *Dissent* magazine. His talk was followed by workshops, conducted by members of the CCSA, on specific types of action appropriate for local and individual initiative. Fifty people attended, mainly from the Cleveland area. In February 1970, we held the two-day Midwest Regional Conference on Soviet Jewry, with the AJCSJ as a third cosponsor. Our two speakers were Dr. Maurice Friedberg, professor of Slavic languages at Indiana University, and Zev Yaroslavsky, a college student from Los Angeles who had recently visited the Soviet Union. The conference concluded with four workshops: on CCSA's projects, by Herb Caron; on mass participation projects, by Don Bogart; on youth organization, by Zev Yaroslavsky; and on tourist briefing and political action, by me. The conference attracted seventy-five participants from Illinois, Indiana, Kansas, Kentucky, Michigan, Pennsylvania, and Ohio.

Greeting Cards to Soviet Jews

The impetus for this project grew out of a new reality unfolding in the USSR. The euphoria over Israel's stunning victory in the 1967 Six-Day War emboldened a number of Soviet Jews to publicly petition their government for permission to leave for Israel. Many also sent appeals for support to the UN General Assembly and other international bodies. Audaciously, each person had signed an appeal with his or her name and address. By early 1970, we had assembled names and addresses of seventy-two petitioners. My idea was to make available to ordinary Americans a special holiday greeting card for mailing to one or more of these petitioners, as a gesture of support. I checked on the merits of the project with Sovietologists in the United States and with authoritative sources in Israel and was encouraged to proceed.[2]

My next move was to discuss a Passover card project with the JCFC. I met with Sid Vincent and Ed Rosenthal, laid out the project and the results of my research, and got a thumbs-up to the JCFC partnering with us on the project. Next was the matter of the cards. Ed arranged for a luncheon meeting with Irving Stone, a federation trustee and chairman of the American Greeting Card Company. I described the project to Irving over the salad, and by the main course, he was on board. He offered to have his calligrapher lay out our text message, provide the artwork for the face of the card, do the printing and folding, and only charge us for his outside costs—paper and envelopes. Ed and I came up with a Russian and Yiddish text that read "Happy Passover . . . The Jews of the USA to the Jews of the USSR: We have not forgotten you." Lastly, there was the packaging: five cards and envelopes in a clear plastic pouch, together with mailing instructions and five names and addresses of Soviet Jews from our list of seventy-two names.

In the weeks before Passover, the CCSA, the federation, and grassroots Soviet Jewry groups elsewhere sold a total of about ten thousand cards. A month later, we began hearing from people who had purchased greeting cards. Bingo! They were delighted and thrilled. They had received responses from the Soviet Jews to whom they had mailed their cards. For them, Soviet Jewry was no longer an abstraction. It was personal and immediate—embodied in the individuals or families who replied to their cards. What an eye-opener! This one-to-one approach offered a powerful way to engage Americans in the

Soviet Jewry issue. It suggested a whole range of new opportunities, several of which we subsequently developed into discrete people-to-people projects. Together, these projects were a major factor in transforming Soviet Jewry from a cause into a mass movement. That summer, thirteen of the Soviet Jewish families on our mailing list received exit visas for Israel.

We repeated the project in the fall for Rosh Hashanah, again with specially prepared cards from the American Greeting Card Company. The list of Soviet addressees now encompassed 196 names. Approximately forty-five thousand cards were purchased, and the responses from Soviet Jews were comparably greater. The card project—for Passover and Rosh Hashanah—continued as a national project of the Union of Councils for Soviet Jews (see the later discussion) for several years with great success.

Addressing the Needs of Soviet Jews Intent on Learning Hebrew

Project Sefer addressed the needs of Soviet Jews intent on learning Hebrew. The resurgence of interest in Hebrew was twofold. First, it was a connection with one's Jewish roots—Hebrew is the language of Jewish liturgy and the Bible. Second, for those whose goal was *aliyah* (immigration to Israel), fluency in Hebrew would speed integration into Israeli society. Beginning in the late 1960s, nonofficial groups were formed and classes held in private homes. I became aware of this activity in 1971, in telephone conversations with Soviet Jewish activists. Subsequently, Project Sefer was set up to meet the various needs of the Hebrew learning groups throughout the Soviet Union. Top on the needs list were textbooks for all student levels. A people-to-people mass mailing of books started in 1973 and continued through 1977. Our Israeli partner in this endeavor was a group of former Soviet Hebrew teachers that mailed books from Israel. By the most import measure of all, our combined effort was a resounding success. Michel Goldblat, a Hebrew teacher in Moscow during the entire period of the mailings, told us, "The number of books that you have sent us was the critical element—the keystone—in the development of the Hebrew language in Moscow."

Lastly, I want to mention two special undertakings that peculiarly benefited from the talents and enthusiasm of Cleveland Jewish educators and institutions. The first enterprise, begun in December 1971 in association with Reuven Yalon of the Cleveland Bureau of Jewish Education (CBJE), was the preparation of special recorded language tapes and material for the self-study of Hebrew by Russian speakers. Other individuals also volunteered their help: Dr. Alexander Conrad, head of the Russian Department at Case

Western Reserve University; Isadore Reisman, of the Cleveland Hebrew Schools; and Aaron Intrater, Rita Epstein, and Frank Stern of the CBJE. The JCFC provided a grant to defray part of the material expenses not covered by the CCSA. Ten months later, the job was completed, and I arranged for copies of the tapes and an associated study book to be channeled to Hebrew study groups in twelve cities in the USSR.

The second of the special undertakings was in direct support of the teachers. Soviet authorities long regarded the study of Hebrew with great suspicion—teachers were harassed and Hebrew books confiscated. When this failed to dampen Hebrew language studies, the government announced that teaching without certification was illegal. In January 1973, my Soviet Jewish contacts suggested it would be useful for a representative of an internationally recognized Hebrew training institution to visit the USSR and certify Hebrew teachers. Soon after, I met with Henry Margolis, director of the CBJE, and filled him in on the situation; we discussed the part he could play in the unfolding Jewish drama in the USSR. Henry understood and was eager to join the effort. With the help of his staff, a standard teacher's license was translated and inscribed in Russian. Travel arrangements were made. (Henry decided to take his college-age son, Jed, along for support and companionship.) Well beforehand, I informed my contacts in Moscow, Leningrad, and Kiev of his schedule. Expenses for the trip were covered by the CCSA. In June, Henry spent two weeks in the Soviet Union, met productively with many teachers and students, and tested and certified thirty-two teachers in all.

UNION OF COUNCILS FOR SOVIET JEWS

As mentioned previously, from 1964 to 1969 all attempts to move the CoP to provide the resources necessary for transforming the AJCSJ into an effective national organization had come to naught. What did change during those years was the number of grassroots Soviet Jewry councils, which grew from two to eight. (Since my NASA responsibilities entailed periodic travel to both coasts, in my off-hours I was able to meet with and assist the leaders of the emerging councils. In this way, bonds of friendship and trust were established all around.) By the beginning of 1970, six councils concurred that the time was ripe. They would wait no longer for the "Jewish establishment" to get its act together but would unite to form a national confederation. On April 6, the Washington Committee for Soviet Jews, the Southern California Council for

Soviet Jews, California Students for Soviet Jews, the South Florida Conference on Soviet Jewry, the Bay Area Council on Soviet Jewry, and the Cleveland Council on Soviet Anti-Semitism jointly announced the formation of the Union of Councils for Soviet Jews (UCSJ).[3] I was elected chairman, and the UCSJ national office shared the CCSA office in Cleveland during my four-year tenure. The UCSJ grew rapidly—by 1971 to 10 member councils, by 1972 to 16, by 1973 to 18, and by 1985 topping out at 32. In 1972, in support of our political activities, I supervised the opening of a Washington, D.C., office, staffed by one salaried employee who acted as congressional and media liaison.

POLITICAL ACTION

In the late 1960s, to check the growing wave of applications by Jews to immigrate to Israel, the Soviet government resorted to several strategies. Among these were the imposition of increased financial and procedural requirements for an exit visa and the criminalization of Jewish national feelings by the arrest of persons possessing books on Jewish history or Hebrew language on charges of "anti-Soviet" activities.

In regard to arrests, between late 1968 and late 1970 a number of show trials throughout the Soviet Union resulted in the sentencing of forty-six Jews to the gulag. The most publicized by the Western press was the Leningrad "hijacking trial." Eleven people—nine Jews and two Russians—were tried for planning to seize a twelve-seat plane and escape the country. They were arrested on arrival at the airport: the KGB had been monitoring their activities. They were charged with fleeing the country—a capital crime in the Soviet Union. Two were sentenced to death, and the others were given long sentences in a special regime labor camp—the worst of the worst. The strong outcry from the free world at what was called "juridical murder" caused the Soviets to back off a bit and commute the death sentences to fifteen years in a special regime camp.

All of this did little to stanch the flow of applications to emigrate. By 1971, it was estimated that a million Jews sought permission to leave the Soviet Union.

In the fall of 1971, the UCSJ decided, in convention, on a policy shift to open political action—that is, to promote legislation in the U.S. Congress that would entail economic sanctions against countries that restricted freedom of emigration. On January 1, 1972, I met with two political pros (associated with the Washington Committee for Soviet Jews). One of them, Nat Lewin,[4] quickly produced a draft of an amendment that could be applied to a foreign trade bill then scheduled for renewal. The other, Harvey Lieber,[5] sketched out plans for the preparation of position papers and legislative tactics by his graduate students. Our Southern California Council lined up California congressman Tom Rees, a member of the Banking and Currency Committee, to introduce the legislation. On May 4, 1972, Reese, with several cosponsors, introduced in the House of Representatives HR 14806, *A Bill to Amend the Export Administration Act of 1969 in Order to Promote Freedom of Emigration.* In mid-July, unfortunately, the bill went down, two votes short of approval by the Banking and Currency Committee of the House. Nevertheless, a precedent was set for a freedom of emigration bill with teeth, rather than the periodic congressional resolutions deploring Soviet behavior.

On August 15, 1972, the Soviet Union upped the ante for Jews wanting to leave. A *ukase* (decree) was issued that imposed an exorbitant "education tax" on all Jews granted exit visas—in short, a ransom. This was a wake-up call for Congress. On October 4, Representative Charles Vanik (D–Cleveland, OH) in the House and Senator Henry Jackson (D-WA) in the Senate introduced legislation that would deny most-favored-nation status (conferring the lowest tariff rates on exports to the United States) to any nation that denied its citizens the right to emigrate.

Over the next two years, President Richard Nixon and his secretary of state, Henry Kissinger—intent on détente with the Soviets—did all in their power to derail the legislation. The UCSJ threw its weight into the struggle by firming up congressional support: through Action Central, a rapid-response group of forty regional political activists, coordinated by CCSA member Carol Mandel from Cleveland; through the UCSJ Washington office; and by feeding to the news media and Congress up-to-date reports of events in the Soviet Union, as transmitted to the UCSJ by Soviet refuseniks. My personal involvement in this power struggle started in September 1972 with a visit to the White House, by invitation, to meet with Leonard Garment, special counsel to President Nixon. It concluded two years later with a trip to the Soviet Union to confer with Jewish activist leaders on ways they might influence the outcome of the tripartite endgame negotiations among Jackson, Kissinger, and Soviet president Leonid Brezhnev. It was quite a roller-coaster ride.

The Jackson-Vanik legislation passed in Congress with a veto-proof majority in October 1974, and President Gerald Ford signed it into law on January 3, 1975. In the sixteen years between that time and the collapse of the USSR, over a half million Jews and tens of thousands of other persecuted minorities emigrated from the Soviet Union.

CODA

My involvement locally, nationally, and internationally continued until the end of 1978. My decision to leave the movement was conditioned by three considerations. First of all, I owed it to my wife, Evy, and our four children to return a distracted husband and father to the family. Then, I needed to put in more time on my job at NASA—between 1975 and 1978, the number of R&D programs in the division I headed had doubled. Lastly, my presence in the movement was redundant—there were capable and dedicated people at the helm of the UCSJ and in the various councils who would carry the work forward.

I believe that for the Jewish people, the struggle for the right of Soviet Jews to freely emigrate stands as the great redemptive event of the latter part of the twentieth century. In the end, over one million Jews left the USSR and Russia. This modern-day exodus was made possible by the dedicated work of hundreds of ordinary people in the United States, Canada, England, Israel, and the Soviet Union. I am proud and privileged to have played a part in this historic event.

NOTES

1. *Report of Justice Arthur Goldberg's Discussion on Soviet Jewry,* prepared by the Conference of Presidents of Major Jewish Organizations, marked "Confidential," December 3, 1963, Cleveland Council on Soviet Anti-Semitism Records, 1963–1983, MS 4011, Western Reserve Historical Society, Archives, Cleveland, OH.

2. I consulted with two sources: Ann Shenkar and the Action Committee of Newcomers from the Soviet Union (ACNSU). Ann Strauss Shenkar, born in 1923 in Cleveland, was a graduate of Bryn Mawr College. She was descended from prominent Cleveland Jewish families. One grandfather was Solomon Halle, co-owner of the Halle department store; her mother, Marion Halle Strauss, was president of Hadassah in Cleveland; and her father, Abraham Strauss, was head of the surgical department at Mt. Sinai Hospital. Ann worked as a mapmaker for the U.S. Navy during World War II and settled in Palestine in 1947. About 1967, she became active on behalf of Soviet Jewry and worked closely with the ACNSU to prepare news bulletins on Soviet Jewry for distribution around the world. The ACNSU, an association of former Soviet Jews, was dedicated to helping family, friends, and colleagues in the USSR.

3. Two other grassroots organizations—the Student Struggle for Soviet Jews (New York City) and the Minnesota Action Committee for Soviet Jews—opted not to affiliate formally with the UCSJ but, throughout the 1970s and 1980s, did work hand in hand with us on several national projects.

4. Lewin was a nationally prominent trial lawyer who worked under Robert Kennedy in the Department of Justice and pleaded cases before the Supreme Court.

5. Lieber was professor of political science at the American University School of Public Affairs.

Section Five

Philanthropy and Service

Cornerstone ceremony for Mt. Sinai Hospital, 1915 (Western Reserve Historical Society).

MICHAEL SHARLITT (1884–1966)

Excerpt from *As I Remember*

Michael Sharlitt grew up in one of the large Jewish orphanages, the Hebrew Sheltering Guardian Society, in New York City. He later served as the executive director of the Jewish Orphan Home, which became known as Bellefaire, the Jewish Children's Bureau, after its move to the Heights area. He served in this capacity from 1922 to 1941 and initiated many reforms during his tenure.

The document that follows is a chapter from his book about the Jewish Orphan Home of Cleveland, privately published in 1959. In this chapter, Sharlitt describes the process of preparing for and building the new home. He discusses the legal battle for "the right to build" on the new site. He also writes about how the name was chosen and why the French spelling was used. The architect, a graduate of the architecture program at Harvard University, was a former resident of the Jewish Orphan Home. Sharlitt explains the reasons for the use of the cottage model and how the decision was made to build the chapel as a separate building. Overall, the process, from the beginning of the planning to the move to the new facility, took fifteen years.

Source: "The Jewish Orphan Home of Cleveland," chapter from Michael Sharlitt, *As I Remember: The Home in My Heart* (privately published, 1959).

CHAPTER 9
The Jewish Orphan Home of Cleveland

I would like to anticipate here the period of waiting for the completion of the new Home. Graduates everywhere seemed to have learned of the prospective removal, with actual building on the new site going on. An unusual number made a final pilgrimage to the old place. One man in particular who called paid his tribute in a manner not easily forgotten. He stopped at my desk, and without too much introduction or greeting of any kind, requested that he be given permission to go through the place. An hour or so later, he dropped in to see me and I understood his blunt manner. It seems his doctor had advised him that he was doomed to pass away in a few months. "I wanted to see the old place, my old bed if possible, before I closed my eyes in the last sleep. I have just done so. I hope you did not mind my abruptness."

The new home began to cast its shadow in several directions. Not necessarily related to my personal story but nevertheless an episodic detail of interest was the struggle to get an authorization from the municipal authorities for building in the suburban section which was to be the site of the new Home. Looking back on the effort now, it is not surprising that we encountered opposition, for a similar effort on the part of one of the big temples experienced the same "screening difficulty" very recently. In both instances, I believe, appeal from the negative decision of the local zoning commission was carried to the higher courts of the state, with affirmation of the right to build granted in both cases. I wonder if the matter of adding to the tax burden of this small, underdeveloped municipality in our instance or the anxiety about parking headaches in the instance of the temple were the true bases for the difficulty confronted. Aesop, in his tale of the wolf and the lamb, probably gave the actual reason.

Incidentally, the attorney for our home in its battle for the right to build was the distinguished Secretary of War in President Wilson's cabinet. I understand he contributed half the fee for his work to the building fund. I bring in this reference because of an incident which brought me face to face with him in the pleasantest way.

My mother-in-law made it a practice each summer to visit with us, coming from New York City. She was not a much-traveled person and her sons would invariably put her on the train for Cleveland. She had learned to alight from the Pennsylvania train at the next to the last station in Cleveland, where we would meet her. But one summer the boys put her on the New York Central, and when the train did not make the expected stop in mid-town, she was dismayed and expressed her worry, at which a gentleman inquired as to the cause of her anxiety. He gave her confidence with his gentle word that somebody would surely be waiting for her at the terminal; and if not, she would be helped to her destination. I was waiting for her at the terminal. When the train eventually pulled in, I scanned the passengers as they came through the rickety corridor down to the old waiting room. (This was before the fine, new terminal was built.) I spied her, of course, but there was a gentleman with her, carrying her old suitcases. Like the great man he was, former Secretary of War Baker turned the elderly lady over to me, saying to her, "Well, I knew you would be met." It was a delightful incident which I understand the old lady never lost an opportunity to talk about. One could hardly blame her. I addressed a letter to the gentleman, telling him what an inspiration it was to see a really great American in action.

The problem of site for the new Home had been settled. Immediately the question arose as to a name for the place. All agreed there should not be a continuation of the original title because of its out-and-out flourish of its eleemosynary character. Throughout the country at this time, wherever there was rebuilding or the establishment of an institution, there was this desire to break away from a designation that might put on the marquee of the institution an illuminated acknowledgment of charity. And while I was a party to the change of name for the new Home, I am not so sure today that sparring for an attractive and euphonious front accomplishes all that is expected. It is too suggestive of the tendency of the foreign-born to change continental names into those that suggest an American background. It may be old age, with its philosophical re-evaluation of verities, or it may simply be an impatience with presumption. Note that the famous Charity School in England, now at least a few centuries old, has never lost standing and respect in that country. The content of its life and tradition have maintained its high esteem.

At any rate, there was the agitation for a new name. There was even talk of a contest with an award for the best name suggested. At one of the sessions considering the subject, the secretary of the Board proposed the name "Bel-fair," which was a combination of the first syllables of the boulevards that intersected where the new Home was to be built, a not uncommon real-estate promotional device. Almost immediately there came to me a flash of inspiration to give the name suggestiveness, as a kind of French word, by simply adding the letters *le* to "Bel" and an *e* to "fair." And so the name "Bellefaire" was born, with its hybrid connotation to signify and do the beautiful. The name has remained and has gained favor and appreciation with the passing of the years. I'll confess that by all observations the children took kindly to the new designation and the public has graciously demonstrated its appreciation of it also.

Building plans had to be prepared. An architect had to be chosen. Obviously it would be necessary to have the most intimate professional relationship between the architect and myself in the conception of the new Home. It was to be a cottage home, we both understood. That was the skeleton around which must come the body and personality and spirit of the place. And I stop here with such descriptive implications because the architect and superintendent, as individuals, both understood to its depths the opportunity and challenge.

The reader knows, of course, my institutional background. But in addition here, the architect himself was an alumnus of the Jewish Orphan Home. He had come up the hard way, working his way through Harvard and later the graduate school of architecture. By the time the new Home was contemplated, he had established quite a reputation in his field. Later he was to serve Uncle Sam as a major in his professional capacity in World War II, and still later to be the architect for a building project in a slum area. Today he enjoys an enviable reputation and is one of the busiest men in his specialty. He was selected for the task simply and basically for his professional skill. I doubt whether the Board stopped to realize how unusual this combination was that was to create the new look for the Home.

It was a veritable joy working with him. He had as much hope, ambition, optimism, courage, and philosophy for the new place as I could have, and I believe the beautiful campus must reveal this. An illustration of the understanding and sympathetic bond between us developed in connection with plans for play facilities. If the reader will recall it, I mentioned in the Pleasantville section something about wet grounds shortening to a very discouraging extent the baseball playing season. The architect had his answer to that, and expensive as it was, he included in his plans the tiling of the baseball field to make sure of drainage after a heavy rain. I really was surprised that the Board did not regard this as a luxury. But there it was, and as a result the Bellefaire teams could take the field within hours after a downpour. The wonderful play facilities of Bellefaire reflected the appreciation shared by the architect and myself of the part recreation plays in the lives of growing children, particularly of the psychological advantages of it for children under care. A separate gymnasium building, later to be known as "Alumni Hall," for basketball, campus gatherings of every nature, an indoor swimming pool, tennis, and outdoor basketball courts were the features of play facilities provided, together of course with the good-sized baseball field, without the usual restriction of playing space in the outfield. To get into the spirit with which the architect and myself approached this factor of play, in the earliest blueprints we had arranged an asphalt boundary to the ball field to allow for roller skating, but mechanical and technical and financial questions entered and we reluctantly had to abandon the idea.

When the children finally made their entry into the new place, they must have been captivated not only by the silken novelty of furnished living rooms and bedrooms for from three to six persons, with tiled bathrooms adjoining, but by as fine a spread of recreational facilities as would be the boast of the elegant boarding schools of the country. It was a gift not only of liberal philanthropy but from understanding and a good memory.

It was the architect, I believe, who conceived the idea of a chapel with classroom facilities to be placed in the center of the campus, with diagonal walks from all cottages leading to it. I heartily concurred with him in this arrangement, particularly regarding its central location. I liked the notion of a chapel deep in the heart of the campus body, with a spiritual reflection of its own.

However, the elaborate building plans increased building costs beyond the budget originally allocated, and serious revision seemed necessary. One of the changes recommended was a combination gymnasium hall and synagogue, the fine chapel to be abandoned. Decision seemed final about this and both architect and myself were very much disturbed. Fortunately, the suggestion was made that my wife and I study the two new cottage plan institutions on the West Coast, one in San Francisco and one in Los Angeles.

We made the trip and I returned all the more anxious that the separate chapel building be reinstated as a reflection of the spiritual pulse of the new surroundings. And the Board, in its wisdom, agreed, despite the additional cost, with the happy result that the specialized appeals of Alumni Hall and the chapel have continued now for over a quarter of a century. The chapel, in my opinion, lifts the entire campus, for it quietly radiates like the sun by day and the moon and stars by night the suggestion of something not brick and stone, something not always reflected in curriculums. That the children in their own way caught this is evidenced by the fact that a number, later in their lives, returned to be married in this same chapel.

Building plans were finally complete and acceptable to all concerned. It would be nearly two years before we would actually move. Successful efforts were made to sell our old property to the City of Cleveland, the intention of the city at the time of purchase including plans for a recreation park on the site. The reader will recall that the institution began as a suburban property. Later, it was in what might be referred to as "the golden ghetto." At the time of its sale to the city, it was in the heart of a slum section of town. An understanding in the sale was, pending the actual removal to the new site, that the playground of the Home with its facilities be opened to the public, which meant of course, to the children of the neighborhood, who were almost all Negroes.

I give this detail in my story because I had an unusual opportunity to practice what I felt so strongly about—the common fellowship of all, no matter what the race or creed. We arranged as many tournament games as possible between our group and the neighborhood children. We engaged a special supervisor whose duty it was to promote playground good will. Our playground was thus opened to the neighborhood for two successive seasons. I was much gratified then and am now that there were no "incidents" between the two so called "underprivileged" groups.

Just another reference to our Negro neighbors. The city councilman who had facilitated the purchase of our property by the city made it an annual practice to issue holiday gifts to the men and women voters at holiday time in December. Our Home was in his district. To my surprise, one late December afternoon I found some men setting up tables on our spacious lawn which fronted the avenue, loaded with goodies of all kind. I tried to locate the man responsible for this and was advised that the district councilman had given the orders and arranged everything, that it was his annual party for the neighborhood. The councilman was not available at the time. The next morning I located him and demanded—I think the correct word is "demanded"—just what he meant by such an exhibition on our lawn. The city may have owned the property, but we still had underprivileged children under care and I did not like the handout exhibition before their eyes.

The councilman at first seemed puzzled by my manner and my point of view. He was silent for a minute or so, and then he smilingly acknowledged his mistake and promised that the lawn would be cleared as quickly as possible. Finally, like the sensible citizen he was, he declared that it was good to know that a fight could be made for such a cause. We later became very good friends.

The big day for departure was approaching. Fortunately, the maintenance staff took over the dismantling of the old buildings. As I review it now, it must have been a masterly job, for there was little regret about oversights once we were established at the new suburban location. We carried away whatever could be used that was in harmony and taste with the new surroundings. Contractors took over the remainder, and of course much was left to them. In a way, it is amazing that the removal was accomplished with little confusion. Sleeping and dining in one place one day, nearly four hundred children slept and dined at Bellefaire in the next twenty-four hours. Speaking of it in this speedy fashion does not express the ease and wonder of it all.

But, as can be imagined, there was an abundance of anticipatory planning, particularly in reference to staffing and preparation for the marked change in manner of living. The reader will recall that one of the early changes introduced after I assumed duty was the organization of the children on both sides of the house into vertically arranged groups, with each group having young and old together, after a family pattern and that the oldest children took over the meanest and heaviest chores. It was not too difficult therefore, to plan for a pre-removal period of several weeks to be a seminar in cottage management for all group leaders and the newly appointed housemothers.

The architect and I had agreed on a duplex cottage arrangement, one side for the girls and the other for the boys, with a common kitchen between. The idea behind this was to promote the propinquity of brothers and sisters, who were to be in all instances on the opposite wings of the same duplex. Occasional suppers, occurring weekly at least, and duplex parties would thus bring them together.

Accordingly, since the great departure was to be in August, 1929, we opened up one of the duplex units for training purposes early in July. The older group leaders of the boys were on one side, the older group leaders of the girls on the other. A group of housemothers established residence on each side. After breakfast, actual household management got underway, housemothers and group leaders learning the routine by doing. Then, two hours in the late morning were given over to actual seminar sessions for the housemothers.

Our psychiatrist, our physician, my wife, and I led in talks and discussions sensitively pertinent to the new life. For the most part, the four of us in this seminar faculty appreciated that we were facing a dramatic change of life for the institution, tremendously realistic, and that we could hardly anticipate the host of difficulties certain to develop with new and obviously novel horizons for the children. The separate entity of each child, the precautions for good health, the domestic mechanics for running a household, the overall administration of group living, all received consideration in the daily class attendance of the new cottage mothers.

Afternoons were taken up in a similar realistic way. The older children, under supervision of the housemothers, each of whom took over at once the equipment of the cottage which was to be her permanent home and responsibility, assisted the maintenance staff in setting up furniture, bedding, and general supplies, so that all would be in readiness when the mass of children would eventually arrive. It was a busy, fruitful, and happy month for all of us, I suppose as might be the case of a newly married couple setting up house, with the adventure of working out new arrangements for living together. I do not recall anything but the excitement of fervent anticipation that marked this trial by living. I believe we were as well prepared for the actual "opening" as could be anticipated theoretically.

That this statement is not too much of an exaggeration was attested to by the fact that less than three months after the new Bellefaire was underway, the old place was deep in the background of memory, sentimental and legendary of course, but irrevocably of the past. I remember a conversation I had with one of the Board members at the time, a woman devoted to the Home for many years, who commented that so much had been accomplished since the removal that it was difficult to believe we had only been in our fine new surroundings for less than three months.

Setting foot on the fine new campus, particularly into the fairy-tale spread of furnishings in such contrast to barracks playroom benches, might have been more of a fantasy to the children had it not been for the fact that up to the time of completion of the buildings we made it a practice to drive out groups of children to see the new place. Mentally at least, the older children were prepared. But there is a magic of its own in possessive occupation of surroundings that reflect the possibility of a brand new kind of life; a magic that only actual occupation can suggest. And this only "D for Departure Day" could supply.

I am unable to resist at this juncture, before going into the Bellefaire section of my story, repeating the lines recited in one of the early musical revues at the Home, and I repeat it here because the great ambition of the patient children and the Board had been realized.

It was fifteen years or longer
    that our very worthy Board
Said us kids would grow up stronger
    if the country air we stored.
So they planned a cottage city
    where the air would be distilled.
Won't you listen to my ditty—
    We'll have whiskers when they build.

It was close to twenty years from the decision to establish a new home to its actual fulfillment. The fine panorama of cottage homes and campus was well worth the long waiting.

A. R. WARNER, JAS. F. JACKSON, AND MARTIN MARKS

Petition to the Trustees, Western Reserve University

Although the backgrounds of A. R. Warner and Jas. F. Jackson are not known, Martin Marks was a businessman and community leader. Born in Madison, Wisconsin, he left school at the age of thirteen. He moved to Cleveland in 1886 after he married Belle Hays, the daughter of Kaufman Hays. He first became active in B'nai B'rith and was appointed to the board of the Jewish Orphan Asylum. He served as the president of The Temple–Tifereth Israel (1890–1904, 1906–1915) during the time when Rabbi Moses Gries was employed there. He helped establish the Federation of Jewish Charities in 1903. Marks was a founder of the Federation for Charity and Philanthropy (1903). On behalf of eighteen Cleveland philanthropic organizations, he and Warner and Jackson presented a petition to the Western Reserve University Board of Trustees on December 18, 1913, asking that the university establish a school to teach "philanthropy, social service and public welfare." In 1914, the university established the School of Social Science and Research.

This petition describes the need for a school to prepare social service workers and presents a strong rationale in support of that proposition. The petition asks that the program be a postbaccalaureate offering and part of the Western Reserve University.

Source: A. R. Warner, Jas. F. Jackson, and Martin Marks, petition to the Western Reserve University Board of Trustees on December 18, 1913, asking that the university establish a school to teach "philanthropy, social service and public welfare," Series 1DB6 17:7, Records of Charles F. Thwing, President, Western Reserve University, 1890–1920, Case Western Reserve University Archives. Courtesy of the Case Western Reserve University Archives.

December 18, 1913

To the Trustees,
Western Reserve University

Representing the will and wishes of eighteen philanthropic organizations of Cleveland, we respectfully present the following for your consideration:

For at least ten years there has been a growing conviction among the various public welfare workers that there was in Cleveland a need and an opportunity for a school to teach sociologic sciences. From time to time, as your President can relate to you, this need has been discussed by those interested in all kinds of welfare work and plans for such a school have been considered. The recent increased demand for public and social service workers and the scarcity of tutored or practically trained candidates for these positions has compelled philanthropic organizations to give temporary courses of instruction that their workers might at least be partially trained: however, such courses have uniformly proven entirely inadequate and no other result was ever expected. This condition and the constant stream of applications from high grade, educated and suitable but entirely untrained persons for positions to do any and all kinds of social work has made these pleas for such a school more numerous and more emphatic.

At a public meeting held November 24, 1913, the following resolutions were unanimously adopted:

"We resolve that there be appointed by this body a committee to prepare a petition to the Trustees of Western Reserve University asking that the University establish a school to teach philanthropy, social service and public welfare, and that this school, in co-operation with the public and private institutions of the city, offer opportunities for instruction, practical field work and for research."

(A list of the persons present and the organizations represented is appended.)

Cleveland with its great and varied business activities, its cosmopolitan population and its rapid growth is a fitting place to teach the sociologic sciences and to train in social work. No informed Clevelander will admit that any city has on the whole more advanced, varied or active philanthropic institutions, municipal or private, or a more efficient fabric of social organizations working for the common welfare; and it is justly so. Therefore no city offers greater opportunity for desirable practical experience, for popular extension courses, for properly supervised survey or original research work: no city has better material to study or from which to teach. Between New York and Chicago there is no university which now has the talent in the various medical, legal, philosophical, sociologic and economic branches already in its organization to combine and assemble for such a school in any way equal to that at Reserve. Reserve has the necessary standing and prestige to attract properly prepared students to sociologic courses carrying University credits and leading to degrees. Reserve also has the confidence and the friendship of every social institution of Cleveland, so that practical extension courses could be given in co-operation with each and all of such institutions, and opportunity given to prepare for any special field of work. Such a combination of courses, academic, practical, liberal, would, we believe, constitute a school in harmony with, but in advance of, the recent trend of sociologic teaching and one more popular, because more practical and of more value to promote public welfare than the older established conventional schools of philanthropy.

We do therefore respectfully but earnestly ask that you give serious consideration to the needs of and the opportunities for such a school in Cleveland and to the organization of such a school as a part of Western Reserve University.

Respectfully submitted,

A. R. Warner, M.D.
Lakeside Hospital
Jas. F. Jackson
Associated Charities
Martin A. Marks
Cleveland Federation for Charity and Philanthropy

ORGANIZATIONS REPRESENTED AT PUBLIC MEETING
December 18, 1913

Alta House
Anti-Tuberculosis League
Associated Charities
Babies' Dispensary and Hospital
Cleveland City Hospital
Cleveland Department of Charities
Cleveland Department of Health
Cleveland Federation for Charity and Philanthropy

Cleveland Kindergarten Training School
Cooperative Employment Bureau
Episcopal City Mission
Goodrich House
Hiram House
Humane Society
Lakeside Hospital
Normal Training School
Visiting Nurse Association
Young Women's Christian Association

"I Remember Hiram House"

Efforts to "Americanize" immigrants in the late nineteenth and early twentieth centuries found one expression in the settlement house movement. The movement's full-service family and children's agencies provided basic health care as well as programs to socialize the newcomers to America. George Bellamy's Hiram House opened in 1896 in the lower Woodland Avenue neighborhood, serving both Jews and non-Jews. Its operations began in a small house, but by 1899, the settlement had constructed a substantial brick building with an adjacent playground at 27th and Orange Avenue.

Social worker Lillian Strauss recalls her early childhood and adolescent experiences with caring adults within the nurturing environment of Hiram House. As many before in similar circumstances, Strauss returned to the settlement house as a college student to help a new generation "Americanize." Hiram House had a profound impact on those it embraced—and prompted Strauss to devote her life to aiding others.

Source: Lillian Strauss, "I Remember Hiram House," Hiram House Records, 1960. The Western Reserve Historical Society.

I Remember Hiram House

It does not seem like such a long time ago when I first began to toddle in the yard of my parents' first home. It was such a big world to explore. There was the garden in front of the house where the bright flowers grew. We were allowed to help sprinkle them with the watering can every afternoon, and in the fall we picked the black four o'clock seeds to put by for the next spring's planting. There was the strange box under the earth where my mother stored the ripe vegetables to be used on colder days. There were the fat hens strutting in the back yard as though they owned the earth. Each day they left a few eggs in the straw nests for us to find. There were the friendly horses in the stalls of the barn. The stalls were rented to neighborhood peddlers, most of whom were newcomers to this land, and could speak but little English. We watched the masters unhitch the horses, both tired at the end of the day's journeying to far away places. Then we watched with eager eyes while the peddlers sorted the treasures people had given them. Sometimes there was a worn story book or a bright piece of cloth for our dolls, given generously to the delighted and unabashed recipients.

The first real excursion into the outer world was thru the little weather-beaten door of the wooden fence in the back yard. There were two houses next door. In the front lived some fine ladies and gentlemen. In the rear house was the most wonderful room. There were small chairs into which a little girl could climb. There were blocks, good strong hard things that would stay together and become houses, wagons, or anything you wished to make. There were books too, with pictures about things you had never seen, a brown and white cow in a field of green, water sparkling in the sun. I was too little to go to the kindergarten, but some grown up let me play in the room after the children had gone home. My mother told me years later, that very often some of the ladies in the front house would call her thru the window to come and help them with the buttons or hooks in the back of their dresses. So much I remember of the first Hiram House, only that they were friendly and neighborly.

But later, in the great red brick building a few blocks further down Orange Street, that was different. My grandmother took me by the hand, and there at last, dancing down the street, I could go to the kindergarten. What a wonderful world, where they gave you colored papers out of which to make things, and let you wash the doll's clothes with real soap and water. The teachers who told stories, sang songs, and played games with us seemed to have only one mission in life, to see to it that we had fun. There was the beautiful Christmas tree, which of course we never saw at home. When the dolls were given to the little girls to take home, and I wanted the one with the flimsy gaudy dress another child already had, instead of mine in the checked pinafore, the teacher kneeled down, put her arms around me and gently explained, "But see, dear, this dress you will be able to wash and iron, and it always will be fresh and nice if you take good care of it!"

Such a beautiful large room with the sunshine pouring into the many windows. Such a big warm friendly house, with everyone knowing your name, your mother's name, and even your grandmother's.

That was only the beginning. When we were older and went to the new public school, we could run to Hiram House after school as fast as our legs would carry us. There were books to read, children to play with, music to sing around the piano, that unforgettable refrain, "Then sing happy children, the birds and the bees are here. The May time is a gay time, the happiest time of the year!"

There were the Mitchells, Grace the older, the cheery, plump one who always greeted you with a smile that warmed you like the sun. She patiently taught our clumsy little fingers how to hold and use the crochet hook. Those white washcloths were grimy indeed by the time row upon row of the horribly complicated stitches were finished. We cared not so much for the washcloths as for the moment she would open the new Wizard of Oz book, and in her cheerful, warm voice each week read another of the exciting adventures.

The younger sister Margaret seemed more like one of the angels we would conjure up, when we first heard about angels and tried to imagine what they were like. Her occasional visit to our home was an event. We brought forth the best chair, and a glass of water in a saucer. My mother, who was a sainted good neighbor herself, would tell her about people who were having difficulties of all sorts. We children always sat with them and listened. We knew that Margaret Mitchell would find a way to help them. And we knew in our hearts that if anyone were in great, great trouble, there was the wonderful Mr. Bellamy who would surely save them. There was the time of the terrible trouble in the peddler's family upstairs. The face of the peddler's wife was white, as he and she sat trembling in our kitchen. We heard the ominous words "receiving stolen goods," "He didn't know," "arrest," "jail." My mother reassured them. "I will go to Mr. Bellamy myself tomorrow morning. He will help you." The peddler was away only for a few days, but every day seemed like a century to us, as we suffered with the frightened, bewildered wife.

Then came many new people to our neighborhood, the hunted and the driven. One family came to our house, the young father, mother, little girl, and boy, and the baby sister born enroute in Paris, after a hasty flight from Russia. Their ragged clothes had a strange pungent odor. We thought for a long time that that was the way the sea smelt, but perhaps it was only a heavy disinfectant our country gave them as a first gift. We listened horrified to their tale. The whole family had hidden in two barrels in the cellar, while the hate maddened heroes of the pogrom beat down the doors of their house, smashed all of their furniture, and carried away anything of value. My mother collected a few dollars from our relatives and friends, and helped them find a place to live, three small rooms behind a tiny store where the father opened a bicycle repair shop. We went there often, my mother to teach her how to cook, we to play with the children, and to see how quickly they could learn the English words. One night a great dazzling event took place. There was a party for mothers at Hiram House, in the beautiful big room upstairs. The lights were soft with colored papers. There was music, and of all things, games for the mothers to play, while we watched. Who ever heard of mothers playing? They were always so busy, they only worked, how could mothers play games? But with the quiet urging out of their shyness by the friendly leaders, play they did. They took hands and made a circle just like children. One mother wore a funny hat and carried a bell. Another who was blindfolded, tried to catch her. The mothers laughed so much. It was music to our ears. We did not know mothers could laugh so much. But the face of our friend, the wife of the bicycle repair man, whom my mother had taken along for the first time, was an unforgettable sight. It was shining so with joy, that for the first time I knew what it was like to weep inside of yourself with no tears on your cheeks. After that evening she went to Hiram House often, to learn to speak and to read English, to listen to the talks that were given to the mothers about their children. I remember after one of these talks, a long thoughtful discussion in our kitchen among a few of the women on the subject "Should you never slap a child."

The most wonderful experience of our childhood was going to the country. Our first glimpse of the great green world was in the Hiram House camp—the first one. There was a race track. Men came on Sunday afternoons and sat in funny little wagons behind the horses that trotted so quickly. Many people came and watched them while we children jumped up and down the steps. During the week it was very quiet. The sky was so large over the field. The sun was a great ball of fire at the end of the day. I did not know the sky could be so big. We went out into another field one morning, and everyone carried a tin. We wondered what it was for. We were told to wait and see. Soon we came upon bushes where hung the largest, blackest, juiciest berries we had ever seen. Just hung there, and we could take all we wanted to put in our tins. What a beautiful world. So many delicious berries. You could take all you wanted and fill your tin to overflowing. When we played in the cool shade under the race track seats, there were hundreds of grasses, all kinds. Mostly we played store, and one kind of grass was sugar, another flour, another money. So many different kinds of grasses in this new world, they made a store full of things.

And later we went to the new camp each summer for two unforgettable weeks. How exciting to climb into the big red country car with the other children, your clothes tied in a bundle, your heart pounding. You rode out of the city past strange streets, then as the first green fields came into sight again, the same joy that grew only more intense with the years, the same clean, fresh smell that one can never forget. There was the big house again, with the same woody country fragrance, the fireplace, the enormous porch, the dormitory where you fell asleep at night listening to the quietness, a dark quietness that was not fearful because it was full of friendly chirping sounds. There were the familiar paths thru the woods, and the great adventurous walk thru the deeply shaded ravine where you once learned that the strange waxy pink and white plants were called Indian pipe, and you were forever seeking them so you could show them to new children who did not know. There was the piano in the play room, open all day. You could shyly run your fingers over the keys, and no one ever seemed to mind the noise. There was the cold, cold refreshing water with the queer iron taste you drank from the pump, or dashed over your face in the morning out of the basin. There was the great bell on the tall pole that clanged for meals, and the new kinds of fragrances of gingerbread or blackberry jam that came out of the kitchen with its good country smells. There was the pond where you learned to swim by holding on to the tall grasses at the side, kicking your feet out behind you, until the day came when you could let go with one hand and then the other, and surprisingly you stayed up.

In the big playroom, evenings, there were the songs, the folk dances, the stories in the flickering shadows of the fireplace. That all seemed a dream out of a book you lived with the year round. There was the long hike to the beautiful Chagrin River, the adventure of crossing on the stones in the spar- kling water to get to your destination, the big rock with its strange carvings. There you climbed up and rested and ate your lunch as you gazed in awe at the tall trees, the rushing water and the green, green woods. One could speak endlessly of the wonders of camp, but the greatest wonder of all was the peaceful hill across from the porch. It was always there, year after year, the sun shining on its head, the sun making a new picture for your eyes every hour of the day and evening, the kind of scenes you take with you wherever you go the rest of your life.

During the busy high school years, there seemed to be little time for Hiram House except to go once a week to the dramatic club. There in our awestruck adolescent way, we were coached in the play "Ingomar" by a young married woman who had been a real actress on a real stage. There we learned the poetic lines, and went eagerly each week to do our part until finally the play was drawn together into a whole to the climax, "Two souls with but a single thought, two hearts that beat as one!"

In the early college years, that was the time Hiram House became so dear and familiar. There you could go on hot summer evenings to play by the hour with the children, not to play just as a child, but to help the teacher who had so many to take care of. The children followed at your heels with the greatest enthusiasm to play all the old games you knew and the new ones you read about in books, and tried out with them. They were always ready for the stories you told them. Their hungry eyes drew them out of you. The young leader, the fledgling, was trying out her wings and growing stronger every day. In the winter you went to the gymnasium because you loved so to play games and to get others to play them too. You were happy to help the teacher with your spirited enthusiasm. Sometimes, when she could not come, you took the class yourself and made sure that every girl had a wonderful evening. One could always help in the busy camp fire cottage, that little dream house that belonged to the girls. You stayed to talk with the leaders after the children had gone home, and gradually you began to visit with the residents in their rooms, to have lunch with them in the dining room. You began to understand more of the grown up points of view about the varied work of Hiram House. You had known for quite a long time that this was the kind of work you wanted to do the rest of your life. Of course you then selected all the sociology and psychology courses you could take, and discarded the easy math and language courses which seemed to have no bearing on work with people.

One day Mr. Bellamy called in some of the older girls. He seemed worried about the coming fortnight of 55 adolescent girls at camp. He wanted them kept busy. Then and there we outlined a plan, and thru that vacation used every ounce of energy to help give them an active, varied program. To honor a request from Mr. Bellamy himself was a great privilege. Thru all the activity there was the keen desire to have the girls become articulate about all the wonderful experiences of camp, and so a newspaper was compiled. I sat alone editing it in the big dining room after everyone had gone to bed. They had been lulled to sleep by the beautiful singing voice of the camp leader, not the least of the spiritual experiences of the day. I thought of all the things Hiram House had meant to me. I wrote only a few of them that night. It was an unfinished story. For years I have been wanting to finish it. And so I have written more of the story thru the years, not on paper, but in my life. I knew always when I was a growing young person at Hiram House what I wanted to do. I knew I wanted to do what Hiram House did for people, to care for them, to help them care for each other, to bring to children all the happy, joyful experiences of play, and thru play to open their eyes to the wonders of books, music, poetry, to quicken their hearts with the sight of green fields, to taste the sweetness of kindly human relationships, and to contemplate in the end the goodness of the universe and the noble qualities with which man is fundamentally endowed to live in it.

BY LILLIAN J. STRAUSS
Social Worker—New York

"The Federation Idea: Cleveland Model"

Henry L. Zucker defined his career during his senior year at the Western Reserve University, when he served as an untrained caseworker at what is now the Cleveland Jewish Family Services Association. Understanding the importance of academic training, he earned a master's degree before joining the staff of the Cuyahoga County Relief Administration, where he later became assistant to the chief executive. He became associate director of the Jewish Community Federation of Cleveland in 1946, its chief professional in 1948, and its executive vice president in 1965.

After World War II, he traveled as a consultant to the American Jewish Joint Distribution Committee and helped to restore Jewish life in ten European countries. He remained active in Jewish communal affairs even after he retired as the Cleveland Jewish Community Federation's chief executive in 1975. His impact on the profession extended beyond Cleveland: at one point, professionals Zucker helped train in Cleveland headed eight of the ten largest federations in the United States.

At an event to honor him and Sidney Vincent on their retirements, Zucker delivered a speech summarizing his views, honed over a lifetime of service, on the ever-changing Jewish condition, the significance of federated giving, the spirit of the Jewish universalist tradition, and the responsibilities of leadership—all as seen against the broad canvas of world and national events. Though he applauded the uniqueness of Cleveland's Jewish community, he anguished over the city's fall from its former greatness. Cleveland's Jewish federated system accepted responsibility for the larger Cleveland community as well as the Jewish community because Jewish tradition requires engaging society to help improve it, a task facilitated through building consensus among community members, lay leaders, and professionals. (See also the chapter on The Jewish Community Federation in this volume.)

Source: Henry L. Zucker, "The Federation Idea: Cleveland Model," speech delivered at the community recognition dinner, Jewish Community Federation, June 29, 1975, Henry Zucker Papers, Western Reserve Historical Society.

THE FEDERATION IDEA: CLEVELAND MODEL
By Henry L. Zucker, Executive Vice President
Delivered at the community recognition dinner.
Jewish Community Federation
Sunday, June 29, 1975
Cleveland Sheraton Hotel

When Mort Mandel broached the idea of this Testimonial, Sid and I said "no" a thousand times. We had sat through too many such evenings on the other side of the proceedings, and when it came our turn, we thought, "not us." But Mort out-voted us both.

Then, when the invitation came, people kept asking whose pictures were on the front of it. Ruth and Harriet thought that Sid and I had a reprieve, the Testimonial was for two other guys. And then, the "Two in a Generation." Two of what? We offer a prize for the best answer to that one!

Anyhow, here we are, and we thank you for being here.

Tomorrow will be my last day as the chief executive of this wonderful Jewish Community Federation. I am not capable of conveying the depths of my feelings on this happening. My Pavlovian reaction is to express deep, deep appreciation for the opportunity to have had such a rich and happy experience with you over so long a period of time. I am not imaginative enough to have dreamt up a career more satisfying to my spiritual needs, nor better suited to my personality, temperament and training.

Mine has been a blessed opportunity to help in a modest, and to me a deeply meaningful way in the rescue, relief, rehabilitation and binding the wounds of 2,500,000 people; to assist in the restoration of total communities; to add a few bricks to the upbuilding of the house of Israel; to minister to the needs of the neediest people at home; to participate in the never-ending struggle to build a better America; and to work with thousands of the best motivated and ablest members of our imperfect society. What more could one hope for in his life's work?

For this great opportunity, I am truly in your debt.

I brooded over tonight's speech for some weeks, challenging myself to produce something that is worth the time of this knowledgeable audience, at the same time complementing the thrust of Sid Vincent's brilliantly philosophical presentation at our Annual Meeting in March. It's a tough assignment.

I came out this way: I owe you a report of my Federation stewardship of almost thirty years. That, and 14 prior years in general community social work, have offered me some insights into the practical operation of our community which are worth sharing with serious-minded community leaders. Perhaps, too, this sentimental occasion is the one time when it is permissible for me to be highly personal in public.

YOU SHOULD LIVE IN INTERESTING TIMES

The Chinese have a curse which says, "You should live in interesting times." The thirty years which have passed since World War II coincide with the years of my service at Federation—and, believe me, they have been interesting.

We are now at the end of the post World War II era.

Thirty years ago, a self-confident United States was the world's dominant military, economic, and political power. Today, after two more big wars, its confidence shaken, its people in a questioning mood, it remains the somewhat reluctant free world leader; and its dominant position is challenged by Russia, and pecked away at by friend and foe alike. The country's tremendous potentiality is seriously undermined by a lack of commitment and directed purpose, and by evidences of moral decay, self-seeking, and a substantial inroad of hedonistic and anarchistic thinking.

The Cleveland community is a reflection of the national condition. Indeed, it has lost position relative to the rest of the country. Its central city is almost ungovernable. Large numbers of its best young people choose to live elsewhere. There are signs of a renewal of leadership, true; but Cleveland has a long way to go to re-establish the position it held in my boyhood days as one of America's great urban centers.

THE JEWISH CONDITION

The Jews of the United States—and of Cleveland—have prospered in the hospitable atmosphere of this country and community. They are the freest, best educated, most affluent Jewish community in history, rooted in American tradition, committed to its history and fate. They make up a substantial part of its intellectual, professional and commercial leadership.

The perspective of the past thirty years requires also a recitation of tragic aspects of the Jewish condition.

World War II and the years leading to it were a low point in Jewish history. The genocide which Hitler and an indifferent world inflicted on the Jewish people left twelve million Jews in a world which had eighteen million; and of these, more than three million were locked behind the Iron Curtain.

In my early Jewish education, I was told that there were Jews in trouble at all times, that there was never a day when there weren't Jews running from some place where they could not live to a place of refuge. I regarded this as an exaggeration and as a figure of speech.

I came to the Federation in 1946, in the immediate post-war period when the destruction of European Jewry was exposed for all to view. Our preoccupation then was to save the pitiful remnant—and, thank God, that we did. But there has not been a single day since then when I did not know personally of Jews who were moving from the land of their birth to a new and strange home. I came to realize that the tragic Jewish wanderings were not exaggerated, and that it is literally true that for 2,000 years, not a single day has passed which has not witnessed Jews running.

Even today, peace has not come for three million Jews in Israel. After four wars, there is still the constant threat of more meaningless destruction and conflict. A generation after the end of World War II, and two generations after the Russian Revolution, millions of Jews remain locked behind the Iron Curtain, hostages to what Elie Wiesel has called "the most tenacious hatred in history."

Once again, after a generation of relative quiet, the strident voice of anti-Semitism is heard in many lands.

Finally, the malaise of our society—reflected so dismally in our statistics on violence, crime and juvenile delinquency, mental illness, and family breakdown is infecting Jewish life as well, threatening the very basis of our capacity to perform as a useful, purposeful and contented people.

These are the realities of 1975, and thoughtful leaders must be conscious of them.

THE MIRACLE OF FEDERATION

What of the Federation during these thirty years?

By 1946, the Federation had already been in operation for forty-three years and had established a fine record. The small group of philanthropists who founded the Federation in 1903 had the simple concept that it would be more effective and efficient to raise money for eight Jewish health and welfare agencies in one annual drive than in a variety of separate campaigns. Allocation of funds soon led to budgeting, and budgeting to planning. Emergencies affecting Jews—an earthquake and fire in San Francisco, a flood in Dayton, pogroms in Russia, the wanderings of the homeless of World War I—greatly expanded the tasks of this fledgling organization. The continuing demands at home of the new immigrants from Eastern Europe, the adaptation of the federation idea to the general community, the overwhelming social needs created by the depression, the virulent anti-Semitism of the 30's, and the special responsibilities that grew out of the Second World War—all of these things and more matured the Federation to the point where it was well prepared to face the greatly expanded demands of the post-war period.

Federation was challenged in 1946 to raise its share of a national United Jewish Appeal goal of $100,000,000—almost three times the amount raised the previous year—an imaginative and magnificent response to the needs created by the newest crisis in Jewish history. Cleveland—the two percent city—sent more than $2,000,000 to the U.J.A.

Every year since 1946, Cleveland has played a leadership role in this life-saving enterprise. Our Jewish Welfare Fund, which raised $1,000,000 for the first time in 1943, has raised more than $220,000,000 in the thirty post–World War II campaigns, almost $40,000,000 of this in the last two campaigns.

After 1946, Federation greatly intensified its traditional budgeting and planning functions; it moved into the community relations and internal relations fields, and created a community forum through merger with the Jewish Community Council; it expanded its special women's activities through merger with the Federation of Jewish Women's Organizations; it enlarged its commitment to Jewish education and Jewish cultural activities, and its work with college youth; it intensified its relationships with the United Torch Services, the Federation for Community Planning, and the Cleveland Foundation, and its activities in the inner city, in inter-faith work, and on behalf of public welfare and community development programs; it embarked on a new endowment program to protect it against emergencies and to add a new quality dimension to its work; it developed a variety of central and joint services to improve the management of its agencies; it helped its agencies to expand and improve their services and to raise unprecedented sums for capital programs; and it provided leadership to many of our most important national agencies.

These and other positive developments were made possible by the voluntary involvement and commitment of a large number of motivated citizens. Today, almost 1,000 different persons are engaged in the governance of Federation through the Board of Trustees and more than fifty committees—a seven-fold increase since 1946. There are 28,000 contributors to the Jewish Welfare Fund, averaging more than one for every Jewish family; and something on the order of 3,000 campaign workers.

The miracle of Federation is that this is a completely volunteer enterprise—a citizens' movement. Federation's authority derives entirely from its acceptance by individuals and groups, and the moral authority it acquires through satisfactory performance. It has no power to legislate, tax, or coerce.

Federation is the American Jewish community's answer to the age-old Jewish search for the right organization form to meet the problems of its economic and socially needy, and promote and enhance Jewish group values. The Jewish component in the Federation idea is the ethical concept of help to the needy, the recognition of the need for each Jew to help every other Jew, and the stubborn insistence on transmitting a distinctive way of life and a value system to future generations. The American contribution is a genius for organization and the emphasis on voluntary participation. The combination creates an indigenous instrument, capable of harmonizing and utilizing the energies and good will of even so sensitive, stubborn, individualistic and intelligent a group as we American Jews are.

Are there limitations on what the Federation should do or can do successfully? Decidedly, yes!

One of its limitations derives from its voluntary character. This requires that Federation be a consensus agency, not a cause agency. It gains its authority from performance in areas where the vast majority want Federation to act. It proceeds with peril in trying to impose its will on a large minority or on autonomous agencies and organizations. It moves cautiously and deliberately, even in the face of criticism by passionate and impatient advocates. It eschews most activity in political and religious areas, where Jews—as others—find it difficult to submerge their differences and control their emotions. Indeed, even with assistance to Israel—where there is consensus that Federation should help in every possible way—the limitation on political activity holds: Federation's help is to people and their needs, not to government.

There are other cautions. The very quality of our leadership and its enthusiastic support of Federation derives in part from personality traits which are not always easy to handle. As a result, a lot of staff and lay leadership time is necessarily devoted to reconciling individual differences, soothing ruffled feathers, greasing the wheels to make the Federation machinery work smoothly. No description of a Federation executive's job mentions this, but believe me, it could be fatal not to take into account this tremendously important function.

There is also the practical limitation which Federation shares with all similar enterprises, namely, that "in philanthropy, demand will always exceed supply" (Ford Foundation). Constructive compromise is the only viable answer to the inevitable disappointments which this fact of life invites.

The budget process requires that a great deal of objective information be assembled so that rational judgments can be made. But one must admit that value judgments and emotional factors also count for a great deal in ultimate decisions. Policy decisions, in the end, remain largely intuitive. This limitation will disappoint the purist who believes that the only way to bring about change is through a rational social planning process, ignoring the fact that wise decisions require the input of real, live, involved, and committed people.

Federation is a sophisticated idea, learned most effectively through participation, by doing rather than from lectures. The community leader who works in Federation gets to understand the give and take which is necessary for a total community system to work effectively.

THE JOY OF GIVING

What is the place of fund raising in our Federation, and what should it be?

Many people look on Federation as simply a fund raising organization. Some are satisfied that this should be the beginning and the end of its activity. Others deplore the fact that Federation puts so much emphasis on fund raising and wish it could go away. What are the facts?

The historic responsibility which faced our generation required a voluntary fund raising apparatus of huge proportions, one with staying power. To the credit of the American Jewish community, it rose to the occasion.

The $220,000,000 which our Federation has raised since World War II was part of a multi-billion dollar effort by the American Jewish community, and Cleveland has played a leadership role in the total enterprise.

It is true that for several years fund raising dominated Federation's work; indeed, [it] squeezed out some other activities which should have been undertaken. But it was never true that Federation was only a fund raising organization. It was regularly and heavily committed to careful planning and budgeting, and to working cooperatively with the total community in the health, education, welfare and community relations fields. Progressively, since 1948, it has devoted its energies proportionately more and more to these activities, at the same time that it has continued to apply itself intensively to the very necessary fund raising activities.

Those concerns which lie at the heart of the Federation could not possibly prosper without the huge and unprecedented fund raising efforts. Yet, we know that fund raising is only the beginning of our program. It is the means to an end, which is service to the community. We have always tried to keep this in mind.

We hear the criticism that people cannot be Federation leaders if they are not big givers and campaign workers. There are also complaints about solicitation techniques and about the so-called ulterior motives of generous givers. Many of these criticisms are helpful. But sometimes they come from people who do not understand the Federation's responsibilities or who do not catch the spirit of giving.

The fact is that Federation has many leaders who are not big givers. I believe, moreover, that the chief reason why people give generously to the Jewish Welfare Fund—large and modest gifts—is because they believe in the cause.

When friends ask me to what I attribute the tremendous response to the Jewish Welfare Fund, I reply that we have the greatest cause, and that intuitively most Jews understand this. Beyond the philanthropic response, most Jews know in their hearts that Jews should "never again" expose themselves to being the unwanted guests of unfriendly nations. This insight was the catalytic agent that brought to reality in our time the 2,000-year-old Jewish dream of a return to a spiritual anchor in Jerusalem—the only people in history to have returned "home" after so long an absence. And this understanding is the reason why millions of American Jews who are completely committed to America will continue to lend moral, spiritual and material support to Israel.

Most Jews know that this is a Jewish obligation, or, to put it constructively, a Jewish opportunity.

The fund raising effort of the Jewish Welfare Fund requires no apology.

It does not aspire to perfection. It is, after all, a human and a volunteer enterprise. If we continue to try to improve it, I think that we shall continue to receive the generous support of the vast majority of the community.

There is one aspect of fund raising that has impressed itself on me more than any other, which William Rosenwald has called "the great joy of giving." In a tribute to his late father, Julius Rosenwald, he said that "in Dad's mind, the most important motivation for giving was his belief that giving does at least as much for the giver as it does for the recipient." He then goes on to say that "these (fund raising) activities have enriched my life in many ways: They have developed abilities which I never knew I possessed; they have immeasurably broadened my horizons and have resulted in wonderful friendships with some of the finest people I know."

He quotes this from one of his father's speeches: "Shall we devote the few precious days of our existence only to buying and selling . . . only to shuffling our feet in the dance . . . only to matching little picture cards so as to group together three jacks, or aces or kings . . . and, when the end comes, to leave an estate that is as little taxable as possible as the final triumph and achievement of our lives? Surely there is something finer and better in life, something that dignifies it and stamps it with a touch of the divine.

"My friends, it is unselfish efforts, helpfulness to others that ennobles life, not because of what it does for others, but more because of what it does for ourselves. In this spirit, we should give . . . **gladly, generously, eagerly, lovingly, joyfully, indeed, with the most supreme pleasure that life can furnish.**"*

OUR UNIVERSALIST TRADITION

If my community experience has given me a deeper insight to the Jewish commitment to the Jewish people, it has also taught me that this is thoroughly compatible with the universalist spirit in Judaism. Leviticus says to us, "Thou shalt love thy neighbor as thyself." The Jew is expected to love all of his neighbors, not just Jews.

How does this apply to the Federation?

*"The Great Joy of Giving"—Jewish Federation of Metropolitan Chicago—October 14, 1962.

For years, Federation has committed itself to helping the public to understand the needs of all the socially disadvantaged in our community. Federation is related in this work to a myriad of local, state, regional and national organizations. What is new is the degree of involvement.

No one can examine Federation's calendar without being aware of the large amount of our time which is spent on the problems of the total community. We work extensively with the Federation for Community Planning and the United Torch Services, with a variety of church groups, associations of churches and inter-faith organizations, a large number of local, state and federal public officials, schools of social work, colleges and universities, boards of education, and a great many national organizations.

Federation engages in this type of activity as the most representative of Jewish community organizations. It is unthinkable that in our complicated and inter-dependent society, a progressive federation would not be heavily involved in the broad problems of the Cleveland community and in national health and welfare concerns.

I wish we had the time tonight to discuss this aspect of Federation's work in detail. That isn't feasible. But, on this occasion, I do want to take a few minutes to comment on our relationship with the United Torch Services.

The predecessor agency of the UTS was organized something [sic] on the model of our Federation, and in 1919 our Federation helped to organize it. Ever since then, we have had a close and harmonious working relationship.

We consider the UTS to be *our* United Way. Our total and enthusiastic commitment to it is based on the fact that it is a practical means of mobilizing support for Jewish and other voluntary agencies, and also—and this is even more important—it remains the best example of an organization through which the positive forces of the total community work together for the community's good. Nothing is more desperately needed in our society than those things which bring us together.

Our Federation is very heavily involved in the annual United Torch Drive and in the year-round governance of the UTS. Are there problems? Yes. Are they capable of being resolved? Of course.

At the present time, the UTS is engaged in a thorough analysis of its planning and allocations process. There are a number of ideas afloat which could bring about major changes in relations with member agencies, and these will require careful auditing by our Federation and other UTS agencies. If the process of the study is deliberate—and up to now it has been—it should result in a stronger United Torch Services and a renewal of excellent relationships between the UTS and our Federation and other partners in the UTS enterprise.

This is certainly high on the priority list of matters which require our careful attention, because we believe deeply in this great community asset which we call the United Torch Services, and because we want to continue to be an enthusiastic partner in it.

ON PERSONNEL AND LAY LEADERSHIP

One of the special satisfactions of a veteran Federation executive is to witness the development of executive staff and to graduate this staff to even more important responsibilities.

Nothing in my Federation experience has made me feel better than to have played a small part in helping to develop a cadre of professional leaders in community service. We have graduated about thirty persons from our staff to positions of greater opportunity. Today, the Cleveland alumni are leaders in many of the country's largest Jewish federations, and in a number of important national and international organizations. In this way, our Federation has had a national impact far beyond its size.

I have been asked on many occasions why so many Jewish professional leaders were born and/or trained in Cleveland.

The main reason, I believe, is that no city has had better lay leadership. Think of the magnificent presidents with whom I have worked: Henry Rocker and Max Simon, the peace-makers and unifiers of our community; and Max Freedman, the powerhouse fund raiser and practical doer—all three, unfortunately, no longer with us. And the presidents who are here tonight, each one still a dedicated leader in current Federation affairs, Mike Glass, Dave Myers, Lee Neumark, Maurie Saltzman, Lloyd Schwenger, and, of course, Mort Mandel. Add to this distinguished group the perennial unofficial presidents of the Federation: Bill Treuhaft and our dear departed Leonard Ratner—and at least another dozen outstanding leaders who have attained prominence in national as well as in local leadership—and you get some idea of the quality of citizen leadership in this Federation.

I hesitate to name others for fear of leaving out too many—but through these examples I want to bring to your mind the image which comes to my own: of the devoted, generous, thoughtful, kind, tremendously capable leaders who make this such a great Federation. I doubt that there is any enterprise in this country—commercial or philanthropic—whose Board of Directors surpasses ours in quality and commitment.

The staff, expectedly, has responded to the warm and wholehearted support of this outstanding lay leadership. The exemplary partnership which exists between our volunteer and professional leaders creates a work climate in which professionals flourish and grow. Staff realizes that nothing at Federation work beats professional harmony and lay-professional understanding and compatibility.

Sid Vincent and I have tried to make the most of the opportunity which this spirit creates. We have tried to keep in mind that the Federation is a citizens' enterprise, and that while the professional has the obligation to contribute his knowledge and insights into all areas of Federation program and policy, the determination of policy remains always the laymen's province. Or, to put it negatively, we have tried to disprove George Bernard Shaw's clever dictum that "every profession is a conspiracy against the laity."

We have also developed a philosophy of staff operation which I hope will become common practice in large federations. Every member of our executive staff considers himself generally responsible for the total Federation, as well as specifically responsible for his special assignment. Thus, you will frequently find members of the staff operating in areas which don't show up at all in their slot on our organization chart. Every Federation executive "worries" about the whole Federation.

Federation has good personnel standards and tries to maintain a climate in which a professional can work effectively. The officers and board have established excellent salary standards and other benefits, as well as good working conditions.

Finally, we try to make it possible for our executive staff to have a range of experience and to give full expression to their talents. They and we recognize that this enables them to grow on the job, and this adds materially to our total production.

Ned Lynde, my mentor for ten years at the Welfare Federation, taught me this by example: You help young staff members to grow by loading them down with meaningful work, giving them maximum autonomy, supporting them as they need and ask for help, being willing for them to make an occasional mistake, and never letting them down in public. He knew that responsibility is the way to development. He also showed me that, as another wise man once said, "There is no limit to what you can do if you don't care who gets the credit," and that the boss can afford to be generous toward the fellows who make him look good. I can say of Ned what Henry Adams wrote of Thomas Jefferson, that "the leadership he sought was one of sympathy and love, not of command."

If I want to claim a small part in the development of Federation staff—and, immodestly, I do—I want at the same time to share it with Sid Vincent, my good friend from boyhood days, my colleague in Federation since 1951, and my partner in Federation's management for I don't know how many years.

Incidentally, Sid and I once tried to set down our division of responsibilities, and we gave it up as a lost cause. I can just say of it that it is a partnership of love, mutual respect and loyalty; an intuitive sharing of responsibility, and a darned good deal for both of us—and I hope for the Federation as well. I'd say of Sid something I heard said about someone else a long time ago—I don't remember where—that when God created Sid, he was so pleased with himself that he didn't do another thing the rest of that day.

I am tempted to talk about each member of our tremendously loyal staff, but I don't dare name names—even starting with Angela Galione, my long-suffering secretary, who sweated through this speech with me—because that would take far more time than we have tonight. I want only to add that I think of many members of the staff almost as members of my own family, and I am eternally grateful to them for making my work days one great thirty-year celebration.

ON RETIREMENT

Since this is a retirement party, it is fitting to conclude by sharing with you Sid's and my views on "retirement." I put "retirement" in quotes because our interpretation of the word leaves no room for putting ourselves on the shelf.

We do both sincerely believe that at age 65—or some other predetermined arbitrary cutoff point—the chief executives of large federations should retire from these positions. Every forward-looking large enterprise needs new blood, new ideas, energy renewal, and opportunities to promote younger executives.

We have seen cases in the Jewish communal and religious enterprises where the failure to recognize this has caused deterioration in the quality of the institutions involved.

On the other hand, we do not advocate "retirement" from the work world for those executives who like to work, and who have the appetite to continue to live in the real world. Many people at 65 have some of their best work years ahead of them. I feel confident, for example, that Sid will continue to offer this community and the national community outstanding leadership in the fields of education, community relations, program analysis, leadership development, and in writing and talking about these things, which he does so magnificently.

Specifically, both Sid and I are committed to make our headquarters at and to spend not less than half of our time with the Federation. We shall both assume specific responsibilities, and will be available to Stan Horowitz and his staff in any way which Stan believes we can be helpful. I expect to specialize in the endowment-foundation field to help Howard Berger develop what he and I hope will be the outstanding program of this type in the country; and to do a limited amount of consultation work in this area. I also expect to enlarge my volunteer activities, especially in the field of higher education. Additionally, I shall be available for special studies in fields where my experience qualifies me, and I am currently involved in one such study.

In short, Sid and I look on this coming Tuesday as the first day of a new career, during which we shall trade a title and the constraints and pressures of administrative responsibility for the opportunity to work at those things which most appeal to us at this point in our careers.

This arrangement, so thoughtfully worked out during the past two years by Presidents Saltzman and Mandel and the Federation Officers, is just the latest of the many considerate actions which have marked the partnership of this Federation's lay and professional leadership.

In closing, and for Sid and me both, I want to thank every one of our friends in this magnificent audience for sharing this lovely evening with us, and especially for being so kind to us over the years.

Documents from the Montefiore Archives

Cleveland's Jews established a network of religious, cultural, educational, and social service organizations in keeping with the mandate *kol Yisrael arevim zeh bazeh*—all Jews are responsible for one another.

Montefiore was established in 1881 as the Kesher Shel Barzel Home for Aged and Infirm Israelites. It was located on East 55th Street and Euclid Avenue. At first, it served male residents sixty-five and older who were in good physical condition but impoverished. In 1884, the name of the home was changed to the Sir Moses Montefiore Kesher Home for Aged and Infirm Israelites. By November 1916, the home was sold for $155,000, and the next year, the Dean Dairy property on Mayfield Road in Cleveland Heights was purchased to construct a new facility. In 1923, the home was renamed the Montefiore Home. Montefiore prospered and expanded, and the need for a new home once again became apparent. Montefiore moved to its present location, 1 David N. Myers Parkway in Beachwood, in 1991.

These letters from the Montefiore archives present a glimpse of the manner in which new admissions to the home were overseen in the 1910s. At the time, Montefiore, like many other social service agencies, was using increasingly formalized procedures; these were some of the hallmarks of the professionalization of social work in the Progressive Era in the United States.

Source: Various documents that appeared in the "Minutes of the Proceedings of the Meeting of the Board," Montefiore Home Records, Western Reserve Historical Society. n.d.

Sir Moses Montefiore Kesher Home for Aged and Infirm Israelites
Corner Wilson and Woodland Avenues
I. Simon, Secretary,
Cleveland, O.

August 3, 1917

Mr. A. C. Wurmser:
Kansas City, Mo.

Dear Sir:

On May 29th last Mr. Mandelbaum wrote you in reference to the application of Meyer Kayser, your city which application yourself and Mr. Nathan Schloss signed as recommenders.

In this letter you were advised that the application had been accepted subject however to a proper and complete application being made on our new Application Blank one of which was enclosed for that purpose.

Up to the recent writing we have not been favored with a reply and we are therefore unable to act intelligently in the matter.

Will you kindly give this your immediate attention and return the application properly made out or else advise disposition of same.

Yours very truly
I. Simon,
Sec'y.

May 29-1917.

Mr. A.C. Wurmser,
Kansas City, Mo.

Dear Sir:

The application of Meyer Kayser, which application was signed by yourself and Mr. Nathan Schloss as recommenders, has been accepted subject to a proper and complete application being made on our new Application Blank, one of which I enclose herewith for that purpose.

The Board has recently adopted a ruling that no applicant will be admitted unless all questions on this new form of Application are answered. The last question on the third page will be answered by the Local Committee who have been investigating this matter.

If you will give this matter your prompt attention, or see that it is properly taken care of, Mr. Kayser's acceptance into the Institution will be advanced to that extent.

Truly yours,
Treasurer.
MJM:F
Encl.

Jewish Educational Institute
Admiral Blvd. and Harrison Street
Jacob Billikopf, Supt.

Officers:
Alfred Benjamin, Pres.
Al Rothenberg, 1st Vice-Pres.
Julius Davidson, 2nd Vice-Pres.
Mrs. H. H. Mayer, 3rd Vice-Pres.
M. Oppenstein, Treas.
Mrs. E. D. Dreyfus, Sec'y.
3437 The Paseo

Home Phone. MAIN 7274
Bell Phone. MAIN 2513
Kansas City, Mo.

May 22nd, 1917.

Mr. Fred Seligsohn
23 E. 24th Str
City.

My dear Mr. Seligsohn:

The case of Mr. Meyer Kaiser, 3411 Central which you called to our attention, we are in a measure, familiar with. Mrs. Hebbel, formerly of Chicago is a niece of Mr. Kaiser, and asked my advice about placing him permanently in some home and I advised her to communicate with the Montefiore Kesher Home in Cleveland, Ohio.

Mr. Kaiser is 84 years old, bordering on childishness. He has no other relatives than a sister in Chicago, Mrs. Simon, who through her children have been paying his expenses here which is about $40 a month. He has been living with one family 8 years. He is too much of a care now for them to look after. Mrs. Hebbel, his niece has a sister living near Cleveland and she has influence at the Home to have him entered and taken care of and I personally would recommend his admission to the Home. If there is anything more I can do in the case, please let me know.

Very truly yours,
Rudy J. Cohen
Sup't.
(Mrs. Henry Cohen)

Menorah Park, "Rules for Synagogue," ca. 1920

Menorah Park Center for Senior Living, founded as the Jewish Orthodox Old Age Home, opened its doors in 1906 with five residents in a house on Orange Avenue near East 40th Street, the second facility to serve the Jewish elderly in Cleveland. A forty-six-bed facility was built at 59th Street and Scovill Avenue in 1911 to serve the facility's growing population; the home moved again, in 1921, to Lakeview Avenue in Glenville. Continued growth required an additional wing in 1929 and another in 1948. The facility was renamed the Jewish Orthodox Home for the Aged in 1950.

The increasing number of Jewish elderly coupled with Jewish movement to the eastern suburbs prompted the home to move to a newly constructed facility in Beachwood in 1968; it changed its name to Menorah Park that same year. Now known as Menorah Park Center for the Jewish Elderly, it provides a variety of services, from nursing home care, assisted living, and independent living to day care, home care, and more on a daily basis to more than one thousand seniors and their families.

The following document, although brief, gives some insight into the nature of the institutional care provided to the elderly in the early twentieth century.

Source: "Rules for Synagogue, Jewish Orthodox Old Age Home," ca. 1920, Menorah Park Records, Western Reserve Historical Society.

RULES FOR SYNAGOGUE

רולס פאר דיא שוהל

1. Under no circumstances is it allowed to Speak or Whisper during Services
2. None of the Inmates are allowed to reprimand each other.
No mather [sic] what rules or
regulations one may violate the
Superintendent is the only one
authorized to act in such cases!
3. Knocking on the prayer books is
positively prohibited
4. A Yom Tehilim after each service
should be recited to which every
one exept [sic] the sick or diss-
abled [sic] ones must be present.
5. Work or Learn, is one of the
strictest rules of our Institution.

[signed] M. A. Haas, Sup't.
By Order of the President and
   Board of Directors

1) עס ווערט שטרענג פערבאטען
ציא רעדען אין דיא צייט פין
דאוונען אפילו ציא ריידען שטילל

2) קיין אלטער טאר ניט מוסרן
דעם צווייטען אויב ער זעהט וואס
אומרעכט זאלל ער זאגען דעם
סופעראינטענטעענד וועגען דעם

3) מען טאר ניט מאכען קיין
טומעל אין שוהל עס מוז זיין
זעהר שטילל אונד רוהיג

4) יעדע אלטער מוז זיין אין
שוהל ביא יעדעס דאוונען ער
טאר ניט אויספעהלען אויסער דיא
וועלכע זיינען קראנק אין בעט

5) ארבייטען אדער לערנען איז
די הויפט רולע אין אונזער
אינסטיטוטיציאן   Time for Services

מ. א. האאז סופר'ט

By Order of the President and
Board of Directors

Chronology of the Beginnings of the Mt. Sinai Hospital, 1915

The efforts of young Jewish women to aid the needy sick in the 1890s resulted in the establishment of Mt. Sinai Hospital in a remodeled home on East 37th Street in 1903. The need of the community for a larger institution soon became apparent, and after other locations also proved unsuitable, Mt. Sinai Hospital built a large modern facility on East 105th Street, which opened in 1916. The hospital served both Jews and non-Jews and soon became a leader in outpatient care, research, and the training of nurses. The hospital became notable for its service to the residents of Cleveland's east side, but financial difficulties in the 1990s eventually led to the hospital's closure in 2000. During the demolition of the building, workers uncovered a time capsule placed in the cornerstone at the site in 1915. This selection was found in the time capsule.

Source: Chronology of the Beginnings of the Mt. Sinai Hospital, 1915, Mt. Sinai Hospital Records (time capsule contents), Western Reserve Historical Society.

On December 2nd, 1912 was held the first meeting to consider the Hospital problem and the same time a temporary organization was formed.

The regular meetings were held on Monday evening at 7:30 P.M. at the Wise Building on Euclid Ave.

A Committee on permanent organization was appointed.

On December 23 a list of names was compiled from which the personel [sic] of the Finance Committee was to be selected.

The committee on permanent organization reported through Mr. Lewenthal who presented a tentative "Code of Regulations" for the Hospital and after discussion the same was referred back for correction. Application for articles of Incorporation was made and the name of the organization to be "The Cleveland Jewish Hospital."

After incorporation the Board immediately set about to further the project and as its first consideration, cast about for a suitable site for the future hospital.

The Committee on Permanent Organization having had their report, submitted the same to the incorporators at the meeting on June 20th, 1913 and at that meeting the first trustees of The Cleveland Jewish Hospital were elected and consisted of the following men:—

A. Lewenthal, Paul L. Feiss, John Anisfield, J. K. Arnold, Hascall C. Lang, Sam D. Wise, Salmon P. Halle, Louis Black, N. L. Dauby, Louis H. Hays and Max Myers.

The trustees met and elected their officers who were: Paul L. Feiss, President; Salmon P. Halle, Vice President; John Anisfield, second Vice President; N. L. Dauby, Treasurer; Max Myers, Secretary. At this meeting $75,000.00 was subscribed without solicitation.

Throughout the entire period, the foremost thought in the minds of the incorporators and the trustees was a campaign for the funds, and at the same time the determining of a definite property for the Hospital. To that end option was taken on various pieces of property and investigations were conducted continually.

About this time an organization was formed among the Orthodox Jews of the city, the purpose of which was to build a Kosher Hospital of Orthodox tendencies and which was beginning to solicit the community for funds.

On September 18th, 1913 the Federation of Jewish Charities authorized the Hospital Board to solicit from the Jewish Community of Cleveland, a sum up to $400,000.00 to be used for the purposes of the Hospital and it was decided to begin active work at once.

Simultaneously with this the Board entered into negotiations with the representatives of the Jewish Orthodox Hospital, with the end in view that the latter projects should be dropped and support given the wider campaign. Meetings were held and progress was made.

On June 26th, 1913 the Finance Committee was appointed and was headed by Mr. Barney Mahler.

As the climax to the work of the Board in the selection of a site, on November 5th, 1913, the Board empowered the site committee which consisted of Messrs. Halle, and Myers to arrange for the purchase of the property upon which the Hospital is now being erected.

About this time active work on the project was started. Temporary quarters were rented with an assistant secretary in charge. Stationary [sic] printed and the active work of a far reaching campaign for funds was put in motion.

Meetings of the Finance Committee were held and representatives of all congregations and societies took active part.

By November 26th, 1913, about five weeks after the start to raise funds, the total of $202,000.00 had been subscribed and the work continually progressed.

At the meeting held early in December, it became apparent that funds would have to be collected in order to pay for the land and current expenses and with that in view, the larger subscribers were asked to make payment on their subscriptions. It was also provided that the first call for payment be issued and the same prepared.

The Hospital offices were moved to larger quarters to meet the demand of more space.

It was decided at this time to call a meeting to change the name of the corporation to the Cleveland Jewish Hospital Association.

The Kosher Hospital organization offered to give the Hospital whatever money was left from their campaign and the action taken was that we would accept an unconditional gift of the money.

At the next meeting held on December 28th, 1913, the question of engaging an architect was taken up and thoroughly discussed, and also the question of starting the active work of the Building. With this end in view the Building Committee was appointed, consisting of Messrs. S. P. Halle, Chairman, Max Myers, Louis H. Hays and N. L. Dauby, in whose hands was placed the actual building of the Hospital.

On December 15th, a meeting was held of the corporation and at which time the corporate name of the institution was changed to The Cleveland Jewish Hospital Association.

On the 7th day of January, the second meeting of the Corporation was held at which time the officers in office were re-elected and reports given which showed the rapid growth of the institution.

The Committee appointed to investigate architects and experts made reports from time to time and on January 26th, the Board selected Dr. S. S. Goldwater of New York, as hospital expert.

Because of the absence from the city of Mr. Mahler, Mr. Lewenthal was elected Vice Chairman of the Finance Committee.

On February 26th a vacancy in the Board was filled by the election of Mr. Max Rosenblum, and at this meeting it was decided to request of the Federation of Jewish Charities permission to collect over $500,000.00.

During all this time the Building Committee was actively engaged in the investigation of plans, etc., submitted by Geo. B. Post & Sons, New York, which firm had been retained as architects.

From time to time various men efficient in hospital construction appeared before the Board and set forth their views which assisted the Board in the determination of what was wanted for this Hospital.

On May 20th the first tentative plans for the Hospital were presented and discussed and after modifications, etc., had been made were accepted by the Board. At that time the total cost was estimated to be $450,000.00.

On June 3rd, the Federation approved the expenditure of $500,000.00 or over and the Board proceeded to work on a flexible type of Hospital which would involve a little greater cost.

In order to further the work of collection of funds a bureau for subscriptions was established at the Hebrew Institute and subscriptions there received.

On June 1st the second call for funds was issued and the problem became apparent as to how the delinquencies were to be handled and the same problem has extended up to the present time.

About this time a committee consisting of Mr. Feiss and Mr. Myers was appointed to investigate persons eligible for the superintendency of the Hospital and with this end in view the committee began to look around and make inquiries. In carrying out the desires of the Board, the medical profession was invited to inspect the plans for the Hospital.

On August 23rd, 1914 a number of the Jewish doctors of this city met with Dr. Goldwater and went over the plans for the hospital.

On September 2nd the Building Committee presented a set of preliminary plans to the Board and asked for ratification of the same. At this meeting the Board approved of the plans and authorized the Building Committee to proceed with the plans as set forth. A publicity committee was appointed in order that the project may more forcibly be brought to the attention of the general public.

The first payment to the architects was authorized at this meeting.

On September 8th the Board met with the executive committee of the Federation and outlined the general policy of the Hospital proposition which met with the approval of the Federation.

At the meeting of October 21st, it was decided that the third call for funds should be issued on the first of November in accordance with the contracts entered into with the subscribers.

On November 4th the Building Committee reported that the final plans for the Hospital have been received and that the same will be presented for approval as soon as the Committee has passed on them.

The third call was issued and again the question of delinquent subscribers presented itself.

About this time the question which had been considerably discussed, namely the name of the Hospital was discussed and a committee was appointed to investigate appropriate names.

Preparations were made for the annual meeting. On January 6th was held the second meeting of the Corporation and the trustees whose terms expired were again re-elected. The Board then proceeded to re-elect the officers in office. Mr. Mahler submitted the final report of the Finance Committee and the same was met with unbounded praise for the work of Mr. Mahler in this connection. A total of $522,266.00 had been subscribed from 3197 subscribers. The said report was accepted and a vote of thanks extended to Mr. Mahler.

Mr. Halle for the Building Committee reported progress on the work.

On January 14th the Federation of Jewish Charities authorized an expenditure up to $600,000.00 for the Hospital.

At the meeting of January 19th, the Board authorized the Chairman of the Building Committee and the Secretary of the Hospital to sign all contracts on behalf of the Association.

After having received bids on the plans and specifications from various contractors and builders and after having opened same and thoroughly investigated all conditions surrounding the estimates, etc. the Building Committee awarded the general contract for the construction of the Hospital to The Reaugh Construction Co. of Cleveland, and on January 27th, a contract with the said company was entered into.

On the second of February 1915 the Reaugh Construction Co. started actual work on the Building and on February 7th at 12 o'clock noon the Board of Trustees dug the first earth on the site. The Property being situated at East 105th St., Ansel Rd. and Hough Avenue.

From that time to the present continued progress has been made and the Building advanced to this stage.

Sub contracts were let as rapidly as possible and work continued by the Building Committee.

At the meeting on March 17th, 1915 it became necessary that the name of the Hospital be definitely decided upon, and after considerable discussion the new Hospital was named Mt. Sinai.

The laying of the Corner Stone was decided to be held on June 6th, 1915 and Mr. Lewenthal placed in charge of a committee on arrangements.

Appendix

Chronological List of Documents

DATE	AUTHOR/DOCUMENT
1839	Lazarus Kohn (?–ca. 1846), Alsbacher Document: Ethical Testament
1910	Kaufman Hays (1835–1916), Excerpt from "Autobiography of Kaufman Hays"
December 18, 1913	A. R. Warner, Jas. F. Jackson, and Martin Marks, Petition to the Trustees, Western Reserve University
1915	Mt. Sinai Hospital, Chronology of the Beginnings of the Mt. Sinai Hospital (time capsule contents)
August 3, 1917	Montefiore Home, Documents from the Montefiore Archives
1917 (published)	Joseph Hays (1838–1916), Excerpt from Oral "Autobiography of Mr. Joseph Hays"
1920s and 1930s	Leon Wiesenfeld (1885–1971), Excerpt from *Jewish Life in Cleveland in the 1920s and 1930s*
ca. 1920	Menorah Park, "Rules for Synagogue"
1933 (unfinished autobiography)	Rose Pastor Stokes (1879–1933), Excerpt from *"I Belong to the Working Class"*
May 2, 1937	Abba Hillel Silver (1893–1963), "What I Would Say . . . "
July 23, 1953	The Jewish Community Federation of Cleveland, "Memorandum on Housing Situation, Lee-Harvard Area"
1954 (published)	Clara Lederer (1907–1987), Excerpt from *Their Paths Are Peace*

1957 (published)	Julius C. Newman (ca. 1876–1958), Excerpt from *Smoke Dreams*
1959 (published)	Michael Sharlitt (1884–1966), Excerpt from *As I Remember*
1959 (published)	Samuel M. Silver (1912–2008), Excerpt from *Portrait of a Rabbi*
1960	Lillian Strauss (?–1959), "I Remember Hiram House"
1962 (published)	Sidney Z. Vincent (1912–1982), Excerpt from *A Tale of Ten Cities*
1967 (published)	William Zorach (1887–1966), Excerpt from *Art Is My Life*
January 14, 1972	Alfred A. Benesch (1879–1973), "Oral History Interview"
May 2, 1975	Laura Porath (1958–), Handwritten Account
June 29, 1975	Henry L. Zucker (1910–1998), "The Federation Idea: Cleveland Model"
1986 (published)	Libbie L. Braverman (1900–1999), Excerpt from *Libbie*
1990 (published)	Howard W. Brody (1916–), "The Life and Times of a Jewish Farm Boy"
1993 (published)	Jo Sinclair (1913–1995), Excerpt from *The Seasons: Death and Transfiguration*
January 10, 1993	David Guralnik (1920–2000), "The Yiddish Theater"
2003 (unpublished)	Judah Rubinstein (1921–2003), "The Jewish Press in Cleveland"
Original for this volume, ca. 2007	Louis Rosenblum (1923–), Excerpt from *Involvement in the Soviet Jewry Movement*

Index

Academy of Music, 152

Activities in the Religious School, 257, 262

Adler, Aberle, 197

Adler, Alfred, 212

Adler, Besle, 197

Adler, Deile, 197

Adler, Hinle, 197

Adler, Rabbi Hirsch, 197

Adler, Lazarus, 197

Adler, Moses, 197

Adler, Weirle, 197

Advertising Club of Cleveland, 218, 219

Agudas Israel, 267

Alcott, Horton & Co., 152

Aleichem, Sholem, 56, 57

"Alfred A. Benesch: Oral History Interview," 112–23

Alfred A. Benesch School, 112

Alsbacher, Assar Loeb, 199

Alsbacher, Babet, 199

Alsbacher, David, 199

Alsbacher document, 2, 6, 195–201

Alsbacher, Hanna, 99

Alsbacher, Isaak, 199, 200

Alsbacher, Jachet, 200

Alsbacher, Jetta, 196, 199, 201

Alsbacher, Jittel, 200, 201

Alsbacher, Madel, 200

Alsbacher, Moses, 5, 195, 196, 201

Alsbacher party, 5

Alsbacher, Sara, 199

Alsbacher, Yetta, 5

Alta House, 294

Althof, Bergman & Co., 150

American Greeting Card Company, 275, 276

American Israelite, 61

Americanization of immigrants, 296

American Jewish Archives collection, 62

American Jewish Committee, 267

American Jewish Conference on Soviet Jewry, 268, 269, 274, 277

American Jewish Congress, 267

American Jewish Joint Distribution Committee, 303

American Zionist Emergency Council, 223

Anisfield, John, 324

Anna Teller, 15, 24, 26

Anniversary Celebration of Israel, 59

Anshe Chesed, 5, 12, 114, 120, 122; and Rabbi Barnett R. Brickner, 9, 205, 208, 212, 214, 216, 217; and Beachwood lawsuit against, 10; establishment of, 7; and Euclid Avenue Temple founding, 206; and Rabbi Israel Porath, 203; known as Fairmount Temple, 10; and Reform Judaism, 7; and Tifereth Israel founding, 5. *See also* Fairmount Temple

Anshe Emeth Beth Tfilo, 234, 235. *See also*
  Park Synagogue
Anshe Grodno Congregation, 252
Anti-defamation League of the B'nai
  B'rith, 267
Anti-Tuberculosis League, 294
Apfel, Aber, 198
Apfel, Feibel, 198
Apfel, Guedele, 198
Apfel, Nathan, 198
Apfel, Rachel, 198
Apfel, Seligmann, 198
Appeal to Conscience to Soviet Leaders, 266
Arnold, J. K., 324
Arsham, Ben, 63
Associated Charities, 294
Association for Jewish Communal Rela-
  tions, 67
Atkin Farm, 173
Atkin, Mayer, 63
Auld, William, 50
Avner, Jane, xi, xvi
Axworthe, Thomas, 133

Babcock, Mayor, 133
Babies' Dispensary and Hospital, 294
Bach, Hanna, 198
Bach, Heffel, 198
Bach, Mayer, 198
Bach, Samuel, 198
Bach, Simchel, 198
Baehr, Herman, 113, 119
Baer, Morris, 59
Baker, Newton D., 111, 113, 116, 117, 118, 119
Barnes, Harry Elmer, 221
Bay Area Council on Soviet Jewry, 278
Beckerman, Solomon, 122
Before Our Eyes, 274
Bein, Joesel, 198
Bein, Juettle, 198
Bein, Mariana, 198
Bein, Sander, 198
Bein, Solomon, 198
Bein, Tarz, 198

Bein, Zerle, 198
Bellamy, George, 296
Bellefaire Jewish Children's Bureau, 8, 11,
  114, 120, 289, 285. *See also* Jewish Orphan Asylum
Benesch, Alfred A., 8, 111, 112; and Alfred
  A. Benesch School, 112; and anti-Semitism, 116, 117; and Benjamin C. Starr,
  113; and Bohemian Synagogue, 114; and
  Cleveland Board of Education, 111, 112;
  on the Cleveland City Council, 111, 113;
  confirmation at Anshe Chesed, 122;
  correspondence with Harvard University President Cole, 117; defense of
  Cleveland City Hospital, 113; as director of public safety, 113, 118; education
  of, 112, 113; elected to Cleveland school
  board, 117; firm with Jerome Friedlander and Robert Morris, 119; and Harvard
  University quota on Jews, 111, 117; law
  career, 112, 113, 114; member of Bureau
  of Jewish Education, 122; membership
  in B'nai B'rith, 120; membership on
  boards, 114, 120; and *New Era Magazine* article, 116; and Newton D. Baker,
  113, 118; participation in charities, 120;
  and Peddlers' Self Defense Association,
  111; as state director of commerce, 113,
  119; and Tom Johnson, 113, 118, 119
Benesch, Isadore J., 112
Benjamin, Alfred, 319
Benjamin, Rabbi Samuel, 62, 232, 233, 234,
  237; arrest of, 236; attacked by Philip
  Rocker, 236; establishment of *Der
  Yiddisher Waechter,* 235; and Jewish
  Center, 234, 235; replacement by Rabbi
  Solomon Goldman, 235
Bennett, Alan D., xi, xiv, 2
Berger, David, 203
Bernon, Maurice, 259. *See also* Bernon,
  Maurie
Bernon, Maurie, 115. *See also* Bernon,
  Maurice
Bernstein, Harry, 37

Beth Israel—The West Temple, 263, 264, 265, 270

Bialik, Chaim Nachman, 9, 49

Bianchi, Don, 58

Billikopf, Jacob, 319

Bingham, Edward, 154

Black, Louis. 324

Blazys, Alexander, 51

B'nai B'rith, 7, 51, 120, 292; Balfour Auxiliary of, 51; Cleveland Auxiliary of, 51; Cleveland Heights Auxiliary of, 51; Cleveland Lodge of, 50; and Women's Grand Lodge District No. 2, 51

B'nai Jeshurun, 7, 10, 235, 246, 252, 255

Bogart, Dan, 264, 265, 266, 268, 274

Bohemian Synagogue, 114

Borstein, Pesach, 58

Bozyk, Max, 58

Brandeis, Louis, 48

Brandis, Wolf, 200

Brandus, Abraham, 197

Brandus, Gerschon, 197

Brandus, Guedel, 197

Brandus, Jakob, 197

Brandus, Mariana, 197

Brandus, Merle, 197

Braverman, Libbie, 12; and Activities in the Religious School, 257; and B'nai Jeshurun, 252, 255; Board of the National Council for Jewish Education, 251; death of mother, 253; education of, 248, 252, 254, 258; and the Jewish Chautauqua Society, 248; move to Chicago, 251; move to New York, 251; musical of, 260; pageants of, 256–57; and Purim Carnival, 258; and Religious Pageants for the Jewish School, 257; and Social Service Project for Hanukah, 259; teaching experience, 248, 254, 255–56, 257

Braverman, Sigmund, 215, 260

Brecht, Bertolt, 59

Brezhnev, Leonid, 279

Brickner, Rabbi Barnett R., 232, 242, 257; and Anshe Chesed, 205, 208, 212, 214, 216, 217; approach to education, 214–15, 216; and arbitrator in labor disputes, 213, 214; campaigning on behalf of Zionism, 9; Central Conference of American Rabbis, 217; and Reverend Charles Coughlin, 210; Conference on Jewish Rights, 222; death of, 245; debate with Clarence Darrow, 218–21; forum at the Euclid Avenue Temple, 211–13; and Senator Huey Long, 210; influence on Jerome Lawrence, 221; interview with Cleveland Plain Dealer, 207; lectures of, 209; and the "Message of Israel," 209; move to Cleveland to lead Anshe Chesed, 205, 206, 207, 243, 244, 256; and Pierre van Paassen, 212; as president of Jewish Educational Bureau, 245; and "Rabbi Brickner Scholarship Fund," 208; radio broadcasts of lectures, 209–11; and Reform Judaism, 208, 212, 216, 217, 218; and Rabbi Samuel Silver, 205; and Rabbi Solomon Goldman, 242, 243; speaking at the opening of the Philosophers' Circle of the Hebrew Garden, 49; wife of, 52; and the World Zionist Congress, 222

Brider Luria, Di, 54

Briggs, Paul, 118

Brilliant, Nathan, 215, 256, 257, 258

Brody, Anna. See Anna Goldman

Brody, Ethel, 172

Brody, Freda, 173

Brody, Herman, 189

Brody, Howard, 9, 171, 191; education of, 175–77, 182, 183, 185; and farm life, 174, 177, 178, 179, 180, 183, 184, 187; and the Great Depression, 181; Hebrew School, 189; the Jewish farming movement, 171; as president of the Cleveland Hill School Board in Buffalo, New York, 176

Brody, Morris, 171–75, 178–80, 185, 191; death of, 190; death of brother, 189; Jewish Agricultural Society, 181; move

Brody, Morris (cont.)
to Fort Lauderdale, 190; and Ohio Leg-
islature, 182; organization of farmers,
183; and Stock Market crash, 184
"Brody's Fruit Farm," 190
Brody, Shirley, 177, 179, 185, 190
Brody, Stanley, 177, 178, 179, 180, 187, 191
Brown, John, 50
Brudno, Emil, 211
Brudno, Zelig, 88, 89, 99
Brush, C. F., 132
Bryan, William Jennings, 164, 218
Buloff, Joseph, 58
Bureau of Jewish Education, xiv, 122
Burkholder, Norman, 173

Cahan, Abraham, 232
California Students for Soviet Jews, 278
Carnovsky, Morris, 58
Caron, Herb, 264, 265, 266, 268, 272, 274
Case Western Reserve University, xv,
276–77, 303
Central Conference of American Rabbis,
217, 223
Central High School, 112, 252
Changelings, The, 15, 24, 26
Chernin, Al, 269
Childers, Norman, 183
Church Federation, 73
Citizens Savings & Loan Co., 132
City National, 132
Clark, John H., 116
Cleaveland, Moses, 2
Cleveland: Board of Education, 8, 111, 112,
226; City Council, 8, 111, 127, 133, 266;
City Hall, 194; Community Relations
Board, 102, 104, 105, 107, 108, 110; Cul-
tural Gardens, 47, 52; Hebrew Garden
in Rockefeller Park, 9, 47–52; Shake-
speare Garden, 47, 49, 52
Cleveland Area Church Federation, 266
Cleveland Arts Prize, 25
Cleveland Bureau of Jewish Education,
276, 277

Cleveland City Hospital, 113, 294
Cleveland College, 21
Cleveland College of Jewish Studies. See
Siegal College of Judaic Studies
Cleveland College Skyline, 22
Cleveland Committee on Immigration, 72
Cleveland Committee on Soviet Anti-
Semitism, 266, 270, 271
Cleveland Council on Soviet Anti-Semi-
tism, 270, 272–79
Cleveland Department of Charities, 294
Cleveland Department of Health, 294
Cleveland Electric Illuminating Com-
pany, 76, 182
Cleveland Federation for Charity and
Philanthropy, 294. See also Federation
for Charity and Philanthropy
Cleveland Foundation, 307
Cleveland Hebrew Schools, 277
Cleveland Jewish Archives, xv
Cleveland Jewish Center, 9, 25, 234, 235,
237, 240, 241, 245, 246
Cleveland Jewish Family Services Asso-
ciation, 303
Cleveland Jewish News, 61, 63, 190
Cleveland Jewish Publication, 61
Cleveland Kindergarten Training School,
295
Cleveland People's Theater, 21
Cleveland Press, 116
Cleveland Public Hall, 226
Cleveland Public Library, 9, 15, 16
Cleveland Railway Company, 214
Cleveland School of Art, 28, 254
Cleveland School of Education, 252
Cleveland Zionist District, 50, 244, 245
Cleveland Zionist Society, 232
Cohen, Gustavus, 206
Cohen, Rabbi Armond E., 245
Cohen, Jessie, 61
Cohen, Rudy J., 320
Cohodas, Norman, 190
Cohon, Rabbi Samuel, 252
Colbert, Ralph A., 101

Communist Party in the United States, 78
Community Chest, 72
Community Hebrew Schools in Cleveland, 252
Community Temple, The, 246
Conference for Human Needs (in Israel), 67
Conference for Jewish Communal Service, 67
Conference on Jewish Rights, 222
Conference of Presidents of Major Jewish Organizations, 268, 269, 277
Conrad, Alexander, 276
Conservative Judaism, 9
Cooke, Edmund Vance, 49
Cooley, Harris Reid, 119
Cooperative Employment Bureau, 295
Cooper, Bernard, 49
Coughlin, Reverend Charles, 210
Coulton & Sprague, 131, 132
Council Educational Alliance, 8, 9, 34, 54, 114, 120
Council for Jewish Education, 248
Council of Jewish Women, 8, 76, 121
Cramer, Miriam E., 51
Crane, Billy, 40, 41, 42
Cultural Arts Advisory Committee, 57
Cuyahoga County Relief Administration, 303

Daily Press, 62
Darrow, Clarence, 218, 219, 220, 221
Da Silva, Howard, 55, 58
Dauby, N. L., 324, 325
Davey, Martin L, 113, 119
Davidson, Julius, 319
Dawidowitz, Harry, 241
Dembo, L., 52
Dienstag, Fradel, 200
Dimov, Osip, 54
Dinkel, Gulde, 198
Dinkel, Hayum, 198
Dinkel, Hirsch, 198
Dinkel, Jakob, 198
Dinkel, Sara, 198

Dinkel, Schenle, 198, 201
Dinkel, Schmule, 198
Dobrynin, Anatoly, 267
"Dr. Nichol," 167
"Doctors' Plot," 264–65
Donnerstag, Aber, 198
Donnerstag, Esther, 198
Donnerstag, Fradel, 198
Donnerstag, Geller, 198
Donnerstag, Guedel, 198
Donnerstag, Maennle, 198
Donnerstag, Rifka, 198
Donnerstag, Seligmann, 198
Donnerstag, Voegel, 198
Drama Advisory Committee. *See* Cultural Arts Advisory Committee
Dreyfus, E. D., 319
Drucker, Rabbi Eleazer, 249, 251
Drucker, Lewis, 52
Drucker, Louis, 245
Duchess Theater, 54

Eagle's Hall, 106, 108
Eastman, Max, 212
Eisendrath, Rabbi Maurice N., 217, 218
Eisenman, Charles, 114, 120
Eisenman, Chas, 154
Elsinger, Joseph, 154
Engel, Abraham, 198
Engelberg, Rabbi Louis, 246
Engel, Isaakloeb, 198
Engel, Klerle, 198
Engel, Miriam, 198
Engel, Roes, 198
Epstein, Mort, 263, 273, 274
Epstein, Rita, 277
Erskine, John, 212
Espionage Act, 78
Euclid Avenue National Bank, 127, 133
Euclid Avenue Temple, 57, 221, 243, 244, 248, 252, 255, 256, 257–58. *See also* Anshe Chesed
Excelsior Club, 7, 115, 158. *See also* Oakwood Club

Fairmount Temple, 221, 266. *See also* An-she Chesed

Federation for Charity and Philanthropy, 292

Federation for Community Planning, 307, 312

Federation of Jewish Charities, 12, 100, 292, 324, 326, 327. *See also* Jewish Federation of Cleveland

Federation of Jewish Philanthropies, 208

Federation of Jewish Women's Organizations, 50, 307

Feder, Ethel, 56, 58

Feder, Joseph, 54, 55

Feder, Mark, 10, 53, 55; Anniversary Celebration of Israel, 59; cameo as Mendele Mokher Sforim, 59; construction of new theater, 57; and Drama Advisory Committee, 57, 58; Jewish Community Center theater, 56–59; meeting of David Guralnik, 55; plays produced by, 56–59; and Warsaw Ghetto Commemoration, 59; and *Yiddish Kultur Gezelshaft*, 59

Feinberg, Jennie, 81, 82, 83, 84, 92

Feis, Julius, 114, 121

Feiss, Paul L., 324, 326

Fibich, Felix, 58

First National Bank of Cleveland, 127, 133

Fitzsimmons, Bob, 36

Fleischhauer, Ruben, 201

Ford, Gerald, 279

Ford, Henry, 212

Forward, The, 62

Franco, Francisco, 19

Frank, Benno, 58

Freedheim, Eugene, 115

Freedman, Max, 121, 303

Frey, Berle, 200

Frey, David, 200

Frey, Fradel, 200

Frey, Israel, 200

Frey, Sara, 200

Friedberg, Maurice, 274

Friedland, A. H., 49, 50, 52

Friedlander, Jerome, 113, 119

Friedlander, Sam, 115

Gaertner, Abraham, 199

Gaertner, Berla, 199

Gaertner, Besle, 199

Gaertner, David, 199

Gaertner, Eva, 199

Gaertner, Gudel, 199

Gaertner, Hayum, 200

Gaertner, Michael, 200

Gaertner, Moses, 199

Gaertner, Perle, 199

Gaertner, Rechle, 199

Gaertner, Sara, 199

Gaertner, Voegel, 199

Gaines, Sam, 115

Gamoran, Emanuel, 257, 262

Gan Ivri Women's League, 48, 49, 50, 51, 52

Garment, Leonard, 279

Gartner, Lloyd P., 1

Geneva, Ohio, 172, 173, 188, 189, 190

German Jews, 135, 228

Gitlin, Dave, 264, 265

Glass, Mike, 121, 313

Glenville Jewish Center, 67

Globe Theater, 54

Goebbels, Josef, 224, 226

Goldberg, Arthur, 266, 267

Goldblat, Michel, 276

Goldenberg, Eliahu, 58

Goldfaden, Avrom, 54

Goldfaden's Kholem, 57

Goldfarb, Samuel, 260

Goldman, Abner H., 52

Goldman, Anna, 171–73, 176, 179, 180, 183, 184, 189, 191; death of, 190; journal of, 185–87

Goldman, Rabbi Solomon, 49, 50, 122, 208, 232, 234, 242, 245; and Orthodox Judaism, 238; Orthodox lawsuits against, 237, 238, 239; reforms of, 237;

replacement of Rabbi Samuel Benjamin, 235; resignation of, 240, 241
Goldmark, Karl, 48
Goldwater, S. S., 325, 326
Goodrich House, 295
Gordin, Jacob, 54
Gottgetreu, Idel, 200
Gottgetreu, Jetta, 200
Gottgetreu, Miriam, 200
Grabowski, John J., xv
Gracemount School, 102, 108
Gratz, Rebecca, 48, 50, 51
Great Depression, 22
Greater Cleveland Chapter of the American Red Cross, 22
Greenberg, Chaim, 264
Greenberg, O. K., 52
Green, Fred, 133
Gries, Rabbi Moses, 121, 127
Groll, George, 39, 40, 41, 45, 46
Gross, Jerry, 115
Gross, Jonas, 62
Grossman, August, 112
Grover Mendelsohn Company, 161
Grove, Isaac Van, 259
Guralnik, David, 10, 53–59

Ha'am, Achad, 48, 49, 50
Haas, Adolph, 62
Haas, M. A., 322
Hadassah, 49, 50, 76, 248
Hahn, Rabbi Aaron, 112, 122
Halevy, Jacques, 48
Halle brothers, 116
Halle, Salmon P., 324, 325, 327
Halle's Hall, 115
Halpern, Moses, 54
Halpern, Oscar, 54
Hammer, Albert W., 154
Handbook for Community Action on Soviet Jewry, 273
Hanna, Mark, 36
Harvard Club, 116
Harvard University, 117, 248, 283

Hatton, A. R., 49
Hays, Abraham, 136, 137, 138, 157
Hays, Bella, 292
Hays, Bertha, 154
Hays, Betty, 136, 137
Hays Brothers, 135, 148, 149, 150, 153; and Albert W. Hammer, 154; closing of, 155; and Joseph Elsinger, 154; move of the store, 151, 152, 154; name changed to Hays Bros. & Co., 154
Hays, Clarence, 154
Hays, Eugene, 154
Hays, Fanny, 127, 136, 137
Hays, Hiram, 154, 155, 158
Hays, Joseph, 6, 128, 135; arrival in New York, 138; attending Spencerian College, 143; birth of, 136; birth of children, 154; and Civil War, 155; death of, 159, 160; death of father, 157; death of mother, 136, 156, 157; death of wife, 157, 159; and Excelsior Club, 158; and fundraising for Hebrew Benevolent Society, 135; and Hays Brothers, 135, 148, 149–55; immigration to America, 136, 138; jobs of, 136, 139, 140–48; and Joseph Hays & Co., 156; learning English, 143; marriage to Rosette Henry, 154; move to Cleveland, 138, 139; politics of, 155; and Schwarzenberg, Hays & Co., 156; and Seth Sauter, 141; and S. Mann, 144, 147; and start of Hebrew Relief Association, 158, 159; will of, 159–60; and William Taylor, 142
Hays, Kaufman, 6, 138, 140, 143, 146, 148, 292; as acting treasurer of Cleveland, 133; birth of, 128, 136, 139; and City National Bank, 132; death of father, 157; death of mother, 128, 157; election to City Council, 133; and Finance Committee of Citizens Savings & Loan Co., 132; and First National Bank, 133; and founding of Euclid Avenue National Bank, 127, 132; and Hays Brothers, 135, 148, 149, 151–54; illness of, 149,

Hays, Kaufman (cont.)
151; immigration to America, 127, 128, 135, 136; jobs of, 128–31, 139; marriage to Lizzie Thorman, 130, 145; move to Cleveland, 128, 135; organization of the Teutonia Insurance Co. of Cleveland, 131; as president of Hebrew Benevolent Society, 127; and Simson Thorman, 130–31; trip to Europe, 130; and Turner Manufacturing Co., 133; and Turner Worsted Co., 133, 134; as vice president of Cleveland City Council, 127

Hays, Louis H., 136, 154, 324, 325

Hays, Rosa, 128, 129, 136, 137

Hays, Yetta, 136, 137, 138, 139, 143

Hayum, Aron, 197

Hazeldell School, 175

H. B. Claflin & Co., 150

Hebrew Academy, 10

Hebrew Benevolent Society, 127, 135

Hebrew Cultural Garden, 9, 47, 48; and Achad Ha'am, 50; and A. H. Friedland, 52; and B'nai B'rith, 51; and Chaim Weizmann, 51; and the Cleveland Lodge of B'nai B'rith, 50; dedication of, 47, 49; dedication of the rock garden, 50; descendants of Simson Thorman, 51; description of, 48; design by T. Ashburton Tripp, 48; and Edward J. Schweid, 52; and Emma Lazarus, 48, 50, 51; establishment of, 51; and Esther Samolar, 51; and Federation of Jewish Women's Organizations, 50; and Gan Ivri Women's League, 48, 49, 50, 51; and Henrietta Szold, 48, 50, 51; and Jennie K. Zwick, 50, 51, 52; and Julius Schweid, 49; and Keren Hayesod Women's Club, 51; and Leo Weidenthal, 51, 52; and Lewis Drucker, 52; and Max E. Meisel, 51, 52; and Max Kalish, 51; and Miriam E. Cramer, 51; and Milton B. Schweid, 50; and Moses Maimonides, 50; and Moses Mendelssohn, 49; and the Philosophers' Circle, 49, 50; and the Poet's

Corner, 48, 49; and Rae Roodman, 50; and Rebecca Gratz, 48, 50, 51; and the Shakespeare Garden, 49, 52; and Walter Sinz, 51; and William Auld, 50

Hebrew Free Loan Association, 114, 120

Hebrew Institute, 326

Hebrew Observer, 61

Hebrew Orthodox Old Age Home. *See* Menorah Park Jewish Home for the Aged

Hebrew Relief Association. *See* Jewish Family Service Association

Hebrew Shelter Home, 114

Hebrew Union College, 189, 205, 207, 223, 252

Heights Jewish Center, 247

Heights Temple, 252

Heller, Rabbi James G., 218

Henry, Louis, 154

Henry, Rosette, 154, 157

Herman, Rabbi Jack, 246

Herrick, Myron T., 132, 155

Herwald, Robert, 62

Herz, David Ralph, 245

Herzl, Theodor, 223

Heschel, Rabbi Abraham, 267

Hexter, Bertha, 136

Hexter, Herman, 61

Hexter, Sol, 121

H. F. Klein, 135

Highland View Hospital, 114

Hiram House, 6, 295, 297, 298, 301, 302; camp of, 299, 300; opening of, 296

Hirshbeyn, Peretz, 54, 58

Hitler, Adolph, 19, 22

Hoffman, Stephen H., xiv, xv

Holmes, John Haynes, 212

Holy Blossom Temple, 209, 217, 243

Hopfermann, Sara, 201

Hopfermann, Seckle, 201

Hopfermann, Simson, 201

Hopfermann, Voegele, 201

Hopfermann, Zerle, 201

Hopkins, William R., 49, 52, 208

Horowitz, Hyman, 62

Horowitz, Rabbi Philip, 215, 266
Hostetler, Joe, 119
Humane Society, 295
Hungarian Benevolent and Social Union, 7
Huron Road Hospital, 115

Infant Orphan Mothers Society, 8
"Inherit the Wind," 221
Institute for Jewish Life, 67
Institute on Judaism, 72
International Conference for Jewish
    Communal Service, 67
Intrater, Aaron, 277
Israelitic Society of Cleveland, 5. *See also*
    Anshe Chesed
Israel's Technion, 248
Isserman, Rabbi Ferdinand, 208
It's a Living, 55

Jackson, Henry, 279
Jackson, Jas F., 292, 294
Jackson, Leo, 266
Javits, Jacob, 266
J. C. Newman Cigar Company, 161, 167,
    168, 169, 170
Jewish Agricultural Society, 171, 173, 181, 183
Jewish Book Council of America, 25
Jewish Chautauqua Society, 248
Jewish communal existence, 2, 5, 6
Jewish Community Center, 8, 208; forma-
    tion, 11; and Jewish theater in Cleveland,
    10, 53, 55, 56, 58, 59; and Mark Feder,
    56, 59; move to Beachwood, 11; move to
    Cleveland Heights, 11; planning of new
    Jewish Community Center, 58
Jewish community of Cleveland, xii, xv,
    xvi, 1, 2; 6, 7; and Beachwood, 10, 74–
    75; and Black-Jewish relations, 70, 101;
    city's first Jewish congregation, 5; and
    Cleveland Heights, 70, 75; contribu-
    tion to the rescue and resettlement of
    European Jewry, 10; and Czech-Jewish
    immigrants, 8; and East European
    Jews, 6, 7; employment discrimina-
tion, 76; formation of the Federation
    of Jewish Charities, 8; German-Jewish
    community, 6, 135; Hebrew Garden in
    Rockefeller Park, 9, 47, 48–52; Hebrew
    schools in, 49, 50; Hungarian Jews, 7;
    and integrated neighborhoods, 11; inte-
    gration of, 70; and interreligious con-
    tacts, 72–73; involvement in the found-
    ing of Israel, 10; Jewish immigration to,
    5, 6; Jewish institutions in the eastern
    suburbs, 9, 10, 11, 67, 68, 69, 70; Jewish
    press in Cleveland, 60–63; move away
    from the Woodland neighborhood, 9;
    move to Glenville, Mt. Pleasant, and
    Kinsman neighborhoods, 9; opening of
    Mount Sinai, 9; and Orthodox Jewish
    community, 11; Polish Jews, 7; Prob-
    lems of church-state relationships in
    public schools, 74; religious exclusions
    in the suburbs, 75; restrictive covenants
    against, 10, 75; and the right of syna-
    gogues to build in suburban areas, 74,
    75; segregation of, 76–77; serving in
    U.S. military during World War II, 10;
    and Soviet Jews, 11; and speaking Yid-
    dish, 6; Yiddish theater in Cleveland,
    10, 14, 53, 54, 55, 58
Jewish Community Council, 12, 67, 100, 307
Jewish Community Federation of Cleve-
    land, xiii, xiv, 11, 114, 195, 265; and
    agreement with the Cleveland Council
    on Soviet Anti-Semitism, 272; and aid
    to Soviet Jews, 11; and the Cleveland
    Council on Soviet Anti-Semitism, 270,
    272, 273, 274, 275, 277; and Community
    Fund, 72; and Community Relations
    Board, 110; and Community Relations
    Committee, 110; election of Charles
    Eisenman, 120; expansion of, 9; and
    federal aid to parochial schools, 74; and
    Federation for Community Planning,
    312; formation, 8; fundraising, 309–10;
    and Henry L. Zucker, 303, 304, 306,
    307, 314; Jewish Education Center of

Jewish Community Federation (cont.) Cleveland, 12; and Judah Rubinstein, 60; and Lee-Harvard area housing situation, 101–10; and merger with the Federation of Jewish Women's Organizations, 307; and merger with the Jewish Community Council and the Jewish Welfare Federation, 12, 67, 100, 307; and the Osipov Balalaika Orchestra, 271; and political activity, 308–9; and the Protestant Church Federation, 104; and St. Cecelia's parish, 102; and subcommittee on Soviet Jewry, 265; and support of the Cleveland Jewish Archives, xv; and United Torch Services, 312; and the Welfare Federation of Cleveland, 72; Young Adult Division of, 66

Jewish Daily Forward, 232

Jewish Diaspora, xii

Jewish Educational Bureau, 244, 245

Jewish Educational Institute, 319

Jewish Education Center of Cleveland, 12

Jewish Family Service Association, 8, 114, 120, 158

Jewish Farmer, 175

Jewish Farmers Association of Geneva, Ohio, 190

Jewish farming movement, 171, 188

Jewish Guardian, 62, 232, 233, 234, 235, 237

Jewish Historical Museum, 260

Jewish immigrants, 6, 7

Jewish Independent, 51, 61

Jewish National Fund of Cleveland, 204, 248

Jewish newspapers in Cleveland, 61, 63. *See also specific newspapers*

Jewish Orphan Asylum, 283; and Board of, 287, 290, 292; and building of new home, 284, 285, 286, 287, 291; move to new home, 287–88, 289, 290; name changed to Bellefaire, 285. *See also* Bellefaire Jewish Children's Bureau

Jewish Orphan Home. *See* Jewish Orphan Asylum

Jewish Orthodox Home for the Aged. *See* Menorah Park Jewish Home for the Aged

Jewish Recorder, 62

Jewish Review, 61, 211. See also *Jewish Review and Observer*

Jewish Review and Observer, 61. See also *Jewish Review*

Jewish Singing Society, 59

Jewish Star, 62

Jewish Theological Seminary, 60, 250, 251

Jewish Vocational Service, 76

Jewish Voice, 62, 63, 232

Jewish Voice Pictorial, 63, 232

Jewish Welfare Federation, 12, 67, 100. *See also* Jewish Federation of Cleveland

Jewish Welfare Fund, 66, 71, 228, 307, 308, 310

Jewish World. See *Yiddishe Velt, Die*

Jews in Eastern Europe, 265

Jews in Egypt, 260

John Hay High School, 16

Johnson, Tom L., 36, 111, 113, 118, 119, 120

Jones, Francis C., 44

Jones, Robinson G., 117

Joseph Hays & Co., 156

"Julius Caesar," 49

Kaiser, Meyer, 319. *See also* Kayser, Meyer

Kalb, Estherle, 197

Kalb, Huebchele, 197

Kalb, Rabbi Loeb, 197

Kalish, Max, 51, 52

Katz, M. A., 233, 239

Kaufman, Tom, 119

Kayser, Meyer, 318–19. *See also* Kaiser, Meyer

Kehilla movement, 62

Kennedy, John F., 172, 267

Keren Hayesod Women's Club, 51

Kern, Herr Von, 131

Kesher Shel Barzel Home for Aged and Infirm Israelites. *See also* Montefiore Home for the Aged

Klein, Aberle, 198
Klein, Abrahamloeb, 198
Kleinberg, Rabbi, 189
Klein, Falk, 198
Klein, Golde, 198
Klein, Hirsch, 198
Klein, Juedle, 198
Klein, Reichel, 198, 201
Klein, Rifkele, 198
Kohn, David, 208
Kohn, Lazarus, 5, 6, 195, 196, 200
Kohn, Rifkele, 200
Krauss, Kuney, 131
Kroner, Leonard, 190
Khrushchev, Nikita, 266
Kuhl, Abraham, 199
Kuhl, Bela, 199
Kuhl, Gabriel, 199
Kuhl, Golde, 199
Kuhl, Hayum, 199
Kuhl, Joseph, 200
Kuhl, Maedel, 199
Kuhl, Simon, 200
Kuhl, Zerle, 199

Labor Lyceum, 54
LaFollette, Bob, 34
Lake, Charles H., 118
Lakeside Hospital, 294, 295
Lamm, Deile, 197
Lamm, Falk, 199
Lamm, Hinele, 199
Lamm, Idel, 197
Lamm, Isarias, 199
Lamm, Israel, 197
Lamm, Kallmann, 197
Lamm, Loeb, 199
Lamm, Schenle, 199
Lang, Hascall C., 324
Laufman, Art, 274
Lawrence, Jerome, 221
Lazarus, Emma, 48, 50, 51
Lederer, Clara, 47
Lerner, Max, 212, 213

Levenson, William B., 118
Levin, Harry, 249, 250
Levin, Jack, 249
Levin, Rabbi Morris A., 249; and Community Hebrew Schools in Cleveland, 252; and move to Chicago, 251; "Pedagogy Among the Jews," 250; and Rabbi of the Anshe Grodno Congregation, 252; remarriage, 254
Levy & Stern, 115
Lewenthal, A., 324, 326, 328
Lewin, Nat, 278
Leybovitch, Sarah, 54
Liebenthal, Heinemann, 197
Liebenthal, Issak, 197
Liebenthal, Moses, 197
Lieber, Harvey, 279
Lieberman, Rabbi George, 270
Liebgold, Leon, 58
Liliana, Lil, 58
Lilienfeld, Bule, 197
Lilienfeld, Hirsch, 197
Lilienfeld, Moses, 197
Lilienfeld, Rifkele, 200
Lilienfeld, Simon, 197
Lindsey, Ben B., 219
Liph, Samson, 183
Lipman, Eugene J., 1
Listen to My Heart, 22
Literarish Dramatishe Gezelshaft, presentations of, 54. See also Progressive Dramatic Club; Yiddish Kultur Gezelshaft
Literary Dramatic Societies of the United States and Canada, 54
Literary Dramatic Society. See Literarish Dramatishe Gezelshaft
Litt, Dan, 264
Locher, Ralph, 266
Loeb, Sam, 128, 129
Loeser, Irwin, 214
Long, Senator Huey, 210
Lothenman, Daniel, 112
Lubavitcher Hasidic movement, 267
Lubliner, Sara, 200, 201

Lubliner, Seligmann, 200
Lupton, Dilworth, 208
Lustig, Abraham, 197
Lustig, Baruch, 198
Lustig, Baruch, the younger, 200
Lustig, Bela, 198
Lustig, Debora, 200
Lustig, Eisig, 197
Lustig, Hinn, 197
Lustig, Kallmann, 197
Lustig, Lea, 198
Lustig, Loeb, 198
Lustig, Mamel, 198
Lustig, Mayer, 198
Lustig, Menke, 197
Lustig, Mesche, 201
Lustig, Miriam (daughter of Baruch Lustig), 198
Lustig, Miriam (daughter of Baruch Lustig, the younger from Schweinshaupten), 201
Lustig, Rifka, 197
Lustig, Sara, 198
Lustig, Seligmann, 197
Lux, Lillian, 58
Lynde, Ned, 314, 315

Machol, Jack, 61
Machol, Michael, 122
Machol, Rabbi Michaelis, 206, 207
Magnes, Judah L., 49
Mahler, Barney, 324, 326, 327
Maimonides, Moses, 48, 50
Mandelbaum, Jacob, 115
Mandelbaum, Manny, 115
Mandel, Carol, 279
Mandel, Mort, 304, 313, 316
Manger Hotel, 116
Manhattan Theater, *14*, 54
Mann, Thomas, 227
Mantel, Elias, 63
Margolies, Rabbi Samuel, 62, 122
Margolis, Henry, 277
Margoshes, S., 242, 243, 245

Margulies, Rabbi, 234
Marks, Martin, 8, 114, 120; birth of, 292; and B'nai B'rith, 292; board of the Jewish Orphan Asylum, 292; establishment of the Federation of Jewish Charities, 292; Federation for Charity and Philanthropy, 292; marriage to Belle Hays, 292; and petition to Western Reserve University, 292–94
Martin, Sean, xvi, 12
Maschke, Maurice, 111, 119, 120
Masonic Auditorium, 218–19, 220, 221
Mavo Hatalmud—Outline of the Talmad, 204
Mayer, H. H., 319
McKinley, William, 36
Meir, Golda, 123
Meisel, Lampy & Co., 150
Meisel, Max E., 50, 51, 52
Mendolssohn, Moses, 48, 49
Menorah Park Jewish Home for the Aged, 9, 11, 321, 322
Merchant, Cyrus, 155, 156
Merging Traditions, 60
"Message of Israel," 209
Mestel, Yakov, 57
Metropolitan Theater, 54
Meyerbeer, Giacomo, 48
Miles Standish Elementary, 176
Miller, Rabbi Uri, 267
Ministerial Alliance, 73
Minkoff, Isaiah, 269
Mintz, Eli, 58
Mitchell, Margaret, 298
Mitchells, Grace, 298
Mittel, Hanna, 199
Mittel, Isaak, 200
Mittel, Joseph, 199
Mittel, Nathan, 200
Mittel, Reiz, 199
Mittel, Simchele, 199
Mittel, Simon, 199
M. & M. Halle's, 150
Moiseyev Folk Dancers, 271

Montefiore Home for the Aged, 8, 11, 319–20; construction of new facility, 317; established as the Kesher Shel Barzel Home for Aged and Infirm Israelites, 317; letters from the Montefiore archives, 318–20; name changed to the Sir Moses Montefiore Kesher Home for Aged and Infirm Israelites, 317; renamed the Montefiore Home, 317
Morgan Lithograph shop, 39, 40, 41, 42, 44, 45
Morgenstern, Elliot, 56
Morris, Robert, 113, 119
Moses Boarding House, 128
Mother and Child, 28
Mount Sinai Hospital, 8, 114, *282;* Building Committee, 325, 326, 327, 328; building of new facility, 323, 327; "Chronology of the Beginnings of Mount Sinai Hospital," 323; and "Code of Regulations," 323; and the Committee on Permanent Organization, 324; establishment of, 323; Finance Committee, 324, 326, 327; funds collected for construction, 325, 326, 327; incorporation as The Cleveland Jewish Hospital, 324; name change to the Cleveland Jewish Hospital Association, 325; named as Mount Sinai, 328; negotiations with the proposed Jewish Orthodox Hospital, 324, 325; time capsule of, 323
Mueller, Krieger, xv
Munro, Thomas, 259
Muskin, Rabbi Jacob, 247
Mussliner, Bela, 197
Mussliner, Besle, 197
Mussliner, Jokel, 197
Mussliner, Loeb, 197
Mussliner, Schlome, 197
Mussliner, Seligmann, 197
Mussliner, Terz, 197
Mutter, Abraham, 200
Mutter, Feibel, 200

Mutter, Perl, 200
Mutter, Samuel, 200
Mutter, Sara, 200
Mutter, Voegel, 200
Myers, Dave, 121, 313
Myers, Max, 324, 325, 326

National Conference of Christians and Jews, 25, 72
National Council for Jewish Education, 251
National Council of Jewish Women, 57
National Foundation for Jewish Culture, 67
National Jewish Community Relations Advisory Council, 268, 269
N. E. Crittenden, 146
Neshkin, Fishel, 54
Neshkin, Sam, 54
Neumark, Lee, 313
New Era Magazine, 116
Newman, Julius C., 8; arrival in Cleveland, 161, 163; brands of cigars, 162, 167, 168; education of, 162, 163; immigration to America, 162; J. C. Newman Cigar Company, 161, 168, 169, 170; jobs of, 161, 163, 164; and Katherine White, 166, 167; move to New York, 164; move to Tampa, Florida, 161; purchase of the Grover Mendelsohn Company, 161; start of cigar manufacturing business, 164, 165; and Teddy Roosevelt, 166
New Masses, 17, 20
Nixon, Richard, 279
Normal Training School, 295
Nowak, Rabbi Abraham, 49, 246

Oakwood Club, 7, 115, 122
Ohioana Library, 25
Ohio Farmer, 175
Ohio Legislature, 182
Ohio State University, 263
Ohio Supreme Court, 74, 245
Ology cigar factory, *126*
Oppenheimer, Rabbi Moses, 137
Oppenheimer, Sam, 61

Oppenstein, M., 319
Ornstein, Frances, 189–90
Ornstein, Jacob, 189
Orthodox Judaism, 7, 9, 10, 237, 238, 246
Osipov Balalaika Orchestra, 271
Ostrovsky, Chaim, 55
Outhwaite School, 112

Paassen, Pierre van, 212
Park Synagogue, 7, 9, 245
Payne, Rhoda, 58, 59
Pearlman, David, 215, 256
Peddlers' Self Defense Association, 111
People's Theater, 54
Performing Arts Advisory Committee, 56
Peskin, Allan, 1
Phi Beta Kappa Society, 116, 117
Phillips, Nathan, 209
Piatagorsky, Gregor, 212
Pinsky, Dovid, 55
Pinza, Ezio, 212
Plain Dealer, 55, 61, 175, 207, 208, 221
Pollock, Channing, 212
Porath, Rabbi Israel, 7, 123, 202; birth
    of, 203; death of, 203; funeral of; 202;
    Heights Jewish Center, 247; immigration
    to America, 203; and the Jewish National
    Fund of Cleveland, 204; marriage to
    Peshe Miriam Tiktin, 203; and Mavo
    Hatalmud—Outline of the Talmad, 204
Porath, Laura, 7, 202
Powys, John Cowper, 212
Progressive Dramatic Club, 54. See also
    Literarish Dramatishe Gezelshaft; Yid-
    dish Kultur Gezelshaft
Project Sefer, 276, 277
Protestant Church Federation, 104

Ratner, Leonard, 121, 313
Reed, C. A., 133
Rees, Tom, 279
Reform Judaism, 7, 10, 203, 206, 216–18,
    239; and education, 122; and Jewish
    Center, 235

Reinhardt, Max, 58
Reinthal, Sol, 114, 121
Reisman, Isadore, 277
Religious Pageants for the Jewish School, 257
Rembrandt, Elaine, 59
Reyzn, Avrom, 55
Rhinewine, Abraham, 243
Ribicoff, Abraham, 266
Rice, Elmer, 59
Rikoon, Sanford, 190
Rockefeller, John D., 165
Rockefeller Park, and Hebrew Cultural
    Garden dedication, 9
Rocker, Henry A. 245, 313
Rocker, Philip, 236
Rocker, Samuel, 62
Rogers, James H., 208
Romaine, Isaac, 78
Roodman, Rae, 50
Roosevelt, Franklin D., 18, 210, 211
Roosevelt, Teddy, 34, 166
Rose, Abel, 54
Rose, Falk, 199
Rose, Heinemann, 199
Rose, Jane, 54
Rose, Jendel, 199
Rose, Jerry, 57
Rose, Mariana, 199
Rosenbaum, Abraham, 197
Rosenbaum, Esther, 200
Rosenbaum, Frumet, 198
Rosenbaum, Golde, 198
Rosenbaum, Hanna, 197, 201
Rosenbaum, Isaak, 198
Rosenbaum, Jakob, 197
Rosenbaum, Kaufman, 198
Rosenbaum, Kuselloeb, 198
Rosenbaum, Liebman, 198
Rosenbaum, Loeb, 200
Rosenbaum, Moses, 197, 201
Rosenbaum, Natle, 200
Rosenbaum, Rachel, 198
Rosenbaum, Rifke, 197
Rosenbaum, Roes, 198

Rosenbaum, Simson, 197
Rosenbaum, Tendel, 197
Rosenbaum, Weinle, 200
Rosenberg, Bunle, 199
Rosenberg, Cheske, 199
Rosenberg, Hienle, 199
Rosenberg, Hinele, 197
Rosenberg, Levi, 199
Rosenberg, Loeb, 199
Rosenberg, Marmias, 199
Rosenberg, Mayer, 197
Rosenblum, Evy, 280
Rosenblum, Louis, 12, 263; agreement with the Jewish Community Federation of Cleveland, 272; and the American Jewish Conference on Soviet Jewry, 268–69; *Appeal to Conscience to Soviet Leaders,* 266; *Before Our Eyes,* 274; Beth Israel—The West Temple, 263, 264; as chairman of the Union of Councils for Soviet Jews, 278; and the Cleveland Committee on Soviet Anti-Semitism, 266, 271, 275; formation of social action committee, 266; *Handbook for Community Action on Soviet Jewry,* 273; meeting with Sid Vincent, 271; and the Moiseyev Folk Dancers, 271; and Project Sefer, 276, 277; publication of *Soviet Terror against Jews: How Cleveland Initiated an Interfaith Protest,* 266; and Soviet Jews, 264; and *Spotlight* newsletter, 272–73; and subcommittee on Soviet Jewry, 265; *To the Leaders of the Soviet Union,* 266; and trip to the Soviet Union, 279; and visit to the White House, 279
Rosenblum, Max, 326
Rosenthal, Ed, 275
Rosenthal, Rabbi Rudolph, 246
Rosenwald, Julius, 311
Rosenwald, William, 311
Rosenwasser, Marcus, 115
Rose, Reichel, 199
Rosewater, Addie, 257

Rothenberg, Al, 319
Rubinstein, Judah, xvi, 1, 2, 112; creation of the Cleveland Jewish Archives, 60; death of, xi, 1; dedication to, xiv; publication of work, xii; historian of Greater Cleveland Jewish community, xi, 60; and the Jewish Community Federation of Cleveland, 60; and the Jewish press in Cleveland, 60–63; and *Merging Traditions,* 60; and the Western Reserve Historical Society, 1, 2, 60
Rubinstein, Z. H., 242
Rusk, Dean, 267
Russell, Bertrand, 212

Saalman, Joseph, 199
Sachs, Abraham, 233
Sachsenheimer, Breinle, 199
Sachsenheimer, Guedel, 199
Sachsenheimer, Hanna, 199
Sachsenheimer, Roes, 199
Sachsenheimer, Samuel, 199
Sachsenheimer, Serle, 199
Sachsenheimer, Zerle, 199
Salb, Breinle, 201
Saltzman, Maurie, 313, 316
Samolar, Esther, 51
Sapiro, Aaron, 212
Sauter, Seth, 141
Schiff, Jacob, 117
Schloss, Nathan, 318
Schwab, Flora, 121
Schwartz, Maurice, 58
Schwarzenberg, Ephraim, 156
Schwarzenberg, Hays & Co., 156
Schwarzenberg, Henry, 156
Schwarzenberg, L. H., 129
Schwarzenberg, Phoebe, 154
Schweid, Edward J., 49, 52
Schweid, Haskell H., 49
Schweid, Julius, 49
Schweid, Milton B., 50
Schwenger, Lloyd S., 62, 313
Scolnik, Max, 54

Scott, Walter, 50

Scovill Avenue Temple, 114, 120. *See also* Anshe Chesed

Seamons, Frank, 45, 46

Seid, Ida, 16

Seid, Nathan, 16, 19

Seid, Ruth, 9; adoption of pen name Jo Sinclair, 16, 17, 18, 20; anthologies of, 26; awards of, 24–25; birth of, 16; and Chaim Weizmann, 51; and the *Cleveland College Skyline,* 22; and the Cleveland Public Library, 15, 16, 17, 18, 20; education of, 15, 16, 17, 21; and first published story, 15–16, 17; and Franklin D. Roosevelt, 18; and Harper Prize, 15, 24; and the Jewish Book Council of America Annual Award, 15; jobs of, 17, 18, 22, 23, 24; memoir of, 27; move to Cleveland, 16; and *New Masses,* 17; nomination for the Pulitzer Prize, 15; novels of, 15, 23–24; plays of, 21; 22, 24; republication of novels, 26; story sold to *Coronet,* 21; story sold to *Esquire,* 20; story sold to *Ken,* 21; and the Works Progress Administration "Foreign Language Newspaper Digest," 18, 20, 21; writing of, 19, 21, 23, 24

Seligsohn, Fred, 319

Severance Hall, 56, 57

Severance, S. L., 132

Shakespeare, William, 49

Shane, Sam, 55

Sharlitt, Michael, 11, 283

Sherwin Williams Co., 183

Shver Tsu Zayn a Yid, 57

Sidlo, Tom, 119

Siegal College of Judaic Studies, 11, 248

Silver, Rabbi Abba Hillel, xii, 190, 232–33, 240, 241, 252; campaigning on behalf of Zionism, 9; as head of the American Zionist Emergency Council, 223; immigration to America, 223; on Nazi propaganda and German student exchange program, 7, 224–28, 231; and

Nazi treatment of Jewish Germans, 228–29, 230; ordination at Hebrew Union College, 223; and the Philosophers' Circle of the Hebrew Garden, 49; as president of the Central Conference of American Rabbis, 223; as president of the Jewish Educational Bureau, 244, 245; as president of the Zionist Organization of America, 223; and Rabbi Barnett R. Brickner, 208, 244; as rabbi of The Temple—Tifereth Israel, 223

Silver, Dorothy, 58, 59

Silver, Rabbi Samuel, 205

Silverstein, Abe, 270, 271

Simon, Max, 122, 245, 313

Simon, Sam, 189

Sinclair, Jo. *See* Seid, Ruth

Sing at My Wake, 15, 24

Sinz, Walter, 51

S. J. Lichtenstadter, 135

Slepak, Vladimir, *195*

Sokol Hall, 101

Sommer, Baruch, 200

Sommer, Bess, 200

Sommer, Jittle, 200

Sommer, Kallmann, 200

Sommers, Bill, 40

Sommer, Schmule, 200

Southern California Council for Soviet Jews, 277–78, 279

South Florida Conference on Soviet Jewry, 278

Soviet Jewry movement, 263, 266, 268, 269–73, 277, 278; Cleveland's contributions to, 263, 269, 274, 275, 276

Soviet Jews, 264–67, 270, 273, 275, 276, 278, 280

Soviet Terror against Jews: How Cleveland Initiated an Interfaith Protest, 266

Soviet Union, 264, 265, 267, 278, 279, 280

Spencerian College, 143

Spinoza, Baruch, 48, 50, 51

Spirit of the Dance, 28

Spotlight, 272–73

Stafford, O. M., 133

Stamm, Lil, 57

Starr, Benjamin C., 113

St. Cecelia's parish, 102, 107

Stearn, Abraham, 121

Steinberg, Phil, 57

Stein, Herman, 236

Stem, Louis, 112

Stern, Frank, 277

Stewart, Wendell, 107

Stockwell, John, 119

Stokes, J. G. Phelps, 78

Stokes, Rose Pastor: arrest of, 78; arrival in New York, 80; and the birth control movement, 78; death of, 78; divorce of J. G. Phelps Stokes, 78; founding of the Communist Party in the United States, 78; immigration to America, 79–80; and Jennie Feinberg, 81, 82, 84, 92; jobs of, 78, 79, 81–87, 89, 90, 91–94, 97; letter to the *Kansas City Star,* 78; marriage to Isaac Romaine, 78; marriage to J. G. Phelps Stokes, 78; move to Cleveland, 78, 81; move to London's East End, 78; move to New York, 78; participation in strike, 98, 99; writing for *Jewish Daily News,* 78; and Zelig Brudno, 88, 89, 99

Stone, Irving, 275

Strange, Michael, 212

Straus, Hiram, 61

Strauss, Lillian, xii, 6, 296, 298; and Hiram House, 297, 298, 301, 302; and Hiram House camp, 299, 300, 301

Suburban Temple, 10

Suitcase Theater, 59

"Sunday, Inc.," 73

Szold, Henrietta, 48–51

Taylor Road Synagogue, 246

Taylor, William, 142

Temple Emanu El, 10

Temple-Tifereth Israel, The, 5, 189; and Rabbi Abba Hillel Silver, 9, 223; build-ing of Beachwood branch, 11; dedication of building, 9; establishment, 7; and Martin Marks, 292; and Rabbi Moses J. Gries, 127, 292

Teutonia Insurance Co., 131, 132

Thorman, Esther, 130

Thorman, Lizzie, 130

Thorman, Sam, 130

Thorman, Simson, 5, 6, 51, 130, 131

Tiktin, Peshe Miriam, 203

Toch, Abraham, 197

To the Leaders of the Soviet Union, 266

Town of the Little People, The, 56

Treuhaft, Bill, 313

Tripp, T. Ashburton, 48

Tuch, Beierle, 199

Tuch, Estherle, 200

Tuch, Fradel, 199

Tuch, Hayum, 199

Tuch, Jakob, 199

Tuch, Jochevet, 199

Tuch, Moses, 199

Tuch, Simchel, 199

Tuch, Simson, 200

Tuch, Zipar, 199

Union of American Hebrew Congregations, 209, 217, 218, 257, 268

Union Club, 116

Union of Councils for Soviet Jews, 276–79

United Jewish Appeal, 307

United Torch Services, 307, 312–13

Vanik, Charles, 279

Vincent, Sidney Z., 10, 305; and "Cleveland—City without Jews," 1; and Henry L. Zucker, 314, 315; Jewish Community Council, 67; Jewish Community Federation, 67, 271, 275, 315; memorandum on the Lee-Harvard area housing situation, 101–10; organization of the first Cleveland community mission to Israel, 67; president of the Association

Vincent, Sidney Z. (cont.)
  for Jewish Communal Relations and the
  Conference for Jewish Communal Ser-
  vice, 67; retirement of, 303, 304, 315, 316;
  and Western Reserve University, 67
Visiting Nurse Association, 295
Vitkovich, Bertshi, 54
Vorspan, Albert, 1

Walker, Ernie, 274
Ward, E. M., 44
Warner, A. R., 292, 294
Warrensville-Center Synagogue, 247
Warsaw Ghetto, 59
Warshawsky, Abe, 43
Washington Committee for Soviet Jews,
  277, 278
Wasteland, 15, 24, 26
Watson, John, 212
Weed, L., 155
Weidenthal, Leo, 51, 52, 61
Weidenthal, Maurice, 61
Weil, Kurt, 58
Weil, Rae, 112
Weissberg, Lillian, 56
Weiss, David, 274
Weizmann, Chaim, 51, 212
Welfare Federation of Cleveland, 72
Welfare Fund Appeal, 76
Werfel, Franz, 58
Wertheimer, Dan S., 61
Wertheimer, Howard, 211
Wertheim, Sally H., xi, xiv, 2
Western Reserve Historical Society, xv,
  xvi, 1, 60, 126, 282
Western Reserve University, 21, 60, 67,
  248, 254, 264; establishment of the
  School of Social Science and Research,
  292; petition to establish school for so-
  cial science, 293, 294
Weyne, Arthur, 61
White, Katherine, 166, 167
Whittemore, Bruce, 266
Wiesel, Elie, 306

Wiesenfeld, Leon, 9, 62, 63; arrival in the
  United States, 232; and Rabbi Barnett
  R. Brickner, 244, 245; and Brooklyn
  New Journal, 233; and creation of Jew-
  ish Voice Pictorial, 232; as director of
  Jewish Orphan Home, 232; founding of
  Die Yiddishe Stimme, 232; and Jewish
  Daily Forward, 232; and Jewish Day,
  242; move to New York, 236; organiza-
  tion of the Cleveland Zionist Society,
  232; and Rabbi Solomon Goldman, 238,
  239, 240; and Der Yiddisher Waechter,
  232, 233, 234; and Die Yiddishe Velt, 232,
  233, 236, 241, 244
Willard, Archibald, 40
William Edwards Company, 165
Wilson, Woodrow, 168
Wise, Isaac M., 217
Wise, Sam D., 324
Wise, Stephen, 212, 217
Witt, Peter, 113, 119
Witt, Stillman, 132
Woldman, Albert A., 50
Wolpaw, Harry, 57
Wolpaw, Lucy, 57
Wolsey, Rabbi Louis, 207, 244, 252, 255, 256
Women's Welfare Organization, 249
Woodland Public Library, 54
Woods, J. L., 132
Works Progress Administration, 9, 18, 22
World Zionist Organization, 51, 222
Worstman, Charles, 62
Wortsman, Ezekiel, 233–37
Wulff, Norma, 117
Wurmser, A. C., 318

Yaroslavsky, Zev, 274
Yiddishe Kemfer, 264
Yiddishe Stimme, Die. See Jewish Voice
Yiddishe Velt, Die, 62, 63, 232–38, 241, 244
Yiddishe Waechter, Die. See Jewish Guard-
  ian
Yiddish Kultur Gezelshaft, 54, 55; and
  Howard Da Silva, 55; and Mark Feder,

59; name changed to *Di Yidishe Teater Studyo,* 55; production of *Dem Tsadik's Nesiye,* 55. See also *Literarish Dramatishe Gezelshaft;* Progressive Dramatic Club

Yiddish theater, 10, 14, 53, 54, 56; in Cleveland, 53, 54, 55, 58; and *Literarish Dramatishe Gezelshaft,* 54; and Progressive Dramatic Club, 54; and *Yiddish Kultur Gezelshaft,* 54, 55

Yidishe Teater Studyo, Di. See *Yiddish Kultur Gezelshaft*

Yom Hashoah Commemoration, 59

Youth Aliyah, 50

Zangwill, Israel, 206

Zionist Organization of America, 223

Zorach, William, 6; and Abe Warshawksy, 43; adjustment to American life, 30, 31; apprenticeships of, 29, 40, 42; and Archibald Willard, 40; art of, 39, 43; and Bill Sommers, 40; and Billy Crane, 40, 41, 42; and Bob Fitzsimmons, 36; and Bob LaFollette, 34; childhood in Cleveland, 33; education of, 28, 31, 37–39, 43, 44; and E. M. Ward, 44; and Francis C. Jones, 44; and Frank Seamons, 45, 46; and George Groll, 39, 40, 41, 45, 46; and Harry Bernstein, 37; in jail, 37; jobs of, 38–42, 44, 45, 46; leaving Russia, 29; and Mark Hanna, 36; move to Cleveland, 28, 32; move to Port Clinton, Ohio, 31; as a newsboy, 36, 37; sculptures of, 28; surname changed to Finkelstein, 28; and Teddy Roosevelt, 34; trip to America, 30

Zucker, Henry L., 11; and Case Western Reserve University, 303; on Cleveland, 305; and Cleveland Jewish Family Services Association, 303; and the Cuyahoga County Relief Administration, 303; and Jewish Community Federation of Cleveland, 303–4, 306, 307, 313, 315, 316; speech of, 303–16

Zwick, Jennie K., 50, 51, 52